PERMANENT REVOLUTION

PERMANENT REVOLUTION

Totalitarianism in the Age of International Civil War

SECOND EDITION

BY SIGMUND NEUMANN

FREDERICK A. PRAEGER, *Publishers*

New York • Washington • London

FREDERICK A. PRAEGER, PUBLISHERS
111 Fourth Avenue, New York 3, N.Y., U.S.A.
77-79 Charlotte Street, London W.1, England

Published in the United States of America in 1965
by Frederick A. Praeger, Inc., Publishers

This is a second edition, with a new supplementary bibliography, of a
work first published in 1942 by Harper & Brothers under the title
Permanent Revolution: The Total State in a World at War.

© 1942, by Harper & Brothers
© 1965 by Frederick A. Praeger, Inc.

Library of Congress Catalog Card Number: 65-21107

Printed in the United States of America

CONTENTS

PREFACE TO SECOND EDITION

Sigmund Neumann was born in Leipzig in 1904, where he received his Ph.D. in 1927. Although his career in Germany was brief, it nonetheless revealed an inherent trait of his character: he was as much an original scholar as he was a dedicated educator. In Berlin, he served as professor of history and social science at the Deutsche Hochschule für Politik and as Director of the Academy of Adult Education. The two books he wrote in Germany, *Die Stufen des Preussischen Konservatismus* (1930) and *Die Deutschen Parteien* (1932), remain lasting contributions to the theory and analysis of political parties. They combined sociology and political science in a manner new in the Germany of that day.

In 1934, Neumann was appointed a member of the faculty of Wesleyan University in Middletown, Connecticut. He frequently was a visiting professor at Harvard, Yale, Columbia, and other leading institutions of higher learning, but throughout the twenty-eight years of his life in the United States he remained faithful to his permanent ties with Wesleyan. He saw in a small university of high standards a unique educational challenge that could be "fountain and frontier of scholarly pursuit and a training ground for the coming generations." He had an unflagging interest in his students and exercised a deep influence upon an entire generation of young political scientists. He served Wesleyan, and scholarship, also as Director of Wesleyan's Honors College and as founder and first director of its Center for Advanced Studies in the Liberal Arts, Sciences, and Professions.

In 1949, he returned to Germany to help reform the study of the social and political sciences in the German universities. His special interest belonged to the re-establishment of the Hochschule für Politik, which had been abolished by the Nazi government in 1933. He was instrumental in making it part of West

Berlin's Freie Universität. In recognition of his work on behalf of German higher education and scholarship, Neumann received honorary doctorates from the University of Munich and the Freie Universität. Thus his activities in the last decade of his life served the interests of the two countries with which his life had been connected: the country of his birth and young years, and the country in which he developed to full maturity.

Neumann had brought with him to the United States the tradition of German scholarship, the close connection of political science with intellectual history, and he tried to steer German scholarship in the direction of American liberal and international-minded democracy, with emphasis on public service and concrete research on vital issues of contemporary society. When he died, prematurely and at the peak of his creative power, in October, 1962, he left behind him both here and in Germany many former students and devoted friends who admired him deeply and who responded warmly to his sympathetic understanding of people, his concern with and pride in his students, his ever-present helpfulness, his cheerful and active nature. No ivory-tower scholar, he was a humanitarian who was conscious of the fact that "man can redeem and fulfill himself only through his social existence."

Among Neumann's books and articles written in the United States, *Permanent Revolution* (1942), long out of print, stands out as a classic study of the social structure of totalitarian rule. It is high time that it be made available once more, for it has lost none of its immediacy and relevance in the quarter of a century since it was first published. Much has happened in the intervening years: Stalinism has been replaced by the "milder" dictatorship of Khrushchev and his successors; the apparently monolithic and highly centralized structure of the Communist world movement has given way to a pluralistic polycentrism; the Fascist dictatorships of Hitler and Mussolini, which loomed so large in 1940, have come to a disastrous end; the democratic parliamentarism of Britain and the United States has survived the crisis of the war astonishingly well; capitalism, which seemed doomed in the 1930's, has shown a new vitality in the welfare state of the

1960's. These changes could hardly have been foreseen by anyone in 1942. Yet the problem of totalitarianism and democracy is still with us, and Neumann's dictum that "it is much more than a problem of constitutional structure or economic progress, it is above all the difference in basic human concepts" is as valid today as it was in 1942. Neumann knew that the totalitarian dictatorships were rooted in the challenge of a world revolution, the first in history, and that this challenge could be met only by an awakened democracy, conscious of the longing of the "lower" classes and the "less developed" peoples for full equality. Only after the destruction of Fascism did this revolution—of the masses in the West and of the peoples in Asia, Africa, and Latin America—enter into the full limelight of history as an irreversible fact.

With clear foresight, Neumann in 1942 stressed the diversity of dictatorships, the many shadings between democracy—which is often identified today in the United States as part of a "free world," a term which includes every non-Communist dictatorship —and dictatorship. "Even the modern autocracies" (Fascist and Communist), he wrote, "are worlds apart from one another. . . . But in actual fact, significant and numerous as their structural similarities and common human traits are, the dynamic movements of our day—the awakening nationalism of the Near East, Latin-American one-man rule, Far Eastern neo-feudalism [the regimes of Japan and of Chiang Kai-shek], Russia's Bolshevism, even German National Socialism and Italian Fascism—must be differentiated in time and space. They have their distinct national climate. They arrive from a specific historical background. . . . Hence a full definition of modern dictatorship must include this diversity with all its shades and conflicting aims. Any sweeping formula should therefore be regarded with suspicion."

Neumann's analysis of dictatorship opens a new approach to political dynamism for the democracies. In 1942, he demanded a redefinition of democracy, its revitalization, giving it a new meaning in a new world. This has begun to happen in the 1960's, with the drive for the full integration of its Negro citizens in the American democracy, with the welfare state which respects indi-

vidual freedom, with the liberation of Asia, Africa, and Latin
America from the political and economic control of Europe and
the United States. Twenty-odd years after its first appearance,
Neumann's wise book should find many attentive readers. For it
deals ultimately with a lasting problem: the dignity and personal
responsibility of the individual, this precious heritage of that
modern Western civilization which arose in Britain and the
North Atlantic area in the Age of Enlightenment.

HANS KOHN

Philadelphia
April, 1965

INTRODUCTION

Rooted in the crisis of democratic government, nourished by the grievances of modern society and raised to world-wide import by the quest for international order, totalitarian dictatorships have presented themselves as the only alternative to chaos. Even where they have emerged as sheer reaction reverting to antiquated solutions, they have claimed to be progressive and post-democratic. To be the forger of a New Order and the champion of a Permanent Revolution is their proud claim. Regardless of whether they are the master or a mere exploiter of a world revolution, their challenge must be met by an awakened democracy. This can be done only when the nature and design of the total state are fully understood.

Is modern dictatorship the "one-man rule" of Messianic liberators or power-ridden megalomaniacs as is often claimed in stirring interpretations pro and con? Or does it result from the inevitable clash of economic forces which, following the cold logic of natural laws, have now reached the "last stage of capitalism"? Or is modern totalitarianism, and National Socialism specifically, simply the outcome of an unjust treaty system, the militant reaction of a proud people who want to avenge their defeat and to renew a drive toward world conquest which they failed to achieve a generation ago?

Each of these interpretations and many more may signify an important aspect of the picture, and in specific stages of the development such formulae may characterize the most essential driving motives of rising dictatorships. But, appealing and reassuring as they may be to people in a hurry who want a quick and definitive answer, all such one-track explanations are dangerous.

If any generalization is possible, it is that modern dictatorship is ready to make use of any elements of unrest that will feed the fire of permanent revolution, and to relinquish them after they have outlived their usefulness. The total state of today above all implies continuous dynamics which cannot be stopped unless stopped permanently. The first aim of totalitarianism is to perpetuate and to *institutionalize revolution.* Paradoxical though it is to put revolution on a permanent basis, the conscious creation of quasi-institutional structures is the most significant political feature of modern totalitarian rule. It is exactly this fact that distinguishes the present-day dictatorships from earlier forms of despotism. True, Hitler, Mussolini and Stalin are in the limelight today. Each seems to stand for his whole nation, and these modern dictatorships are synonymous with the names of these men. But symbols of the "awakened" nation though they may be, there is a party machine which represents the life line of present-day autocracies. Even the end of the Number-One Man does not guarantee the end of the dictatorial system—Lenin is dead, but Bolshevism lives on. The existence of a machine promises the survival of autocratic rule beyond the life span of its creators. A sober analysis of the institutional framework undoubtedly presents a less glamorous picture than the story of superhuman heroes or villains, but it strikes nearer to the real forces behind this permanent revolution.

Modern dictatorship is a Leviathan of the machine. While its far-flung organization and clock-like machinery have attracted many keen analysts, its efficiency, especially in waging total war, has equally impressed "the man in the street." Few observers, however, realize that what makes this machine run is human material; and the price paid for its success is high. Human loyalties and sacrifices, social relationships and controls, as in any political body, form the life blood of modern totalitarianism. In order to understand clearly the inner dynamics of these systems—their power and their peril—one must understand the social fabric of totalitarian control. Such control rests on a specific relationship between *leaders and followers*. It is this political pyramid that is the primary concern of this study.

There are leaders and followers in democracies as well as in dictatorships. Only a period ripe for dictatorship could invent the idea of a leaderless democracy. In order to survive the dictatorial onslaught, democracy will be in bitter need of leaders, for eventual post-war reconstruction will unquestionably depend on the presence of courageous leadership.

It would be no less misleading to regard the followers in modern autocracies as a blind herd led by an all-powerful ruler. True, it is one of the major tenets of totalitarianism that man is manageable and that the whole problem of modern society thus boils down to a question of techniques and strategies for mastering the "human material." Yet, such a significant approach to man makes it more necessary for dictatorships to create a definite hierarchy which binds all its members in all layers of society. Needless to say, the democratic and dictatorial pyramids in every stratum are diametrically opposed to each other in meaning and reality. This is true of their leaders, their party, their masses. It is unfortunate and misleading that our political vocabulary uses the same labels to cover such divergent phenomena.

Even the numerous modern autocracies are worlds apart from one another. Dictatorship is a catchword of our era. Only twenty years ago every government prided itself on being democratic. Today, the success of modern demagogues and the law of imitation make every noisy fellow in any country a little dictator. But in actual fact, significant and numerous as their structural similarities and common human traits are, the dynamic movements of our day—the awakening nationalism of the Near East, Latin American one-man rule, Far Eastern neo-feudalism, Russia's Bolshevism, even German National Socialism and Italian Fascism—must be differentiated in time and space. They have their distinct national climate. They arise from a specific historical background. They claim to meet specific crises and to answer specific needs. Hence a full definition of modern dictatorship must include this diversity with all its shades and conflicting aims. Any sweeping formula should therefore be regarded with suspicion.

Permanent Revolution is confined to the *totalitarian dictatorships* in Europe, with special emphasis upon the Fascist autocracies. Only by comparison will other and different dictatorial types be considered. This limitation is justified by the fact that these European dictatorships represent the paramount challenge to western democracies. Long before World War II officially began, their world-wide repercussions were clearly apparent in the international scene. Now they dominate the design and fate of the world at large. Their success or failure is decisive in internal politics as well for the very existence of democratic institutions. In this sense, they are democracy's contemporaries.

Moreover, many essential features of modern autocracies are the result of democratic experience. Their demagogical leadership and their party machine, their propaganda techniques and gigantic schemes of social and economic planning are answers, misleading though they may be, to a social query which likewise confronts democracy. Above all, dictatorships demonstrate crisis elements of democratic organization and thus throw light on the driving forces which make and break modern government.

For the student of politics the analysis of dictatorial government thus opens a new approach to political dynamics, bringing to the fore inherent discrepancies and hidden strata in the body politic. The clash of political ideas in our time may disclose the vital forces of democracy. In fact, to meet the Fascist attack, it will be imperative to *redefine democracy*, to revitalize its great institutions, to prove its own virility and to give it new meaning in a new world.

The historical setting of this study is Europe during the Armistice period; the main theme, a comparison of the dictatorial hierarchy with the democratic framework. From the top of the pyramid—the leader and his elite—through the intermediate layer of the dictatorial party down to the mass base of a totally organized and controlled nation, this study analyzes the social structure of totalitarian rule as compared with democratic government. Since modern dictatorship is a total revolution infiltrating all agencies and activities of the body politic, its nature cannot be altogether discerned by a single approach, economic or social, psychological or historical, ideological or otherwise. Emphasis therefore shifts in practically every chapter and runs the gamut of the social sciences. Historical circumstances and personality patterns, economic and social forces, psychological motivations and institutional structures must be equally comprehended for a full picture of modern totalitarianism. Such concrete analysis of integral dictatorship will alone provide the perspective necessary to evaluate the strength and weakness of its dynamics within the international scene. In fact, belligerence in world politics denotes a major element in the definition of modern totalitarianism. War is its beginning, its demand, its test. It is in the twilight of a world at war that the flames of revolution break through. A constant state of war is the natural climate of totalitarian dictatorship. Its psychological roots and human drives become apparent in an analysis of the "impact of permanent war." It is against this background that the challenge of "dictatorship in international politics" will be perceived fully and against which it must be weighed accordingly.

On Methods

The sources of information in the field of contemporary history are manifold. Each stands in its own right. Though usually covering the same area of knowledge and often addressed to the same reading public, the participant, the publicist, and the scholar are possessed of divergent traits. They differ in focus and intention and, therefore, in prerequisites and methods necessary for a proper fulfillment of their specific tasks.

Much of the confusion in "current events" derives from writers who have never learned to distinguish, as George Dangerfield so neatly puts it, "between three quite distinct things: contemporary journalism, a sermon, and a chill down the spine." True, such a combination makes for best-seller material; in fact, such a dangerous mixture of intentions is partly due to the reading public itself. Many of the most successful books on contemporary politics, such as Valtin's *Out of the Night*, are frequently read as modern substitutes for wild "westerns."

It is even more understandable and justifiable that the writer on contemporary affairs should feel the urge to take a stand and to propagate his convictions. The obvious difficulties of such an attitude become especially apparent in the numerous semi-autobiographical studies which are flooding the market today. Only a few outstanding publicists have succeeded in finding the proper balance between reporting and personal confession. These dangers have been avoided by such writers as Vincent Sheean, *Personal History*, Louis Fischer, *Men and Politics*, and Walter Duranty, *I Write as I Please*.

The disturbing situation in the field of contemporary history is not in the least a result of the virtues of Anglo-American journalism. Its high-class performance has all too often led to imitation by the scholarly world. Similar tendencies can be seen in the field of literature. The vigor and color of modern journalism have misled young writers and social scientists to accept the well-proved techniques of on-the-spot observers. The results of this "cultural borrowing" have often shown only the transfer of the bad features of journalism to contemporary writing. It seems to be most pertinent to separate the different sources of information concerning contemporary events and to define clearly the domain and techniques of each.

There are three major groups of writers: participants, observers and scholars. Each of them fulfills a specific function and has distinct advantages and danger elements at the same time. Participants have the obvious advantage of direct contact with the action concerned, but the disadvantages of subjectivity and bias in reporting are just as manifest. Their natural interest in only one side of the cause gives to their writings an intentional (or at least unconscious) desire to spread "propaganda."

The observers are above all fact-finders. As many differentiations in reporting are possible as there are types of men. Yet every foreign correspondent has to fulfill definite requirements. His profession may be full of excitement and suspense, but it presupposes hard work, substantial knowledge and a long training just the same. The good journalist must be familiar with his domain; and in a constantly shifting world this is a big order. He must know how to tap sources (not only official ones) and how to cultivate them. Above all, he must be able to evaluate the news and to present it to his specific public. Before he can reach the public, not only may he have to face difficulties with his employer, but he most certainly will have to pass or circumvent stringent censorship in obtaining and delivering the facts. All this work demands that he be a well-trained and experienced specialist. He is rarely the daring glamour boy of news exploits commonly presented to the outside world. On the contrary, when the story of present-day publicists is written, the crown may well go to the man who preserved poise and calmness. No doubt, the most effective among the modern radio commentators have been those who, like Edward Murrow and Elmer Davis, apply a policy of factual reportage and even understatement.

Great as the contributions of the participants and observers are to current history, a definite place is left for the responsible student of contemporary affairs. He depends largely on the first-hand information available to the eyewitness (though to some extent he may be a participant and observer in his own right); but this distance from the day-to-day events gives him an opportunity to see them in a wider range. He must sift and compare, interpret and weigh the findings of the fact-finders. But his task is not fully accomplished even with the most careful and critical collection of the available source material. His main concern is the attempt to fit the facts into a frame of reference and into their historical perspective. Only such "systematization" gives meaning to the science of current history, which must serve as a guide to man in the crisis of our age.

On Concepts

Historical reality often changes without having managed to create a new language. If there is any need for proof that we are living in a time of transition, this is a visible test. Our political vocabulary is antiquated and thus by necessity full of misnomers. It has ceased to possess meaning. Basic concepts have "lost their spell." We must either acquire a new vocabulary or renew the old. This is of primary importance for the survival of democracy which, of all forms of society, is most dependent on "mutual understanding." It is in such a twilight zone that the stability of vital meanings is lost.

Modern dictatorships have capitalized on this intellectual vacuum, just as they have filled the social vacuum in which the crises strata of contemporary society have found themselves. In fact, many theoretical concepts of modern autocracies are borrowed from their enemies—such diverse origin is visible in dictatorship's nationalism and conservatism, its socialism and slogans of an "ennobled democracy." But these ideas lose their original connotation in the hands of the dictators and the result is a dissolution of the basic ideas of the 19th century. These ideas were developed against the background of an ordered world of institutions which are now shaken. This usurpation, devaluation, and actual transformation resulting from the dictators' use have caused havoc in democracy's camp no less than dictatorial blitzkrieg tactics have destroyed democracy's ordered battle lines—the remainders of yesterday's wars.

All social concepts must be seen in their historical context. They are defined in time and space. They must be tested anew in every generation and in every society if they are to have meaning for their adherents and to render effective resistance to their challengers.

A continuous misinterpretation of basic concepts is visible

and extremely dangerous within the fast-moving social and political sciences which are especially affected by the time lag between ideological perception and historical reality. A heritage of a quarter of a century's standing is often used. In a time of transition such a situation may be deadly. A strategy of confusion is a powerful weapon in the hands of an unscrupulous enemy. In order to be on guard, every democratic society needs a regular conceptual housecleaning.

The Bibliography, although no claim is made to any comprehensiveness, is intended for the expert, and can be discarded by the uninterested layman, thus relieving the text of heavy ballast but still comforting the "scholarly conscience." Thus the book may serve two masters, as it should. The conflict between democracy and dictatorship is everyone's concern; it must be faced with courage and open-minded realism. There is no place for the Cynic or the Utopian. An esoteric discussion between "academicians" seems to be as irresponsible as an oversimplification for popular consumption is dangerous. In fact, the fight for clarification of these vital issues must proceed in both camps at the same time. It must make intelligible to the responsible citizen the results of research in the realm of political science. At the same time it must push forward into unexplored regions, the conquest of which is the perpetual goal of scientific endeavor.

Lord Bryce after having completed his *Modern Democracies* poignantly remarked to Dr. Eliot: "When you have been so long over a book, the ideas which pleased you at first have come to seem commonplace." Such a sentiment is particularly pertinent in an epoch dominated by this ever-pervasive and ever-present theme of totalitarianism. Yet one may find consolation in the words of William James: "If you say everybody knows that— that is a thing worth discussing."

ACKNOWLEDGMENTS

_____

Unlike Montesquieu's *L'Esprit des lois*, whose title page carries the proud (and unjustified) statement, ". . . prolem sine matre creatam," *Permanent Revolution* is most certainly not "an offspring born without a mother." But it is impossible to trace all the influences which have contributed to its making. Modern scientific endeavor is essentially the product of a cooperative enterprise.

The theme followed for years and finally brought together in this volume is partly based upon earlier writings. For generous permission to draw upon material from previously published articles of mine, due acknowledgment is made to *Foreign Affairs, Virginia Quarterly Review, Journal of Politics, American Sociological Review, Review of Politics, Vital Speeches*; and to Guy Stanton Ford, *Dictatorship in the Modern World* (University of Minnesota Press) and R. V. Peel and J. S. Roucek, *Introduction to Politics* (Crowell). Specific acknowledgment for quoted material is made in the Bibliography.

A primary purpose of this study is to translate European experiences and realities into a meaningful challenge for an American audience. In this endeavor I have been greatly supported by my students at Wesleyan University and elsewhere who have always been an inspiring and most understanding testing group. I am no less grateful to Eugenia May Henry, Waldemar Gurian, Chester J. Hill, Edward F. Kornblith and Ralph D. Pendleton, who read the manuscript and made valuable suggestions; to Arlene Beckley, Frances Beardsley and Harriet Cheney, who assisted me in its technical preparation; and to Dorothy Thompson of Harper & Brothers, for her work on it.

To the Wesleyan Research Committee I am indebted for encouraging support. The Olin Library of Wesleyan University, the Widener Library of Harvard University, and the Sterling Library of Yale University have extended many courtesies.

Chapter 1

MODERN DICTATORSHIP DEFINED

THE HISTORIC SETTING

Dictatorship is neither new nor novel. In fact, throughout the recorded history of organized government "absolute authority vested in one man" (dictatorship's dictionary definition, misleading though it is) has prevailed as a system of political control. "Government of the people" signifies a relatively recent development only.

In the light of this definition the new "age of tyrannies" may seem to be a mere reversion to the earlier traditions of autocracy. Yet present-day dictators are not at all the direct offspring of the despots of the past.

The very meaning of the term dictatorship has undergone basic change. In classical Rome where it found its first institutional form, the dictator was always regarded as an exceptional, irregular type whose function was to grapple with such emergencies as war, sedition, or constitutional deadlock. The normal processes of government would replace the temporary ruler as soon as the emergency was over. The possession of unlimited power by one man was accepted by the citizens because of this temporary character of his control. "The man of the moment"—real or presumed superman—would disappear just as quickly as he had made his appearance on the political scene. When the task was finished (or his incompetence exposed) his power ended. Cincinnatus returned to the plow.

G. P. Gooch in his masterful essay on Dictatorship thus describes the function of the Roman magistrate: "Like a strong cordial or a subcutaneous injection administered to a sick man, his function was to grapple with a major emergency, to restore tone to the system at a moment of confusion, to steady the nerves after a formidable shock."

One may even go so far as to define as the very aim of the dictatorial office in the Roman Republic the preservation of the constitution as a whole by suspension of some constitutional features. The extraordinary magistrate in the Roman commonwealth in fact can well be regarded a forerunner of "Constitutional Dictatorship" which is provided as a "safety valve" in emergency articles of certain modern democratic constitutions. An often-quoted example of such a provision was the ill-fated Article 48 of the Weimar Constitution. On the other hand, the famous Article 17 of the Spanish Constitution of 1876 seemed to have successfully furnished such a safety valve, thus allowing the Constitution—in the words of Madariaga—"to go to sleep now and then."

Until most recent times the concept of dictatorship as a temporary emergency rule prevailed. In this sense, it is compatible with democratic government. In emergencies democracies may in fact be compelled to suspend temporarily their dependency on the consent of the governed. If in the process they can preserve their constitutional fiber and an open road to normalcy, they do not lose their essential nature.

Since the end of the First World War, however, dictatorship has seemed to convey a very different meaning. It is often identified with autocracy or absolutism. Misleading as such a definition may be, it rightly connotes the aspiration of modern dictatorships to *permanence*. It is not the Romans' six-month rule but at least the "millennium" that the modern dictator aims to establish.

The design of modern dictatorship is essentially different from that of its nominal antecedents. Present-day autocracies are not just departures from the democratic norm. They claim to present a system of government outliving their dictatorial creator and extending their sway into a *totalitarian rule* over practically every sphere of human interest and activity. It is their quasi-institutional and totalitarian character, this virtually limitless extension in time and space, that holds out the challenge to democracy.

Modern democracy has not only to meet this challenge, but also to recognize in this dictatorial growth its own quandary; in spite of the fact that dictatorships today represent the opposite of what democracies stand for, they are in many respects the direct outgrowth of our present system with its discords.

Resulting from the recent rise of mass democracy and the threatening breakdown of institutions, two elements of crisis loom for modern government. The same elements constitute the historic premises of the new despots. Their primary claim is leadership in the mass state and substitution for shattered institutions. This two-fold promise, indeed, determines important social features and at the same time fundamental discrepancies inherent in modern dictatorial rule.

In the sense of this promise present-day dictators are children of a democratic era, much as they seem to despise it. In fact, this democratic background constitutes the basic difference between the absolutism of the *ancien régime* preceding the French Revolution and that of modern tyrannies. Pre-democratic autocracies had a comparatively easy task to fulfill. They hardly had to stifle the voice of the people. Control of court factions and of aristocratic intrigues was all that mattered. Then democratic revolutions awakened a mute populace. Since that time every recurrence of autocracy arising in a nation which has gone through a democratic experience (transient though it may have been) has had to answer the queries of people who still remember a pre-dictatorial past. To overcome this historic memory and at the same time to respect and to counteract it, a proper "public opinion" becomes a necessity.

The new tyrannies whose historic hour strikes in the age of mass democracy are "popular dictatorships." Avowedly they exemplify the antithesis of democracy but at bottom they show a pseudo-democratic basis. Their "legal" seizure of power, their pretense to elections, their constant craving for popular acclaim

—all these intricate schemes of a quasi-democratic existence are preconditional for the very survival of the new dictatorships. This fact is among the important explanations of the predominant place yielded to propaganda in the daily life of modern totalitarianism.

Important as these propaganda techniques are, these new dictatorships are, however, not simply the result of an unscrupulous and technically perfected system of propaganda. These propaganda techniques undoubtedly reveal most significant symptoms, but they should not be mistaken for the essence and basic impulse of these movements. Propaganda to be effective must answer real needs and desires. This must be especially true of political movements as successful as modern dictatorships are. Justified or not, grievances toward the existing order generate the seekers of change whose greatest strength is often simply their enemy's weakness. Negative characteristics far more than any positive creed serve as a point of departure for a concrete definition of modern dictatorships. They are anti-parliamentarian and anti-capitalistic, anti-Semitic and anti-western, anti-rational and anti-individualistic. They arise as movements of protest; and even if they do not reach beyond this stage of negative criticism, this sheer negativism represents a focal point of crises elements in modern society. Like all the various types of historic dictatorship, they are children of a crisis, in this case a totalitarian crisis reaching into all ways of life and sweeping over the whole planet.

The impetus and extent of this social and political upheaval largely depend on cultural standards and political traditions in the different nations. Hence scientific observers of the spread of dictatorial rule in Europe have often regarded the educational standards of the different nations as a key to explain its expansion. Countries, so they said, where the percentage of illiteracy is high are likely to become dictatorships. This rule seemed to apply well to Russia, Poland, Italy, Spain, and the Balkans; but when Germany joined the autocracies, the weakness of this argument became manifest. If, however, one looks at the standard of what might be called political illiteracy, their explanation would have

been more convincing. In none of these countries had the tradition of self-government and of free institutions been strong and
lasting. Beyond this, it is a fact that the political system of the
central and eastern European countries was changed suddenly and
without adequate preparation from the more or less benevolent
paternalism of semi-absolute governments to the independent responsibilities of free democratic institutions. There was no time to
build up new traditions and to adjust the institutions to so rapid
a social development.

Notwithstanding national deviations in political maturity, a
lack of adaptation between social structure and body politic seems
to be a characteristic problem of all modern nations, with the
possible exception of England. The rise of modern political democracy coincided with the sweeping social changes of modern
industrialism and urbanization, with the breakdown of a fixed
social order, of basic religious concepts, and of old institutions.

The impact of these great social disturbances on political institutions became especially manifest with the change from liberal
democracy, i.e., the rule of the classes of property and culture,
to mass democracy. Steady extension of the electorate throughout
the 19th and 20th centuries made the problem of leadership in a
mass state the crucial issue of modern government. With the
sudden rise of the mass state the historic hour of the *demagogue*
seemed to have arrived—demagogue in the classical sense of the
word, the "leader of the people."

The modern dictator is even more indicative of the breakdown
of accepted institutions. When an economic system becomes questionable, when a social order is shattered, when religious ties are
loosened, people look for new authorities, for substitutes. The cry
for the "leader" is the result of the weakening or non-existence of
political institutions, of a ruling class, and an accepted code of
values. Wherever these institutions and their governing elements
are strong enough not only to preserve but also to adjust the
society in its evolutionary development, the danger of the demagogue does not arise. This is the great test for the strength of
institutions. When they fail, demagogues arise. They are the

substitute for institutions in time of transition. Here, if anywhere, lies the historic justification of this new personal rule of the modern dictator. It may fill a gap between two social orders. This was the historic function of the absolute monarchy which helped to develop modern capitalistic society. But the new dictatorship is differentiated from the earlier absolutism by its other historic element: its origin in the age of mass democracy.

All these crises elements in the age of democracy—its changing social basis, the breakdown of social institutions, the shattering of the predominant system of values—have already been perceived by observers in pre-war Europe, such as Tocqueville and Burckhardt, Dostoevski and Kierkegaard, Nietzsche and Sorel. Indeed the war only hastened and accentuated this process. Yet, though it may not have created anything essentially new in the web of time, it gave new impulses, broadened the attack, focused the issues. Thus were prepared the national climate and the international scene most suitable for the unfolding of dynamic totalitarianism.

The time setting of modern dictatorship is Europe of the Armistice period—a fertile breeding ground of war. The peace treaty following this "war to end war" and "to make the world safe for democracy" certainly was not so false and free from any constructive spark as Versailles may look to many today. Yet there were the conflicting expectations of a well-entrenched victorious nationalism (fed by slogans such as "Hang the Kaiser" and "*Le Boche payera tout*") and an inexperienced budding internationalism, abundant in its hope to ban forever international anarchy. The result was the Paris Treaty System, which embodied a mixture of contradictory motives and solved none of Europe's pending problems.

The Armistice period was laden with political passions, economic misery, and psychological strain. These tensions were the heritage of the World War, the result of the forces which had led to this conflict and which had sprung from its outcome: integral nationalism, economic imperialism, belligerent rivalry.

Nationalism, the driving force since the French Revolution, seemingly reached in the Armistice period its greatest victory in the recognition of national self-determination as the basic principle of the Treaty System. The newly created succession states followed this principle with the additional result—most welcome to the victorious powers—of the complete destruction of the Dual Monarchy in the name of this national self-determination. Yet the dictated peace did not solve the acute prob̄ f national minorities, though it did cut down Europa irredenta.

This Balkanization of Europe, creating thirty-four separate political units out of twenty-five, certainly intensified the nationalistic spirit of a new tribalism. On the other hand, bitterness of defeat among the vanquished, fanned by forced cession of territories, unfulfilled restitution of its own national irredenta, a humiliating warguilt clause, military and financial control—such grievances aroused the passion of a proud people. What was worse, this nationalistic feeling also spread into economic spheres.

The new economic nationalism—an obvious contradiction to natural tendencies of world-wide economy on a shrinking planet of interdependent markets—was largely based upon the war experiences of submarine warfare and blockade. National self-sufficiency—the new slogan of economic orientation—had, above all, a political motive: to be prepared "in case of emergency." The post-war attempts to reconcile this inflated nationalism with an effort toward international order led inevitably to difficulties which became manifest in the tragic failures of the League of Nations and of international relations at large. Those failures served as the mainstay of the new dictatorships.

Rising demagogues also took full advantage of the "economic consequences of the war" unheeded at Versailles in spite of Keynes' severe warning. A continent in ruin, unheard-of material losses, the burdens of reparations, universal dislocations of economic interrelations, the unequal distribution of the world's possessions—these and many other factors were fuel for new dynamics in world affairs. Especially the uncertain formula of the "Haves" and the "Have-nots" became effective munition in the arsenal of the "young nations" fighting for a place in the sun and their share in the wealth of the world's resources. In a way it was pre-war imperialism all over again. Fight for colonies, raw materials, and markets, even the demographic imperialism of population pressure was nothing novel. What was new, however, was the fact that these dynamics of imperialism could now inflame the masses—excited, restless, awakened as they were by post-war experiences. To be a "Have-not" nation made the quest for redistribution of worldly goods a moral issue. Such a slogan was also useful in diverting internal unrest into international channels. In a time of great socio-economic upheavals and the loss of all security (partly the result of the inherent discrepancies of the economic system, partly the after-effect of the World War), the proletarian among the nations could find in international adventure a most suitable safety valve against internal revolutions. No doubt, economic tensions in a politically unsettled world provided additional dynamite for dynamic forces.

Last but not least there was the moral issue. Basic concepts of the 19th century—the Victorian faith in human progress and the ultimate goodness of mankind—were definitely shaken by the war. Liberalism, individualism, rationalism—the war had emptied them of meaning. Gone were generally recognized standards of conduct which had promised to a degree at least a common code of social behavior. Four years of war had bred a cult of violence. Martial spirit, heroic virtues, the daring had their day. No room was left for balanced compromise and *juste mesure*. Unpredictable perpetual motion took possession of a young generation. The stability of a world at ease was no more. Moral anarchy loomed. It opened a spiritual vacuum into which any new force could rush.

Such a fundamental revolution did not imply the definite destruction of all pre-war concepts. But no longer could they be taken for granted. They had to be reaffirmed and filled with a new meaning by a strong and positive generation. Yet this is the last thing the manly business of warfare seems to breed. In fact, those who returned home, tempestuous youth or tired cynics, made the worst agents for a necessary reconstruction that asked for patience and perseverance above all. The post-war dictatorships are children of these political, socio-economic, and moral upheavals. They are crisis governments in the fullest sense of the word.

In spite of many striking similarities between the modern autocracies, they are worlds apart in political background, ideological traditions, social context. This fact naturally limits comparisons. To illustrate these differences in national expression, the rise of three outstanding contemporary dictatorships must be outlined before an evaluation of common patterns can be ventured. Blurred as their historic origin may often become in the later development of the mature dictatorship, the design of the origin still remains a distinctive feature of every dictatorial reality.

THE ORIGIN OF MODERN DICTATORSHIP: THREE CASE STUDIES

Soviet Russia

The Bolshevist Revolution, undoubtedly, has unique features, just as the Soviet system takes a unique place among modern dictatorships. Three facts stand out in a definition of the Bolshevist Revolution: its long ideological tradition, its inner Russian character (the peculiar conditions of Eurasian Russia), and its specific historic circumstances. In complete opposition to the Fascist revolutions, Communism was based upon a fully developed system of thought, complete in its radical criticism of the existing order and scientifically rational in its vision of a new society. Bolshevism was the revolution of a radical intelligentsia. In that respect it followed the pattern set in Russia since the first uprising of the Decembrists of 1825: a revolt of officers without an army. A similar situation faced the Russian officers who, having served in the Napoleonic wars, brought back French revolutionary ideas of liberty and democracy. Their mutiny was quickly crushed. No better fared the young students who returned from European university centers in the mid-19th century. Full of European liberal culture and philosophy, they enthusiastically turned their recent experiences into socio-political action in the

Narodniki movement with the slogan of land and liberty for the peasant serfs, only to be denounced to the police by the distrustful Ivan Ivanovitchs whom they romantically had embraced. The professional revolutionaries of the 20th century such as Lenin and Trotsky, preparing in Zurich and Paris for their historic hour, were no less lone fighters.

Russian upheavals were primarily revolutions from above and from outside, and very European movements at that, transplanting essentially European rational thinking into Asiatic soil. In fact, revolution and westernization in Russia were so strikingly blended and inextricably mixed that their attacks seemed to become only a twofold advance of one and the same movement. This holds especially true of victorious Bolshevism which claimed to be the genuine continuation of the great French Revolution. Lenin has often been called the Peter the Great of the 20th century. The revolution was as much an attempt at bringing Socialism on earth as it was at bringing Europe to Russia.

This fact suggests the specifically Russian features of this revolution. It introduced Socialism into a country which Marx would have regarded the least fit for such an experiment. Russia was just beginning to experience capitalism. Significantly enough, foreign capital played an important part in the growth of Russia's industry, trade, and railroad communication. It has been estimated that about one-third of the capital invested in Russian stock companies in 1914 was of foreign origin. This large-scale participation of foreign capital above all reflected the weakness—one might almost say the non-existence—of a middle class in czarist Russia. (This active interest of western capital in the inner Russian development was obviously of great consequence for the hostile attitudes of western powers toward rising Bolshevism.) In spite of the westernization by Peter the Great, the reforms of Alexander II abolishing serfdom and redistributing land (in 1861), and the economic transformation under Alexander III and Nicholas II, Russia still remained, in the words of its great historian, Klyuchevsky, "in the rear guard of Europe." She was basically a feudal country when the Bolshevist Revolution came, and she was an Asiatic nation too.

The short interlude of the Revolution of 1905, though it gave Russia a pseudo-representative parliament in the Duma, did not essentially change the political structure of the country. New electoral laws soon did away with the popular basis of the Duma and made it a most conservative body representing only a small propertied minority. Thus in contrast to the possibilities in western nations the masses were denied any chance of constructive participation in Russian politics under the czarist regime. If they did not live the animal existence of the dumb creatures of their environment as the huge majority did, they tended toward a revolutionary interpretation of future development much more than western Socialism did. The lack of direct channels of political activity drove the opposition by necessity into underground movements. The adversaries of the ruling system became outsiders of state and society. Compromise was thus ruled out. Such a plight affected the specific revolutionary tactics of growing Bolshevism. It at least partly explains the cruelty of the final revolution when hitherto checked forces broke the dam. Victory meant extermination of the enemy.

In many respects, Soviet Russia was czarism, its symbols reversed and its ruling elite changed—a pyramid upside down. It is therefore idle to ask which was worse, the Red or the White Terror. The fight was going on on practically the same level, though its meaning was no doubt worlds apart in the two camps. Triumphant Bolshevism had learned its lesson. It was heir to the temper and methods of the czarist regime. It inherited not only the Ochrana of the imperial rule, but also its general Asiatic features. These facts make many elements in the Russian picture hard for the European mind to understand. The centuries-old dualism of western and eastern influences is still alive. A generation after the Bolshevist Revolution Russia still preserves her oriental character. For this split, Europe herself is partly responsible in having pushed Russia out of the western world. In fact, early Sovietism had tried to bridge the two worlds (again in this respect following old traditions of a ruling class) in making up for a delayed development. The industrialization pursued in the Five-Year Plans and the emancipation of the women, to cite only two outstanding attempts, will always stand out as great marks of the Soviet regime. It may even be ventured that they could not have been accomplished without such a centralized system of government. These achievements are so much a part of Bolshevism that they can hardly be eliminated from an evaluation of this great social experiment—a fact that must be kept in mind in every attempt to transfer this venture into other societies which had already accomplished this stage of industrialization half a century and more ago.

Specific circumstances of victorious Bolshevism have to be considered also in regard to its historic hour. The "Imperialist World War" played an essential part in Lenin's doctrine. In fact, imperialism, the monopolistic period of capitalism, and its inevitable outcome—the fight over colonial markets in imperialistic wars finally leading to the proletarian revolution—were a cornerstone of his theory. This postulate presented one of Lenin's chief contributions to the original Marxian edifice. The intercapitalist battle line became to Lenin the strategic front on which the Socialist victory could be achieved. Thus a Russian defeat was counted upon by this lonely revolutionary sitting in the Central Library of Zurich in Switzerland, reading Hegel and waiting for his hour to come. It came in the fall of 1917, as Lenin had predicted with almost mathematical accuracy. The spring revolution of 1917 under middle-class leadership introduced a constitutional regime (belated and not wholeheartedly pushed forward on account of its primary interest in the successful continuation of the war) and collapsed principally because it did not bring the peace longed for by the masses.

Lenin's victorious revolution in the autumn of 1917 was in fact a combination of three revolutions, as such completely separated: the seizure of land by the peasants (for more than half a century the crucial issue of Russia's social question), the liquidation of war, the Bolshevist fight for power in the cities. The Bolshevists, far from initiating the uprisings of the peasants and soldiers, soon took the lead in all three upheavals. Victory came to the greatest tactician. Lenin's realistic genius proved, in this earl' 'age as in later and often more dangerous situations, his gr....... n adapting his theory to present-day political needs, in unifying divergent masses in the revolutionary cause even if it meant at times compromising basic revolutionary tenets.

The Revolution certainly did not solve basic contradictions between the Bolshevists and the peasants. They finally had to clash, but they were brought together in the revolutionary hour by bold leadership. This was exactly what the numerically much stronger social revolutionaries lacked, although they were backed by the core of the peasant masses; they had even represented an overwhelming majority in the constitutional parliament which was elected under the pre-Bolshevik Kerensky government, and which finally met after Lenin's seizure of power to be forcibly dissolved in this session by Bolshevik shock troops. The first declaration of the revolutionary government made all three revolutions—fight against the big landowners, liquidation of the war, and Bolshevist control of the industrial production—a part of its program.

The following civil war undoubtedly helped in blending differences. The peasants, though suspicious of the urban proletarians, had to take their side in the fight against the White army led by feudal landlords whose manors they had just expropriated. The Red army miraculously created by Leon Trotsky consisted in its great majority of peasant boys. This fact, though of some importance in post-civil-war peasant revolts, solidified the Soviet regime in these crucial years from 1917-20. These fighting experiences welded together the future leading elite of the nation. The intervention of the Allied powers backing up the White armies of Kolchak, Denikine, Yudenich, and Wrangel was another contributing factor in consolidating the revolutionary regime. It made the Soviets' fight a national struggle against foreign invaders, and persuaded even old czarist high officers like General Brusilov to take sides with the Reds.

The final victory of the Bolshevists thus presents itself as a most complex picture in which consistent theory and national characteristics, historic circumstances and strategy of leadership played their part in leading to the establishment of the Soviet state. As soon as the White armies were defeated and peasant revolts suppressed, i.e., as soon as the Bolshevists had definitely won the power, the structure of the Soviet system slowly found its shape. To be sure, it was a revolutionary process with ups and downs passing through different and extremely divergent stages. Even a quarter of a century after her hour of birth Soviet Russia is still far from any definite structure and form. Such evasiveness may be a chief characteristic of this dynamic government which it has in common with other post-war dictatorships though they represent themselves as its arch enemy.

Fascist Italy

Fascism and National Socialism no doubt arose as a reaction against Bolshevism and the presumed danger of its infiltration into central and western Europe. This fact gives the phenomenon of Bolshevism a greater perspective and certainly a much greater stake in European politics than its actual challenge may have presented in these post-war years. In spite of this obvious importance of Sovietism for the definition of rising Fascism, the essence of the new movement is not in the least circumscribed by the "defense of western civilization against the Red peril." As a matter of fact, Fascism, and even more so National Socialism, in themselves are a challenge to basic concepts of European traditions. Growing out of a specific and for each of them a different national situation, they by now represent a world problem in their claim that the 20th century will be a Fascist era.

What made Italian Fascism? Again national characteristics, political heritage, and historic circumstances serve as a background for its rise. There is first the socio-economic structure. In contrast to Great Britain, Germany, or the United States, Italy of the 20th century is still in the early stage of capitalism. There is no bankers' atmosphere there, no large factories—with the possible exception of the northern Po Valley. Italy is a nation of cities, but not of metropolitan size. Handicraft of the artisans and small middle-class life are predominant. Experiencing no clear-cut class differentiation, no outspoken class consciousness or strife as other countries did, Italy has been relatively unaffected by highly developed capitalism. Local interests and patriarchal family ties have typified social relations. Conflicts have represented almost medieval clashes between urban oligarchies. Even the early fights of Fascism and Socialism have been reminiscent of the activities of the Guelphs and Ghibellines.

The pre-Fascist party structure reflected this social setup. Just as in the German states of the mid-19th century and in Republican France to some extent until her breakdown, local rather than national interests were represented in the political factions. They were far from being based on social class alignments or even party programs. They were above all personal followings. Personality factors played a much more important part than ideas did. "The leader" is a pre-Fascist invention. In a way Depretis, Crispi, Giolitti already answered the Italian desire for a leader. Politics meant to the Italians least of all the realization of a program, and principally a personal fight for power where speech-making, big gestures, and colorful shows were necessary requirements. Indeed, rhetoric was a desperate effort to reach the imaginations and emotions of a small bourgeoisie which was definitely not politically-minded. Italians are actors. Their lively imaginations and fantasy make them grateful listeners and spectators too. They even like to be participants in the acting presented on the stage. Thus it could happen in a Roman opera house during the Italo-Ethiopian War when the victorious general in the second act of *Aïda* asks the king, "Sir, liberate the imprisoned Ethiopians," that a chorus of excited spectators shouted, "No! No!"

Politics even before Mussolini did not mean political responsibility to the Italian people. In fact it was no essential part of their life. The Risorgimento, the unification of Italy, came very late, not before the second half of the 19th century, and even then it was essentially the movement of an elite rallying behind Mazzini,

Garibaldi, and Cavour. As late as 1860 the patriot Massimo d'Aze-
glio declared, "Having made Italy we must now make Italians."
The Italian people as such—a large minority of them being illiterate—had no national conscience. Divided for centuries into a
dozen semi-feudal principalities, allied with or oppressed by foreign royalty, every Italian city-state had its own history, and was
often in closer contact with foreign countries than with its Italian
neighbors.

Regional differences dominated the national picture. Geography
also played its part. The climatic differences in a country extending from the Alps down to Sicily run through the whole scale
of a continent. No less divergent were the racial and economic
differences. This diversity made the wealth of Italy—so attractive
and impressive to every visitor to the country—but it also explains this great cultural center's Cinderella fate in politics. Absence of lasting political traditions and only short experience
with responsible government prevented the emergence of a ruling
class. Untried parliamentary institutions had to meet the continued pressure of provincial interest groups. Italian democratic
politics was the art of manipulating local patronage. The national
government was the slave of local bosses. This fact did not make
for efficient government. It certainly did not strengthen young
parliamentarianism in this country lacking traditions in self-rule.

Such weak and often corrupted government was confronted
with a most delicate international situation. When Italy finally
succeeded in her national unification—one of the last to arrive—
it was due only partly to her own efforts. From the Congress of
Vienna, to the Franco-Austrian War, to the Austro-Prussian war,
to the Franco-Prussian conflicts, to the First World War her triumphs were only the reflected glory of her allies and brought her
scarcely deserved laurels. Opportunism has been her traditional
national policy. Leaving aside the much-discussed question of
militant fighting spirit in the Italian soldiers, one sees that unfavor-
able geography and economic weakness dictated such an oppor-
tunist attitude. Italy has no coal and a very limited supply of iron,
to mention only two of the most crucial raw materials necessary

for national self-sufficiency and independence "in case of emergency," as fashionable formulas put it.

Long before the First World War, however, the economic plight of Italy was full of dynamite. Then the increasing population pressure could still be at least temporarily eased by export of labor. In 1914 about 6,000,000 Italians lived abroad in the United States and South America. Those countries absorbed 150,000 emigrants yearly, who in turn sent home half a billion lire annually. This outlet was suddenly stopped by the strict immigration legislation of post-war years, especially in the United States, which in this indirect way is partly responsible for the rise of the nationalistic temper of a bottled-up country in this "danger spot of world population."

Since the turn of the century, demographic imperialism based upon population pressure had made headway in Italy, leading to the enterprise in Libya and Tripoli. Yet such expansion could not relieve Italy's population pressure. Post-war Fascism certainly knew well how to make use of this popular unrest for its nationalistic dynamics.

There were other grievances typical of the post-war situation which Fascism succeeded in directing into its own channels. Indeed, Italy's plight was an unhappy one. Though she had won the war, she felt that she had lost the peace. True, Italy had achieved two major aims of her program: the liberation of her irredenta and the destruction of the Dual Monarchy, her arch enemy. Still not all the great promises of the secret Treaty of London (1915)—promises that enticed Italy to enter the war on the side of the Allies—had been kept. Above all, she felt cheated in her share of colonial spoils. The disappointments of the Peace Conference which even the tears of Italy's representative, Orlando, could not prevent (though they certainly touched Mr. Wilson) led to disillusion and discontent, to a spirit of desperate adventure and of obstruction against the treaty system. It was not difficult for a daring movement to find support with the young who felt that their nation had missed its hour. They were even ready to line up with the Have-not nations as if they themselves

had lost the war. "Fight against this mutilated peace"—this slogan
of the great phrase-maker D'Annunzio especially fired the circles
of active war officers. They had gone through the bitter experience of feeling the Italian people's contempt for their returning
officers wherever they appeared in uniform. These officers were
the first recruits of nascent Fascism.

To be exact, the first soldiers of Mussolini were the interventionists who had joined with him soon after the outbreak of the
World War, fighting for Italy's entrance on the side of the Allied
powers. Those interventionists were the forerunners of a post-
war Fascism. The Socialist leader, Labriola, had called this movement a "phenomenon of primitive militarism." This militant spirit
was just as prevalent when the movement was officially created in
March, 1919, as the *fasci di combattimento*. Its members called
themselves the aristocracy of the trenches, a claim which was to
be heard again and again from rising nationalist movements all
over Europe. No doubt the war was in their blood. The *Popolo
d'Italia*, the Fascist daily, addressed itself above all to the warriors
(and the producers). The two mottoes in its heading were telling
enough: "He who uses a sword has bread" (Blanqui) and "Revolution is an idea that has found bayonets to support it" (Napoleon).

But militant spirit was not the only appeal. The disappointed
soldiers were not the only followers of the young movement.
Small as it was even at the time of the march on Rome, it could
not have grown as big as it did if it had not attracted more substantial strata of society. The economic depression, a necessary
result of the crisis of demobilization in every country which was
changing from war economy to peace economy, hit Italy especially hard. The devaluation of the lira, particularly painful for a
nation dependent on foreign raw materials, the corresponding rise
in the cost of living, the uneven readjustment of incomes and
salaries, the new distribution of wealth creating a small group of
showy *nouveaux riches* (*pescecani*—sharks, they were called in
Italy) and a large class of impoverished citizens, the disillusioned
peasantry which had been promised in vain a redistribution of the

land and a dissolution of the huge estates in central and southern Italy, and last but not least the mounting population pressure—all this great social unrest and discontent created a mood receptive to social and political adventure. Especially the groups hardest hit—the young professionals, the small independent middle class, the white-collar people—were ready to listen to the promises of a new security twice as sweet since this security had been lost in their own lifetime.

There was one other set which joined forces with young Fascism, or at least played with the idea of joining it. Small as this group of capitalists was—and by no means all or even the majority of this group joined hands with Mussolini—their alliance was at times of paramount importance for the survival of the movement. Not only could its precarious financial situation, especially in the early days, often be bridged by the big bosses, but above all their approval (silent though it usually was) gave social prestige to this group of often disreputable characters.

The credit of Mussolini's Black Shirts especially rose after the so-called "Bolshevist attempt" of September, 1920. In fact, this "seizure of the factories" by labor groups was not such an important event as the Fascist legend afterwards liked to make it. Nor was the attitude of the Black Shirts beyond doubt. As a matter of fact, they even sympathized with the workers on several occasions.

This occupation of the factories must be seen against the background of the revolutionary post-war situation which cast its shadow on this Italian attempt too. Desperate and embittered groups were full of expectations for a new social order. The Russian example from afar was at least a talking point, though by the summer of 1920 the decisive Battle of Warsaw had already stopped the Soviet march to the west. The Italian workers certainly had not too large a scheme in mind when they seized their factories. The real occasion for the proletarian action was the workers' demand for increase in wages. It was refused. Consequently, they used the old device of passive resistance. The employers threatened a lockout. This the workers prevented by seizing the factories. If any basic concept could be found behind this action, it was a typical syndicalist attempt to win the control of production by making the factory and not a centralized organization the essential unit of social action. In fact only a part of the workers took possession of the plants. The others took vacations with their relatives who still lived on farms. (In spite of the fact that the Socialists were numerically strong and the only organized mass party in pre-Fascist Italy—apart from the Popolari recently founded by the priest, Don Sturzo—there was hardly a class-conscious proletariat in Italy. Many laborers were peasants, transplanted to the cities not more than one or two generations before; they still had their roots and relations in the country.) After twenty days the attempt collapsed, not only because of the resistance of the bankers denying credit and the entrepreneurs canceling orders and refusing to give necessary raw materials, but also because of the want of skilled labor and the lack of general support.

The main importance of this episode was its after-effect. From then on class tensions became more evident than ever before. Workers were radicalized or—under the impress of this failure—fell into political inertia. Embittered entrepreneurs showed their interest in "nationalist" movements or at least were no longer opposed to an anti-Socialist action. The final victory of the relatively small Fascist party was largely due to the general apathy of the masses, to the tacit acquiescence of the upper middle classes, and last but not least to the "don't-care shrug of the shoulder" of the non-political millions. Undoubtedly Fascist squads prospered in an atmosphere of civil strife and "threatening Bolshevism" which called for "strong-arm measures" in defense of the nation. This became the standard justification for the final seizure of power in the fall of 1922 when the Fascists marched on Rome.

Yet Mussolini himself had written in his own paper on July 2, 1921: "To say that there still exists a Bolshevist peril in Italy is to substitute certain insincere fears for the reality. Bolshevism is vanquished. Nay, more, it has been disowned by the leaders and the masses. The Italy of 1921 is fundamentally different from that of 1919. This has been said and proved a thousand times."

Such a strong statement by Il Duce himself did not, however, hinder young Fascism from making itself the savior of the nation from the Bolshevist peril. This was the beginning of the "myth of the Red danger"—from now on the most helpful device of rising Fascism everywhere.

True, there were economic contradictions, political confusion, and parliamentary weaknesses in post-war Italy, but even the most careful and circumspect interpreters of these years were skeptics in believing that Fascism was inevitable. It was equally doubtful that it stood for the new creed of a social revolution mobilizing harassed masses. As a matter of fact, young Fascism was proud in having no program. "Fascism as an idea is undefinable. It is a fact which is taking place," its leader stated. It certainly was not backed up by an elaborate and comprehensive theory of society, as the new Bolshevism was. In the words of one of Fascism's main spokesmen, Alfredo Rocco: "It is, above all, action and sentiment." In fact, the vague doctrine full of contradictions and inconsistencies, at least in the early stage, was of no consequence for the victory of Fascism.

Important, however, for its final success was the personality of Mussolini. Without Il Duce, Fascism was not inevitable. More than any post-war dictatorship (with the possible exception of Kemalist Turkey) it was, above all, the reflection and expression of its dynamic leader. He is the essential part of its definition. Even today, Fascism is Mussolinism.

National Socialist Germany

The rise of German National Socialism unfolds a picture fuller of contrasts and deeper in color than that of Italian Fascism. To begin with, Germany represents the complex social structure of a more highly developed capitalist country, complicated by the fact that she preserved, more than any other contemporary leading power, remnants of an earlier feudal order. But this is not the only complication. Battlefield of the Thirty Years' War, she has not yet overcome the centuries'-old religious contrasts. Further-more, dynastic division, at least until recent years, separated her states. Those time-honored traditions not only created centrifugal forces and competitive strife among the brother states leading to its climax in the historical dualism between Prussia and Austria, but these inner frontiers were also unsurmountable dividing lines of a European consciousness. The "Limes" (the boundary path distinctly separating "the barbarians of the north" from the Roman Empire) ran, and still runs, right through Germany.

When unification was belatedly brought about by Bismarck as a unification from above, it did not solve any of the social, re-ligious, and cultural conflicts. It decreed and enforced the specific formula for the imperial Germany which was, above all, feudal, Protestant, and Prussian. The new German Empire still remained a country of conflicting loyalties.

All these unsettled problems resounded through Germany's post-war history. They received an additional stigma because of defeat and a harshly dictated peace. Versailles undoubtedly brought new grievances and reemphasized old ones. Tremendous as was such a burden, it would be a mistake to make this peace settlement the villain really responsible for the rise of Hitler. The "legend of Versailles," cleverly exploited by National Social-ism, aroused within the western powers so bad a conscience that every unilateral change on the part of Nazi Germany seemed to be morally justified. Late as this discovery of a guilty conscience came (and undoubtedly under the pressure of German rearma-ment), it completely broke the moral defense lines of the *status quo* powers. Step by step Hitler could destroy the essential parts of the Treaty System: by introducing compulsory military service and thus creating the powerful army, remilitarizing the Rhineland, seizing Austria, Czechoslovakia, and the Memelland. His great victory in foreign affairs, indeed strengthening his home front tremendously, made it most plausible to see in the "shame of Versailles" the driving force of National Socialism.

The Paris Treaties (and even more their unwise and rigid appli-cation during the following Armistice period) were no doubt a live expression of the basic failures and a typical illustration of the lack of understanding in the post-war period. Yet it would be shortsighted to see in rising National Socialism nothing but the natural and powerful reaction of a proud people against a grievous defeat and merciless treaty. The roots of the unrest went much deeper into German history. Its real driving force derived from more vital social conflicts. A complete misunderstanding of the real meaning of National Socialism has led old western statesmen to believe that it could be appeased. If it could, it would not be the radical dynamic power that it really is. Hitler's rise must be attributed far more to inner German sources than to international constellations.

True, Versailles was of unfortunate importance even in internal politics. The German Republic was an outcome of the defeat; and though it was certainly not responsible for such a failure, this fact inextricably associated the young Republic in the popular mind with the humiliation of Versailles. After the treaty acceptance, Max Weber, Germany's outstanding social scientist and co-founder of the German Democratic party, prophetically exclaimed, "In ten years we all shall be nationalists." Such was the hour of birth for the German Republic. Yet Versailles was not its only dilemma.

The Weimar Constitution—most progressively democratic as it was—reflected the perplexities of the internal situation. It was the result of a compromise between the parties of a coalition. The Constitution left many basic issues undecided; and thus representing only a temporary framework, it marked the battlefield for coming constitutional struggles. True, the three partners in the coalition—the Social Democrats, the Catholic Center party, and the Middle Class Democrats—had much in common. They were the centers of a staunch opposition in the Empire. Even during the war their alliance had found expression in the July resolution of 1917, a binding declaration of the Reichstag's majority for a "peace without annexations." Yet they were called to political responsibility in November, 1918, rather suddenly and much against their own will. Though another legend today tries to make them the "November criminals," one may say that they became victims of their national conscience. They took the responsibility not because they desired to do so, but because those really responsible left it to them to master the chaos. They were confronted with a beaten army and a hungry nation which had suddenly lost its belief in its traditional leadership.

The alliance between Ebert and Hindenburg, the saddler and the general, often blamed as the Social Democratic treason against the young Republic even before its legal establishment—was in fact a symbol of the best Prussian tradition within the Social Democratic party and within army circles. The first President of the Republic and the monarchist military leader agreed upon collaboration to bring the soldiers home. It was above all a sincere attempt to save Germany. It was national consciousness *sans phrase*. The same sentiment was the basis of the Stinnes-Legien understanding, when the industrial organizations and trade unions united in action to lead the economy of chaos into an economy of peace. If there was a "Socialism of the trenches" (a slogan often abused in later days by the right-wing opposition), here it found its great political expression. The "November criminals" saved the country from Bolshevism by calling upon veteran troops of the old regime to suppress revolts in the early days of the Republic. The distress of the following years, an excellent propaganda campaign, and the poor memory of human beings made many Germans forget what had really happened in those nine months from the November revolution until the Constitution was proclaimed.

But this young Republic not only had to pay for the military defeat of the old regime, it also suffered from being successor to a political system which did not know the concept of "His Majesty's opposition." The Republic's new leaders had been "outsiders of the state" in pre-war times and deprived of all political responsibility. Even if these untried leaders had possessed greater statesmanlike caliber (which they did not), they certainly could not rise overnight to match a traditional ruling class of experts. In fact they lacked self-confidence and still retained something of an inferiority complex toward their former superiors. They further felt indebted to the bureaucrats and officers of the old regime who in spite of their monarchism went on to serve as experts for a republic to which they only paid lip service.

In view of these difficulties at the start, it is the more amazing that the young Republic after five years succeeded in overcoming the first post-war period of a "war after the war." The Weimar Republic defeated internal revolts from the reactionary right and the Communistic left. It steered through one reparation crisis after another. It even survived the climax of the crisis, the occupation of the Ruhr, and the incredible inflation, an era which, critical everywhere, had overthrown the men who had won the victory and made the peace: Clemenceau, Lloyd George, Wilson, Orlando, and Venizelos.

When, by 1924, the internal and external stabilization finally came, it meant a new lease on life for the whole of Europe. The five short years that followed offered to her the great chance for building up a new Europe based upon the Wilsonian principles. The League of Nations became the meeting ground for this policy of understanding, the Locarno Pact between the Allies and Germany its great symbol, and such statesmen as Briand, Stresemann, and Sir Austen Chamberlain its personification. This confluence of European statesmen was not just a tactical maneuver. It was possible because here representatives of the same European burgher class met, speaking the same language, holding the same values, adhering to a common human ideal. They were liberals. They saw great perspectives opening up where others scarcely perceived first feeble tendencies. Their approach, to use a formula of Lord d'Abernon, British ambassador to Berlin at that time, rested simply upon a lack of mistrust. Especially Stresemann, grown up with the ideals of 1848, seemed to be the clear expression of a reawakened liberalism. In him the German middle class and the German Republic found their political representative.

The German Republic indeed offered the great chance for a transformation, for the rebirth, of a political middle class. Contrary to western bourgeoisie, the German middle class had twice been defeated in the 19th century in its fight over political control: in the premature Revolution of 1848 and in the so-called "conflict over the Constitution" (1862-66)—the struggle between Bismarck and the Prussian parliament over the control of the army. Bismarck's Empire, born of the Iron Chancellor's victories on the battlefields of three wars, represented a working compromise between the Junkers and the bourgeoisie. Recognizing the vital importance of the capitalist middle class in economics, it still left the political control entirely in the hands of the old conservative ruling classes. They in return promised to win for expanding capitalism colonial markets abroad and protection against growing proletarian unrest at home. As a matter of fact, the middle classes relinquished their influence upon internal affairs. What remained was only an apparent retention of the Constitution. The middle classes were deprived of all sense of political responsibility in Germany. While a Victorian compromise merged the British middle class with a ruling aristocracy which from now on complied with middle-class standards, the German bourgeoisie accepted the social concepts and images of the traditional ruling classes. A "feudalization" of the German burgher was the result; but it was only after the World War that the serious consequences of this fact became evident. With these developments a decisive change in the middle classes themselves took place, characterized by the substitution of a solely economic "bourgeoisie" for a politically-minded "burgher."

Seen against this background, the Weimar Republic was the belated attempt at a middle-class rehabilitation. Unfortunately, however, even the short period of prosperity from 1924 to 1929 (a period when Europe's burning problems should and could have been settled peacefully) was only a boom produced by foreign loans for German finances. Thus the consolidation of the Republic in this epoch proved to be only apparent. This was true in a much deeper and non-economic sense. At the beginning came the inflation, in many respects the price paid for stabilization. Business, freed from debts and obligations, found a new starting point.

But it was not until five years later that the social effect of the inflation, and the political consequences, became evident. It meant the beginning of the end for the middle classes. And this occurred just at the advent of an epoch which promised under Stresemann's leadership to give the middle classes predominance. From then on it was not only a middle class broken by the pre-war development in Germany and handicapped by its own lack of political consciousness; now it had been shaken to its foundations. The year 1929 demonstrated how far "property and culture" of the former liberal middle classes had disappeared. From then on they were without their original power of resistance and capacity for influencing their environment. After this convulsion the kingpin of middle-class values—the idea of security—was shattered.

The process began with the shrinking of all economic security in the period of inflation, which withdrew the guarantee middle-class people enjoyed by virtue of their training, occupation, and standard of life. The authority of money was diminished. Money had been the measure of social prestige in the 19th century, identifying, according to Guizot's well-known formula, wealth and the moral good in middle-class civilization. A hierarchy of property still existed *de facto* but no longer *de jure*. The possession of property was more and more generally condemned in the popular judgment and even among well-to-do people. In any case, with the loss of property the burgher ideals of property and saving lost ground. Here is the social psychological root of Socialism, even though of a vague and ambiguous variety.

The disturbance was of course not restricted to the business world. It touched all spheres of life, including foreign politics. Established order, treaties, contracts, mutual understanding in arranging a dependable sphere of action, are no longer valid when the foundations crumble. The burgher, feeling that his internal economic security had been betrayed, was ready at such an hour to speak for an extreme revolutionary foreign policy—even if only to gain thereby compensation for his lost security in the internal sphere. This was the more true of a younger generation grown up in wartime and revolutionary chaos, which never knew the security of a bourgeois existence and which could hope to alter the entire uncertainty and hopelessness of its future only by a bold stroke. The "revolutionary dynamics" of National Socialism no doubt could recruit ardent supporters among the impoverished and embittered middle classes. This was even more true of their sons and daughters, "the dispossessed" who had sunk into the "lower" stratum of salaried employees.

It has often been said that National Socialism found its definite social backing in this "new middle class" of dependent employees who accepted this young movement as a last line of defense against threatening proletarization. Though this formula undoubtedly is a rough simplification, considering the more complex character of the Nazi following—restless military free lances, dissatisfied peasants, rootless unemployed, resigned idle youth—the white-collar class still presents a typical picture of the psychological elements of National Socialism's magnetic attraction and driving force.

The salaried employees were the product of monopoly capitalism (grown bureaucratic) and its victim, too. They were the children of an independent middle class which had been hard pressed by capitalist concentration, weakened by war derangements, and finally broken by the inflation.

Even if one may not accept the harsh judgment of Borgese that the "petty bourgeoisie" represented nothing but a "border-zone inhabited by people with white collars and grey consciences, proletarians who mimic the colours and manners of the bourgeoisie," the plight of the "new middle class" was deplorable indeed.

Such a plight offered a life without future, no hope for individual advancement, constant danger of replacement, an existence at the margin of society. A generation before, the working class had experienced a similar fate and had met it with a proletarian mass organization, which, counting on the rationally predictable self-defeat of the capitalist system, in the meantime promised reasonable betterment of the class plight. The newly dispossessed in post-war Germany, however, did not accept the proletarian formula. Instead of the class, it was the nation on which the confused white-collar man pinned his hopes for a fuller life. This turn toward nationalism also corresponded to the psychological attitudes and traditional experiences of the middle class. Their social esteem was based upon nationalist sentiment. Especially in Germany, military traditions had been formative for the nation that had found its first focal point in Prussian militarism and that had been united by victorious armies. Militarism as an attitude of human behavior had infiltrated all social institutions and relations.

The average German is undoubtedly a gregarious animal. It is, however, not the mannered reserve of British club life ("Manners makyth man" is the motto of one of the most ancient Oxford colleges) that satisfies his social ambitions nor is it the informal fellowship of the American Rotarians, Lions, and Elks. True happiness and comradeship the average German finds in the ranks, within the organized group, most glorious of all within the regiment. Soldierly thinking and the military way of life; the army's discipline, duty, authority, and obedience characterize the average German mentality. The cult of uniforms and flags, the goosestepping of the uniformed men appeal to a people who react *en masse* to the spectacular.

Such a reaction was especially powerful in a proud nation that had been made a "proletarian among the nations" by an intolerable treaty. The fight for national liberation and independence thus was easily identified with escape from personal distress. Glory in foreign affairs would not only dispose of internal national troubles but also remedy individual perplexities. Thus, to overcome a national inferiority complex, to count as a first-ranking nation again, being looked up to and if possible feared by the others, could regain for the Have-not nation a place in the sun and for the middle class the lost position in the social hierarchy.

Such militant dynamism calling for a *levée en masse* to break the chains of Versailles of course fascinated youth which by its very nature hated an all too temperate and sober "policy of fulfilment." Yet in order to set free all these forces and to direct them into one political stream the social circumstances of a depression were needed.

In 1929 the economic world crisis began. In Germany it revealed the breakdown of a surface boom. Simultaneously Germany experienced—as did other countries in lesser degree—the rebirth of the war as reflected in literature. After a period of ten years there was a peculiar revival of interest in war experiences. The soldier had never been absent in Germany, not even during Stresemann's period. His unrest had not been overcome and subdued. He had only stepped into the background. He lived on in many military political leagues. Now he got in touch with the new social groups that were pushing toward an "anti-bourgeois" reaction. The social revolution massed them together and gave them a revolutionary impulse.

The peculiarities of this growing revolution can be fully understood only if an additional source of support is clearly detected: unemployment. During the economic crisis it had continuously increased until in the early '30's it reached a point where it threatened the whole social fabric of the country.

The principal victim of the depression was youth. Children of the war and the inflation period, grown up in a world of insecurity, they needed the special care of society. They were hit hardest while they served as apprentices. They were dismissed after completing their training. The universities became the waiting halls of an unwanted youth. With no prospect for jobs on hand, even school work and study seemed to be a waste of time. At an age when fundamental impressions are formed, it became impossible for them to take root in labor, to acquire industrial habits. The only thing they cared about was how to kill time, for they had not learned how to fill it with life. Idleness became a habit. Disintegration of home and family, an increased number of young tramps and gangs, juvenile delinquency and pathological life—these phenomena are telling examples of the social effects of permanent unemployment.

The political consequences were of even greater import. Such a crisis created political radicalism of a special kind. The danger of this radicalism had already been seen by Karl Marx. According to him, it is not the mob proletariat (*Lumpenproletariat*) which should lead the labor movement, but a proletariat trained in industrial habits and factory discipline. The unemployed can never be an efficient opponent of the ruling economic system. He is an outsider of society and, therewith, he is losing his political impulse. The permanently unemployed is helpless, indifferent, apathetic.

This resignation alone explained the relative stability of an economic system with 20 per cent unemployed among the working population. Political revolutions were never led by the lowest, most miserable stratum of society. In the same way in post-war Germany, the vanguard of social revolt was the academic youth, especially the many thousands of Ph.D.'s without an adequate job. The salaried employees were in a similar plight. They were troubled and disturbed but not desperate and discouraged. They had at least a living memory of better times that aroused their political will. They became the leaders of the new movement.

Political propaganda found no difficulty in making these young men who saw no future for themselves hate this system which had accepted the humiliating Treaty of Versailles, hate an older generation which they made responsible for this crisis, despise a science unable to solve the burning problem of unemployment. These disillusioned young were anxious for a new faith, for new activity, for new vitality. In their eyes the old ideas of peace, equality, justice, had lost their spell. The heroic ideals of a non-bourgeois life, combined with the longing for the protection within a group to fight for and obey and thus to overcome the bitterness of personal and national resentment—those impulses were responsible for a sincere following in the leading group of young nationalists.

But underneath a very different mass following flocked to the new party. It came not the least from the unemployed. They represent, one may say, the "political reserve army" of our days. They are not the leaders, not the pioneers. They are certainly not constant reliable fighters. The often-observed fluctuations in parties of right- or left-wing radicalism are largely due to such followings. They are easily won. Yet if promised success does not soon materialize, they as quickly leave the revolutionary party. They are political driftwood. They simply indicate the high tide which can burst the dikes. The permanently unemployed endanger the existing order; they also endanger the revolution. Their radicalism is not genuine. It does not go back to basic issues, to the roots of social and political evils. It has no roots because they themselves are not rooted in society. Their revolution is above, all destructive. It is action, but not responsible activism. It is a "revolution of nihilism."

That the revolution of nihilism became the core of the movement is, however, due to another group of outsiders: the irregulars. More will be said later about this most crucial class among the National Socialist following. Suffice it to mention here that they were largely recruited from the young war generation who, though they returned from the battlefields, did not find home. War became their profession. They were the early fighters of the movement. They probably represented its driving force all the time. They certainly decided more and more the course of events.

Such a manifold and often incongruous social backing largely explains the complexity of National Socialism. Certain German traditions and particular post-war experiences contributed to make it a strange amalgamation leading to the characteristic ambiguity prevalent even years after the seizure of power.

The story of the turmoil years preceding the National Socialist victory has been often told. Only a few milestones of this thorny road toward the end of the Weimar Republic may be here enumerated. The political crisis was not in the least a result of the great socio-economic upheaval that had undermined crucial social strata. In the spectacular September elections of 1930 the right and left, the National Socialists and Communists, had risen to such numerical strength that their tactical collaboration in a negative opposition made the normal functioning of the parliamentary machinery practically impossible. The Republic's electoral system, proportional representation, was also instrumental in the destruction of this "most progressive" democracy.

Chancellor Bruening, at the wheel during the next two critical years, had to rely upon a slim and often shifting majority of coalition parties which to be exact did not altogether support him but—as was the case with the most important Social Democrats—only "tolerated" him as the lesser evil compared with threatening National Socialism.

The result was an extremely unstable political situation which the Chancellor sought to master almost entirely with the help of the emergency powers of Article 48. No doubt, the Weimar Republic provided for a "Constitutional Dictatorship." The Reich's President may, "if the public safety and order are considerably disturbed or endangered, take such measures as are necessary to restore public safety and order." These extraordinary powers in the hands of the President and his Chancellor did not preclude parliamentary control because (in the words of the same Article 48) "the Reich's President shall inform the Reichstag without delay of all measures taken under this article. On demand by the Reichstag the measures shall be repealed." But misinterpretation of his constitutional duties by the Reich's President and practical self-abdication of the Reichstag led to a slipping of such constitutional checks and responsibilities. Continuous emergency legislation undermined the weak parliamentary structure. Bruening himself tried to keep up at least its legal substance. After his brutal dismissal by Hindenburg in May, 1932, the last remnants of constitutional procedure went.

The presidential or authoritarian Cabinet of von Papen, Chancellor according to Hindenburg's own choosing, was illegal from the start. Neither could it expect to find parliamentary confidence (prerequisite for its constitutional existence), as its smashing electoral defeat of July 31, 1932, definitely proved, nor did it have any backing within the nation. It was nothing but an attempt to put the clock back to a bygone imperial Germany—and an amateurish venture at that. The principal deed of this "Cabinet of the Barons" was its coup in Prussia, when it ousted the legally established coalition government, last stronghold of republicanism in Germany. Papen thus broke the last defense line against rising National Socialism, whose onslaught could certainly not be stemmed by the most unpopular government Germany ever possessed.

Whether General von Schleicher, Papen's successor in the Chancellery, could have turned the tide; whether his Cabinet might have broken the constitutional deadlock in establishing new political fronts welding together the Reichswehr, trade unions, and other extra-parliamentary forces; whether such new alignments could have revitalized a deathly sick German democracy if given sufficient time to develop—all such considerations were conjectural in view of the fact that, presidential appointee as Schleicher was, his political existence depended on Hindenburg's confidence. When he lost this confidence it was not least the work of a camarilla whose web around the Old Marshal he himself had helped to spin.

On January 30, 1933, Hindenburg, following the advice of Franz von Papen, his choice confidant, made Hitler Chancellor of the Reich. The "Custodian of the Constitution" handed over the keys of the republican citadel to its arch foe. The German Republic was dead.

In addition to those historical elements, specific to the German social and political situation, there were of course general crisis elements of democratic government also responsible for the growth of this anti-parliamentarian revolution. Difficulties were manifold in the turbulent post-war world. The basic belief of liberalism and democracy, the belief in human progress and the ultimate goodness of mankind, had been definitely shaken by the war and the disturbing post-war experiences. So was the idea of compromise which is fundamental to the working of democratic institutions. It was jeopardized at a time when a fight over ultimate issues seemed to prevail. Agreement on fundamentals is a precondition for an effective contest of democratic parties. The prolonged economic crisis striking at the essence of the existing economic order by necessity questioned the political system too.

Democracy had grown up together with capitalism. No wonder that in its critical hour it was easily identified with that economic system. The anti-capitalist almost automatically aligned himself with anti-democratic forces.

In most countries a perplexed electorate enlarged after the war and, suddenly called to responsibility, quickly accepted the proffered expedients. The average voter, and not seldom his parliamentarian representative also, could not understand the increasing complexity of modern life. The oftener he was called to the polls, the more disturbed he became. The year 1932, the one preceding the National Socialist seizure of power, saw no less than four national elections, to say nothing of numerous state and municipal elections. Such frequent polling could, in fact, become a part of the political strategy of anti-parliamentarian forces controlling key positions in Germany by then. "Let them vote until they pop off," ill-fated General Schleicher had sarcastically suggested.

More and more people preferred to leave decisions in the hands of a strong executive. In fact, a new balance between legislative and executive power often had to be struck when legislative and executive functions inextricably merged in emergencies—and in the last quarter of the century Europe never came out of this state of emergency. Rapid and decisive action was needed, for which democratic institutions were not adequately prepared. A dictatorial government, unhampered by democratic control, seemed at first view more efficient for handling the crisis and for giving jobs, bread, and security to the harassed masses. They in return were often ready to surrender a large part of liberty for economic security and thus to hail the oncoming Caesar.

Such a breakdown of the functioning democracy comes neither as fate nor as sudden surprise. Vital democracies, alert to their functions, can adjust themselves to new necessities. The disintegration of their institutions is usually a slow and not at all inescapable process. At almost any stage of this critical development, a self-confident democracy may call a halt to such a decline, especially if it can fall back on traditional reserves. The following chapters will describe in detail what has actually happened to basic democratic institutions, such as political parties, in countries which became the dictatorships of today. Here this much should be stated: the final destruction was due not just to the inner dynamics of democratic institutions, but to a number of circumstances some of which have been outlined above for the three major revolutions. Personalities also played their part. Even intrigues entered into the story of the breakdown of democratic governments, though a *histoire scandaleuse* has given them an exaggerated importance. No doubt the advisers close to King Vittorio Emanuele in Italy's hour of danger were of definite influence; so was the camarilla (von Papen, Meissner, Oskar von Hindenburg, etc.) around Reichspresident Hindenburg during the last years of the Republic. Yet intrigues enter only when the constitutional machinery is already losing its grip, when the normal channels of governmental processes are disrupted; i.e., when democracy is in crisis. The intriguers are certainly not the miracle men and the extraordinary, wise planners they are often played up to be by sensational publicists. They have only one thing in common with the owl of Minerva: they do not start their flight until twilight.

PATTERNS OF MODERN DICTATORSHIP

Modern dictatorships—as the three case studies on their origin in Russia, Italy, and Germany amply prove—are conditioned by national characteristics and historic circumstances, by ideological foundations and social alignments and not least by personality factors. Manifold as their national variations may be, there are, however, a number of common features which typify modern dictatorship and indeed constitute a part of its definition.

Five basic patterns stand out, almost invariably discernible in the gamut of modern dictatorships and visible in all strata of their existence: the promise of security, action instead of program, quasi-democratic foundations, war psychology, and the leadership principle.

Strange as it seems, the basic appeal of dynamic dictatorship is its *promise of stability*. The masses longing for rest are ready to

Such comfort was especially welcome to a generation over-strained by war and post-war experiences, overtired and longing for rest. The rise of dictatorships found its complement in a re-nunciation of politics by the masses. In these post-war years sport had become popular with the European people as never before. It was a refuge long before dictators discovered the usefulness and propaganda value of Olympics to demonstrate the efficiency and glamour of a totalitarian state. It might almost be said that politics itself was judged like a football match or a bullfight. Let the best man win. Success became the only measuring rod and no moral code could affect it. The right of the stronger nation was accepted. That was the way of legalizing revolutions and conse-quently of causing their *fait accompli* to be accepted in interna-tional politics. Thus a bourgeois society became reconciled to dynamic post-war politics.

All modern demagogues, however, have instinctively felt the necessity of building *quasi-democratic foundations* underneath their dictatorial rule. Their "legal" seizure of power, their all-em-bracing propaganda machine, their effective policy of *panem et circenses* give daily evidence of this intrinsic feature of post-demo-cratic autocracy. Yet it should be understood that their concept of democracy, if it may be called that, is militant in character. Such a turn may be the simplest way of arriving at some kind of democratic organization especially appropriate to nations with intrinsically military traditions and without the long political training of the Anglo-Saxon people. The nation is seen as an army. Its life is a constant battle. Its citizens are political soldiers. The "new democracy" is nothing but the introduction of the military vision into political life.

In fact these dictatorships were born in the World War and this is their fourth common feature—they are borne along by *war psychology*. Lamartine in his Manifesto to Europe (1848) had said, "War is nearly always a dictatorship. Soldiers forget institu-tions for men." This is even more true in modern warfare. There are no longer any frontiers. Air raids and hunger blockades affect civilians as well. The civilians' morale is a deciding factor in the

outcome of modern warfare; and since it is a war of all groups—
men, women, and children alike—the whole nation must be organized. The idea of the totalitarian state was born in the last
World War, which became a totalitarian war. In wartime all
opposition and discussion must cease. Personal liberty no longer
exists. As a matter of fact, the best argument for this sort of suppression is the country's peril. Thus, the claim to absolutist control
by the dictatorial parties in post-war Europe has always been
based on a real or presumed danger from abroad. War is a dictatorship's beginning, its demand, its test. Therefore modern
dictatorship focuses its machinery for propaganda on building up
a fighting spirit. No actual warfare is needed in order to create
this warlike atmosphere and reaction. As soon as it is aroused, it
works almost automatically and reaches ever-widening circles.
Alarmed neighbors naturally respond by gathering their forces
against menacing aggression. The dictator in return calls for even
stronger power to counter threatening encirclement. When the
League of Nations proclaimed its sanctions in the Italo-Ethiopian
War, it was a godsend to Mussolini's power: it strengthened the
control and prestige of Fascist dictatorship.

This predominant militancy of the dictatorial parties undoubtedly made them especially attractive to the armed forces. In spite
of obvious reservations, raised particularly among the higher
military caste, against the irrational and unruly elements in these
dynamic dictatorships, their continuous call to arms promised
dominant position and prestige to the soldierly profession. No
wonder that in many lands army circles took a friendly view of
rising Fascism, not without flattering themselves that they could
easily control these irregulars in the end. This sympathy or at
least responsive reserve toward the revolutionary upstart assured
their successful coup d'état. It was good strategy, therefore, for
the new dictatorships to establish the best relations possible with
the military.

The warlike temper of modern totalitarianism, however, was
not meant only for home consumption in order to win over a
restless populace and the military cadres of the nation. The con-

sequences of this militancy for international politics are so obvious
and so often told in the daily news that there is no need for further proof. "War" is in fact inseparable from the meaning of
Fascism. In one of his few outspoken programmatic declarations
Mussolini stated: "And, above all, Fascism believes neither in the
possibility nor the utility of perpetual peace. . . . War alone
brings up to its highest tension all human energy and puts the
stamp of nobility upon the peoples who have the courage to
meet it."

This driving force of militant dictatorships is raised to high-
pitched intensity by a quasi-religious missionarism. Every revolution which claims to be more than a mere change of government
and which pretends to create a new social order must also stir up
neighboring countries and awaken in them a spirit of deep unrest.
The idea of the great mission is indissolubly mixed with national
ambitions. Such a combination characterized the ideas of the
French Revolution. It also holds true of the modern ideologies of
the Third International, the revival of the Roman Empire, and
the Nazis' "New Order."

A dynamic foreign policy is essential for totalitarian dictatorship. As a matter of fact, with the exception of Soviet Russia,
the separation between democracies and dictatorships may be
identified with the often-used division of the powers into the
Haves and the Have-nots. It is obvious what an important role
national frustration has played in the rise of modern dictatorships.
Their design is to liberate the country from national humiliation.

This holds even more true in internal affairs. Here the claim to
power is based upon the necessary destruction of the nation's, or
the classes', arch enemy; and when power is won, the *permanent
revolution*—even if renounced in foreign affairs, at least at times,
for tactical reasons—has to go on in internal politics. Opposition
groups have to be seized, the party has to be regularly purged,
trials and expulsions have to take place. All this means stamina
to a dictatorship, and even the most peaceful work of daily life
must show the touch of warlike activity. There are a thousand
battles going on: the battle of grain, the battle for raw materials,

the fight for joy after work, the battle of the birth rate. And they are all merely preparations for the supreme battle for world power.

Scarcely any modern demagogue wears civilian clothing when he appears before his masses, and when he does he always looks as if he were wearing a disguise. The uniform almost becomes the measuring stick, the shibboleth, for real demagogical leadership in Europe. He who does not wear a uniform—like Turkey's Inonu, successor to militant Kemal Ataturk—is not a genuine, one hundred per cent dictator.

Politics itself has been defined by Carl Schmitt (belated partisan and for a time crown jurist of the Third Reich) in terms of the irreducible category of Friend and Foe. Fully militarized social relationships have been basically conceived on the battlefield. No concept of civil government is left. Militancy reflects all activities of modern dictatorship. It becomes its organizing principle. It shapes its party structure and its *Wehrwirtschaft*, its totalitarian control and its revolutionary missionarism. It is the "permanent revolution" in foreign affairs and in internal politics that makes possible the strange mixture of dictatorship's promise of stability and at the same time the belief in revolutionary action. Victorious dynamics become the only security of a war society.

There is, finally, the *leadership principle*, perhaps the most dangerous element of modern dictatorship. "Power corrupts, absolute power corrupts absolutely," in the words of Lord Acton. Says Goering in his *Germany Reborn*: "We National Socialists believe that in political affairs Adolf Hitler is infallible, just as the Roman Catholic believes that in religious matters the Pope is infallible. His will is my law."

The decree of August 4, 1939, definitely establishing the Fascist Falangist organization as sole party in Franco Spain reads as follows: "Interpretation of the statutes and documents of the movement rests with El Caudillo [the leader], who alone may determine the circumstances and the pace of the movement." His position is tersely defined: "El Caudillo is the supreme chief of the movement and personifies all the power and honor of the movement. As the author of the historic era in which Spain has the opportunity to rule her destiny, he assumes absolute authority. He is responsible only before God and history."

It is characteristic of the leader that he is responsible not to those below him but only to those above him, and therefore is finally responsible only to a supreme Fuehrer or Duce who is responsible not to any man "but to God and the nation."

This twofold justification of political authority reverts to the two premises of modern demagoguery: its character of a substitute and its democratic element. How important the democratic or pseudo-democratic responsibility to the nation is regarded even by the leader state has been indicated above. Modern dictatorship assumes the place of a religion for people who have lost their faith in transcendental power. It ministers to the human yearning for worship. This explains the subsequent and deadly conflict of a totalitarian state with religious authorities. At the same time such a revival of the divine right theory serves as a useful device for shifting final responsibility to an agency deprived of efficient means of control and coercion. It fortifies dictatorship. It transcends human power to combat, thus removing it from the realm of human criticism. It makes the dictator a superman, a demigod.

The leader epitomizes the dictatorial system. He is its beginning, its moving spirit, its fate. The analysis of his power and position, therefore, will lead to the core of modern totalitarianism.

Chapter II

THE LEADER

Leadership is the prominent theme of any political order. The very existence of society by necessity leads to a differentiation between leaders and followers. Selection, character, and function of political leaders, however, will be varied according to the institutional and conceptual framework in which this relationship is placed. In fact, this social context of modern leadership reveals the basic discrepancies between democratic and dictatorial governments in our day. A comparative analysis of the Number One Men thus may serve as a key toward an understanding of their irreconcilable differences.

The study of the star performers on the stage of history has always attracted the inquisitive mind. It undoubtedly offers a natural and convenient approach to politics. It deals with "human nature in politics," thus dramatizing highly technical phenomena of modern government. It has won additional impetus in our day because of the appearance in the political arena of the spectacular leader type of modern dictators. The exciting rise of unknown soldiers from darkness to world position invites an interpretation of politics in terms of personalities—an interpretation indeed most welcome to a mechanized age longing for color and glamour in the drab of its daily grind. It is no mere accident that the two schools of thought concerning the interpretation of history which flourished especially in the aftermath of the First World War, the "debunking" school and the "heroic" school, center around personalities. A "devil theory of history" blames everything on the villain, thus relieving the betrayed masses of any responsibility. "Hero worship," on the other hand, pins all its hope on the rise of the liberator who will lead suffering society to a better morrow.

In a way, such an interpretation is a return to Treitschke's and Carlyle's "It is men who make history" and a reaction against an economic interpretation of history which had made leaders nothing but functionaries of the driving socio-economic forces in history. Just as this theoretical controversy over character and personality in history, and individuality in society, represented an unreal simplification of social phenomena, so the unfortunate separation labeling political organizations as leaderless democracies and programless dictatorships is far from the reality of existing tensions. True, such a simplification somehow represents the extremes and, one may say, the danger elements of the two systems. Democratic leadership is often in peril of being suffocated by program and organization. On the other hand, dictatorship frequently tends toward uncontrolled personal autocracy alone. Yet the real life of democracy and dictatorship moves on between these two extremes.

The essence of modern dictatorship is not explained merely by the need for leadership. In fact, the rise of modern dictatorship is no mere accident due to a few dynamic personalities in contemporary affairs. There have been dynamic leaders and potential dictators at all times. The rise and acceptance of modern dictators are due, as was shown above, to social circumstances which are connected with two historical premises: the ascendancy of modern mass democracy and the breakdown of institutions. Modern democracies have to answer the problem of leadership in the mass state if they want to survive the challenge of dictatorships. Modern dictatorships, autocratic as they may be, have to fulfill the social needs for security and material welfare for their mass following if they expect any degree of permanence. In this sense, both systems—rivals though they are in contemporary politics—belong to the same historic era.

The type of leader prevalent under a political rule is always conceived within its institutional setup. The difference between the British Prime Minister and the National Socialist Fuehrer cannot therefore be simply resolved into a personality pattern of two different men with different temperament and different life experience. This divergent leadership, above all, reflects on the varying political orders which they represent and may have even themselves created. Certainly national climate, historic experiences, and, to some extent, personality factors are most important in creating or preserving specific political systems and in bringing to the fore particular types of leadership. One may well presume that a type like Hitler would be utterly unacceptable to the British people should they ever choose to accept dictatorial control. Even a comparison between Mussolini's and Hitler's rule indicates an extraordinary degree of differentiation in Fascism itself.

Greatly though they vary in time and space, two main types of political leadership can be distinguished: *institutional* and *personal*—types roughly corresponding to the contrasting political systems: *democracy* and *dictatorship*.

Democratic leaders always remain representatives of institutions and not substitutes for them, as dictators claim to be. Stanley Baldwin rose to political preeminence in his historical Carlton Club speech of 1922 when he smashed Lloyd George's war coalition. Baldwin said of the then Prime Minister, "A dynamic force is a very terrible thing. It may crush you, but it is not necessarily right." This speech was a declaration of war against Lloyd George, the demagogue, by Baldwin, the defender of institutional politics. It was the good fortune of this same British statesman to reach the climax of his political career in his adroit handling of the monarchical crisis of 1936 (years before his blunders in international affairs had become manifest). Baldwin epitomized the institutional character of British statesmanship.

This structure of democratic leadership is also visible in the personality features of democratic leaders. The long gallery of Prime Ministers from Walpole to Chamberlain illustrates this. Again Baldwin represents an outstanding example of this species. He is, above all, the plain man. His inevitable pipe is the visible bond of union with the plain man. One may say that he had the English-

man's "genius for appearing an amateur in a game" in which in
fact he was "a superb professional." Sir Austen Chamberlain was
often described as the most English of Englishmen; and what was
said about Herriot—"an average Frenchman, a stronger dose, but
the same mixture"—holds true also of the average party leader in
a democracy who tends to be, as Bagehot said, "an uncommon
man of common opinions." The same thing could be repeated of
Stresemann, who even had a face and figure very common in
central Germany. He was always praised for his ability to meet
his adversaries halfway. Balance of mind, distaste for violence of
expression, a faculty for spreading conciliation on all sides—these
are characteristics of democratic statecraft. "I am not a lawyer
pleading a case," said a great Swiss leader, "I cannot put an argument in such a dazzling light that all the other arguments must
retreat into the shade."

There is, as a matter of fact, a demagogical element within
every modern democratic government too. Its mass democratic
character makes it necessary. It would be an oversimplification
therefore to identify demagoguery and dictatorship. However,
the preeminent elements of leadership in a democracy are institutional. This fact of course leads to variety in democratic leadership according to different institutional structures. The unlike
character of the British Prime Minister, the President of the former
French Council, and the American President is only a reflection
of different institutional setups of these democratic governments.

The extraordinary position in power and prestige the *British
Prime Minister* enjoys no doubt makes him the most influential
prototype of institutional leadership. The preeminence of the
British Premier is attested to by his extraordinary function in
British politics. He is majority leader in Parliament, leader of the
ruling party in the country, chairman of the Cabinet, and his
office is the main channel of communication between the people
and the Crown. The fact that he must perform these institutional
functions of course must be taken into account in the selection of
a Premier. Especially in recent decades it has become an unwritten law that he shall be a member of the House of Commons. In

the two-party system the leader of the majority party, successful in the elections, almost automatically becomes the embodiment of the highest political power. Strict party discipline and the right of dissolution guarantee the Premier a strong lead in the Parliament. No statute settles his position as Chairman of the Cabinet. Officially speaking, he is regarded as *primus inter pares*. Actually he is the "keystone of the Cabinet arch." He can call for the resignation of any of his colleagues. The Prime Minister's close contact with the Crown might give him additional strength.

Recent development of the British Cabinet system has led even to emphasis on an Inner Cabinet which makes the crucial decisions, especially in time of crisis. This trend, however, does not mean that the British Prime Minister has lost his chief quality, "the gift for getting difficult people to work together." Collective responsibility in the British Cabinet system creates the necessity for teamwork. These institutional limits of the British Prime Minister certainly do not preclude variations in the importance of individual Premiers according to their personalities. An incapable Prime Minister, not infrequently, has ruined his conventional position. The actual power of a Peel, Gladstone, or Disraeli might easily outgrow the institutional framework. It is this happy combination of institutional tradition and individual initiative, of control and vigor, of representation and responsibility that can find its personification in Great Britain's highest office.

The position of the *President of the French Council of Ministers* (before the debacle of 1940) was somehow complicated by the existence of a multi-party system in the Third Republic. The French Premier, of course, was not a majority leader of the English type. One of his main tasks was to maintain a working majority in the Chamber of Deputies and a most uncertain accord between Cabinet members of more than half a dozen parties. Skillful conciliation therefore became the first and most momentous quality of his leadership. Even a Prime Minister who was the unchallenged leader of the predominant party in the coalition, as were Herriot and Blum, had to use persuasion as his chief weapon. He certainly could not whip together an obstinate

Parliament with the threat of dissolution—a power which the British Prime Minister possesses and which is largely responsible for the greater stability of the British government. Indeed, since 1870 England has had only one-fifth the number of Cabinets that the Third Republic had. The fact that this high rate of casualty was not more detrimental to the French political system may be attributed largely to the civil service. Guarantor of continuity in governmental policies in the midst of constant reshuffling of Cabinets, it was the real executive power in France.

But this fact discloses the enervating task that confronted a French Premier. His primary function—to serve as the connecting link between the legislative power and the executive power— put him "between hammer and anvil, between his two deadly enemies, Parliament and the bureaucracy." To be called upon perpetually to restore the balance between hostile agencies was a great test of ingenuity and skill in statesmanship. The numerous "stopgap ministries" of second-rate politicians should not obscure the fact that the French Republic had had great ministers who succeeded in striking such a balance and winning a leader's prestige. It is no less significant that in time of crisis, France—that country of suspicious individuals—has always been willing to accept the authoritative leadership necessitated by national emergency. This was true with Thiers after the debacle of 1870, with Clemenceau during World War I; it would have been also true with Daladier and Reynaud if they had had the courage to accept this challenge.

Contrary to some opinions raised in the heat of electoral campaigns, the *American President's* leadership, colorful and personal as it often appears to be, also is far from any dictatorial pattern. His constitutional power and prerogatives are ample as compared with those of British and French political leaders. He is the national leader, the head of the Cabinet, the director of administration. He has an extensive power of appointment. He can exercise wide influence on congressional legislation, and he is a legislator in his own right. Especially in the field of foreign and military affairs, he is much more than a mere executive. To the public he is the personification of the American government. In fact, the whole American system is largely influenced by the President's office. The major parties have often been described as "loose leagues to capture the Presidency." The maintenance of the two-party system is in large measure due to orientation to this situation.

Yet the fact that the concentration of power and responsibility in the presidential office is so great seems to have invited a number of checks upon the actual authority of the President. The presidential selection itself effects in a way the curtailing of his power. Men of outstanding authority in the Senate are never chosen. A candidate may not be selected, as French Presidents were, because he is weak, but he had better not show much self-willed resolution before election. Soon after he enters the White House the principle of separation of powers makes itself felt, thus restoring a delicate though hardly definable balance. Not infrequently the second Congress of an administration contains a majority politically adverse to the President in either one or both of its houses. Further, the party which brought him into office and which looks at him as "chief patronage dispenser" will be most influential in all his decisions, including appointments officially left to his discretion. "The President," as Peter Odegard poignantly remarks, "is not only the leader of his party; he is in a very real sense its prisoner."

All of which does not mean that the President cannot exert a tremendous influence on public opinion, especially when he proves to have the "capacity to get along with people." But even in foreign affairs—a much-talked-about domain of presidential power—it may be doubted whether an American President, even if he dared to sign a Munich Pact as the British Premier did, could have "got away with it."

Much will depend, it is true, on the President as a personality. He may take a narrow view of his prerogatives or he may take a wide view of his functions; yet when a President's actions and achievements are viewed in historical perspective, they seem much less the result of personal whims and much more the reflection, in the words of Charles A. Beard, of the "spirit of the times" and the "state of the country." The institutions may make themselves felt in a looser manner in this spacious continent of great riches. They still hold the President as their representative no less than other countries which define more strictly the position of their institutional leader.

A time of crisis opens a new challenge to institutional leadership in a democracy. This holds especially true of the Premiership in a war Cabinet. It certainly would be a misleading simplification, though often suggested in our daily use, to believe that the fact of necessary concentration of power and decision in the hands of a war Premier inevitably leads to dictatorial government. This shift of responsibilities only proves that different qualities are needed for leadership in war and peace.

A shrewd observer of Great Britain once stated, "The four most powerful people in England are the Prime Minister, the governor of the Bank of England, the editor of the London *Times*, and the Archbishop of Canterbury." This is hardly a combination that any country but England could offer to the observer. It contains the name of no "rich man," and each name is a symbol of a representative and, in a way, a unique institution. Such a catalogue somehow reflects Burke's ideal conservatism: the disposition to preserve and the ability to improve. Men like Baldwin and Neville Chamberlain in their Victorianism were typical representatives of such institutions. In recent times, however, doubt has sprung up in the minds of many thoughtful observers whether this preservation of the Victorian compromise has not led to a petrification of the ruling class in Great Britain and thus taken the spark out of constructive leadership in post-war England. Whatever one may think of Great Britain's morale— low in the '30's—and of "the danger of being a gentleman," she was put to a new challenge in September, 1939.

In wartime even democracies call for dynamic leadership. The shift from the Premiership of Neville Chamberlain to that of Winston Churchill no doubt meant the end of an era, brought to a climax by the financial crisis of 1931. This government of mid-

Victorian businessmen had a primary mission to pull Great Britain out of the depression. But while it succeeded well in this thorny task, it characteristically failed in mastering the much greater international perils by approaching them with familiar and orderly techniques of skillful traders. Yet the temper of the era was not any longer that of peaceful competition. The sedate and complacent were hopelessly out of place long before the actual shooting started and were swept out of office when war came in earnest to the British Isles.

Churchill was the natural, in fact the only, choice in succession. In a way, this change in Cabinet was the procedure of World War I all over again, when Lloyd George took the place of Mr. Asquith, who—though a perfect Premier in peacetime—was out of place in time of war. "What an occasion was the whirlwind of the war. Here was place for no holiday magistrate, no fair-weather sailor." These words of Emerson on Lincoln could be repeated of Churchill, too. In fact, they remind us of Addison's classic lines praising Churchill's great ancestor, John Churchill, first Duke of Marlborough, "who rides in the whirlwind and directs the storm."

When the storm broke, Winston Churchill became Britain's pilot. In peacetime, the realization of this greatest ambition might have been forever denied to the *enfant terrible* of the Conservative party. War leadership called for all the qualifications he so fully possesses: passion and perseverance, vigor and vision, bold daring and independence of mind, self-confidence and the ability to create trust, and even the "power of drawing from misfortune itself the means of future success." He may lack patience and caution, so often praised as the great qualities of Asquith. Yet he may well defy the dictum, attributed to the same Asquith, that he "has genius but not judgment." Neville Chamberlain might have thought similarly of his tempestuous critic and colleague. These statesmen speak a different language. They belong to a different spiritual climate.

Churchill could be called almost pre-Victorian. As a critic once said: "He has brought back the arrogance and splendor of Elizabethan language. He has recovered the spirit of those rough vibrant days when men of affairs were buccaneers at heart, but poets in their leisure time, and fierce implacable patriots always." Perhaps in the mixture of British and American blood which flows through his veins lies the clue to his tempestuous career and meteoric temperament. From his British ancestors he inherited and represented institutional traditions and a full share of "bulldog British tenacity." From his mother, the former Jennie Jerome of New York, he may have received his bold daring, his boyhood rebellion against authority, and his independence of mind.

Churchill's mental make-up, to use William James' well-known classification, is not that of the tender-minded but of the tough-minded. He is great as an orator: "When Churchill thunders, all Britain takes heed." He is great as a writer and critic; in these trying days he is his nation become articulate, its thoughts cast into form. Yet as an orator and writer Churchill shows the qualities of a soldier. Since early youth, adventurous war was the chief factor in his life. Today, as a sober elderly statesman, he is a fighter just the same. He is not the unreliable and unstable erratic, as Asquith saw him. In fact, even in his military blunders there were brilliant conceptions and sound strategy. "All Mr. Churchill needs," said Harold Begbie prophetically almost twenty years ago, "is a direction in his life of a great idea. . . . To be saved from himself, Mr. Churchill must be carried away by enthusiasm for some great ideal, an ideal so much greater than his own place in politics that he is willing to face death for its triumph, even the many deaths of political life." This great ideal came with his crusade against Hitler's Germany and its challenge.

In this life-and-death struggle of modern society, where respect for human individuality and preservation of social traditions are at stake, where a new balance has to be struck between individuality and institutional heritage, it is not the cynic who can revitalize the concepts of democracy worn thin, but the courageous and self-assertive fighter. It seems to be no mere accident that in order to find such a man Great Britain had to go back to a time when England was young—old Merrie England.

He had warned his compatriots "while England slept." A modern Cassandra, he clearly foresaw the world nearing the abyss "step by step." When the "peace" of Munich came, like a Biblical prophet he exhorted Parliament: "Do not suppose that this is the end. It is only the first foretaste of the bitter cup which will be proffered to you, unless by supreme recovery of moral health and martial vigor we rise again to take our stand for freedom, as in olden times."

DICTATORIAL LEADERSHIP: PERSONAL CONTROL

The Demagogue

Confronted with the institutional leadership in its British, French, and American version is the personal leadership of the dictatorial type. Here again will be found differentiations due to national traditions, historic circumstances, and personality patterns, but all modern dictators are characterized by specific elements of leadership. In the first place they are anti-institutional. As a matter of fact, their very rise is the expression of the crisis of institutions. Modern dictatorships, substitutes for institutions in the age of mass democracy, create by necessity a specific type of leadership. The modern dictator is, above all, a *demagogue*. He has to be a "leader of the people" who rises from the dark. This illustrates the democratic chance of everyone. You yourself may become the leader tomorrow. In fact, you address in the leader the masses whose humble son he is and continues to be. He is "the cottage-bred man." He lived the simple man's life and understands it. He is proud of having been poor. He harps upon the hardships he has experienced. He never risks losing his class ties with the people. An extensive propaganda machine daily proves that he still belongs to the people. He is so genial. He plays with children. He chats with the plain man. He takes simple breakfasts in the fields with the peasant folk. Puritan simplicity, or at least the appearance of it, is the motto of the modern dictator's standard of life. The noble-born is suspect in popular dictatorships. Primo de Rivera in Spain and De la Rocque in France could not make the grade of modern dictatorial rule. On the other hand, Mussolini, who never tasted coffee until he was twenty, was reared in a family on the margin of starvation where "one potato more or less" meant a critical issue. Hitler, too, had to eke out a precarious existence from his earliest days. Even Napoleon confessed in his early letters to his father from the officers' school in Brienne "that he was fed up with having his poverty the butt of jokes of his aristocratic comrades."

The demagogue's way of rising to power is most democratic. Mussolini since his early political beginnings as a radical and ardent Socialist was determined to revive the "power of the market place," the spontaneous voice of the mob. For a projected autobiography he had devised the significant title: "Della Strada al Potere"—from the street to power.

Applause from the multitude is pleasing music to Il Duce; to Hitler it is a matter of life. Like William II of imperial Germany before him he may exaggerate the importance of oratory: "All enormous world revolutionary events have been brought about— by the spoken word," he claimed. Yet his rise has been brought about by mass meetings in a Wagnerian setting. Like a live wire they electrify him as much as he hypnotizes them. When he awakens the masses, they bring him into being. "The Drummer," as he proudly called himself in the early days, is "nothing but the flint which strikes the spark out of the German nation." This contact with the aroused masses becomes his real life and nature, so much so that he loses the meaning of personal conversation; as one astute interviewer once remarked, "He talks to you as if you were a public meeting."

Only recognition by the people can legitimize the demagogue. He is nothing without the masses. The acclaim of the multitude means everything to him.

The histrionic abilities of modern dictators are outstanding features of their technique. The character of their oratory of course will depend on the national climate of their country. As a matter of fact, it can serve as a symbol of modern demagogical dictatorship. Those who do not like to be in the limelight of an aroused mass, such as Salazar of Portugal, actual rulers of their nation though they may be, are not demagogical dictators.

The Master of the Machine

In addition to the demagogical elements so significant in the life of modern dictators, there is another element connected with contemporary autocracies which seems to be contradictory to these emotional dynamics. The modern autocrat is the *master of a political machine* because his rule is based upon strong organization, one may almost say upon a quasi-institutional setup. The dictator may delegate many functions of its technical process to his lieutenants, but he has to keep final control over the machine. That is the reason why in the succession of dictatorship not a Trotsky, the glamour boy of the Revolution, but a Stalin, the cold master of a powerful political machine, finally won the power.

The historical conflict between Stalin and Trotsky was more than a personal struggle. True, they were antagonists by character. They cordially disliked each other because they belonged to different worlds. Stalin called Trotsky "an aristocrat and an actor," the worst two things a Bolshevist could call his co-revolutionary. (It has been rightly stated again and again that Trotsky was an aristocrat in all save the social sense: he had brains, courage, and style.) Trotsky called Stalin "a boor, treacherous, barbarous, and corrupt." There is no doubt that just as Trotsky was a violent individualist, so was Stalin a creature of committees. The lone wolf stood against a patient politician. "Stalin," the synonym for "steel," was all patience and caution. He could wait for his hour while the dashing dynamics of Trotsky made him overshoot his mark and thus miss his historical chance. The great theorist could not measure up to the supreme organizer. Also, Stalin, the partisan of the early hour, had been an ardent party worker when it meant dangerous underground work. He had taken part in the notorious hold-up of the bank of Tiflis in 1907 which to him meant only the exploitation of capitalist wealth for the good Socialist cause. Such a man had merely contempt for "the lover of the abstract who was horrified by sporadic violence." There is a story in the New Testament about the laborer in the vineyard. Trotsky joined the party only in 1917; and if there were no other reason, this would be sufficient to make him hateful in the eyes of a man who had been Lenin's faithful disciple as early as 1902.

But the conflict between Stalin and Trotsky is also an antagonism by circumstances. Their difference in political ideas somehow represents two basic stages of the Bolshevist Revolution. Trotsky's doctrine of the "permanent revolution" was the definite expression of the first period of wartime and civil war Bolshevism. The passing of the "revolutionary situation" in Europe after the Battle of Warsaw in 1920 marked the beginning of a second stage. Soviet Russia retired from world politics and Stalin's formula of "Socialism in a single country" came nearer to expressing the task before the new Soviet fatherland. "Russia, as Stalin saw it, was settling down to the prosaic order of married life, while Trotsky, the incorrigible romantic, wanted a permanent revolution as a perpetual honeymoon." The failure of Trotsky, therefore, to seize Caesar's mantle after Lenin's death was not due only to tactical blunders (such as bathing in the Caucasian sun and worrying about his own health at the time of Lenin's funeral). Russia, turning away from Europe and settling down to the attempt at an inner reconstruction, had no room for a great revolutionary tactician and fighter who had lived in exile far from his country in his most impressive youth.

The patience and shrewdness of the Oriental won out. What is more important, Stalin, the professional revolutionary who had become secretary of the Communist party and had built up this position to strategic importance, lining up behind him a group of reliable co-workers all over the country, finally created a most powerful political machine. The future by necessity belonged to the great organizer. In this stage of revolutionary reconstruction it was not the intellectual capacity and colorful personality but the efficient organization that commanded prestige and control. There were greater theorists, like Bukharin, in the leading circle.

There were no doubt better orators among the Number Two
Men; but that did not count in this situation. In fact, it may be
said, as one shrewd observer once cleverly remarked, that Stalin's
writings sound "like those of an applicant for a Ph.D. degree at
a minor university." His intelligence may be slow. His speech
may be simple and businesslike, but what counted in this situation
was the complete control of the machinery, tied up with an amazing sense of details, an extravagant ruthlessness, and—perhaps the
most important element of a political tactician—an extraordinary
sense of timing. In fact, the Trotsky opposition had a point in
stating that Stalin got all his ideas from Trotsky, who had always
stated them years ahead. This was true of the necessary industrialization of agriculture, of the Five-Year Plan, and of the military preparation for a new revolutionary situation. But the fact
that he could wait for his hour made him succeed where Trotsky
would have failed.

Stalin's classic article, "Dizzy from Success," put a stop to a
hurried collectivization. It showed at the same time that he had
the courage to admit errors. Stalin today may be an oriental autocrat (and all biographies published in recent times in the English
world, such as those by Souvarine and Lyons, make this point,
as much as the earlier biographies tried to show the revolutionary greatness of Stalin). But he certainly is a crafty realist. His
foreign policy has proved that sufficiently. If we had insight
into his political machinations we might discover that he shows
cunning and shrewdness in internal politics no less. Years ago he
himself stated, "The art of leadership is a serious matter. One
must not lag behind a movement because to do so is to become
isolated from the masses. But one must not rush ahead, for to
rush ahead is to lose contact with the masses. He who wishes to
lead a movement must conduct a fight on two fronts—against
those who lag behind and those who rush on ahead." But in order
to put such a statement into the right perspective—as it otherwise may just as well become a standard for an efficient American President—one may be reminded that it was Stalin who also

coined the phrase that "no revolution can be made with silk gloves."

Such an analysis proves that the failure of Trotsky, meteoric though his career was, is due not simply to personal accident but to basic changes in dynamic leadership. Revolutions in the age of technology and the emergence of amorphous masses necessitate a new pattern. They lose all the glamour of the 19th-century upheavals, when the courage of an individual fighter and the underground movement of a few conspirators could kindle a flame and make great revolutions. Modern upheavals are carried on by leaders who command a large and all-inclusive machine. These new revolutionary leaders most certainly cannot be defeated by a revolutionary tactic that was coined in a pre-industrial era. This fact explains the difficulty of a counterrevolution against totalitarian dictatorship.

The Marginal Man

The modern dictator is the *"man of the people"* and the *"organizer of the masses."* Voice of the market place though he may be, he is yet strangely remote from the people themselves. All dictators strictly adhere to this aloofness and distance from the people. In spite of the democratic pretense of the demagogue, he has no friends, no equals. He must abstain from the comfort of intimacy. He trusts nobody. He is lost to the world. That is the price he has to pay for being a "superhuman leader." He is so big, so strong, so lonely. Mussolini never misses making this point when he meets his former journalist colleagues, especially when he can arouse the pity of American ace women publicists. Of course this aloofness is not the reserve of a shy man who hates the limelight. In this respect, as in many other ways, Salazar's reputation of being inaccessible goes back to different motivations. It may be added that the "leader" cultivates this aloofness as a weapon of defense, too. He knows men and he knows it is dangerous to be too close to them.

This remoteness from the people strictly adhered to by all dictators leads to an important question: Is the leader the representative of his people or a stranger to them? Almost all modern dictators and demagogues who claim to be the self-expression and exclusive representation of their nation were born either outside of the country in which they live or along its frontiers. Napoleon, Pilsudski, Ataturk, Stalin, Hitler, Hess, and Alfred Rosenberg are examples. Whether they come from Ajaccio to Paris or from Braunau to Berlin, they do not belong to the most representative national group of their people, and often their most receptive years are spent outside of the country which has raised them to leadership. This may account for the intense and often exaggerated nationalism of the modern demagogue. He grew up in an atmosphere of defense of something which was too obvious, a matter too much taken for granted for the average citizen reared in the midst of his fatherland. At the same time, the fact that he is different from his countrymen in this respect gives him a specific appeal. He is different and therefore he may even lead to new expressions of nationalism, to a new heaven.

As a matter of fact, the dictator is usually an unsociable individualist by nature. Young Mussolini, brought up in the smithy of his anarcho-Socialist father and a group of his political cronies, was a restless, pugnacious, combative, and domineering type of a fellow. He certainly honored, though in a very Romanesque way, Benito Juárez, the Mexican revolutionary after whom he was named. There are tales of stone-throwing fights similar to stories told of Napoleon. Of course many other boys threw stones. Yet young Mussolini does not seem to have been a good mixer. He was an unsociable individualist, and in one of his weak moments he confessed to Emil Ludwig that Max Stirner, the great theorist of anarchism, was his beloved author. There is something to the psychologist's observation that those who do not like to take orders want to give them.

The childhood and early youth of Hitler were probably even more full of revolt and resentment. He certainly was never at ease with his environment, one of the basic preconditions for a balanced social relation. Revolt against an overstrict, narrow-minded, bureaucratic father, against school discipline, against non-

German nationalities—experiences of this kind shaped his entire boyhood and colored his political ideas. This revolt was carried on into the young man's life. The dreams of a painter's career were thwarted by the refusal of the Vienna Academy of Art to accept him. A casual laborer and a postcard artist, he lived the life of a *déclassé* at a time when others were building up a career, a home, and a stake in society. The frustrations, the wounded pride of an outsider combined personal humiliations with national resentments. Those are elements at the base of the political Hitler.

The World War to him seemed "as a redemption from the disagreeable experiences of youth and, overcome by fervent enthusiasm, I sank to my knees and thanked Heaven from an overflowing heart that it had given me the good fortune to live at such a time" (*Mein Kampf*). The "private" Hitler, the Austrian dilettante, who is still real today and who shaped the "official" Hitler, the Prussian militarist, is the "little man" personified. He somehow symbolizes the whole social group which is on the edge of social existence and in many respects is living a borrowed life.

He was a lonely man, even during the war which melted away social class distinction and created to some extent a feeling of solidarity among combatants—a Socialism of the trenches. The fact that Hitler, according to his biographer Heiden, had no one to whom to appeal in all his four years in the trenches, explains a great deal. Neither on his birthday nor at Christmas did he ever receive a soldier's comfort kit. Such loneliness certainly is far from the proud isolation of the Napoleon with whom Hitler is all too often compared today. Though colorful history books describe Napoleon's rise also as an emergence from the dark depth of poverty, his father was, after all, a successful lawyer, and his mother, Laetitia, a "born lady." It is surely significant, too, that Hitler did not have a mother who, in the day of his greatness, could stand above or even behind him, as Napoleon's mother did, saying, "If only it lasts." In intellectual background and human concepts they are worlds apart. One has only to compare the *Memorial of St. Helena* with *Mein Kampf*. Napoleon after all was an admirer of the classic world, a son of the French Revolution. Brutus had been the hero of a young Napoleon who "took a wrong turn and became a Caesar himself." The driving force of the wars of the Empire derived from the fervor of the French Revolution, spreading its mission of a new era beyond the frontiers. Napoleon was thoroughly modern. He has been often regarded as the first prototype of bourgeois success. Hitler, on the other hand, is a romantic to whom German mythology, a misunderstood Nietzsche, and Wagner operas represent an appealing image.

The modern dictator is a *marginal man* of a marginal group. It is no accident that he becomes the mouthpiece of the crises strata of society: of an impoverished middle class which lost property and security in an inflation, of a white-collar group which lost all hope for advancement and for a real stake in the community, and of an unemployed class which forsook even the right to work and therewith to a place in a society which is based upon labor.

The marginal man is an outsider. He moves along the periphery of events. In a dashing move he may push into the center of the political arena. Comet-like he may lighten the scene—and disappear. It is significant that Fascist and National Socialist dictatorship found a prelude in transitory figures who were nothing but marginal men. D'Annunzio's and von Papen's historic roles can thus be circumscribed. The strategic importance and hazardous peril of those transitional types are worth studying. The forerunners always indicate directions. They set the spiritual atmosphere. They are the vanguard of the oncoming army. Voltaire and the Encyclopedists were the mouthpiece of a revolutionary middle class; Marx and Engels, articulate expression of a rising proletariat.

It was a D'Annunzio who gave first expression to the drive of the "problem children of the World War." The adventure story of this warrior-poet was the prelude to Fascism and to Mussolini. D'Annunzio "crazed" the mind of an aroused Italian youth. He coined the phrases of a nascent Fascism. He created its first symbols and images. A modern Cyrano de Bergerac, as a poet— Italy's greatest as he was—he had already made his name as a great sensualist and eccentric, a lover of all excessive pleasures and luxuries. Epicurean, self-indulgent, he at the same time showed a deadly dissatisfaction and insatiability with the world. He had made headlines with the glittering style of his *Dead City* and as a great lover of Eleonora Duse; yet he broke into the political arena only at the time of the First World War as an ardent interventionist. When Italy finally joined the Allies, he entered active service in the cavalry, infantry, navy, and finally as an aviator. He was the man who made the first leaflet bombardment over Vienna, which the British used so much at the beginning of World War II.

Capricious as his military adventures were, his great career started with his march on Fiume in September, 1919. It was the first "direct action" in post-war politics. It became a symbol of post-war activities. D'Annunzio was at war with the world. So was Fiume, his creation. The Holy City, the crucified city, the citadel of the future—all of that was this "oratorical republic" where a poet had done a deed. From the balcony of his palace at the market place in Fiume, in the full military insignia of a self-appointed *commandante* without any command, he addressed his aroused followers. A farce as it was, especially considering its very unheroic ending, Fiume held the seed of almost everything that Fascism stood for in the next twenty years. With Biblical eloquence D'Annunzio had sworn that he never would abandon the Holy City and that the henchmen of Giolitti and Sforza would have to tread on his bleeding corpse. When, however, the Italian troops finally appeared before Fiume after fifteen months of D'Annunzio's unchallenged rule, and when the first shell finally exploded not far from his balcony, the twentieth-century *condottiere* declared, "Italy is not worth dying for," and retired to his St. Helena, the spacious villa on Lake Garda where he lived to the end of his life in 1938—at odds with the world and for most of the time with his successful competitor Mussolini, too.

Almost all the symbols of Fascism were created on the square before D'Annunzio's balcony: the Black Shirts, the Fascist salute, the battle cries. Mussolini, and for that matter, Hitler also, borrowed heavily from the poet's arsenal. Even the *Fascist stato corporativo* had its forerunner in the statutes of Fiume. It was a vain attempt to recover a medieval guild society. It was Wagner, Nietzsche, and the Italian futurist, Marinetti, in one; Fascism only stirred this mixture into a stronger brew.

The strange following of D'Annunzio is even more indicative of future social alliances to be found in the totalitarian movements. A strange conglomerate of enthusiastic idealists and broken-down criminals, they were all united in one characteristic: they were marginal men, they were not living in a world of law and order, they were restless fighters—either in a sincere attempt to win a better world or in a spirit of merely fighting for the fighting's sake. This was the material of which modern dictatorships were made, and the standard-bearers of these movements signified the same psychological trends.

The Condottiere

The new dictator is finally a 20th-century *condottiere*. Like the system itself, he is the creation of war. His social concepts are essentially those of militant experiences which have brought about his political awakening. Said Hitler (in a mass meeting opening the winter relief campaign on October 10, 1939), "We emerged out of war; our conception of the world is derived from war, and if it must be, we shall prove our mettle." Accordingly, politics spells nothing but continuous warfare, struggle for survival, successfully to be turned into a fight for spoils.

There is nothing new in militarism breeding dictatorship. Since ancient times history books have been full of stories of "strong men" seizing power with the help of armed forces. In more recent periods pronunciamentos by army officers have been a stereotyped beginning of dictatorships in Latin America and frequently also in Mediterranean countries. "The age of the Caudillos" is not an invention of General Franco of Spain (he is not even its strongest representative).

Yet the most powerful totalitarian rules were created not by professional soldiers, but by vigorous outsiders whose rise was often viewed with suspicion and alarm by the established military services.

Just as dictators—different from the dynastic autocrats—do not hold power thanks to princely birth or legal title, so their military repute scarcely derives from "official standing."

Demagogic dictatorship is the rule of the amateur. Even its military elements have the features of the irregular. The modern army, a highly rational institution, does not breed irrational leadership of the demagogic type.

When the time is out of joint, the hour of the irregulars comes. They do not conform. They cannot be held by the hard and fast rules of army discipline. They do not accept the methodical and rational orderliness of military experts. They frown upon the tried patterns of the well-regulated services. They take the world by surprise and manifest the unpredictable daring of the amateurish and restless adventurer. Their motto is: *Jeder ist seines Glückes Schmied.* (Everyone forges his own fortune.)

Like the *condottiere* whom the great historian Jacob Burckhardt designated as "the highest and most admired form of illegitimacy of the XVth century," modern dictators evolve from nowhere, build up an army of their own, loyal to their command alone. Knights of the sword who elevate themselves to noble standing by their own choosing, they usurp power, knock down crowns from established heads, and make themselves the rulers of the realm. Nothing is beyond the reach of their ambitions because "might is right," and this might rests with the *condottiere's* faithful army.

From small beginnings he musters reliable henchmen; each happy stroke of fortune—tempestuous and irascible as its master —adds to his following, which is bound to him in unflinching allegiance. The modern dictator is at home only in his armed camp. He celebrates Christmas among his "comrades." There is a close relationship between the *condottiere* and his troops. He is the master of their destiny and they are the guarantors of his future.

Even as ruler of his country, the modern dictator takes pride in picturing himself, above all, in the role of supreme commander. Innumerable photographs from the leader's headquarters thus show him bent over huge maps of military campaigns, his finger pointing at the next steps in war strategy and generals accepting his dictum in awe. Master eulogists daily assure him of his commanding position and praise the military genius of the statesman-soldier. He is Frederick the Great revived.

Flattery is essential in the life of the *condottiere*. He has to be reassured again and again of his self-made position and of his greater power to come. Unsatisfiable ambition makes him restless. Mussolini thus confessed to Margherita Sarfatti (secretary-biographer of his earlier days): " 'Ambition—that last infirmity of noble minds!' . . . and then with a smile of irony on his lips: 'If all shall have gone well, I shall perhaps thirty years hence be accorded a bust which will serve as a rendezvous for nursery-maids and their young men in some public garden. "Behind the Mussolini bust at eight" perhaps some young lovers will whisper. A fine satisfaction that will be! And yet—and yet! Yes, I am obsessed by this wild desire—it consumes my whole being. . . . I want to make a mark on my era like a lion with its claws.' "

Shifting and variable as such personal rule is by its essence, to win a permanent hold on his era becomes the mainspring of the modern usurper. More than that, there is one ardent desire with all *condottieri*—to become immortal as the great Greeks and Romans were. For that purpose, they surround themselves with the artists and poets; for what is Achilles without Homer!

They become the new patrons of the arts. Their glory shall be cut in stone. Great monuments, imperial roads, lavishly rebuilt capitals are the symbols of the modern self-made ruler. This is the way of winning posterity for those who have no ancestry.

The adventurous *condottieri* of Renaissance Italy have come back to life in a 20th-century setting. Yet not all autocratic rulers in our time follow this same pattern.

Metaxas, last strong man of Greece, undoubtedly does not fit this picture because he was a professional soldier above all.

"Little Moltke," they called this brilliant strategist who received his early military training at the Potsdam Military Academy. Like the proverbially silent Prussian army chief, he was no popular hero. The Greeks usually called him not the leader, but Barba Yanni (Uncle Johnny). He lacked all the qualities that make a great demagogical leader. Neither the physique of this stocky little Premier with heavy shell-rimmed glasses and short waddling legs nor his bearing in public lent itself to the spectacular. There was no oratory, no pageantry, no mass appeal from this hard-working, unpretentious administrator.

Throughout his whole political career he failed in all intrigues, lifeblood of Balkan politics. When he finally became master of Greece in August, 1936, it was only because all the other "strong men"—Venizelos, Tsaldaris, Kondylis—had conveniently passed from the political scene. Seven votes out of 300 was all that he commanded in parliamentary backing. The King could only try to silence violent opposition with the assurance, "Yannaki [Little Johnny] gets things done." And this in time a large part of the public accepted.

Differently thought those who were bitterly affected by the ruthless measures of the "Third Hellenic Civilization"—as Metaxas proudly called his rule. In fact, Metaxas not only was pro-German in his international orientation, but as an old admirer of Prussianism he was also deeply impressed by the methods of the Third Reich at the time he organized his own country. He made himself Prime Minister for life; abolished freedom of speech, press, and assembly; introduced land reclamation schemes, minimum wage levels, quick and ruthless efficiency; created a national youth movement (closely patterned according to Fascist organizations, with some interesting borrowing from the Y.M.C.A. and the Boy Scouts) and—as every good dictator does—he built roads.

It is an irony of history that his creation was destroyed, at least for the time being, by the very powers whose institutions he had copied so diligently. Whether he was fundamentally democratic (in a Balkan way, to be true) as the recent legend pictures him since he became in the eyes of his countrymen the embodiment of their love of freedom, may be questioned.

Yet there is no doubt that he was a great patriot and that his international orientation was ultimately dictated by military considerations alone. Despite contrary ideological preferences, he soon recognized Italy as the arch enemy of Greece. It did not hinder him from planning theoretical field campaigns against all his neighbors. He was a military strategist (maybe a genius at it) but an efficient professional, above all.

No more of a daring *condottiere* is Admiral Horthy of Hungary. Though he actually rides on the proverbial white horse into newly acquired provinces, his victories are only by-products of the adroit diplomatic chess game of a Ribbentrop. In fact, the whole political existence of Hungary is an anomaly. Just as Horthy is an admiral without a navy and Hungary a monarchy without a monarch, so is his rule (and that of his son, who recently succeeded him) a dictatorship without a dictator.

Closest to the type of modern *condottiere*—aside from Hitler and Mussolini—come Pilsudski of Poland and Kemal Ataturk. Though both were professional soldiers, they were commanders of a people's army, defending the masses against the privileged. They were rebels themselves, living a soldier's life.

Articulate generals are the exception. Kemal Ataturk and Pilsudski were an exception. They could speak to the plain man and they kept some kind of democratic kinship. They were officers, yet not estranged from the people.

Pilsudski had been a fighter all his life. A character as venturesome and as arrogant, as romantic and as contradictory, as colorful and as grotesque as the history of his country, he became the father of restored Poland.

He was born near Wilno in 1867 in the shadow of the bloody uprising, in the midst of Russification and ruthless suppression.

His mother filled him with the proud history of the Polish nation and he became an ardent patriot. "The Litany of the Traveler" by Mickiewicz, the great Polish poet—was his leitmotiv:

> "Give us, Lord, a War to set us free,
> Arms, our Nation's symbol, Liberty,
> Death in Battle, if the grave will be
> in our Fatherland . . . But let us see
> Freedom for our country—unity.
>   Give us, Lord."

"I became a Socialist. Hatred for the Russian regime grew within me from year to year." It has been rightly doubted whether Pilsudski ever was a convinced Socialist. He was disgusted with the Polish landowners and the new middle class who, discouraged or out for profits, had made their peace with Russia. Pilsudski turned to the Poland of labor. Thus he accepted the slogan of the Polish Socialist party: "Through Poland's liberation to the liberation of the people." Yet despite imprisonment and exile for the cause, he always remained a "lone wolf" in the labor movement and soon forgot its Socialism for his aggressive nationalism.

His was a record of courage and adventure: accidental implications in terrorist attempts on the life of the Czar—Siberia—then underground activities—again arrest, faced with a life sentence —spectacular escape from prison by simulating insanity—short exile in London—return to Poland, then preparing the military cadres of the legionnaires, awaiting only the favorable moment for Polish liberation.

Victor Chernov reminds us that Pilsudski, in a prophetic lecture before the Geographical Society of Paris as early as 1914, had stated that "all hopes for Poland's independence rested upon the result of a war in which the Russians would be defeated by the Austrians and Germans, who in their turn would be vanquished by the English and the French."

Pilsudski stacked his cards accordingly. He fought with the Germans against the Russians first; and then when the peril from the east was in abeyance, he suddenly refused to be lined up with Germany and awaited her defeat in German "custody" at Magdeburg. "One must know the proper time to land in jail."

With the Allied victory and Poland's independence achieved, Pilsudski became the acclaimed hero of the nation. He saved his country in the historic Battle of Warsaw (thanks to the counsel of France's General Weygand and to the blunders of Russia's Generals Tukhachevsky and Budenny). After that victory, however, he retreated from politics, at odds with the established parliamentary regime, only to seize complete power in a coup d'état in 1926. From then until his death in 1935, he remained the actual ruler of Poland.

Pilsudski was above all an activist who at heart had a deep contempt for all theories. When he once saw a copy of the Communist Manifesto published by his party, he shrugged his shoulders and asked, "What for? Can a single Russian soldier be killed with that?" He relied upon force and his devoted legionnaires alone, willfully changing the Parliament and Constitution of the nation. The government of his dictatorial rule was appropriately called "the Cabinet of the Colonels." Yet cruelly as his regime hit his internal adversaries, even though they had been close friends in his revolutionary past, it was not simply the rule of an army general.

Though Pilsudski had none of the qualities of the successful tribune and politician, scarcely anyone among the modern dictators felt so deep a conflict between militarism and democracy as he did throughout his life. As late as 1925 he confessed that he could not solve this contradiction between order and liberty, between honor and right, between military power—always personified in a leader's command—and the abstract principles of civil democracy. For many years he had fought together with democrats. His post-war reaction was that of bitter disillusion. Such a true disappointment sounds even through the speech which Pilsudski delivered before the Polish Sejm after his successful coup in 1926, a speech that did not leave much to be desired in its plain outspokenness: "Within the reborn nation there was no rebirth of the people's soul, save in the army."

In his own lifetime he became to his unflinching devotees a legendary figure, a tradition, a symbol of a legionnaire's state. Yet his colonels could not keep its strength after the great *condottiere* was gone. When the storm broke from the west, Poland was hopelessly lost.

Ataturk, more fortunate contemporary of Pilsudski, was no less a rebel from his early life. A headstrong youth, an unruly officer, a great plotter, and finally the revolutionary founder of modern Turkey—willful independence and jealous militancy were the marks of his career. He ran away from school to become a soldier. He fought the hated Sultan Abdul-Hamid, founded the "Secret Society of Liberty" in Stambul, was arrested and banished to far-off assignments. Finally in Salonika he joined the movement of the Young Turks, but soon quarreled with its leader, Enver Pasha. Then, after a few years of an average Turkish officer's life, came the wars. They brought new exploits of his courage— in Tripoli against the Italians, in the Balkan Wars, and above all, in the World War against the ill-fated Allied expedition to the Dardanelles. He became the hero of Gallipoli. At the age of thirty-six he was made a general (pasha). His rising popularity, however, alarmed his German and Turkish superiors. Sent to the Russian front, he came into conflict with his superior, General Falkenhayn, and threw up his command in protest. Enver exiled him to the German front until the end of the war. But even the drastic armistice of Mudros (1918) did not mean the end of his military career. On the contrary, defeated and prostrate Turkey found in Kemal Pasha her first center of resistance. The Greek expedition to Smyrna (May, 1919) gave him a cue to take matters into his own hands. With only 2000 war-worn soldiers whom he was officially ordered from Istanbul to demobilize, he entered upon an apparently hopeless conflict with the great powers— and won.

From the smashing defeat of the Greeks climaxing in the Treaty of Lausanne (scrapping the peace dictate of Sèvres) led the direct way to his complete seizure of command as first President of the newly established Turkish Republic. The title of Ghazi (conqueror) had been appropriately bestowed upon him; his rise to power was the military conquest of a revolutionary *condottiere*. He was the glorious liberator from foreign sway. He was the hero who gave a new lease on the life of the "sick man of Europe." The nation reborn—smaller in size, yet consolidated in its ethnic homogeneity—praised him as its first soldier.

The great reforms which marked his later rule and which may establish the fame of his regime were only partly his own work; they went back to his devoted collaborators, not least to Ismet Inonu, second in military command and first in political succession.

Even this radical westernization defying all Islamic traditions was a militant crusade. In his new role of the nation's schoolmaster he was a fighter just the same. It was his good fortune to find in Inonu an orderly and systematic organizer who—provided with the proper international situation—could build up and carry on the deeds of the Ghazi. From early youth until his premature death (often ascribed to his scorn of medical advice) Kemal Ataturk's ways (and his private escapades, no less) were bold and boisterous.

If there is any *condottiere* in the modern style, "the perfect Father of all Turks" is one.

The modern dictator is the demagogic leader of the people and the absolute master of the machine. Guide and model of his nation though he is, as the "superhuman leader" he is a stranger to his people—a marginal man, nationally, socially, psychologically. He is finally the fiery *condottiere* of the armed band.

These are the essential features of his existence. Yet dictators like other rulers differ as widely in character as in ability. Viewing the species in its present-day version, one sees kaleidoscopic variations evolve. The basic elements appear in different mixtures, weaker or stronger doses, partly blended, partly sifted out. National mind and design, political fate and fortune, and the inner structure of the dictatorship itself bring to the fore the great protagonist. He is not least the product of his own world. His followers and, no doubt, his lieutenants are a part of his definition.

Chapter III

THE POLITICAL LIEUTENANT

————————————————————————————

THE NUMBER TWO MEN: NATURE AND VARIANTS

The political lieutenants are the forgotten men in most discussions of the totalitarian state. They are overshadowed by their supreme leaders and often unknown to the uninitiated outside world. While the chief actors are always in the limelight of the political scene, actually not much is known about the subleaders, their character, their function, and their achievements.

And yet these lieutenants are an essential feature which differentiates the modern version of dictatorial rule from its classical prototype. Not only do they represent the potentialities for survival of these modern political forms beyond the lifetime of their creators, but they also stand for the very existence of modern dictatorship, because this revolt of the masses, child of machine age and mass democracy, is the creation of an organized party and is carried on by a well-established bureaucracy. The lieutenants reflect the daily life of dictatorship. They are the power behind the throne, the driving force of modern demagogic rule, the backbone of its institutions. The structural characteristics of modern dictatorship, therefore, find in the subleaders their definite expression certainly more than in the supreme leader, who often rises to power through specific opportunities unique and closely connected with anomalous personality patterns. This is not as true of the Number Two Men. They are usually more typical of the peculiar national features of the dictatorship, even though they reflect only distortedly national characteristics.

All this makes the Number Two Man a phenomenon most

significant for an understanding of modern dictatorial systems. Yet he is sadly neglected in the otherwise abundant literature. Such an omission is due to a number of reasons.

Superficially at least, these systems seem to be nothing but the self-expression of their masters: Stalinism, Hitlerism, Mussolinism, Kemalism. Certainly the leader himself is eager to preserve this unchallenged identification of the system with his personality. As soon as his lieutenants gain a competitive position in public esteem, they are doomed. Balbo's triumphant return from his transatlantic flight and his dictator-like reception in Rome brought him exile as governor of Libya, where he found an early violent end. Grandi's spectacular success as Minister of Foreign Affairs and Italian representative at the League of Nations led to a change of guards. He was placed in the Embassy at the far-off Court of St. James's where he was to perform a thankless task as long as Mussolini wanted it to last. "Changing the guards" becomes a regular feature in Fascist Italy. This custom is certainly not solely, as the official version goes, to give new blood a trial. The constant assurance of Achille Starace, until recent years clever secretary of the Fascist party, that every public ovation given to him was in fact meant for Il Duce and only taken in commission by his secretary, was one way of saving himself for a long time from the fate of his numerous predecessors. These techniques have been even more accentuated in Germany. It is no mere accident that Goering always presents himself as Hitler's *treuester Palladin*.

As a rule, subleaders should not be too much in the public eye and, though seen in the nation's big parades, like good children they should not be heard. No wonder that the literature dealing with these lieutenants of dictatorship is scanty and standardized. It usually follows the same pattern: "Robust fiber, a keen and ardent mind, a heart of both gold and iron." They present themselves as types rather than as human beings. Wherever specific studies are available, as in the case of the Nazi subleaders, they are either inflating eulogies by friends of the system or debunking attacks by its enemies, estimates of little if any value for scientific analysis.

A further difficulty in arriving at a valid generalization of this phenomenon is the uneven knowledge that is obtainable about the subleaders in the different countries. While an abundance of material is procurable on National Socialist lieutenants, there is comparatively little information available on leaders in Fascist Italy, to say nothing of Soviet Russia, whose internal development has been for years unknown, even to most of the people who claim intimate knowledge.

This uneven knowledge in itself, however, is a significant fact reflecting the structural differences of the dictatorial nations. Variances, of course, are partly due to personal differences between a Mussolini and a Hitler—one from his early youth more self-reliant than the other and already in pre-war times experienced as a political leader. But there is also a marked difference in the position of the supreme leader in Fascism and in National Socialism. The quasi-religious, apostolic character of the Fuehrer makes it necessary that the real work—not only of execution but also of governing—be done by the subleaders. Hitler (until the start of the Second World War at least) had become almost a legend in Nazi Germany. Like lightning the Fuehrer comes down —frequently against the advice of his collaborators—to execute his sudden decisions before a surprised world, only to return immediately afterward to his remote mountain château on the Obersalzberg. This evolution in Hitler's position, more and more obvious during the last few years, of necessity emphasizes the actual importance of the subleaders. The situation has always been different with Mussolini. He is much more of this world and he always wants to run it. At times he has held many portfolios in his Cabinet. He rides a horse, he digs a ditch, he swings the scythe at harvest time—propaganda though it may be, it is real too, but Hitler would not do any of these things.

The differences are also connected with the historic origin of the movements. While Fascism rose to power in an amazingly short time and thus did not have much chance to set and to build up a quasi-institutional tradition, the long period of preparation in Germany, the slow rise and many disappointments of the movement, created a stronger comradeship among the early fighters. When National Socialism seized power, it was done not only by the speeches delivered by "the drummer of the movement," but also and even more by the combined efforts of a score of subleaders. These tried and well-known lieutenants could only be purged, never changed, as Mussolini changes his guards.

Aside from the deeper national characteristics and traditions, there is finally the difference of national setup. The many-headed National Socialist leadership is, in part at least, an expression of the complexity of Germany's social structure. To win a near majority it was necessary to appeal to all the different groups. And while the cynic Goebbels could conquer Berlin, it needed a Darré to win the peasants, a Prince Auwi (son of the late Emperor William II) to line up monarchists, and a Goering to impress big industrialists and crucial army circles.

In Italy also, different methods were applied in different parts of the country; Farinacci and Admiral Ciano (father of Count Ciano), Rocco and Rossoni, Balbo and Gentile appealed to different groups. Yet by comparison Italy was much more a one-class country and the counterplay of social forces was much less obvious than in Germany. Thus the subleaders did not win the specific significance that was held by some of Germany's Number Two Men.

These comparisons show how much the subleaders are a part of the national climate—a fact which defeats any attempt at a too far-reaching generalization on the phenomenon of the political lieutenants. That such an attempt can be made only with great reservations is obvious in view of our relatively short experience with these new movements and their dynamic character. There is nothing definite: no program, no promise, no power. Dictatorships are essentially in flux and the expression of a time of transition. Still a few salient features of the dictator's lieutenants may be tentatively suggested.

The political lieutenants personify basic traits of modern dictatorships. Not that everyone typifies the whole scale of values and all the qualities of the dictatorial rule. On the contrary, the subleaders are usually split up into various groups which may contradict and even fight each other. They are often held together only by the strong arm of the supreme leader and his ability to compromise their differences.

In this respect the sociology of leaders in a dictatorship is not so different from that of the leadership in a democratic party system. In the latter case the ruling group is differentiated according to the varied types among its following and the manifold functions to be performed. The expert leaders, the representatives of vested interests, the local dignitaries, and the masters of the party machine, they all constitute basic elements of the political organization. These human tensions and real controversies within the party setup necessitate a leader who in his person coordinates and reintegrates these diverse forces. It has been said that the gift of getting difficult people to work together is the primary qualification of an English Premier. The successful dictator no less must show similar strategic abilities. In fact, he is often in a more fortunate position. Because of the national mass mind which he has created and of which he is the high priest, he can exercise a compulsion on his lieutenants that is denied an English Premier who must negotiate and conciliate.

The basic difference between democracy and dictatorship finds its expression in the variant patterns of selection and function characteristic of their respective subleaders. Even though these differences may often become differences only in degree, they disclose essential contrasts. It is in this second layer of leadership that the specific problems of mass control in modern democracies and dictatorships are brought to the fore.

THE COMPOSITE STRUCTURE OF THE ELITE

Four decisive elements make up the composite structure of the leader's henchmen. They are bureaucratic, feudal, democratic, and militant.

The *bureaucratic component* is an outstanding feature of the elite. The subleaders stand above all for the political organization and, in this respect, typify the development of modern mass parties in which the "machine" predominates. Bureaucratization of leadership has rightly been attacked by great social critics like Georges Sorel, but it is a definite fact on which success or failure of a political movement depends. The main strength of the American boss rests on his command of an organization. The primary function of the political lieutenant in a dictatorship is to make the party machine run. This party machine not only is all-powerful in the daily life of the decentralized democratic party of the American system; it is no less influential in the development of modern autocracy.

This is indeed one of the many contradictions of the dictatorial party. Created as an anti-party largely founded on a well-justified anti-machine sentiment, it soon develops an even more intricate and extensive apparatus, thus tremendously increasing the crisis elements in the modern party system. Still the development of political functionaries is certainly no exclusive expression of post-war dictatorship. Such results seem an almost unavoidable outcome of political organization in a mass democracy. What makes the position of the dictatorial functionary paramount, however, is the totalitarian character of the dictatorial party which integrates all human activities. This totalitarianism not only guarantees the partisans' organization from the cradle to the grave and the comprehensive control over the nation as a whole, but it also attempts to stabilize or normalize dictatorial rule.

Modern revolutions have succeeded in reaching a full-grown bureaucratic stage which underlies the whole life of the dictatorship. The political lieutenants in a dictatorship stand above all for the organization. They are the representatives of the party machine. The human equation is almost completely blotted out. These men have to be reliable, not popular. Mussolini's Italy, which apart from Il Duce himself has produced almost no demagogic leaders, prides herself upon her efficient lieutenants, praised in standard descriptions as fighters and organizers rather than as thinkers and orators.

Practically the whole personnel of the Politbureau, most powerful agency of the U.S.S.R., could be thus described. They dislike talking. Industry, memory, efficiency, passion for detail, and "the capacity to make others work and like it"—in short, organizing abilities—are the qualities of the bureaucratic leaders. They perfectly fit Molotov, whom Lenin is said to have rated "the best filing clerk in the Soviet Union."

Such terms no less describe men like Andreyev and Malenkov, Kaganovitch and Mikoyan, who hold key positions in the party bureaucracy. Zhdanov is a master of the machine. The successor of the powerful Kirov (until his mysterious assassination in 1934, the leader of the Leningrad Soviets and heir apparent of the regime), Zhdanov has often been called the Jim Farley of the U.S.S.R. Such an epithet also hints at his popular appeal, which he for one really possesses. But if it were not for his sensational article in *Pravda* preceding and favoring the German-Russian accord and his leading role in the Russo-Finnish War, he would hardly be known to the outside world.

Anonymity is the mark of bureaucratic leaders. Only insiders know, for instance, the key men of the Oberste Reichsleitung (Directorate of the Nazi party), especially if the latter do not hold more conspicuous state positions at the same time. Philip Bouhler, the business manager of the party (a dictator in his own right) and Franz Schwarz, the party treasurer, are unknown giants of the system, to say nothing of its provincial pashas: the Gauleiter and Statthalter, such as Koch and Wagner, Mutschmann and Terboven. And yet the growth and continuity of the movement rests upon these lesser-known lieutenants. Even the leader's successor may well be among them.

They are bureaucrats in all save one important respect: they are entrusted with their specific power and function not on the basis of specialized training and proved knowledge, but because they were found worthy of the supreme leader's confidence. They can hold their office only as long as they can avoid his wrath and purges. The result is, as Hans Gerth has rightly emphasized, a strange fusion within the "inner circle" between bureaucratic and charismatic control leading to a monocratic administration laden with inner tensions, yet strongly disciplined by its orientation to the unchallengeable authority of the infallible leader.

Extraordinary as the position of the leader is and endowed with divine grace in the eyes of his disciples, this aspect of domination points at a second feature typical of the dictatorial elite: its *feudal relation.* The political lieutenants are vassals-in-chief of the overlord. This is symbolized by the oath to the leader taken by his adherents. Sovereignty rests no longer with the people, as it does in a democracy, but with the dictator alone. The political lieutenant, therefore, is his delegate, subject to his confidence and always acting in the name of the supreme leader.

The feudal aspect of the political lieutenants is made further obvious by the fact that they seek patronage from their leader just as the vassals-in-chief received it from their overlords. Elements of this kind of feudal relationship are certainly visible in democratic organizations too, especially in the patronage of the American party system. Spoils are received for services rendered. J. T. Salter, the most diligent observer of "boss rule," states: "The most striking single identifying quality of the division leaders . . . is loyalty. These men are loyal to their leaders just as their leaders are in turn loyal to their own leaders and the organization. It is personal rather than civil loyalty." Yet, granted such feudal elements in democratic party systems, they are limited in time and space. There never has been and probably never will be a national boss in the United States; furthermore, the power of the bosses is often checked, and frequently broken, by federal investigations.

The "boss rule" of present-day dictators, however, is unchecked. Moreover, their feudal empire produces a type of political agent new on the national scene: the personal confidant of the leader.

Confidence can be won in different ways. It may derive from the fact that these lieutenants were the comrades of early and trying conspiracies, "the partisans of the first hour." The leaders of the 1905 revolution in czarist Russia, the quadrumvirs of the march on Rome, the comrades-in-arms of Hitler's beer-hall *Putsch* in 1923, Franco's general staff from the weary civil war years are typical rallying forces.

Another group of confidants no less important in the life of dictatorships are the bodyguards of the leader. They are the guarantors of his safety. Their names seldom appear in the newspapers, but they often wield more power than other much-photographed lieutenants. They are always near the leader, close to his life, and usually close to his heart. They are the only ones, if any, who call him by his first name. Brückner and Schaub are the faithful adjutants of Hitler; they regulate his daily life and decide who shall see the Fuehrer and who shall not be admitted. The head of the secret police fulfills this watchful function for the whole country. For this reason a Heinrich Himmler becomes indispensable to the system; the same seemed to be true of his Italian equivalent, Arturo Bocchini, until his recent death which strangely coincided with the increased appearance of Hitler Elite Guards in Italy.

Often a myth is built up around many of the confidants of the leader: that they actually saved the life of their superior and that this fact gave them their place in the sun of the dictatorship. Such a story has been told about Count Ciano, son-in-law and heir apparent of the Fascist dictator.

There is a third group of confidants whose close contact with the leader is largely due to the personal loyalty of the Fuehrer to the superiors of his past. Again it is significant, for the difference between National Socialism and Fascism, that Mussolini has no confidants of this sort. Much to the dismay of his close collaborators, he has even admitted that he can claim no friends, with the exception of his brother Arnaldo who died years ago. That no loyalties to any superiors of Mussolini's earlier career are known is certain.

The case is very different with Hitler. Some of his closest collaborators are this kind of confidant. Max Amman, the actual owner of the official Nazi publishing house, was his wartime sergeant. His captain in the war, Carl Wiedemann, has frequently undertaken extremely delicate diplomatic missions in recent years. During the early period of the Czech crisis he went to London; well-informed people even see in him the instigator of the Runciman mission. Until the diplomatic break, he was consul general at San Francisco. These services notwithstanding, he was a latecomer to the party. He is one of the interesting examples of the rise of a non-party man to a key position in Nazi Germany. Herr von Ribbentrop—for different reasons, however—is another example of this kind.

The daily shifting of their personal relations to the supreme leader is of paramount importance to the actual power of his lieutenants. An evaluation of the policy predominant at a specific period—whether it is the right or the left wing, the capitalistic or the socialistic group that is at the helm—largely depends upon who has the leader's ear at the moment. Even social charmers and mystery women may play their part in this return to the camarilla policy of uncontrollable court intrigues. At the same time the sway of the overlord often depends on his power to balance the competing factions in his feudal empire.

The fees for services rendered are the prestige and the political power distributed among the subleaders. The possessing vassals-in-chief illustrate the fact that modern dictatorial rule cannot be simplified into one social formula, attractive as it might be for effective political propaganda. All these men with connections and experience in industry and labor, in the army and in foreign affairs contribute in their specific way to the might of the supreme leader. They expect spoils after the final victory, but as vassals they are satellites who derive their power from the supreme leader alone. This factor illustrates the leadership principle in dictatorial party organization which, differing from its democratic counterpart, is organized from above.

However, a third feature of dictatorial leadership seems to introduce, as has already been mentioned, a *democratic element* in this dictatorial organization. Modern dictatorship is by definition a challenge to democracy, and thus originating as democracy's opponent it becomes permeated by its spirit. The veil of democracy conceals its absolutism. The pretense of elections, the dictatorial party itself, an extensive propaganda machine serve the same purpose of bridging the distance between government and the people. To organize an "ennobled democracy" becomes the crucial task of the demagogic experts.

In spite of all pronounced social stratification in the dictator's hierarchy, a democratic atmosphere of comradeship has to prevail. The supreme leader himself sets the tone for it and the subleaders adopt it. Of course, it is of the essence of the system that there are insiders and outsiders. Dictatorship is democracy for the insiders alone. Brutal and merciless as the lieutenants usually are toward their enemies, strutting like the gods of vengeance, they had better not play the boss within the circle of their associates. In this respect the Number Two Men in dictatorships, even more than the supreme leader, have to be men of the people. The noble-born is suspect, useful as he may have been for propaganda purposes before the seizure of power. Only seldom does he reach a commanding position. The leaders of the post-war revolutions spring from modest backgrounds. They speak the plain man's lingo. They are the "people's choice," and they are jolly fellows too. The monthly one-dish meal, the street collections for "voluntary winter help" by the celebrities in the system, play up the idea of union between leaders and the masses. Even the human interest story figures strongly: the happy family life, Christmas celebrations at the home of the higher-ups, etc. Rigid frugality if not asceticism is the preferred pattern of their standard of life; and when it is not followed, extravagance and "conspicuous consumption" are represented as a duty indulged in for the fatherland's greater glory.

Goering, of course, is the perfect instance. He has been most joked about but is undoubtedly underestimated as a unique combination of Lohengrin, Arminius, and Falstaff, with special emphasis on the last. Yet he not only is the most powerful and ablest of Hitler's lieutenants, but he also enjoys a popularity second only to the Fuehrer—for opposite reasons, of course, as shrewd observers like Shirer and Harsch confirm. He is a "jovial, earthy, lusty man of flesh and blood where Hitler is distant, legendary, an enigma as a human being." The people admire Goering because they can make him out, because he epitomizes their secret yearnings and most ambitious dreams. He is like a fairy prince and a promise of what will be coming to every German "when the last battle is won." He is their inflated ego which makes them bear the sad reality of subservience and sacrifice. He is a modern and very German version of Henry VIII.

Master of Karinhall, shrinelike estate of unheard-of pomp, he presides at a banquet table loaded with food beyond other people's means, directs hunting parties which are the meeting ground of the protagonists in the great world theater, and outshines them all in his titles, uniforms, and medals—uncounted and unsurpassable in splendor. "When I get to be an officer," Goering is reported to have said in his rebellious boyhood, according to Erich Gritzbach's official biography, "I want war right away, I want to distinguish myself so that I will have more medals than my father."

He personifies many of the much-talked-about traits of German character—its perennial juvenility and its illusions of grandeur, its self-assertiveness and combativeness, its prowess and perseverance, its tendency to exaggeration, and the strange mixture of sentimentality and brutality, of romantic idealism and ruthless selfishness. Goering is the flying ace of daring exploits and nobody's fool in down-to-earth business. The old maxim, *Divide et impera*, strictly adhered to by modern dictators in regard to their lieutenants as well, seems to be strangely abandoned as far as the Reichsmarshal goes. Hitler has piled on him innumerable honors, responsibilities, and prerogatives. Goering is the only one among Hitler's lieutenants who for twenty years has kept a key position in the leader's closest council. He is also reported to be the only one who can speak up to Hitler. He is no doubt in a class by himself and not at all representative of the lieutenants of modern dictatorial rule. Their appeal to the people does not come as naturally, much as they stress it in their daily bearing.

Indeed, what makes this popular strain in dictatorial leadership somewhat open to suspicion is the fact that it is so obviously organized. Still, the demagogic masters of public opinion perform most essential functions. They are indispensable in the council of the dictatorial elite. Goebbels and Gayda are the one and only mouthpiece of the leader; they are no less the official "fliers of trial balloons." They have to find out how much the people can take. Constantly they feel the pulse of the nation. They keep their ear to the ground. They register as well as mold the people's will and stifle revolutions at their inception.

This close touch with the people, of course, does not make them democratic bosses because their political existence does not derive from the people, but is based upon delegated authority from the leader alone. Much as their power over the masses enhances their chances for survival, it is before the leader and not the people that they have to prove their mettle. This makes them more dangerous as demagogues since they are not checked by the open competition of other demagogues or—if they should win regional control for a time—by appropriate pressure from national authorities.

What is more important, the democratic politician *is* a man of the people—smarter, quicker perhaps, yet one of them just the same. His inherent sense of humor is an indication of this natural partnership. The dictatorial demagogue is different. While he knows how to play upon the people's emotions, he regards himself as above and beyond them—a class unto himself. The strict division of the nation into a two-caste society—the superhuman elite and the all-too-human masses—is at the base of plebiscitary dictatorship. It is Nietzsche and Pareto—in a debased edition to be sure, yet no less assertive and self-confident. The manipulators of the public mind are masters in the rationalization of the irrational. From their commanding bridges they control the moves of the blind and helpless masses. The political engineers channelize the stream of human material. They are definitely no part of it.

The essential difference between the lieutenants and the subleaders in democracies is brought out clearly when the fourth and perhaps most important element of modern dictatorship, the *militant component*, is considered. Modern dictatorship is belligerent; so is an essential group of its leadership, balancing and often outbalancing the bureaucratic component. The one serves as a stabilizing element, the other as a dynamic force in the system. While the bureaucrats function as dams against the second revolution, checking and purging the "perennial revolutionaries," the militia unites the fighters who break the dams when the hour arrives.

The Holy War of the creed makes every partisan a militant fighter. No compromises with the political opponent are possible, no coalitions, no barters, all of which are basic schemes of the politician's life in democracy and yardsticks of his ability. Exemplary fighting spirit, relentless militant discipline, and unconditional obedience to the supreme leader are the virtues of the dictator's henchmen. The subleaders are above all *lieutenants*. In the Fuehrerstaat civic democracy is superseded by the militant hierarchy of an army. The citizens become political soldiers since the nation's life is a constant battle. Super- and sub-ordination are the characteristic features of such a military organization.

The coming of the war certainly accentuated the importance of the military in the "inner circle" of command. There are even indications, especially in Germany, that it has led to a complete reshuffle in leadership. Not only has it changed the supreme demagogue into the greatest *condottiere*, the political leader into undisputed commander and military conqueror, but, what may be even more significant for the future of the political system, it seems to have weakened old-time party chieftains and brought forward as a matter of course the military experts. It is interesting, however, to note that behind the front of official dignitaries of the army like Keitel and Brauchitsch there again evolves a predominant power: the personal confidant of the leader, such as General Jodl, head of Hitler's personal military staff and often regarded as the strategic tactician of the Third Reich at war.

Everywhere war is the occasion for military leaders to rise, and thus is created a new elite. But it is worth noting that it is Hitler who bestows the marshal's baton upon his victorious generals. This epitomizes the Fuehrer's rule.

Dictatorship's lieutenants derive their power and prestige from the leader's recognition alone. In democracies the Number Two Men are not only the bosses of the party machine but also the "ambassadors of the people." They serve, above all, as the human link between the individual voter and the body politic. The supreme quality of the bosses is their skill in the management of men. They are the masters of particular situations, not of principles. True, their power does not depend on this personal element alone. They are the people who are ready to do the work. They start their political career with bell-ringing. They are, above all, vote-getters and masters of the organization, but they try to produce intimacy on a large scale. Their first interest is the individual. As neatly stated by J. T. Salter, "The rights of society as a whole are of little or no concern to the average division leader. Only an individual can cry out in pain, and only an individual can vote."

To the political lieutenant the human equation is almost completely blotted out. He has essentially no interest in the individual's well-being; he is concerned solely with the preservation of the leader's rule. Above all, he has to be reliable for the dictator, not popular with the masses.

And while the demagogical Fuehrer, rising as the substitute for institutions, stands for himself, and the democratic leader always remains the representative of institutions, in this second layer of political leadership a contrasting situation can be observed: the political lieutenant stands for the impersonal organization and the politician is the ambassador of the people. This reversal is no mere accident. As will later be seen, it characterizes the basic difference in the concept of the masses in democracy and dictatorship.

TRAINING AND SUCCESSION IN LEADERSHIP

The different concepts of the elite become finally manifest in the *training and selective process* of future political leaders under the various systems. Again a basic difference appears between democracies and dictatorships.

Institutional channels are the main avenue for future democratic leaders. They are selected through open competition, especially in the national parliament and frequently through a successful career in municipal government. Such a rise to political importance presupposes and trains specific qualities in the future leaders, qualities which, in turn, characterize their future rule. In fact, selection of leaders is one of the most important functions of the parliaments. Success or failure in this decides the very existence of democratic government. The severe apprenticeship which the political aspirant has to undergo in the open forum of parliament tests his availability for ministerial functions. Long before he achieves his first departmental appointment he has to prove his mettle before an extremely critical audience. He has to show his capacity for effective statement, for the framing of legislation, for mastery in parliamentary debate, for teamwork, cooperation, and successful compromise. He has to be acceptable to the house and thereby to the country. A government that is not subject to such criticism may pick its members at will. "Any fool," as Napoleon said, "can govern in a state of siege."

Great statesmen look back at a long parliamentary career before they take the driver's seat in parliamentary government. It has often been rightly remarked that the rapid change of membership in the United States House of Representatives is one of the main reasons why it has been outstripped in power by the Senate.

The time element is also partly responsible for the uneven prospect of different social groups in achieving a successful political career. Great Britain's young aristocrats, reared in a political atmosphere, trained for politics (at Eton and Harrow, Oxford and Cambridge), and entering a political profession at an early age, are at an advantage as compared with businessmen and trade union leaders. This holds true even today when the earlier privileges of aristocratic background and schooling are no longer preconditional for a political career in Great Britain. Only the revolution of total war unfolding before our eyes may open clogged channels of old established institutions and bring to the fore new elements of leadership.

Apart from these extraordinary circumstances there are specific professions which present themselves as advantageous openings for a successful political career in democracies. The prevalent conviction that the man who *knows* the law can also *make* the law gives the lawyer a predominant position in parliaments all over the world. Half of the members of the American House of Representatives have a legal training. The same was true of the French parliaments of the past. From Gambetta down to Poincaré and Briand the lawyer was a preferred type in French public life. The honored position enjoyed by the advocate and notary in French society reflects at the same time the high esteem law commands in a nation that believes in reason and justice, in institutions and codification—a tradition that cannot be destroyed overnight and will not be broken even by a crushing defeat.

It is most significant that the teaching profession was second only to law as a leadership reservoir for French politics. To represent the great cultural traditions and, if possible, to have contributed to their reputation by a literary product of their own seemed to be almost a prerequisite for future statesmen. Herriot, Tardieu, Léon Blum, Daladier—to mention only a few contemporaries—have done so. (Laval is a significant exception to the rule!) In a nation where generals regarded it as their highest glory to be elected members of the Académie Française, to be "educated" was a necessary entrance ticket to public position. The extremely democratic educational system of the Third Republic, however, hindered the rise of an exclusive class of "property and culture." The sifting process of competitive examinations throughout the whole educational hierarchy made possible the ascendancy of the able underprivileged. In fact, one may accept the recent statement of a shrewd observer of politics in the Third Republic: "To succeed in French political life, one must be born humbly, live studiously, enter by the door on the left [Clemenceau, Millerand, Viviani, Pierre Laval], do at least one administrative job well, take quiet note of the weaknesses of one's colleagues but without ever speaking one's thoughts aloud, and then wait for the tide."

Such examples hint at the variations in the selection of leaders due to national ideals and educational standards. No less significant for this selection are structural differences in the political agencies, especially the political parties. The decentralized party system of the U.S.A. gives the local and state boss a predominant hand in making national leaders. Any attempt, such as that recently made by Roosevelt, to purge senatorial candidates, if successful, would break the power of the bosses. Even the chairman of the party cannot successfully interfere in their feudal domain. Like the British King, he may have "the right to be consulted, the right to encourage, the right to warn"; and if he is a shrewd politician this power may carry enough weight, especially if he can make use of national spoils. Yet the selection of political leaders will be primarily decided not by the responsible political officeholder but by the irresponsible local boss. This largely accounts for the enormous waste of personnel in American politics.

There is, in fact, no career that leads directly to the most important political position, the American Presidency, as the frequent selection of a "dark horse" significantly indicates. This does not mean, however, that the candidates finally selected do not carry specific qualities which make them "available" for the highest political office. Certain prerequisites for being elected President could be stated. Protestantism appears to be one. Geographic considerations also enter the picture. No Southerner has been selected since the Civil War. The Democratic vote in the "Solid South" was never so doubtful as to invite such a nomination. Since 1860 the Democrats' successful candidates have come from the East, while the Republicans, sure of the support of eastern conservatives, have looked to the Middle West for presidential aspirants. Though no career leads to the White House, legal practice, and until recently military service, have represented a preferential channel. Governorship, especially of a populous and strategic state (like New York), has proved an excellent stepping-stone. The combination of a successful political contest and some public administrative experience seems to offer an effective appeal. So does the possession of a name long known in politics, or a favorable reputation derived from a popular legend (if possible, not outspokenly political in character). Though the saga of birth in a log cabin, popular since Lincoln's day, is by now somewhat outmoded, to be born on a farm or to have at least worked on one as a boy is still convenient for the political aspirant. The political physiognomy of a presidential candidate should not be too definite (in order not to make enemies), but he must have a human side (even if one has to be manufactured) and a good personality which can be sold to the American people. Above all, he must not be highbrow. His family life must be beyond reproach. Game hunting and trout fishing are suitable avocations for a candidate; they demonstrate his vigor and healthy outdoor life. The publicity build-up will collect these enhancing features of the "presidential timber" after the "king-makers" (a President in office who is not running for reelection, some editors, politicians, etc.) have picked the candidate for the country's highest office.

Not much consideration is given to the qualifications of the Vice-president. His position usually commands no great importance. Two rules, however, can be stated. He should not come from the same geographic district as the presidential candidate and, if possible, he should represent a different wing of the party.

It is even harder to make generally valid statements on the training of "American bosses." Their rise may almost be called a process of natural selection. Politics in the U.S.A. is an open profession recruited from all ranks, but it is a profession. To make a success of it demands a man's whole life, readiness for service at any time. This is one reason why people who have a civil profession at stake are hesitant about entering the political arena. What makes a politician may be his desire to obtain public office or to exert influence and power, or simply the fact that he likes the game. He is a self-made man, often from humble origins and recent immigrant stock, not seldom a social failure. The city boss especially, somewhat different from the often more respectable state boss, usually begins his study of human psychology in the streets of a large city as a newsboy, in the saloons as a waiter, or in similar pursuits. In such daily contact he acquires skill in the management of men, the supreme quality of the successful boss. He possesses a superabundance of physical energy and resourcefulness. He establishes his party position by hard work. If he secures command of the active voters in a precinct, it gives him control to distribute spoils. He is on his way to political power.

Training for leadership is very different under the personal rule of modern dictators. Selection certainly depends to a large extent on the personal choice of the leader, especially in the higher brackets of the political hierarchy. Favoritism plays an important part in it. Even outsiders of the party may enter the leading council of modern autocracies. In spite of this significant importance of the personal element, however, it is characteristic of modern dictatorships that they train the successors to, and the administrators of, their dynamic rule in an almost rationalized and quasi-institutional scheme.

The main channel through which the selection is made is not the parliament and certainly not open competition. Selection is basically made through the party machine. Being a "charter member" of the party is equivalent to tenure in a democratic parliament. In a way such a choice also brings out specific qualities. The "old guard" of the first hour proves to the leader to be ardent fighters and trustworthy confidants and martyrs to the cause, suffering in the prisons of the "system" or in political exile. This glory may not be sufficient after the seizure of power. Indeed it may even be necessary to purge the "comrades of early and trying conspiracies."

The composite structure of modern dictatorship in its all-embracing power requires varied types of leaders, i.e., the demagogic, bureaucratic, militant, and feudal. The party machine has to put forth the necessary leader material, a task seemingly simplified by the non-existence of any opposition. Some thoughtful dictators, however, have realized the weakness of this selective process due to the lack of any testing competition. (An attempt, such as Ataturk's, artificially to create official opposition is doomed to failure in a dictatorship.) Yet even the closed party system of modern dictatorship is not completely free from competition. In fact, it represents a hidden multi-party system, thus defining selection through victorious factions. Here again the personal element of leadership selection enters. The faction nearest to the leader's ear has the best chance for command of the key positions. Such a process accounts for the unpredictability of a leadership career and for the waste of personnel in modern dictatorships.

One important feature of modern dictatorship is its extension of monopolistic control over the body politic to the oncoming generation. Entry into the ruling party and thereby a share in power, position, and prestige are left to the mercy of the party in control. The specific culture patterns of the ruling dictatorship will decide on selective principles. Thus, the new leader schools of National Socialism state as their first requirement bodily strength and skill and, above all, military virtues. Hitler has declared training of the will and courage to be the ultimate aim of all education. "The land of poets and thinkers" is now taught to regard such an epithet as a sign of national decay.

The training of future leaders through a state-controlled youth movement and a completely coordinated educational system represents a bid at perpetuation of the personal rule beyond the leader's death.

The paramount importance of the lieutenants becomes obvious in the crucial problem of *succession in dictatorship*. It is the fearful preoccupation of the dictator's following, the consoling hope of his enemies. It is certainly too early to draw any definite conclusions as to whether modern dictatorships will succeed where classical forerunners failed. However, the few test cases of succession experienced in recent history already disclose the significant role of the lieutenants. Two preconditions for a successful perpetuation of the dictator's rule seem to be indispensable: the establishment of a well-functioning party machine and the destruction or absorption of traditional institutions. The obvious failure of Rydz-Smigly in Pilsudski's Poland and the probable success of Inonu of Kemalist Turkey (international implications notwithstanding) cannot be explained simply in terms of personality. Failure or success is largely due to the degree of internal consolidation of the system. If the shots aimed at Lenin in August, 1918, had killed him, the Soviet regime would probably have collapsed. When he died in January, 1924, an integrated system of power had grown up; and after the short interregnum of the historic struggle between Stalin and Trotsky, the master of the party machine emerged the final victor.

A well-established party is important insurance for the probability of effective succession. No wonder that dictatorial rulers who seized the power without such party backing—in Rumania, Austria, Portugal, Poland, and more recently in Spain and France —tried or are desperately trying to establish this mass democratic foundation. Such artificial or belated attempts can hardly succeed.

Where parties are definitely organized, their internal cohesion reaches beyond the personal genius of their creator. Here dictatorship finds the weighty advocacy of hundreds of thousands who share its profits and cling to their fellows for safety.

The exit of the dictator creates a vacuum that may be filled by other still-existing institutions of traditional standing, such as the army. That is the reason why those outside competitors, especially army generals like Schleicher or Tukhachevsky, are better liquidated by the dictator before his death can break the totalitarian spell.

Even more desirable is the successful infiltration or capture of traditional institutions. As far as the army goes—undoubtedly the dictator's closest competitor—this conquest becomes a life-and-death matter for the safety of the system. To achieve it, even an ardent republican like Mussolini may become converted to monarchism.

One may even go so far as to make a few generalizations in regard to some characteristics of the dictator's successor. One may venture to say that it is not the glamour boys of the revolution—not Trotsky, Farinacci, Goebbels—who have the best chance to succeed the leader. It is, above all, the unostentatious master of the machine who will be in line for succession. Mussolini's Italy, somewhat different in this respect, with son-in-law Count Ciano first in line, seems to have returned to the Roman principle of adoption.

To have the reputation of being a middle-of-the-road man will be a second element in preference for succession. This may mean, as in the case of Stalin, that one cleverly knows how to play off one wing against the other. Choice may finally fall on a "dark horse"—a man who is not so conspicuous as to cause envy, make enemies, or disturb the slow accumulation of power.

The above three characteristics of the possible heir to Caesar's mantle indicate specific features of the future rule of the successor. If ever established, it will unquestionably be different from that of the founder. Though ruling in his name, with the help of the oncoming generation born under the established regime it may liquidate the remnants of the revolutionary generation.

If the new autocracy should live on beyond the lifetime of its creator, whatever may be its specific elements—partly dictated by its international dynamics, unfolded, or checked—it will without doubt take shape from the forgotten men in the totalitarian state, from the political lieutenants of the modern dictator.

Chapter IV

THE AMORPHOUS MASSES EMERGE

THE REVOLT OF THE MASSES

A decade ago Ortega y Gasset's *Revolt of the Masses* caused a sensation in intellectual circles. It was a warning, by a great Spaniard and a liberal philosopher of repute, against the emergence of mob rule, against "the accession of the masses to complete social power. The multitude has advanced to the footlights and is the principal character. There are no longer protagonists. There is only the chorus."

Warning against the oncoming masses had been sounded since the days of the French Revolution. Yet while it was then the traditional battle cry of romantic conservatives, spokesmen of the *ancien régime* like De Maistre, De Bonald, Gentz, to be taken up again and again by anti-liberals like Nietzsche and Spengler, it failed to make any impression on their own age. Throughout the 19th century rational progress of humanity was the theme song of prevailing liberalism. The few discords that middle-class thinkers noticed were dismissed as a product of the irrational behavior of the yet uneducated poor who, according to a Malthusian interpretation, were thus alone responsible for their unfortunate plight.

True, there had been a few far-sighted bourgeois humanists who to some extent sensed the threatening consequences of the machine age. Their criticism, however, was chiefly concerned with the cultural aspects of this phenomenon. When their query turned to political considerations at all, it restricted itself to general criticism of the "rule by the average man," or the supremacy of ignorance over instruction and of numbers over knowledge, or became simply a warning against the "peril of the rising proletariat and of threatening Socialism." These analysts hardly recognized that the "mass man" whom they feared and attacked was a product and therewith a responsibility of their own society. They certainly did not realize that he had infiltrated into wider circles of society and, in fact, attacked the social fabric itself.

The full implications of the great social revolutions did not and probably could not become apparent until recently, when their impact on the future of democracy could no longer be denied. Ortega y Gasset's book was timely and challenging, though it left the querist in search of an answer. The years following his pronunciamento brought home to a world of statesmen and social scientists—equally unprepared for this onslaught—the reality of the rising masses.

In fact, revolt of the masses is the core of modern dynamism. A full appreciation of the fundamental changes within the mass stratum therefore becomes imperative for an inquiry into the nature and momentum of modern dictatorship.

The rise of the masses as such is nothing novel, nor should their disquieting influence upon politics be a matter of surprise. Throughout the 19th century in Europe, one of the main difficulties in political development was the concurrence in time of political revolution and major social change. England obviously presented a different and unique development, because here the Industrial Revolution came more than a century after the parliamentary system had established itself in a political revolution. In all other countries the destruction of the *ancien régime* coincided with the beginning of the Industrial Revolution, i.e., with the economic transformation of society. The consequences of such a coincidence have been well summarized by W. L. Middleton, astute observer of French political development: "It was a misfortune for France that the Great Revolution occurred so late in her history. . . . If absolutism had been overthrown in 1689, instead of 1789, the new constitutional foundations would have been firmly established before the modern collectivist ideas became a powerful force in politics. The social movement might thus have been absorbed without shock in the free play of settled democratic institutions. But the agitation for a total economic transformation of society first reached dangerous proportions in France . . . at a time when the whole question of the political régime was still in momentous dispute. . . . It destroyed the Republic of 1848. It divided the Republicans. It frightened the bourgeois and the thrifty as much as Bolshevism alarms their successors of today. Louis Napoleon succeeded in his coup d'état, partly by the magic of a name, but more because he offered the protection of authority against the monster of Socialism, exactly as Mussolini, at a similarly well-chosen moment, provided the Italian bourgeois with a guarantee against Bolshevism." Similarly, Hitler ten years later whipped together a strange alliance of frightened industrialists and perennial revolutionaries. The revolutions of the 19th and 20th centuries must be regarded as "hybrid products of two distinct revolutions going on at the same time."

The Industrial Revolution, wherever it occurred before political stabilization was achieved, threw into the political arena different and competing principles of division. This became evident within the party systems, thus creating divided loyalties and precarious entanglements for a confused electorate. A significant example of such an intricate political situation was presented by the French Third Republic. The perplexing and utterly misleading nomenclature of her parties was typical of the prevailing confusion; so was the oscillating character of her extremely powerful Parti Radical Socialiste. Politically progressive and socially conservative, it had been wittily compared with radishes (red outside, white inside). In fact, it only reflected the fatal tensions within the socio-political structure.

The multi-party system—gravedigger of democratic institutions —is not least the result of such social confusion. The well-entrenched two-party system of the Anglo-Saxon world is no less due to the more fortunate fate of those nations that won a common ground of political order at an earlier period.

THE INDUSTRIAL REVOLUTION

The Industrial Revolution created one basic tension that became a constituent element of the modern state everywhere. The division into rural and urban sectors presented an inescapable challenge to statesmanship in striking a new balance between these two antagonistic and yet complementary sectors of the social order.

Different nations tried different formulas. France remained a peasants' republic in spite of the rising trends toward industrialization. The Bismarckian Empire instituted the political control of the agrarian Junkers over an otherwise progressively industrialized country. The Weimar Republic, on the other hand, can be regarded as a belated and short-lived victory of the urban west over the rural east in Germany. Great Britain's traditional ruling class, the landed aristocracy, by mid-19th century had definitely entered the "city," merged with an urban bourgeoisie, and become gradually infiltrated with its spirit. In Soviet Russia the industrial proletariat forced upon the numerically superior peasantry a socialization of rural life that was nothing but an attempt to extend industrial society into agriculture. The United States at first glance seems to illustrate the conquest of the country by the city (with all the modern agencies of communication—newspaper, radio, and motion picture—assisting this process by their concentration in urban areas). Closer observation, however, might show the great influence of rural areas on political and social development. This intricate phenomenon of interaction and dominance thus reflects here the balance of forces which modern sociologists describe as the beginning of a rurban society.

The dynamics of rural-urban differences—even if temporary solutions are found—create in every modern state constant bipolar tensions, which since the Industrial Revolution have been a major theme in internal politics.

The *agricultural classes* usually live on the periphery of political activities. They do not command the established means of communication; they are least articulate in the formulation of national politics. In spite of these obvious facts, the political weight of rural society should not be underestimated. Its import is emphasized by the relatively consistent attitude of the farmer toward public affairs. He is predominantly traditional and easily represents the backbone of conservative forces within the nation. One may reject the wholesale dictum of Karl Marx against "the class which represents barbarism in the confines of civilization." One may even raise reservations against more careful evaluations of recent interpreters who see in the farmer the champion of Fascist rule. The suggestion frequently advanced, that "European dictatorships have as a rule been established in rural countries," not only contradicts the evidence, but also conceals the driving forces behind those revolutionary movements that derive primarily from urban radicalism. Still there is no denying that the emotional nationalism of the agricultural classes, fed by economic distress, has been a valuable ally in the rise of modern autocracies. The rule of a military caste in Japan today is no doubt essentially backed by and recruited from a hard-pressed and ambitious peasantry. Mussolini has successfully appealed to discontented and depressed farm areas.

The policy of "blood and soil" so eloquently advanced by Hitler's Lieutenant Darré certainly made deep inroads into politically "unawakened" rural Germany; without such help the "legal" seizure of power might well have been impossible. And yet the agricultural classes have neither contributed leadership material to National Socialism in any degree, nor has their relation to the victorious movement gone beyond a suspicious and sober affiliation of give and take.

The main attraction of National Socialism to the farmer—as to other social groups—consisted of its negative character: its radical divorce from the Weimar Republic, which had never succeeded in extending its sway beyond the eastern gates of Berlin. But while German agriculture in the east was definitely not part of the "bourgeois republic," the farmers' opposition derived basically from pre-capitalistic sources.

The economic and social plight of agriculture in East Elbia no doubt was progressively straitened by the internal growth of industrial society and the rising competition from oversea. Yet this distress with its undeniable unrest among the peasant folk did not cause them to question their entire existence. Certainly the depth of instability was not reached as it was in other social strata. In a way the agricultural sector was materially and spiritually self-sufficient. It was therefore not touched by the disruptive forces in modern economic society. Capitalism and its dialectic twin, Socialism, were equally strange to the agrarian world. Man was still fully embedded in his rural community. He had not progressed to modern individualization, nor had his rural world experienced the dissolution of social groups into amorphous masses —the fateful threat to urban society.

The social and political crisis of modern society crystallized in the cities and seemed to find there in the *proletariat* its first focal point. Its rise undoubtedly heralded great political changes. Whether the city was the exclusive breeding ground of political liberty or not, the "urban way of life" certainly awakened the masses. They called for a voice in political decisions. The question of franchise became one of the predominant issues in 19th-century reforms. England, the pioneer of the Industrial Revolution, was also the pathfinder in electoral reforms. The successive extension of the franchise reached ever wider social groups. This process was finally completed after World War I with the introduction of woman suffrage. Other countries followed, with the characteristic exception of "progressive" France, where women could become undersecretaries of state but never had the right to cast a vote.

This quantitative change in the electorate implied qualitative transformations too. Early in the discussions of the franchise, reservations had been raised, not entirely selfishly, by "property and culture" groups who sensed some fear in the intrusion of the "new masses." True, their reservations were based on mixed motives—such a reaction as can be noted in Madison's classic exhortation in No. 10 of *The Federalist*.

The fact that the propertyless masses had "no stake in society" and thus lacked responsibility was regarded as a justification for their political curtailment. It was at the same time an appropriate excuse to rid the middle class of a rising and numerically superior proletariat. This "great fear" indeed often aligned a bourgeoisie with its political opponents in the conservative aristocratic camp.

In fact, the rise of the urban proletariat was nothing less than a revolution in society. It was the beginning of the "new masses."

The concept of the masses is even more elastic than the concept of the leader. Devoid of precise scientific content, the notion is often used with a moral undercurrent: the canaille, the great unwashed, the rebellious masses, the eager masses, etc. Like any other social concept, the abstract idea of the masses takes on color only against a concrete historic background and thus varies in character and function in different historic periods. Before the French Revolution it designated the heterogeneous elements excluded from the privileges and prerequisites of the *ancien régime*. Post-revolutionary democracy identified the masses with "the people"; a people one and indivisible became indispensable for modern democratic nationalism and a reality in an open American society.

The rise of modern industrialism and urbanization, however, soon created a new differentiation and caste-like immobility in society. Now the industrial proletariat stood for the masses, and brought into focus all the danger elements of a middle-class society and the inner discrepancies of its economic order.

The *proletariat* as a class had neither profession nor property, neither cultural status nor political responsibilities, neither a stake in the present community nor the promise of a brighter future.

In a modern industrial society where work by necessity became mechanized, monotonous, and emptied of all creative value, the separation of work and civilization weighed especially on the class that had nothing to sell but its labor. Whatever personal development could be achieved had to come from outside the occupational process. No impetus could derive from daily work. The proletariat had no profession, no life-filling calling. Occupation stood for nothing but a way of earning one's living, doubly burdensome in view of the autocratic control by industrial management.

Indeed, social criticism of and active rebellion against the prevailing order took their start as a protest against the deadening weight of the machine. Fight against the machine signalized just as much the opening of early anti-capitalist movements as it still represents the natural reaction of young college students today whose social conscience awakens and who turn "radical." Despite short-lived promises of the technocrats to dissolve this basic ill by carrying mechanization to such a point as would relieve man from mechanized work altogether, and despite the even less auspicious attempts by a *stato corporativo* at a romantic recreation of "meaningful professions," the challenge still persists. The lag between technological progress and human readjustments is at the base of the modern crisis of state and society. The proletariat seems to bear the brunt.

Yet its plight is intensified by further discrepancies immanent in the predominant economic system. By definition, proletarian existence represents no longer a transitory phenomenon but a permanent classification, often petrified to caste-like hereditary status; at the same time the fluctuations of business cycles lead to continuous economic insecurity for this group.

One may add the well-known Marxist claim of the maldistribution of produce in a profit economy based upon "accumulation of capital" and upon the exploitation of the proletariat. The mere enumeration of these immanent contradictions and serious maladjustments within the capitalistic system shows how truly the proletariat had become the negative class of capitalistic society, a class that had "nothing to lose but its chains." This very negative stand, however, placed it, according to class-conscious Socialism, in a strategic position making the proletarian masses "standard-bearers of a future society."

Whatever the political prospects of this newly awakened class consciousness were, there is no doubt that it had a tremendous effect on the social morale of the proletariat. It may well be said that cognizance of such an intrinsic place in society saved the proletariat from the threat of amorphous existence.

A century before, Abbé Sieyès had aroused the "third estate" with a similar call to political action: "What is the Third Estate —nothing today, everything—tomorrow!" The 19th century had turned these promises for a middle class into reality. The 20th century has seemed to carry this process of "liberation" into the fourth estate. Yet it was not only the realization of a great mission which thus made the drab daily life of the "awakened" proletarian more bearable. The new ideology transformed his very existence. It gave him self-esteem and confidence. It answered the human urge for power and prestige, or, more simply, man's need for a stake in society. In protest and pride he could warn the world and assure himself: *Alle Räder stehen still, wenn Dein starker Arm es will* ("All wheels will stop when your strong arm wants them to"). The proletariat in such a vision had become the moving center of action which sooner or later had to be reckoned with and would be recognized as a crucial force. And if the individual proletarian had lost his chance of personal promotion, he had gained the promise of continuous rise in the rising status of his social group.

This transformation of his individual hopes into those of the working class as a whole gave him a new self-reliance. In fact, it is the reinstitution of a strong social group which alone could balance the disintegration of urban existence.

The proletariat, urban class par excellence, had fully experienced the dissolution of modern mass society. Immigrants from rural areas, if not from oversea, they had lost the old social ties of family and neighborhood which had made them spiritually self-sufficient, which had held them in a world of constant values and secure customs, which had clearly defined their place in society, their contact with nature and even with supernatural forces beyond human reach. All these guarantors of an ordered life were destroyed in an urban society that did not reintegrate man in a new social order. In the competitive world of the modern city where the continuous encounter with heterogeneous elements constantly created new but only casual relations, man was more lonesome than the farmer in his semi-isolation of family and neighborhood.

It has been rightly stated that the "nervousness of modern man" does not originate merely in the lack of satisfaction of certain personal aspirations; it springs no less from a disturbance of his social character. The neurosis strikes deep into a society of restless and hustling hermits in the midst of a noisy metropolis. The working class (of all groups!) escaped such a fate, at least partly, by reorganizing the proletarian masses into a communal or cooperative existence. The growing trade unions did not improve only the worker's standard of life and his position in industry, but—what was more important—they gave him a group conscience again, thus liberating him from disintegrating isolation.

Apart from all further political aims—in fact, often in contradiction to revolutionary Socialism—such a social organization succeeded in alleviating basic contradictions of proletarian existence. It promised a tentative answer at least to the search for a new social order. This great turn of the urban proletariat is largely due to the sobering and socializing experiences of factory life. It disciplined, matured, and rationalized the proletariat. Its schemes of collective bargaining, of a planned society, of social insurance, of industrial democracy—all of them answers to the immanent contradictions and serious maladjustments of modern society—are the reaction of rational masses.

Marxian Socialism became the political creed of the majority among the urban proletariat. The latter no doubt was largely living by the concepts of a now popularized rationalism. Darwin's *Origin of the Species* and Haeckel's *Riddles of the Universe* became the Bible of the "awakened people."

It is this concept of the rational masses which, justified or not, oriented the rising trade unions and Socialist oligarchies. It decided their approach to the masses, the images they presented, the propaganda techniques they applied. It gave them a new security. Indeed, it made them almost bourgeois-minded, especially the labor aristocracy of skilled workers in pre-depression days. The great German author and liberal, Thomas Mann, could address them as the last bulwark and genuine heir of a middle-class civilization, when fatal attack upon it was threatened with the rise of National Socialism. The proletarian movements even in their most revolutionary forms were children of 19th-century rationalism. In this sense, even the Bolshevist Revolution of Lenin and Trotsky was a rational movement deriving from the spirit of 1789.

THE SOCIAL BASIS OF FASCISM

The Fascist revolutions sprang from different sources. In fact, their advent was preceded by fatal transformations in other social strata which in turn became the mainspring of utterly different revolutionary dynamics. Social unrest found a new momentum, grew in depth and dimension. The amorphous masses emerged. They were recruited, above all, from three social groups which significantly enough had not been reached by the social images of rational Socialism, yet at the same time represented the crisis strata of modern society. A shifting "new middle class," a restless unemployed, and a militia of irregulars were the problem children of post-war Europe. The analysis of National Socialism has illustrated their import in present-day unrest.

In fact, it is in Germany alone that these developments came to a climax and found definite political expressions that challenged the world at large. What had become an actuality in post-war Germany may remain only a latent threat in other highly industrialized countries. Their different social and political structure contains counterbalancing forces (which Germany does not possess), and may arrest incipient trends. The German example, however, serves as a supreme warning which must be heeded; it also manifests the inherent radicalism of the Nazi revolution. This analysis of the amorphous masses will therefore refer primarily to the German experience. Furthermore, the scope of this discussion forbids treatment of the widely different condition of the masses in other countries, such as Mexico and Russia. Illuminating though such an expansion of material analysis would be for a general evaluation of this crucial phenomenon, it is above all the fate of the German crisis strata which has world-wide repercussions and needs all our attention. Here only a few basic elements of this process of social disintegration can be underscored.

The *salaried employees* became the prototype of this social convulsion. The marked and rapid growth of this youngest stratum in capitalist society in the period of highly developed capitalism brought about not only quantitative changes in relation to older social strata, but qualitative transformations too. The social level of the group sank with its increasing extent. The average chance for advancement declined. The rise from office boy to general manager lost its reality and became only a theme reserved for story books. The job no longer required a specified training. Rational scientific business management replaced the personal experience of the individual. Increasing mechanization made replacements a daily routine without effecting any great loss of efficiency. It brought the level of wages (even if they were still called salaries) and the social security of the salaried man down to proletarian status. Inflation swelled the number of the jobholders who had once been independent small capitalists and still could not free themselves from the living memory of better days. The depression in the late '20's and early '30's brought the horrors of unemployment for this hitherto secure group.

What made the fate of this white-collar class especially unfortunate was its awakened realization that it represented a group between big capital and labor that was always in danger of being crushed by these two impersonal forces. The office workers and shop assistants were anti-plutocratic in sentiment, but they were anti-proletarian as well. The proletariat and its Socialism was to them only a product and complement of the capitalism of the monopoly state. If these shaken middle-class sons did possess any social image, vague as it was, it came near the ideal of a handicraft society of small independent artisans where professions were still all-inclusive callings, and where the community assured its members security and a sufficient outlet for the goods they produced, guaranteeing everyone his living and clearly defining his place in society. Such a need-satisfying sustenance economy was no doubt a romantic conception of a medieval world, actually much less harmonized. There was not always a happy Hans Sachs, singing master of the shoemakers. And what was even more important for present-day considerations, this concept of the medieval city was certainly out of tune with modern needs and conditions and far from offering the individual freedom these young and disappointed idealists demanded.

Justified or not, these new employees felt themselves to be the last residue of personal values in a mechanized world of super-organization. They were the victims of that battle cry of highly developed capitalism, rationalization. Large-scale production, big department stores, and banking mergers—indeed, capitalism of the monopoly state grown bureaucratic—was steadily weakening the independent middle class. No wonder their sons revolted against this world of rationalism that gave them no hope for the future, not even personal satisfaction in their daily work.

In reaction against such emptiness in life and work, they fled into a dream world of movie glamour. It had to give them what they missed in daytime. The private secretary marrying the big boss and the little man growing into a figure of national and international import, "by proxy" living dangerously and moving in high society—these familiar themes of escape novels were taken so seriously by the petty bourgeois malcontent that she herself (or he!) became a hilarious movie theme.

Amusing as this respect for the imaginary life of the screen was and profitable as it could be for an alert motion picture industry, this desire revealed the most significant phenomenon of our days: "the depersonalization of individuals."

Such a reaction was not reserved for Germany alone, but there it represented a preliminary to the emergence of the amorphous masses, the bricks of modern dictatorial edifices, because the political turn these discontented *Kleinbürger* finally took followed exactly the same pattern. In fact, politics meant to them nothing but escape from their petty existence through collective emotionalism. The "nationalization of the masses" grew out of the extreme loneliness of urban man. Just as romantic poets and thinkers more than one hundred years ago had sought refuge from breath-taking isolation in their religious turn to the all-embracing church, so a mass conversion to political religions was going on among modern urbanites. It is most significant that their sudden "discovery of politics" was usually preceded by their conversion to religious sects. A disproportionate growth of sects and cults is always a danger sign of a society out of tune, looking for substitutes. Politics itself was actually approached in a spirit of revivalism. A concrete analysis of the rites and symbols of the new mass state and its emotional nationalism will prove that abundantly. The better life promised by the leader was like an awakening from a bad dream. "Germany awake!" became an electrifying slogan for the masses who wishfully pictured their own meager reality as only a nightmare from which one could be aroused by the strong voice of the master of "the day."

The tragedy of the white-collar class was that its whole existence had become a borrowed life—and so dangerously unreal! Its romanticism, its passion, its irrationalism—genuine though they were—did not grow out of superabundant strength but resulted from "collective escapism." It was more a burning urge for a new belief than a real faith that made the uprooted masses passionate followers of a new messiah. Such an escapist attitude found its crystallization within the new middle class, yet it came to include ever wider circles of a society in turmoil.

Two other classes in particular—the unemployed and the irregulars—showed the same symptoms just as clearly, and in a way became even more significant for the final disintegration of freely organized group life. What distinguished them, however, from the new middle class was the fact that they did not go through the slow and painful process of disintegration that has been outlined here as a fate typical of the white-collar class. The other two crisis strata somehow entered the political scene from the beginning as amorphous masses. This was certainly true as far as the *unemployed* were concerned.

Unemployment as such did not represent a completely new phenomenon. It was a characteristic of modern industrial society, a living criticism of the prevailing economic order. But there is a great difference in extent and duration between the industrial reserve army of the pre-war time and the post-war unemployed. The latter is more than a result of cyclical fluctuations to be absorbed by industry in times of prosperity. The post-war phenomenon represents a group of people who by the fact of being unemployed for a long time often become unemployable. Instead of being a threatening menace and an interruption of normal working life, unemployment becomes an inevitable fate, a continuous state—one may almost say, a profession, a fifth estate.

The economic and social implications of this new fifth estate are paramount. A society based as ours is upon labor for its economic well-being and its moral existence cannot bear the continuous idleness of nearly one-quarter of its employables. Even if it could carry the economic waste and burden, the social consequences would be of crucial import. It is occupation, above all, that links man with society, attaches social prestige to him, determines his specific position. Without a job he is an outcast, unwanted. Therefore, if labor is taken from him, the moral basis of his existence begins to weaken.

What is worse: not only are all normal bonds with existing society broken, but the unemployed loses hold on society as such and therewith even the power to challenge an order that left him out. Though unemployment petrifies his position, it leaves the group formless, amorphous. The result is a rootless radicalism—inertia at best, and explosive nihilism at worst—as the example of Germany fully proves. This same very radical experience also shows that unemployment—numerically potent though it is—represents only a latent power to be released or used by outside force.

This impelling force came into being with the rise of a *militia of irregulars* in 20th-century Europe. This group undoubtedly never belonged to civic life. That it entered the bourgeois world in significant numbers at all was due only to the First World War, which was the origin of this militia and as such of modern dictatorship. The full implications of this group's emergence into politics will be seen later, when the intrusion of the militant by "the impact of permanent war" is analyzed. Here only this much must be emphasized: these soldiers of fortune were different from the professional soldiers only in this respect: they did not establish a societal organization as was seen above in the analysis of their *condottiere* leader. None of the institutional frames of the regular army was theirs. They aimed not at new forms but at never-ending revolution. They were the driving force in the new dictatorship; they gave impetus to an apathetic unemployed, and revolutionary *élan* to a desperate middle class.

These dispossessed taken together composed the material of the amorphous masses of modern totalitarianism. They had lost or never possessed real group life. They now were ready to merge into a great stream of political activism giving them direction and fulfillment in a life which was no longer of their own making. "To believe, to obey, to fight" became the motto promulgated by Il Duce. It was the chief political function of the new masses.

The phenomenon of these masses found its complete realization in Germany alone. Italian Fascism, though it showed incipient elements of such a development, did not reach such revolutionary dimensions. Italy had not proceeded to the same degree of industrialization and metropolitanism; thus she did not experience the rise of amorphous masses. Her revolution therefore smacked of pre-war imperialism. Her dynamics were not so nihilistic, not so explosive as those of National Socialism. Fascism represents a much less radical and much less dangerous movement. If it were not for its alliance with or its dependence upon the big brother in the north, it might even have been appeased. In spite of its illusions of grandeur, its Caesaristic gestures, and its promises of a 20th century under Fascist rule, it was definitely not a world revolution. It was German National Socialism that became the prototype of the revolution by the amorphous masses.

To make this surrender to the dictator complete, the "neurotic age" of World War I and the Armistice period was needed. Only societies which had undergone the complete denouement and the catastrophic experiences of a total crisis were ripe for the radical extinction of independent individuality and autonomous group life. Probably a particular national make-up was also preconditional for releasing the full sway of such a sweeping societal change.

The story of National Socialism has indicated the historic circumstances that made emotional nationalism a natural avenue of escape for the new middle class in Germany. Keen analysts of the German national character have even found that the Germans in general seem to be especially disposed toward such self-surrender. From the powerful barbarian invasions of early times to the present-day quest for world domination, the Germans have always impressed the circumspect observer as being torn by inner contradictions. If happiness, following the Epicurean definition, is a state of tranquillity, the Germans have never been a happy nation, never at peace with themselves or with the outside world. The Greek idea of Sophrosyne—balance, sanity, self-control, and moderation—could not take root in a nation laden with tensions and moving in extremes.

In this respect, the "young nation," as German nationalist Moeller van den Bruck proudly called his country, really showed that it had not yet grown to full maturity. By no mere accident have the Middle Ages always enchanted the German people. "All experience had yet, to the minds of man, the directness and absoluteness of the pleasure and pain of child life. All things presenting themselves to the mind in violent contrasts and impressive forms lent a tone of excitement and of passion to everyday life and tended to produce that perpetual oscillation between despair and distracted joy, between cruelty and pious tenderness, which characterized life in the Middle Ages." These masterful lines from Johan Huizinga's *Waning of the Middle Ages* reflect the spiritual climate of a romantic nation that has carried the same "violent tenure of life" into our own days.

Ever since Tacitus gave his account of these hard-headed and courageous fighters who at the same time showed a persistent strain of melancholy, the deep contrasts in German character have puzzled friend and foe. Today reports from occupied Europe and from Germany proper confirm no less that underneath and side-by-side with a fiery fighting spirit is boundless moodiness. One has only to look at German soldier songs and he will be struck by their dismal sentimentality.

No other word has been used in recent Germany more often than *Ordnung* (order)—secret yearning of a people never at rest.

It is certainly not too far-fetched to see in the strutting self-assertiveness and excessive pride of the German nation its utter insecurity and uncertainty. One may be reminded of Guglielmo Ferrero's brilliant and challenging characterization of Napoleon in his recent *Reconstruction of Europe*: "It was not ambition which led Napoleon to mutilate, dismember, absorb, fetter, and violate so many states; *it was fear*—but the result was always the opposite: the more Napoleon maltreated his victims, the more he feared them."

THE IRRATIONAL MASSES

The great change society has been undergoing since the latter part of the 19th century also found expression in the renewed interest of the social sciences in the phenomenon of the masses. Under the impact of modern urbanization and revolutionary episodes in 19th-century European capitals, Le Bon and his school emphasized the irrational behavior of the masses. This most influential school of modern crowd psychology developed a somewhat confusing tendency to identify the masses with the highly emotionalized and unstable mob, thus stigmatizing mass action as devoid of individual self-control. This identification certainly simplified the much more complex interplay between rational and irrational elements in modern mass reaction. Only recently the attempt was made to differentiate between distinct types of masses. This differentiation is especially necessary in an evaluation of mass participation in modern political movements; it parallels the contrasting types of their leaders.

Basic variations will be found in the mass following in the different social layers of a given population. Rural groups will differ from urban masses. Scattered crowds react differently from congregated mobs. It will be decisive whether political action is confronted with a latent or with an aroused mass. Different social classes invite a variety of stimuli and reactions. Political movements have an uneven appeal among the various social strata. The rational theory of Marxian Socialism presupposed the sobering and socializing experiences of a generation trained in factory discipline and living by the concepts of a now popularized rationalism. It was not only because of lack in leadership that these rational schemes failed completely to reach the suddenly rising groups of salaried employees and of unemployed. The irrational politics of new dynamic national movements found a first foothold in these groups because they definitely were not rational masses.

In fact, they offered all the characteristics that, according to recent social psychology, define mob behavior. Cantril has shown in his keen *Psychology of Modern Social Movements* that "the individual mob member is inclined to display specific characteristics of an immature person." He is naïve and blunt, lacking in balance and discrimination. He definitely has not grown to mature individuality, the main characteristic of which is self-containment. Like a child he is completely dependent on his environment for his well-being and his inner equilibrium. The result is his self-identification with the group in which he is submerged.

In a way, this phenomenon of mob existence is the counter and complement to anarchic man who has thrown off the natural and fruitful balance between well-integrated personality and free society.

This complete submission to the group at the same time shuts out the outside world; "the individual world of the mob members becomes circumscribed and confined." Such an exclusion of "counter-propaganda" indeed simplifies life, it stabilizes cultural norms, it guarantees well-predictable actions, it gives promise of security. But while this "psychological autarchy" may serve as a "protective tariff" for the inexperienced child, it definitely destroys the personality of the grown-up but confused mob member who gives himself up to the closed community. His escape into the safety of the tightly sealed citadel makes him unfit for an independent stand and decision just as the spoiled and well-protected child will be unprepared for life.

The psychological effects of such surrender are obvious. It is the strength of self-contained individuality that it recognizes in its own particularity the right of everyone to differ from everyone else. It makes for moderation, open-mindedness, restraint, and tolerance. The mob deprived of individuality is egocentric, prejudiced, fanatical.

Mob psychology, when it seizes a whole nation, destroys the web of its complex social structure. Like the individual differentiations of its members, so the innumerable associations of the living community are melted into one gray mass. This process of "massification"—the dissolution of free organizations, the flattening of the social pyramid—in a way preceded the rise of modern dictators. They were the product of this disintegration of society which in turn became the basis of their established rule.

The classes which had lost their social characteristics, which had been emptied of substance and deprived of forms, became the human material of a political revolution, the essence of which was "the institutionalization of amorphous masses," because modern dictatorship in its sociological meaning is nothing but the substitution of crowds for society. Thus it represents a unique phenomenon, decisively novel—and the great challenge to social order. The transformation of the spontaneous social groups of a pluralistic society into the totalitarian mass state is the real background of Fascism.

The end of independent man obliterates any private sphere for his existence. Civil rights and constitutional guarantees become meaningless. The distinction between state and society—prerequisite of democracy—is definitely dissolved.

Free interplay of spontaneous and responsible group associations is the necessary precondition for a democratic society. Freedom of association not only is a fundamental right of democracy, it furnishes the lifeblood of its existence. This essential is equally denied by the Communist and the Fascist state. The Marxian myth of the "classless" society is in this respect identical with the "superclass" concept of Fascism. Both of them destroy the balancing powers of clashing classes which, as guarantors of freedom, serve as substitutes for the classical liberal belief in a preordained social harmony of rational human beings.

The aim and essence of the revolutionary post-war movements is the pulverization of all autonomous groups (the family included) into an inarticulate crowd which, permanently in need of a tyrannical leader, is kept together only if moved and satisfied emotionally. It must be dynamic, therefore, and it cannot be appeased. This is the basis of the modern "state of the masses." Its success in assault, however, presupposes a long undermining process and the inner destruction of social order.

The crisis strata of society—a shifting new middle class, a rootless unemployed, and a warlike militia—are the first lines of dictatorial attack. They have one element in common: they are negatively united; they do not fit into the rational scheme of the 19th century. These new masses throwing their fate into politics are, above all, irrational in their reaction.

Faith in a rational mass of followers, swayed by reason and progressively educated in rational standards, was the foundation of early democratic thinking and has remained so in spite of obvious setbacks to rational order in world politics today. Democratic institutions stand and fall by their belief in discussion before a reasonable public. Such recognition of the masses as responsible participants by necessity limits the sphere of independent leadership in a democracy, already restricted by its institutional character.

The dictatorial leader of the formless masses views his following differently. To cite Mussolini: "When I feel that mass in my hands, as it yields, or when I mix with it there, it almost crushes me. Then I feel but a lump of that mass, and yet there remains in me something of hostility, like the distaste that the poet feels against the matter on which he is working. Does not the sculptor sometimes break the marble in ire because it does not take, under his hands, exactly the shape which it had in his first vision?"

It is no mere accident that some of the most powerful dictators of our day have shown throughout their life a strong disposition toward an artistic career. In the critical days before the outbreak of the Second World War, Hitler remarked to the British ambassador to Germany, that if his "last" demand in regard to Poland were fulfilled, he would return to the dreams of his early childhood, to the life of an artist. In fact, modern dictators view politics itself in a pseudo-artistic fashion, arousing the emotions of the masses in collective romanticism. "Our policy is an artist's policy," Goebbels pontifically pronounced during the last stages of the Danzig campaign in June, 1939.

Hitler's concept of the masses is not different from Mussolini's: "Like a woman," he says, "whose psychic feeling is influenced less by abstract reasoning than by an undefinable sentimental longing for complementary strength, who will submit to the strong man rather than dominate the weakling, thus the masses love the ruler rather than the suppliant, and inwardly they are far more satisfied by a doctrine which tolerates no rival, than by the grant of liberal freedom; they often feel at a loss what to do with it and even easily feel themselves deserted."

Such statements reveal the human difference between dictatorship and democracy. They stand for a divergent "image of man." Goebbels says, "The ordinary man hates nothing more than two-sidedness, to be called upon to consider this as well as that." Such a philosophy appeals to masses harassed by uncertainties and insecurities. Life becomes clear and simple again under the orders of a dictator. Everything is decided and people merely have to follow. All disquieting criticism dies down according to the classical formula of the servant of the Prophet before the Library of Alexandria: "If those books agree with the Koran, they are unnecessary; if they disagree, they are pernicious."

In a democracy, however, there persists an absolute unwillingness to give up the search for truth and the freedom of choice in the knowledge of good and evil.

These different views on the mass following are not alone a philosophical concern of divergent political systems. They also find concrete expression in the respective party organizations, in the techniques of propaganda promotion, and in the creation of symbols.

Chapter V

THE ONE-PARTY STATE

—— —— —— —— —— —— —— —— —— —— ——

Through its parties the modern state reaches down to the people. Here again, as in all other strata of the political pyramid —and even more so in this first mass layer—divergent political systems are hidden behind the same nomenclature. Just as leaders and lieutenants do, so parties carry a different meaning in democracies and dictatorships.

To be sure, the definition of a party presupposes a democratic climate and makes the term a misnomer when applied to a dictatorship. A one-party system is a contradiction in itself. Only the coexistence of at least one competitive group makes a political party real. To become a party to something always means identification with one group and differentiation from another. Every party in its essence signifies *partnership* in a particular organization and *separation* from others by a specific program.

Political parties furthermore presuppose active *participation* in politics, or at least an attempt at and a chance for participation. Only in such a fight for control and in conscious influence on political forces do parties gain meaning and importance. It is not accidental that the beginning of political parties is closely tied up with the rise of parliaments. When political representation appears and a national forum of discussion looms and, therewith, a constant opportunity for political participation, only then do political parties arise. This happened in England in the revolutionary 17th century, in France on the eve of the great Revolution in 1789, in Germany around 1848. Even where neighborly influences create political groups of an awakened intelligentsia, as in 19th-century czarist Russia, they assume political dimensions only when they find some degree of participation possible.

Thus the hour of birth for the political party in every nation can be well defined by a simple derivation from its original meaning. The same is true of the critical period of the party system. By its very concept the party connotes not only the coexistence of different competing entities, but also the inclusion of every separate group as a *part in a whole*. Only when the specific interests of parties are embedded in a common whole does the political struggle not lead to the disintegration of the entire group. Only when essentials can be constantly reaffirmed, uniting the political adversaries, can differences be balanced. Just as children are ready to accept the rules of the gang only as long as they are willing to continue their group life, so can sacrifices be asked from each political opponent only as long as the preservation of the community seems worth while. A common field of activity, a basic homogeneity, a common language are presuppositions for a functioning party system. Such a common basis alone makes bearable sacrifices, renunciation, and even defeat. Wherever this body politic becomes questionable, the crisis of the parties seems a necessary result. The vitality of its party system thus becomes a test for the stability of a social and political order. The strength of the Anglo-Saxon party system is largely founded upon a basic national unity that makes the differentiations of political groups, in the words of H. D. Laski, "differences in degree and not in kind."

This interdependence of political parties with the fate of the political whole is the result of their "political" character. Political they are, not only because of their claim to political power, but even more on account of the fulfillment of their essentially political function.

Organizing the chaotic public will has been often stated as a primary task of political parties. "They bring order out of the chaos of a multitude of voters" (Lord Bryce). They are brokers of ideas, clarifying, systematizing, and expounding their doctrine. Representatives of social interest groups, they bridge the distance between the individual and the great community. They maximize in the competitive scheme of at least a two-party system the voter's education and sharpen his free choice. The coexistence of a competitor, therefore, is of paramount importance to an effective democratic party system which presupposes that the final choice will reflect the reasonable decision of a free electorate.

In fact, the basic assumption of democracy is the inevitability of differing views and the free operation of conflicting opinions. In the words of W. Ivor Jennings, "The true democrat has a suspicion that he may not always be right." Thus in England the opposition becomes the most important part of the Parliament; its members are "critics by profession." The ruling majority not only highly respects His Majesty's opposition but often incorporates its fruitful ideas—indeed a wise course for the party in power, if it wants to remain so. The opposition is not only the looming "shadow Cabinet," but an active participant in actual control.

The open forum of parliament becomes the clearing house for the policies that the state should follow. The political parties are the proper engine for such a continuous plebiscite. They make the voters choose the lesser of at least two evils, thus forcing political differentiations into a few major channels. Yet, important as this machinery of political concentration may be, the political services of the parties do not stop at that. What is even more essential, the parties transform the private citizen himself. They make him a *zoön politikon*. They *integrate the individual into the group.* Every party has to present to the individual voter a picture of the community as an entity. It must constantly remind him of this whole, adjust his wants to the needs of the community, and if necessary ask sacrifices from him in the name of the community. No less can the so-called "class parties" that apparently call upon only a specific part of the population renounce this essential function. The outstanding example of such a class program, the Communist Manifesto, justifies its position with the claim that the united proletariat will represent the overwhelming majority and that its dictatorship will lead to a dissolution of all classes and therewith to the liberation of society as a whole.

If the party in a democracy fulfills these two first functions of organizing the chaotic public will and educating the private citizen to political responsibility, then it can also lay claim to a third, that of representing the *connecting link between government and public opinion*. Since democracies are pyramids built from below, the connection between leaders and followers becomes a necessity in the two-way traffic of democracy. The avenues of public opinion are vital in a democracy. It is the major function of the party to keep them open and clean. Such a task makes the parties, if not supreme, at least the controlling agency of government in a representative democracy.

This is even more true of the fourth function of a democratic party, the *selection of democratic leaders*. Here, as everywhere in a democracy, it is the competitive scheme, the choice between at least two oligarchies, that guarantees the quality of its leadership. Of course, such a selection presupposes an enlightened public qualified to make the right choice.

The *crisis elements* of democratic parties can be well perceived in the rise of dictatorial parties. In fact, dictatorial parties grow up within the democratic party system. They are a state within the state, alien to its basic principles. One may therefore question their justification in a democratic party system to which they actually do not belong, because they make use of its "instruments" without abiding by its principles. Yet their rise is the expression of a basic lack within the society. They can recruit followers because there are those who no longer are a part of society as a whole, who differ not only in degree but in kind, who cannot compromise (or at least believe so) since they are fighting the predominant society as such. They are outsiders to this kind of society. If they succeed in winning over considerable numbers, then the party system stops functioning; the democratic process enters a critical stage. The rise of dictatorial parties within democracies is a storm signal for the democratic party system.

Dictatorial parties are older than dictatorships. Long before National Socialism rose to power in Germany, as early as the late 19th century, the emergence of a new type of party could be detected. National Socialism has merely accentuated characteristics to be found, for example, within the Social Democratic parties before the war. In sharp contrast to the loosely knit organization and passive membership of most western European parties, the Social Democrats had developed a widely ramified and highly integrated party machinery calculated to reach its adherents in every phase of their activity. Closely associated with the leading trade union organization, consumers' cooperatives, workingmen's sports associations, active youth organizations, and a controlled labor press, they tried to hold their members "from the cradle to the grave." Similar developments could be found within the Catholic Center party, though here the organizations were essentially confined to cultural activities.

Unfortunately these developments meant progressively extended bureaucracies—the starting point of the much-discussed party machines and their functionary, the *Bonze*. Yet what was more important: this development pointed to the inner difficulties of the democratic party system. From then on, disagreement between the parties concerned fundamentals and a fight over ultimate issues. Compromise became impossible and so did any coalition with another party. The main purpose of the new totalitarian parties became the *fight for a new political order*, for a new society. Speaking a different language and living according to a different set of values (at least they thought so), the new partisans had to be segregated from the political and social body of the ruling class and society. They might be enchanted otherwise, taken in by an old order, the destruction of which was the essential purpose of the "guarantors" of the new morrow. With the rise of the dictatorial party, its competitors in politics necessarily became more inflexible, too. Struggle assumed the quality of a religious war; the only possible outcome for any contestant seemed to be overwhelming victory or ultimate annihilation.

Such a situation explains the revolutionary function of a dictatorial party before its seizure of power. It is, above all, the revolutionary vanguard of the future state.

Lenin's fight at the turn of the century for a small centralized revolutionary elite as opposed to the Menshevists' idea of a loose democratic mass organization laid the foundations for such a disciplined totalitarian party. Lenin thus anticipated what revolutionary parties a generation later experienced when they had to choose between thoroughly revolutionary policies and mass following. Only in a "revolutionary situation," i.e., at a time when complete victory enhances the revolutionary cause, is it possible for a radical party to win and hold the masses. The latter are in need of visible rewards. If they cannot reap the fruits now— or at least hold a reasonable expectation of doing so in the near future—they will leave the ranks. This explains the extraordinary fluctuation in membership rolls to be observed in radical groups everywhere. Communist followers of today may turn up tomorrow as Fascism's most "reliable" fighters. Whoever seems to deliver the spoils has the confidence of the fluctuating masses; but if he cannot do this by tomorrow, another deliverer will be sought out.

Revolutionary parties, reckoning on a long struggle, can count only on a small elite of unrelenting fighters who do not care for rewards today and who are ready to stand up for the revolutionary cause even if it takes a lifetime. The young Bolshevist party comprised, above all, professional revolutionaries who took their orders from the central party organization, robbing a bank, organizing a party cell, conceiving a new program without any thought of early victory. The revolutionary intellectual in his great flight into a future morrow and the revolutionary wire-puller in his minute work were worlds apart, but they met in one respect: they did not expect rewards in this world. They had given their life to the party which in return became their life. Thirty thousand was the largest membership the Bolshevists could muster before they became rulers of Russia.

In post-war Europe, however, revolutionary parties changed these tactics and did not fare too well. Partly on the basis of the mistaken presupposition of a revolutionary situation they now opened their ranks to the masses. In Soviet Russia of course they could offer their followers all the spoils of the victor. In fact, many people joined the party for such reasons alone. Exploiters of the revolution, even if they tried to be two hundred per cent Bolshevists, were not sincere revolutionaries. Quite a number among them became renegades when it seemed opportune. Many more were purged when the revolutionary state could dispense with their originally useful services.

The radical parties in other countries did not have to eliminate this ballast of "political profiteers and job-hunters" because there were no jobs to be distributed. As quickly as the prospects of revolutionary changes attracted the driftwood of a political reserve army, so quickly did this army move on to new shores that seemed more promising. The whole tragedy of the German Communist party—and for that matter, of any Communist party that could for a time attract some group following—was its dilemma between its revolutionary character and its mass adherents, between its uncompromising attitude as a party which did not want to sell the revolution for a mess of pottage, and the necessity of offering substantial results at once because the masses would not be satisfied with a promised millennium. They wanted higher wages, social security, political recognition—visible success today. Thus they left the party that was preparing for a revolution not yet in sight.

The significant change in character and techniques to be observed in the German National Socialist party during its rise serves as a test case for this impact of mass following. Leaving aside the short episode preceding the ill-fated beer-hall *Putsch* of 1923, one may say that the National Socialist party before its most impressive victory of September, 1930, was a truly revolutionary party, attracting in particular a small group of "tough fighters" who were proud to be "outcasts." Radical negation of their political environment was sufficient justification for membership. Far-flung programs of utopian character meant reality to them. The day after victory was won, such an attitude had to be completely reversed. Now the party had to show concrete successes to its newly won followers. It had to give them assurance of the forthcoming total conquest of the state. The party had

daily to confirm the idea that they were with the winning battalions. If not, they would leave it for another heaven. The tone
of the party propaganda changed overnight. Only yesterday they
had laughed at the politicians and their small coin of results. Now
every minor success—a secondary ministerial position in a third-
rate German state, an honorary function awarded a party member,
a well-staged intrigue—such little successes were regarded as signposts of impending victory. For a mass party everything depended
on success. Without immediate success it could not survive. Its
final fate became a race against time.

True, the spectacular rise of the National Socialist Party from
seven men to a membership of millions had established a myth
of invincibility. But two years after the victory in 1930, the party
showed signs of disintegration. The lost opportunities of 1932—
Hitler's two unsuccessful attempts to win the Chancellorship—
spelled failure in the eyes of the masses. Not that they trusted
Papen and his machinations, not that they understood General
Schleicher and his policies. Had the "politicians of the system"
outsmarted Hitler? Had Hindenburg put the little corporal in his
place? Were there intrigues around the Marshal? They did not
know, nor did they much care. What counted was the simple
fact that two years after Hitler had received a people's mandate
he still did not rule the Wilhelmstrasse, but at best only moved
around its antechambers, and, incidentally, was rather awkward
at that.

Within a few months, between the elections of July and November, 1932, his party lost two million votes, i.e., one-eighth of
its following. A week after his first major defeat in the Reichstag
elections, a number of state elections showed a 50 per cent decline in votes as compared with the national elections. The rats
were leaving the sinking ship. It was sound party tactics, therefore, for Hitler to concentrate in the following eight weeks upon
a comparatively insignificant state election in Lippe which was
held on January 3, 1933, and comprised all in all an electorate of
100,000 people. The party sent all its big orators, including Hitler
himself, into the little market square of Lippe-Detmold. With all

this energy poured into this effort, the Nazis barely succeeded in holding their own. Yet this was important enough; no price seemed too high to stop the flight of the disappointed masses.

The party finances were running low, and no kind capitalist was ready to raise the ante. One only has to read the diary of Joseph Goebbels, especially his entry on December 23, 1932: "The year 1932 has brought us eternal ill-luck. . . . The past was sad, and the future looks dark and gloomy; all chances and hopes have quite disappeared."

The breakdown of the revolutionary mass party was simply a question of time. Hitler knew it just as well as his overconfident opponents did. Thus since the front door to success seemed to be locked he tried the back door. This was the historic hour of intrigues around Hindenburg's house, and of the Hitler-Papen conversation at Banker Schroeder's home in Cologne. It was the turning point. The national government of Hitler-Papen-Hugenberg was born. The two junior partners (who, old in party tactics as they were, believed themselves the senior partners of the firm) were soon relieved of their "responsibilities." National Socialism was in power. "The revolutionary vanguard of the future state" became the ruler of the Third Reich. The totalitarian party entered a new stage.

CHARACTER OF THE TOTALITARIAN PARTY

The dictatorial party after the seizure of power has three main functions:

1. *It creates the political elite.*
2. *It controls and educates the masses.*
3. *It maintains communication between state and society.*

The first function is the basis of the inner party organization, the nucleus and training school for the ruling class. The second is fulfilled by the institutional framework set up under the dictatorial regime, for which the party serves in its capacity as the system's guarantor and as the exclusive representative of the proper (i.e., National Socialist) world outlook, thus creating "an atmosphere of national discipline and patriotism for the coming generation." The third activity is carried out by an elaborate propaganda machine that reaches even beyond national boundaries. Modern dictatorship, though it may seemingly follow only a one-way road, cannot dissociate itself from public opinion. It must listen carefully to the "voice of the people," especially since this is stifled under the tyrant's rule. The party serves essentially as a listening post.

All three functions, if successfully administered, secure a fourth purpose of the party (a task by no means ascribed to the monocratic party system by its cynical critics alone): the *preservation of the status quo*—and if possible the continuous extension—of the ruling elite's factual power.

This enumeration of the party's services well proves its key position in the political edifice of modern totalitarianism.

Yet to call such a dictatorial organization a party is a misnomer and often a conscious misconception. The right to combine freely, this basic freedom of choice to participate in or to part from, is essentially denied. The dictatorial party's monopoly which prevents the free formation and expression of opinion is the precise antithesis of the party system.

Even Fascist theorists have felt the inadequacy of the term. Many learned studies have been written to explain the *nature of the dictatorial party*. In fact this topic became the preferred, if not the only, theme of Fascist public law. The *Partito Nazionale Fascista* has in turn been defined as an institution of public law, an oligarchical fraternity, the nation in substance, a religious order, a civil militia. All these descriptions depict specific elements of the dictatorial party. It is in fact a blend of these different qualities, and often this gives a most contradictory result.

The dictatorial party indeed has typical characteristics of an *institution of public law*. It not only achieves official standing and recognition, but the state defines its scope and function by specific legislation. The party becomes an essential, if not *the* essential, organ of the regime. The symbols of the party (*Hakenkreuz, Fascio Littorio*, Hammer and Sickle) are adopted as the emblems of the state. But the fact of such a predominant and all-embracing position makes it in the eyes of many critics extremely doubtful whether the party can be called an institution of public law such as are municipalities, churches, public utilities. True, the dictatorial party receives a charter from the state, signifying the latter's interest in its pursuits and therefore the right to control and inspection. But what is the meaning of this "legal subordinacy" in regard to an institution which by its essence claims its identification with the state or even its "irrefutable supremacy" over the state? Such doubts point at the precarious dualism between state and party, indeed one of the foremost problems of the one-party state. Its indissoluble contradictions can be seen within the institutional framework of every totalitarian state.

This much should be said here: while every dictatorship tries to strike a somewhat different balance between state and party, they all agree that to the dictatorial movement should be reserved the exclusive right of political volition, thus relegating to the state the mere execution of the will of the party. National Socialism in particular emphasizes this supremacy over the state in making the party the creator, guardian, and guarantor of the Third Reich. Whether such an interpretation still leaves to the state the sovereignty that is preconditional for its institutionalization of political agencies, may be doubted. The party that merely makes use of the machinery of the state is sovereign. The concept of the party as an institution of public law thus becomes a legal fiction, important though it may be for winning over the conservative (*Staatserhaltende*) and neutral elements of the populace and for creating a continuity of state loyalties.

The creation of "official status" for the victorious movement in the subdued state, problematic as it may be and far from marking the party's true character, indicates, however, a most significant negation of a fundamental democratic rule. Parties in democracies are private organizations with public functions but without public recognition or authority. This fact is not simply a slip of democracy's legal machinery, as some political scientists are inclined to think. This lack of registration is of the essence for "these free associations" within the democratic system. It assures the crucial distinction between state and society. Freedom from control is one of the fundamental preconditions for effective functioning in the democratic process. Its unhampered development would be jeopardized by a minute regulation of the party's place and function in society.

In recent years, it is true, parties even in democracies have become, at least indirectly, more and more subject to legislation. The legalized particulars (regulation of electoral procedures, the working of parliamentary controls, the enforced publicity on election expenditures) necessitated the factual recognition of the semi-official status of political parties. Yet it is not by chance that in democracies like the United States and the Weimar Republic (where the concrete legislation had to consider the legal status of the parties) these most important driving forces were mentioned only incidentally, if at all, in the fundamental law of the nation. Such an omission guaranteed, so to speak, the associational character of modern democracy. Democratic parties stand or fall by their own right. As soon as they are officialized they lose their representative character of a free electorate and can easily be welded into a weapon, an auxiliary of the dictatorial state.

In order to understand the reality of the dictatorial party, one must examine the nature of the dictatorial state. The second definition of the Fascist party as an *oligarchy* may answer such a query. The *classe dirigente*, the ruling class, regards itself as the creator of the revolutionary state which in turn guarantees the survival of the dictatorial minority. The oligarchical character, according to numerous political scientists a significant feature of every political system, is basic for the dictatorial party. This becomes obvious in specific methods of cooptional self-renewal and regular membership purges. This fight of the elite for control against the outsiders of the party, against the non-participants in power, against the majority, against the people, creates at the same time an inner party democracy of the *Parteigenossen*, the party comrades. In fact, as already shown for the upper layers in respect to the leader and his lieutenants, in spite of all pronounced social differentiation in the dictator's hierarchy a democratic atmosphere of comradeship has to prevail among the insiders. The supreme leader sets the tone for it, and the subleaders adopt it. In fact, the "community of trying experiences" may create unity and loyalty, especially among the fighters of the "first hour." On those political battlefields may thus arise a fraternity that can outlive many party crises and may become the backbone of the party state. This political elite, fighting for the coming state and preconceiving its future existence, becomes the guardian of the new state when victory is won. From such a concept, one has to proceed but one step to the definition of the party as the *nation in substance*, the awakened nation.

According to such an analysis, the main function of the party is to represent the conscience of the nation, the true patriots, the trustees of the masses, the formative and driving force of the state, its organized minority—in short, the real state. "The Fascist party is the state." With this claim, it actually governs and administers the country and coordinates all the citizens' activities with its program. This characterization of the dictatorial party again leads into hopeless contradictions between the "sovereign party" and the "strong state," inner conflicts that will be observed in a more concrete analysis of the institutional framework.

The Fascist party has been further called a *religious order*. "The party appears to us as a church, that is to say, a communion of faith, a union of wills and intentions loyal to a unique and supreme end," Panunzio stated. The inner driving forces of the modern dictatorial party are no doubt closely connected with this spiritual, one may almost say semi-ecclesiastical, character. The party is an asserter of faith, a faith that permeates all aspects of human destiny and reaches into the region of the absolute. Its totalitarian nature inevitably turns the party into a religious order, a theocracy. The faithful follow the Fascist guide as the Jesuit Order made its followers ready for Christian service or Mohammed called upon his believers to fight the infidels.

The reality of the Fascist party can be well described by this religious character. The party has its hierarchy, its rituals, its dogmas, its seminaries. It offers spiritual rewards and punishments. It prosecutes its mission also by administering material pain or pleasure. Fanaticism becomes the most significant feature of the zealous followers; heretics have to be converted or they will be burned. To this end churches have always needed their militant orders and their missionaries. Institutions of propaganda were created to propagate the faith. Persuasion, stimulation, charitable works, public worship, and commemoration of saints and martyrs are consequential techniques of this new religious sect.

It is not a well-balanced program but a stirring myth that moves and possesses its followers. Georges Sorel (father of the most effective social myth and in this respect of Fascism also) always stressed the religious origin of the myth. Like religion, myths cannot be refuted. "We have created our myth. It is a belief, a passion. It does not matter whether it is reality. It becomes reality in us because it is faith and courage," Mussolini said shortly before he marched on Rome, inspired by the myth of the nation.

Such secular revelation makes the movement equally dogmatic, total, and intolerant as the *ecclesia militans*. It also helps to fill the empty space which has been created by the dissolution of basic religious concepts.

It is this quasi-religious character, above all, that makes modern totalitarianism so great an object of suspicion to Japan, despite her otherwise autocratic tendencies. The great social changes brought about in the Far East have not yet changed the religious foundations of Japanese society. The Mikado-Emperor remains the religious head of the nation. Prime Ministers may be strong and military castes powerful; national movements may be called upon and strategic alliances with Axis powers played up—Fascism is still not acceptable to a nation which recognizes "one sovereign over all, the Son of Heaven." In spite of the pronounced westernization of Nippon, the secularization of the divine has certainly not progressed to the point of deifying political forces, a point which is the exact core of modern "faith movements" because the Fascist party is, above all, the asserter of a new faith in an infidel world.

Finally, the Fascist party has been called a *civil militia*. In fact, the original meaning of *Fascio* denotes a group of men armed for guerilla warfare. The constitution of the fully entrenched movement defines the party along the same lines: "a civil militia under the order of Il Duce in the service of the Fascist State." Bolshevism is also "government by an armed sect" deriving from a wartime organization far more than from Marxist theory.

Again it might be said that a militia that is subservient to the state cannot be its actual master, as is the Fascist party. Actually it was the maker of the new government through "the armed plebiscite of October 22, 1922, overcoming the demobilized state" and it has been its exclusive ruler ever since.

Yet this concept of the civil militia represents the most vital element of the dictatorial party. As soon as it gives up fighting, it has to make room for a new fighting elite. The militant element indeed not only is the driving force of the early fighting days, but is predominant throughout the lifetime of the dictatorial government. It creates all its essential attitudes and institutions: the readiness to battle, militancy, and discipline, the hierarchy of the party, and warlike obedience to orders from above; these features cannot be removed from the Fascist party, which becomes the creator of the garrison state. This last classification, in fact, comes nearest to the daily reality of the modern totalitarian party.

STRUCTURE AND COMPOSITION

The militant nature of the dictatorial party finds visible expression in its foremost feature: the *military structure*, a strikingly novel element in modern political organization. Fascist parties center around and crystallize in semi-military formations. In fact, the real life of the party begins with the establishment of a "shirt" movement. Mussolini's Black Shirts and Hitler's Brown Shirts became the nucleus of the new movements. This is also true, though with some reservations, of Soviet Russia's Red army, the creation of the actual fighting of the civil war. Indeed, a dictatorial party which does not succeed in organizing such a semi-military group does not establish totalitarian rule.

Because of a real or presumed danger, "defense organizations" are created which are called to "protect" the "peaceful" meetings of the rising party and "to free the street for the brown battalions." The fame of these *Saalschlachten* builds up the myth of the party's defense corps. So do the punitive excursions into the "enemy's land." Red villages and their Socialist mayors are "taught," with the help of castor oil during the small hours of the night, the fundamentals of a new heroic age. Burning trade union buildings and destroying offices of the opposing parties spread fame, fear, and repute of the rising movement, just as the Ku Klux Klan's night riders did in the restless South.

The military character of the party appeals especially to the crisis strata of shiftless irregulars. These first recruits of the movement become its most formative group. They owe everything to the party that takes them back into the society and gives them a stake in it. They become its most ardent fighters. They are fighters by profession now.

The party in the hands of the legionnaires becomes basically a militant group. It prefers to call itself a fighting league (*Kampfbund*) instead of a party. It enrolls military cadres when it ventures a new orientation. Politics becomes a battlefield of two irreconcilable opponents who are out to win or to die. Military expressions become fashionable and this turn toward a new and violent language is certainly more than a fashion. Captain Roehm of *Feme* murder fame and Balbo, a daring youth, became the prototypes of these novel movements. Followers are held in equally ruthless discipline; they have to follow the strict party line or face the party's purge.

The military nature of the dictatorial party is also seen in its second outstanding characteristic: its strict *hierarchical order*. Officers are appointed by their superiors to whom alone they are responsible. They are beyond any control from below or outside. At the top of the pyramid will be found the general staff of the dictator: the Central Directorate (Oberste Reichsleitung) of the National Socialist party, the Fascist Grand Council (Gran Consiglio del Fascismo), the Politbureau of the U.S.S.R. They are the "shadow cabinet" of modern autocracies and usually overshadow the official government as the actual power behind the power. Here again, the dualism between state and party becomes obvious, as it does throughout the whole political hierarchy down to local government by a set of party offices paralleling the state bureaucracy. There is some personal union in both hierarchies, more confusing overlapping of responsibilities, and always watchful control of official activities by the party officers enforcing the National Socialist world outlook everywhere. Constant interference weakening the position of the state representatives is not seldom a preparation only for the final storm of the "neutral" vestiges of the state. The shifts in key positions in the German Ministries of Economics and Foreign Affairs—from Schacht to Funk, from Neurath to Ribbentrop—are cases in question. The supreme party organ, indeed, is the policy-making agency; thus the state offices are often degraded to the mere execution of policies decided in the party's inner circles. The Grand Council is the only forum, if any, before which Il Duce discusses his policies.

The political hierarchy firmly established in a central body at the summit is carried through a whole set of regional organizations down to the smallest local party groups, from district leader to regional leader to local leader. In this thorough planning, modern dictatorships have borrowed heavily from church and army and have copied each other no less. National Socialism has developed the system to perfection—and even beyond. Yet the undeniable frenzy of superorganization that no doubt contradicts the proverbial efficiency of modern dictatorships creates an intricate system of checks and balances which, though an artificial and costly substitute for democracy's open competition, well suggests a secret of dictatorship's efficacy.

This top-heavy mechanism that draws practically every follower into a web of organizational controls from which there is no escape, at the same time manifests a third element of the political pattern: *close-knit organization.* It reflects dictatorial all-inclusiveness—the last step in a party's development from the loose and sporadic vote-getting organization to the totalitarian order.

A cell organization taken over from the Bolshevist arsenal is the
partisan's keeper everywhere, especially in the sphere of his daily
activities—at home, the watchful eye of the *Blockwart*; in the
factory, the help of a circumspect *Betriebszelle*; during his leisure-
time activities, the party's cultural organization. Thus a dictatorial hierarchy is fortified from below and made real by meeting
and controlling its members in their day-to-day pursuits.

Dictatorships usually show a significant differentiation in their
party organization between integral groups and affiliated associations, a differentiation which roughly corresponds to a separation between full-fledged members and mere followers. The
first type represents the active core of the movement (specifically designated in National Socialism as the Storm Troopers
(S.A.), the Elite Guard (S.S.), National Socialist Motor Corps
(N.S.K.K.), Hitler Youth, National Socialist Student Association,
National Socialist Women's Organization); the second type en-
larges the circle into wider areas of working organizations and
professional groups (teachers, lawyers, physicians, technicians,
public officials, etc.). The German Labor Front in particular, with
enforced membership for every working person of Aryan origin
(employers included), reaches down to the people.

Such expansion of the party's sway leads to a change of character on its periphery. In fact, its actual composition shifts with
an extension in space and time. Before the conquest of power,
the Fascist parties had an underrepresentation of farmers and
manual workers and a prevalence of the typical crisis strata in
the middle classes, as outlined above, especially among the hard-
pressed white-collar employees and independent professionals.

Even more significant was the predominance of the younger
age group and its continuous percentage rise before the seizure
of power. Statistics for the total party membership in 1931 and
1932 show in this youngest set, 18 to 30 years of age, an increase
from 37.6 to 42.2 per cent. Compared with the age composition
of the competing Social Democratic party, which comprised
only 19.3 per cent of this age group among its membership, and
with the age distribution of the country as a whole where this

same group represented only 31.1 per cent, the "youthfulness" of the National Socialists becomes obvious.

The victorious party showed a no less interesting change in its age composition. In 1935, only two years after the conquest of the state, a decrease to 35.4 per cent of the youngest age stratum was reported. This shift may reflect the typical fate of every "revolutionary" party grown big, old, and successful. The revolutionary have "arrived." Moreover, victory or nearby victory attracts the band-wagon followers, less active, less daring, less revolutionary. It becomes safe to join.

Now the victorious movement has to ward off two opposite dangers at the same time. It may have to check the praetorian vanguard which alone made victory possible but may thenceforward endanger the stabilization of the "new" system. The victorious *condottiere* thus may accept Oswald Spengler's dictum: "The real master is known by the manner in which he dismisses them, ruthlessly and without thanks." Mussolini had done it; Hitler's June purge of 1934 seemed to suggest a similar move, though the following years brought a different course in Germany. National Socialism was far more aware of the second danger: a weakening of the revolutionary spirit. Closing of the ranks, legalized privileges for the "old fighters," fanatical persistence on fighting strength, and a continuous acceleration of the revolutionary tempo—these became acts of self-preservation. Hitler in his early writings proclaimed, "Thereafter solely the nucleus continues to lead." In fact, the entire leadership (with the significant exceptions of Hitler's personal confidants) was formed from "the basic stock of the old movement"; and even the few outsiders who had been taken in as experts by the victorious revolution were soon dropped, as the fate of Hjalmar Schacht, Karl Goerdeler, and Robert Schmidt fully proves.

The recruiting of party members after the party's seizure of power is almost exclusively reserved to special youth organizations. The party closes its ranks and admits only new members who have risen through the recognized channels of its youth organization, membership in which is made compulsory for every child. The *Hitler Jugend* in the Third Reich, the *Konsomols* in Soviet Russia, the *Balilla* and *Avantguardia* in Fascist Italy not only guarantee the future of the dictatorial party, but serve at the same time as a sifting process for bringing to the front reliable fighters for the cause. With this last link extended into the future, the political party becomes the nucleus and training school for the ruling class.

STAGES OF PARTY DEVELOPMENT

The dictatorial party, definitive as it seems to be in character and structure after the final victory, goes through different stages. In fact, its beginnings are in direct contrast to the all-inclusive bureaucratic machine which it presents at the end. It is an anti-machine sentiment that is at the base of the new movement. Indeed, what in the end turns out to be a party Leviathan began as an anti-party, one of the many contradictions of its real existence.

Anti-party attitude can originate in different places. There may be a conservative disdain for democratic institutions. Such ideas will find appeal in nationalist circles, especially in countries whose long-delayed national unification was finally achieved from above by blood and iron, and not by the people's democratic action. Party organizations in such a country are operating under a tremendous handicap. Forces beyond the parliamentary forum have created the state and afterward continue to make their weight felt in every political decision. The fact that these outside pressure groups do not act in the open market place of politics makes it more difficult to evaluate and to fight them in a concrete national situation.

The anti-parliamentary reaction can also derive from the opposite camp of leftist radicalism. Long before the beginning of the First World War every European country showed a significant split in its Socialist camp between a reformist and a revolutionary wing. While the first group tried to win control and to achieve a Socialist change through parliamentary process, the second group regarded as its only function the preparation of a revolutionary upheaval. It not only had condemned the parliamentary Socialists, but it even feared their popular successes since they might lead to "appeasement" and to destruction of the fighting spirit of a rising proletariat. The syndicalist Socialism of the Latin countries especially emphasized the danger of organized democratic and parliamentarian Socialism. Its political machine, this group felt, would lead toward making the party "bourgeois-minded." Syndicalism therefore, under the leadership of its great theorist, Georges Sorel, suggested direct action beginning at the center of economic activity, at the factory, instead of parliamentary procedure through a centralized party organization. It is no mere accident that rising Fascism represented an intermarriage of conservative nationalism and radical syndicalism because both groups met in their enmity toward parliamentarianism.

It is most significant, however, that the Fascist party before its seizure of power developed a second technique which seemed to be contradictory to its basic principles. It played the parliamentary game. It not only entered the parliament as a political party, but it also affiliated itself in a coalition with other political movements. Italian Fascists used these techniques from 1921 to 1923; German National Socialists did so from 1930 to 1933. During this time they tried to become "respectable," and many members of the nationalist parties reconciled themselves to the wild radicals whose emotionalism and exquisite fighting spirit might become a useful weapon in the hands of well-experienced politicians. The radical movement, so they hoped, could in the long run be directed into moderate channels. As a matter of fact, the leaders of Fascist movements made their coalition partners believe that their radical lingo was meant only for mass consumption and could be easily discarded when the hour of statesmanship arrived.

A careful analysis of the inner party activities, however, could have revealed the revolutionary character of the party even during this time of parliamentary "respectability." The ruthless oppression of the opposition within the party could be seen from the beginning. Party purges were continuously going on within the dictatorial party (long before they received national and international prominence as did the June purge of 1934). The relegation of Drexler, the founder of the National Socialist party, the repudiation of the party organization of Streicher and Feder during Hitler's short prison term in 1924, Hitler's final seizure of power within the party, his successful fight against the revolt of Otto Strasser and Stennes, finally his handling of the crucial Gregor Strasser dissension immediately before the final national victory—these are only a few examples of continuous purges within the party which finally molded it into an absolutely reliable weapon in the hands of its leader. This stage, therefore, was only preparatory for the final seizure of power. It showed the typical twofold technique of separate treatment for an inside and outside world. While the party at this point was above all dictatorial within its own ranks, it still made conciliatory gestures in its relations to possible allies in the outside world.

The seizure of power by dictatorial parties was also achieved in a coalition move. The first Bolshevist government was a coalition government not only as far as its official proclamations went, but also in the actual party alignment. The first Fascist government included members of all political parties, with the exception of the Socialists. A similar claim to have established a national government and not simply a party dictatorship was made by Hitler's new government on January 30, 1933. It had been born in the coalition of the so-called "Harzburg front" of 1931 that united Hugenberg's Nationalist party, Seldte's *Stahlhelm*, and Hitler's National Socialists in a plebiscite against the Young Plan. This coalition move was only the initial stage of the final seizure of power by the National Socialists.

In Italy this last stage of exclusive control was not reached until four years after the march on Rome, the official birth hour of Fascist Italy (October 28, 1922). During the first period victorious Fascism recognized the existence of opposition parties. In fact, the complicated electoral reform of 1923 and the subsequent elections of 1924 guaranteed on the one hand a solid majority of two-thirds of the parliament to the ruling Fascists, but at the same time retained minority parties (though shorn of effective power) as instruments of criticism and advice. The final suppression of all opposition parties came in a way as a defense of Fascism which, cornered by political scandals—above all the murder of Matteotti, the leading spokesman of the Socialist party —was forced into a life-and-death struggle. It is an academic question today whether better political tactics on the part of the opposition parties could at that time have broken the rise of the Fascist dictatorship; but undoubtedly if Fascism wanted to survive this great crisis it had to suppress all opposition that progressively succeeded in convincing the public of the Fascist dangers. Not until 1926 did Italian Fascism stamp out all the other parties and secret societies and thus establish the monopoly of the Fascist party.

German National Socialism proceeded at a much quicker pace. Six months after the establishment of the national government, the law concerning the formation of political parties was decreed (July 14, 1933). It created the machinery for the establishment of the one-party state, giving the National Socialist party the monopoly as the only political party. As soon as this last stage was reached, the party could proceed to develop its dictatorial scheme on the second plane. It became not only an inner party dictatorship, but from then on it reached national dimensions in its suppression of the national opposition, its coordination of all political activities within the national boundaries, its identification of the state with the victorious party.

Again the party showed its Janus head to the inside and the outside world. It was ruthless in its seizure of power within the German nation; it made a conciliatory gesture in the field of international affairs. Only when the one-party state felt sure that the monopoly was guaranteed on the second plane of control, when the nation had finally become the National Socialist Third Reich, only then could the party state with the help of specific agencies of its international arm make its bid for control of the world at large. This is the beginning of the Napoleonic expansion of Hitler's Germany. Significantly enough, one month before Hitler began his march toward the world in his *Anschluss* of Austria he co-ordinated the last two vestiges of political independence in Germany, the Foreign Office and the army. Only then could he begin his fight against the suppression of "foreign interference." Therefore, before the international dynamics of the dictatorial nations can be analyzed, a sketch of the institutional framework of the dictatorial rule is necessary.

Chapter VI

THE CONTROL OF THE MASSES: INSTITUTIONAL FRAMEWORK

BASIC PRINCIPLES

The "control and education of the people" becomes the primary task of the dictatorial party. This function comprises the institutional framework of the totalitarian regime itself since party and state are identical under the one-party system. The party—in all its chameleon-like qualities—plays the most decisive role. All the essential beams of the dictatorial edifice can be derived from the party's work.

The institutional framework represents a most complex system of carefully plotted procedures. One may be deeply impressed by its clocklike accuracy and efficiency; one may easily become lost in the labyrinth of its intertwining schemes. It is one of the many and deep-seated paradoxes of modern dictatorships that they were created as an "anti-party" to destroy the bureaucratic machinery in party and society—it was this aspect of the movement that represented the impetus to the most loyal followers— but they all became super-parties with super-bureaucracies. The dictatorial state is a super-machine: *Leviathan incorporated.*

The totalitarian character of modern dictatorship, which leaves practically nothing within the state to chance, necessitates this bureaucratization, the extent of which far surpasses even the keenest expectations of social scientists who predicted such an inevitable trend in modern society.

Totalitarianism is the basic principle of the party's monolithic control. In politics the consequences are obvious. If a nation has a federal structure, the dictatorial party necessarily will pursue unitary developments. By such a transformation it may fulfill a timely need and thus, for the moment at least, reconcile people who otherwise would fight this dictatorship tooth and nail. "After all they brought unification, long desired and delayed." (Bismarck's unification, for example, made his regime acceptable to many liberal middle-class people.)

As for such a transformation, there is, however, a basic difference in purpose and spirit. The spokesmen of the unitary state in pre-Nazi Germany fought for the abolition of an already defunct dynastic regionalism for which should be substituted greater administrative unity. Thus the economic and cultural diversity of the nation might find an ample field of activities in a larger unit. But this unification, progressively achieved in important steps from Bismarck's Empire to the Weimar Republic, did not definitely succeed in dissolving the dualism between Reich and *Länder*, a major cause of friction within Republican Germany. National Socialism certainly did away with this dualism in the same way as it did with all *Länder*. Yet this unification had a different meaning as applied by the autocratic lawmakers. To the dictatorial party it meant the suppression of any competitive forces from whatever quarter they might arise. It was primarily a question not of administrative efficiency but of rigid centralization—an essential precondition for direct autocratic rule.

This purpose becomes evident beyond doubt in the co-ordination of all political parties and political organizations. The liquidation of the multi-system and the creation of a monopoly by the dictatorial party is, of course, in line with the basic concept of the one-party system. Under this rule only *one* political will can manifest itself, and this is expressed in the dictatorial party that has finally won power. However, what stabilizes the one-party rule and makes it a dictatorial system is the principle of *Gleichschaltung*. The full meaning and far-reaching consequences of this process are not completely set forth by the usual translation of *Gleichschaltung* as "coordination." Coordination, for instance, does not necessarily exclude any spiritual independence, and it may mean a mutual assimilation of social and political forces. But the process of *Gleichschaltung* under dictatorship indicates "enforcement of conformity." It has been rightly called the real beginning of modern dictatorship. The significance of this process is evidenced by the fact that it stops practically nowhere.

From the primary central political institutions down to the most ephemeral organizations, every social grouping is subjugated to the will of the dictatorial party and controlled by its emissaries. The enforcement of conformity is accomplished with equal seriousness whether it concerns a ministry or an association of stamp collectors, whether it deals with political, social, or cultural organizations. This thoroughness guarantees the final establishment of the dictatorial rule and the destruction of any opposition wherever it may be hidden. Such a tactic sufficiently explains the fact that the old revolutionary techniques of undermining an existing order and preparing the coming revolution are hopelessly outdated in an era of totalitarian dictatorships. There are no room and no time left for opposition to crystallize; as soon as it embraces two members, one of them may turn informer, serving as the watchful eye of a circumspect autocracy.

Not much has to be said of the institutional agencies. They are worn away and they lose their basic meaning by the party's seizure. The fact that these old established institutions are preserved at all is largely due to a realization that *institutional symbolism* can well serve a rising dictatorship.

If well-constituted and firmly established, the *monarchy* has a significance for the continuity of a political order that has often been commented upon by keen observers. Monarchy has actually gained ground in recent decades. This institution somehow embodies the abstract idea of the state and, especially in time of crisis, transforms law and order into images the people can grasp. While the institution can thus serve well as a stabilizing factor in a revolutionary situation, it can also be used by adroit dictators to give much-needed traditional support.

The upholding of the monarchy in Fascist Italy serves the need for continuity, especially necessary in the midst of revolutionary upheaval. The only neutralizing factor and the only humanizing element in the dehumanized atmosphere of civil war, the Crown represents the nation above and beyond the party struggle; it is the fountain of honor, the representation of the services, the personification of the people. When Paris was worth a mass for a Henry IV, Rome was worth a sudden conversion to monarchism by Mussolini, the staunch Republican—three days before he "marched" to Italy's capital.

It was equally important to carry on with the institution of the German Reich's Presidency—as long as the "venerable" Hindenburg held office—and thus transmit loyalties concentrated in this office to the Nazi party.

The elevation of Pétain to the position of Chief of State after the breakdown of the French Republic followed a similar pattern. For lack of an established monarchy, the "pure and incorruptible Marshal," the "Victor of Verdun," could well serve as a symbol of unity, perseverance, and national hope, and at the same time represent an ideal screen for the emergence of dictatorial rule in the name of the people and its symbolic leader.

The necessity for institutional symbolism is so much felt by the anti-institutional dictatorial governments that they do not even hesitate to create such symbols artificially if the reality of these institutions vanishes. This explains the attempt to make General Ludendorff a national hero after Hindenburg's exit, and the even weaker attempt to substitute General Mackensen for Ludendorff after the latter's death.

Hindenburg's so-called Political Testament calling upon Hitler to become his successor served similarly as a useful perpetuation of institutional power—and constituted the bridge necessary to lead the neutral army into the Third Reich.

If dictatorship succeeds in continuing its power beyond its creator, his successor can capitalize equally on the founder's myth. Thus as the loyal disciple he can usurp Caesar's mantle, if necessary with faked testaments. Such a procedure almost institutionalizes dictatorship.

Similar considerations are responsible for the preservation of other pre-dictatorial institutions under totalitarian rule. True, to the prolonged *parliament* not much is left of the substance of a people's responsible forum. Unreal are its origins, its work, its achievements: the "free" electoral campaigns made up of an appointed one-party list, the "spontaneous" demonstrations minutely staged for the acclaiming machine of Yes-men, the comprehensive legislation decided beforehand by an uncontrollable Fuehrer's council. Yet the fact of *post facto* national plebiscites gives the people a sense of participation, the mere calling of a parliament creates a public forum, its passing of laws legalizes them in the eyes of "post-democratic" masses. True, all these functions are only seemingly real—they are mere substitutes for institutions.

But substitutes as they are, they are accepted, though with reservations, by the outer world. People abroad smile at the fake of dictatorial elections and the farce of their parliamentary sessions; but still they are somehow impressed by the "unity" of the dictator's nation. The parliament may not serve any longer as a sounding board of public opinion; it is still an impressive audience before which the leader can sound the fatherland's keynotes. (It may also be mentioned that the continuation of the parliament serves as an appropriate source of honors and spoils for deserving party members.)

Such representation, of course, is worlds apart from its original intent. In order to realize the contempt Fascist leaders demonstrate for the democratic institution, one need only read the speech by Mussolini, delivered on November 16, 1922, demanding the grant of full powers from the last freely elected Italian Parliament. These were his words: "What I am doing today is merely a formal act of courtesy toward you, for which I do not ask for any special expression of gratitude. The Italian nation has overthrown a Cabinet and has given itself a ministry outside, above, and in spite of Parliament. I leave it to the melancholy worshipers of superconstitutionalism to make dissertations and complaints, but I say that revolution has its rights. I would add—that the whole world may know—that I am here to defend and to use to its highest capacity the revolution of the Black Shirts, to introduce it as a force of development, progress, and balance in the history of Italy. With 300,000 men fully armed, thoroughly determined and religiously obedient to my orders, I could have punished all those who have decried Fascism and conspired against it. I could have closed Parliament and formed an exclusively Fascist Cabinet. I could have, but for the time being I chose not to. . . . I am not going—so far as I can help it—to govern against the Chamber, but the Chamber must understand the peculiar position it is in, which may entail its dissolution in two days or in two years. We ask for full powers, because we want to assume full responsibility. Without full powers we can carry out no economies. We shall accept all offers of cooperation made in a cordial spirit. . . . No more useless talk."

President Kalinin of the U.S.S.R. thus enumerated during the campaign of 1937 the reasons for elections in dictatorships: "We will show the whole world how great is the unity of the working masses and the Communist party. . . ." And he further stated: "In bourgeois countries election campaigns take much less time than ours is taking. Why should we need such a long election campaign? The election campaign must serve as a great school of education for the masses and for the leaders who will emerge from the masses."

In fact, "representation" in dictatorship is intimately connected with propaganda. Its function is to create "the relationship of confidence between government and people," in the words of a National Socialist writer.

Yet if one does not regard the preservation of the parliament as a "hoax," or—to put it more mildly—as a "tactical concession to the old order" using the emotional attachments of the masses to established institutions as symbols, one will be forced to perceive with René de Visme Williamson, a specific "Fascist concept of representation" that has nothing in common with the established use of the institution but the name. According to such an analysis (which could well be backed by official Fascist statements), representation does not derive from the people but from the leader

alone. The amorphous masses are essentially unable to choose their
own representation, but "the one who has authority represents
directly through his personality. . . . Complete representation is
always personal representation." This authoritative interpretation
by Otto Koellreutter, one of the leading professors of public law
in the Third Reich, brings the Fascist concept of representation in
line with its idea of personal leadership. Paradoxical as it seems
for a "collectivist theory," as it represents itself, Fascism's main
plank is that of extreme individualism, which, of course, is reserved to the "master people" alone, to the elite, to the leader,
not to the followers.

The *plebiscite* is the perfect form for the people's participation
in such organized and centralized authoritarianism. "Plebiscite
and dictatorship," as Fascist authority Panunzio tersely says, "are
the two faces of one and the same political reality." In fact,
contrary to theoretical expectation, the experience of the referendum in modern governments does not suggest, to use H. D.
Laski's phraseology, "that it is a very helpful addition to the
armory of Democracy." Direct government is not the same thing
as self-government; it may indeed, as the experience of Fascist
countries has shown, be the exact antithesis of it.

In the hands of a demagogical leader plebiscites will be presented to the people at the proper moment and on well-chosen
issues which by that time will be accomplished facts. In such a
procedure "popular elections" do not choose representative government nor do they pass judgment upon its record (as is the
business of a democratic electorate). Under dictatorship the people's ballot becomes a useful weapon to "make the masses want
what the leader wants." A plebiscite is not an act of will and
decision by the people, but a ceremonial manifestation of the
people's "identity with the leader."

BUREAUCRACY: THREE ATTEMPTS AT A SOLUTION

Bureaucracy is the life line of the modern state. In the machine
age it is more than a special phase; in the words of Carl Joachim
Friedrich, it is "the very core of all government." In fact, the

beginning of the modern state has been rightly timed with the creation of a bureaucracy. Warning has even been sounded in recent years that the "desk government," which should be kept on "tap" but not on "top," has actually taken control. Though this threat of a "dictatorship of the bureaucracy" has been discounted by most students of government, the constant growth of officialdom in numbers and in powers is generally agreed upon as having significance of the first rank.

This triumph of government services is part of a universal process toward rational management in modern society. Division of labor and selection according to skills instead of social status have revolutionized economics. These principles have also become rules to guide public administration.

The nature of bureaucracy can be described in terms of specific principles that were definitely established in Brandenburg-Prussia as early as the 17th century. Competence and the hierarchy of office are its two outstanding characteristics. Regulated by law or statute, competence strictly defines (1) differentiation of functions; (2) powers of office, safeguarding within these limits the independence of judgment of each member of the bureaucracy; (3) qualifications preconditional for entry and promotion, thus guaranteeing proper fulfillment of functions and powers through a merit system.

The hierarchical principle leads not only to centralization of control and supervision (the life interest of growing absolutism fighting the centrifugal forces of feudalism), but also to coordination and integration of offices. The strict accountability of every civil servant, the regulated procedure through a definite succession of bureaus (*Instanzenzug*), the keeping of records and files, the establishment of a scientific technique in training—all these factors can serve as a safeguard against arbitrary government. They certainly have been greeted as such a check by the rising middle class. They undoubtedly create specific "habit patterns" of the bureaucrat: efficiency and expertness (though often routinized, unimaginative, and lacking in initiative), fear of rash undertakings, objectivity, and impersonality.

All these qualities guarantee the efficient disposal of the complex functions of modern government. The totalitarian state in its all-inclusive activities certainly could not afford to weaken this indispensable instrument. In fact, the attitude of modern dictatorship toward bureaucracy is a split reaction.

Rational administration was once hailed by the rising middle class as an efficient safeguard against arbitrary government. It may again serve as such a check. Indeed, hope has often arisen that bureaucracy will "kill the revolution," or at least take the sting out of its unpredictable dynamics. It has frequently done so. Yet, granted such possibilities, they do not describe the day-by-day reality of the complex relations between modern dictatorship and bureaucracy.

The totalitarian Leviathan has to break the last stronghold of resistance. Administration must be coordinated with the one and only political will, and purged of all "undesirable" elements politically and racially "incompatible" with the new system. This "cleansing" process, usually termed the "restoration of civil service," is only the initial step. In the days of the revolutionary honeymoon, many "deserving partisans expect to take over"— and to secure promised rewards; yet even these spectacular dismissals and replacements can be only limited. They must be stopped by the dictators in their own interest if the state's machinery is not to break down. Dictators must even show gratitude for the bureaucracy's service in bridging the old and the new order. This, however, does not mean simply the final victory of the "neutralizing forces" of the administration, i.e., normalization of the regime. In this new phase, the conflict is often transposed into an inner party struggle between moderates and revolutionaries. Hidden as such a struggle may be from the common man, it becomes a contest between factional formations for the control of the party. It represents the permanent rivalry among the lieutenants and their stooges, and often leads to a greater fluctuation in office personnel than the original revolutionary upheaval brought about.

At this second stage the more significant clash between state and party also becomes apparent. This conflict is inherent in the one-party system and its inner contradictions. After the seizure of power is accomplished, the dictatorial party has fulfilled its revolutionary aim. Having completely conquered the state, this party becomes identical with the "new state" and logically loses its right to further existence. Of course, there may always be counterrevolutionaries, insurgents, enemies of the state, within its own gates. Vigilance may be necessary for the "permanent revolution" because the "nation in arms" always considers itself in a constant state of war; yet all such control can be sufficiently exercised by the state and its machinery.

Confronted with this discrepancy, dictatorial systems vary in their solutions. *Fascist Italy* alone has gone far in at least posing the question of the self-dissolution of the Fascist party. The obvious dualism causing innumerable tensions between the competing hierarchies of state and party in the first years of the Fascist regime led Mussolini to write his famous *Circular to Prefects*, in which he promised them that he would not "hand any prefect's scalp to a provincial party secretary." His strong declaration in his historic speech of September 14, 1929—"All dualism of authority and hierarchy [as between party and state] is extinguished"—suggested the legal regulation of a rather stormy relationship. The subsequent law promulgated in royal decrees reorganized Fascist agencies as institutions of public law.

It is even more significant for the Italian solution that the bureaucracy seems to enjoy relative independence and high esteem and that the regime has been reluctant to purify the higher administrative ranks.

That this specific prestige enjoyed by the bureaucracy may have something to do with ideological orientation, especially with a prevalent Hegelian philosophy of state absoluteness, has often been suggested. The state undoubtedly became in the Fascist system "the point of reference"; the bureaucracy, the "main cog" in the machinery of control. Compare Mussolini's own statement: "The state is the absolute in relation to which all individuals and groups are relative."

This specific development may at the same time serve as a partial explanation of the more conservative character of Italian Fascism, at least as long as it followed its own volition.

The difference in climate of the *Nazi state* is visible in its management of the bureaucratic complex. Of course historic fate and the leading personnel of the party had something to do with the modified procedure. German National Socialism was more revolutionary than Fascism; at the same time, because of its slow rise to power, National Socialism necessitated the erection of a complete party apparatus of its own, a state within the state. In the hour of victory, two complete sets of organizations confronted each other. True, identity was achieved at the apex of the political hierarchy. Just as in Italy where the office of the *Capo del Governo* and that of Il Duce merged, so a fusion was achieved in the "office of the Fuehrer." In Hitler's person the position of the Chancellor of the Reich and the leader of the party were combined. This identification was continued in the office of the deputy leader, Rudolf Hess; in his capacity as Hitler's representative of party affairs until his spectacular flight to Scotland, Hess was at the same time a member of the Cabinet. A similar relation was to be observed even down to the *Kreisleiter* in local government. In these lower strata, however, the dualism made itself felt in the separation of state bureaucracy and party machinery. This fact certainly led to numerous difficulties, yet it presented, especially in the first revolutionary state, a useful device. The separation between the party and the state (the one free from official handicaps expressing the "boiling soul of the people," the other not responsible for this spontaneous outburst) could be cleverly played up in an intricate technique of legalizing revolutionary upheavals. Such a procedure was particularly important in a nation which by its nature is very legalistically-minded. It relieved an official government from responsibility for irresponsible party actions. On the other hand, the movement's aims and ambitions were thus registered and channelized through "respectable" formal legislation. Such devices were successfully used in the first pogrom on April 1, 1933, and in the burning of the synagogues on November 10, 1938.

Though the legal monopoly of the National Socialist party was formally established in the early "single party law" of July 14, 1933, the more precarious relation between party and state was not legally attacked until December 1, 1933. This "law for safeguarding the unity of party and state," however, did not really create an equilibrium. Neither did it expel the fear in some party circles that it might mean only the first step toward the final absorption of the party into the state, nor did it prevent constant tensions and interferences by the party, especially in local politics. These interactions did not reflect merely twilight zones of power distribution. National Socialism erected a dual state.

The existence of a dual state in a more comprehensive sense as fundamental for the legal system, legal theory, and legal reality of National Socialism has recently been suggested by Ernst Fraenkel in a penetrating analysis of the judicial practice of the Third Reich. In fact, he relegates to a secondary position the conflict between state and party so much stressed in Fascist literature, suspecting this emphasis as being "a favorite device of National Socialist jurisprudence . . . to obscure the real significance of certain issues by a clamorous insistence on the importance of incidental ones." The basic issue, according to Fraenkel, is the coexistence of the "prerogative state" (*Massnahmen-Staat*) and the "normative state." While the latter represents "an administrative body endowed with elaborate powers for safeguarding the legal order as expressed in statutes, decisions of the courts, and activities of the administrative agencies," the former stands for "that governmental system which exercises unlimited arbitrariness and violence unchecked by any legal guarantees."

A constant friction between traditional judicial bodies representing the "normative state" and the instruments of dictatorship serving as agents of the "prerogative state" characterizes the legal reality of the Third Reich.

Notwithstanding Fraenkel's conclusion that such a "legal situation" is preconditional for the preservation of a capitalist economic order and appropriate to its imperialistic phase, the strange combination of "arbitrariness and efficiency based on order" is of the essence of the National Socialist state. This fact accounts for the staying power of this rule, and also for its inner contradictions.

These tensions were emphasized by the frenzy of organization, a by-product of a totalitarian party, that spread over the whole scope of its totalitarian endeavor. The party created innumerable divisions such as the Women's League, the Hitler Youth, the Storm Troopers, the Elite Guard, the Motor Corps, the Labor Front, the Handicraft League, the Agriculture Estate, the People's Welfare Organization, Professional Leagues, Cultural Estates, etc. It led to a confusing intricacy of influence and interaction, but throughout all this time the dualism between state and party was preserved. The state stood for the traditional governmental functions. The party became the champion of *Weltanschauung*, the mentor and educator of German life, the guardian against political opponents. This recognition of mutual independence, however, did not prevent continuous clashes between the two hierarchies.

The first major conflict arose, significantly enough, in the clash between the army and the Storm Troopers, and led to the historic purge of June 30, 1934. The preliminary results certainly spelled victory for the state civil service over the party. It reflected at the same time inner party conflicts between a revolutionary and a conservative wing. Yet, as later developments definitely proved, this purge meant neither the end of the permanent revolution nor the abdication of the party in favor of the state. Whether or not there was actual danger of a revolution under the leadership of Roehm, as Goering claimed to have discovered, the steps taken by Hitler were dictated above all by considerations of remilitarization, from then on the primary aim of the National Socialist state. The real meaning of the June purge did not become obvious until February 4, 1938, when the German army, by then a representative body (which owed its rise to Hitler's cunning policies of rearmament, remilitarization of the Rhineland, and international blackmail), became fully co-ordinated with the National Socialist state.

Even in this last stage, army and bureaucracy still preserved some independence. This was the price Hitler had to pay for efficient administration. This compromise, similar to Bismarck's alliance with a de-politicized bourgeoisie, gave honor and prestige to the civil service, whose policies, however, were decided in the party's councils alone. The efficient fulfillment of the tasks set before the experts was largely due to the fact that these branches, especially with their expanding opportunities, attracted the enterprising minds of the younger generation, whether sincere partisans or not. It is not surprising that in this respect the army made a better bargain than the bureaucracy. This preeminence was the result partly of traditions of long standing, partly of the systematic grooming of a new military elite in the days of the German Republic.

While the bureaucracy did not seem quite as attractive as the military profession, particularly to young partisans, the civil service still preserved high status. The surprising successes, especially of the economic agencies of the Third Reich, are largely due to the fact that victorious National Socialism had a well-established bureaucratic staff from which to draw. The career and position of men like Helmuth Wohlthat, Hans Kerrl, Hans Fischboeck, and Karl Clodius were typical of the success of the party government in enrolling "neutral experts." The Economic General Staff, active long before the Second World War began and no doubt more so ever since, consists of well-trained men like the "four horsemen" of Goering's Four-Year Plan (Paul Koerner, Erich Neumann, Friedrich Landfried, and Helmuth Wohlthat). Business circles are said to be talking of "the rule of the State Secretaries."

Indeed, what the "bureaucrats" had to give up in independent political judgment they gained in actual control. There were enormous possibilities for economic expansion in southeastern Europe and oversea, and what expert would not be ready to give up political birthright for all the glories of power and prestige that might lie in international trade and world domination?

Soviet Russia's obvious difficulties in building "Socialism in a single country" are largely due to her failure to find a definite place for the bureaucracy within the one-party system. She certainly "has not yet produced her Colbert nor has she paid much attention to a methodical grooming of administrative talent," as F. Morstein Marx pointedly observes.

The transition to the Soviet state was no doubt more abrupt than in any other dictatorship. There was no "legal" seizure of power, no call to responsibility by legitimate agencies—Crown or President—no recognition of bureaucratic continuity. It was a complete overthrow of the pre-revolutionary state machinery, a total severance of the past from the future.

Backbone of the old regime, the bureaucracy had been practically the undisputed master of the country. It had become the living symbol of czarist autocracy. Perhaps such a judgment was not always fair. Experts like Florinsky gave to pre-war Russia's officialdom the mark of "a fairly high tradition of public service and, in its higher levels, a reputation of reasonable efficiency." Yet all the professional shortcomings of bureaucracy—routinized slowness and unadaptability, complacency and arrogance—were manifest in this atmosphere of stuffy officialdom and oriental inertia. Even if credit can be given to the civil service for some of the pre-war reforms, the decay of government in the latter days of the regime, compromised by Rasputin's personal rule and paralyzed by war strain and mismanagement, finally destroyed the limited prestige that the imperial administration had built up. The October Revolution of 1917 was meant to start with a *tabula rasa*. There could be no adaptation of old institutions.

In addition to this total interruption of the state machinery, the concept of bureaucracy was contrary to Soviet ideology, at least in the early days of the regime. According to Marxian theory, the victorious proletariat had not only to take over the apparatus of government but also to break and destroy it completely. Bureaucracy was regarded as "a dangerous inheritance from the bourgeois regime." The revolution once accomplished, there was absolutely no place for the state. It did "wither away because in a society free from class contradictions the state is both unnecessary and impossible." In line with this interpretation, Lenin instituted two definite measures at the beginning of his regime: first, the abolition of the permanent army and its replacement by a "popular militia"; second, the abolition of the bureaucracy. Capitalistic culture, so he argued, has created large-scale production, and on this basis the immense majority of the functions of the old state have been so simplified and can be reduced to such elementary operations that these tasks can be perfectly accomplished by any literate people. "All should fulfill the functions of control and supervision, all should be bureaucrats for a time, and therefore no one should become a bureaucrat." The same pattern of thought was followed in Lenin's classic statement, "Every cook must learn to rule the state."

This interpretation, no doubt, showed a complete misunderstanding of the actual functioning of the state machinery. Soviet experience during the next decades proved this sufficiently. The state did not "wither away," but became more powerful than it had ever been before in Russian history. Lenin outstripped Peter the Great, Stalin outdid Ivan the Terrible, yet Bolshevism never freed itself from its original theoretical tenets. The split in theory and practice weakened its efficiency and its *Schlagkraft*, especially in the eyes of independent foreign observers. The result was wavering methods, continuous fluctuations between the radical negation of a managerial class and the creation of a huge amount of red tape, suspicion against the "experts," and unlimited administration for the machine. Soviet policies attempted to bridge these discrepancies by substitute solutions. The new economic policy, the calling of specialists, particularly of foreign experts, the praise of the shock-workers (*Stakanoffs*) in industrial production, the temporary independence of Red army officers—all these measures, halfheartedly undertaken and constantly reversed, showed the indecision of the Soviet regime in respect to modern management. These constant oscillations definitely proved that the

Soviet landscape lacked one element that is at the base of every bureaucracy's existence: continuity.

This fact pointed to an essential problem of the Soviet regime since its two vital functions were absolutely dependent on the development of smoothly working machinery. Planning became the keystone of the U.S.S.R.'s social development. Total defense seemed to be the primary precondition for its survival, surrounded by enemies of the Soviet fatherland. Both these attempts presupposed a continuous endeavor by an efficient officialdom. The fate of the Soviet experiment will depend not least on its final success or failure to develop such a state machinery and thus to find an appropriate formula for dictatorship and bureaucracy in the U.S.S.R.

ECONOMICS OF THE GARRISON STATE

The importance and extent of state management in modern dictatorship is evidenced by the fact that this new autocracy does not stop at political control but carries its power into the field of economics. Divergent as the different dictatorships appear in approach and in aim, they all agree on one basic formula: the *primacy of politics over economics.*

In fact there is no autonomous sphere left to economics. Complete subordination to the totalitarian states' will is here, as everywhere under dictatorial rule, the order of the day. The rules of classical economy are abolished—or at least a moratorium is declared on its laws. The government can inflate the currency, can set wages and prices, can decide the standards of life. The state is a law unto itself. This fact is one of the reasons why Nazi economics seems to be beyond the rational comprehension of western democracies. The whole set of values developed by economic science is undermined in the hands of totalitarian politicians. The clever machinations of the wizard, Dr. Schacht, whose master mind during its first years led the Third Reich through its financial labyrinth, surprised and confused the economic experts the more since he seemingly spoke their own language. It was the same confusion that had succeeded so well in the "legal" seizure of power and the electoral manipulations of dictatorship. And just as a von Papen served only as a figure of transition who, as soon as he outlived his political usefulness, left his place in the political sun of the Third Reich to represent Germany under the Turkish half-moon, so Hjalmar Schacht had to make room for Dr. Funk, inferior indeed to his predecessor in genius, yet subservient to the party's political aims in its economic pursuits.

The whole economic system is subordinated to and shaped by the political intentions of the rulers. The new *planned economy* presented by modern autocracies is the result of political needs and not of economic necessity. Again an amply discussed and defined concept is taken over by dictatorships and deprived of its original meaning. Again it carries a different connotation under the different dictatorial systems. In fact, basic discrepancies in Fascist and Bolshevist control and purpose can be well detected in their difference in the field of economics.

The keystone of the Russian economic endeavor is the *Five-Year Plans*. Their main purposes—Socialist planning, large-scale industrialization, and military autocracy—are so inextricably mixed that they confuse the followers of the Third International abroad. They present a specifically Russian plan, gigantic in its extent and bewildering in its aim: an attempt to create the first Socialist country, to defend it against outside aggression, and to industrialize the most backward agrarian nation at the same time. Revolutionary *élan* carried young Bolshevism even further in attempting the industrialization of the rural sector.

This "collectivization of agriculture" was staged in a succession of daring thrusts, strategic retreats, and renewed attacks. It started with the forced requisitions of grain and other foodstuffs in the period of war Communism. At the end of the civil strife, however, victorious Bolshevism was confronted with numerous peasant revolts all over the country. Though these uprisings could easily have been crushed by urban Red army detachments, Lenin the realist well understood that "you cannot betray social classes." Thus he introduced the New Economic Policy (N.E.P.), which made definite concessions to individual enterprise and control, especially in the field of agriculture. Individual tenure and exploitation, a fixed system of taxation, and trade in surplus production were re-established. These steps, taken in order to encourage production, were hailed by an outside world as a return to a capitalistic order; yet the N.E.P. period indicated only that the peasants had won the first round. To Bolshevism it meant a temporary cessation and an attempt to attack the problem differently. "Educate the ignorant peasants" became the party slogan—to convince them that Socialism is for their own best interest. This "cultural revolution," undoubtedly successful in other sectors, failed in rural Russia. By 1927 only 1.5 per cent of the total grain marketed was supplied by collective farms which represented "mere islands in the sea of individual peasant farms." It was the period of the rise of the kulak, the enterprising small peasant who became the scapegoat of Bolshevist propaganda in the following years. The "liquidation" of this class ended the respite given to the agrarian sector. A new drive for complete collectivization was launched in the winter of 1929-30; but soon Stalin (true disciple of Lenin) warned his followers in his classic article, "Dizzy from Success," against too drastic steps that might destroy the basic purpose of collectivization. Yet awareness of peasant antagonism did not spell surrender. The passive resistance of the peasantry, aggravated by the poor harvests of '31 and '32, finally led to the historic famine which, no doubt, was largely also a politically staged famine. Stalin with extravagant ruthlessness made this famine a lesson to his class enemies. Estimates place the destruction of human life at from one to four million peasants. Stalin was perfectly frank about this transaction. To Lady Astor's question, "How long are you going on killing people?" he bluntly replied, "As long as it is necessary." This great crisis broke the resistance. From that time on, the social collectivization of agriculture seemed to be accomplished.

If successful, the collectivization of the farms would disprove the idea, predominant even in Socialist circles since David's *Capitalism and Agriculture*, that "property" is a basic quality of agrarian existence. This collectivization no doubt dissolved a dualism of rural-urban relations which up to now has been regarded as axiomatic for society. It did, at least for the time being, create a monolithic urban structure. This extremely radical endeavor to change "human nature" may one day be regarded as a most significant attempt and the ultimate test for the success of the Soviet experiment.

The development of Soviet control in the hinterland shows the basically political intent of Soviet economics. The central theme, the industrialization of the predominantly agrarian country, was full of political meaning. To build up the resources and to utilize them in newly created industries is a belated attempt not only to raise the standards of a backward country but also to make it a chief competitor in the industrial world markets. Yet behind this seemingly economic endeavor looms the major political aim, national self-sufficiency and industrial preparedness "in case of emergency." Modern mechanized warfare gives the chance of survival only to the highly industrialized nations, and the threat of foreign invasion—a major theme in Soviet policy since its beginning, and a well-justified fear it was—became the focal point of orientation in Soviet planning while the years passed. All economic activities were now directed and overshadowed by the thought of a defense economy that organizes the whole body economic in terms of the national protection of the Socialist fatherland against foreign aggression. The bloody test came with Hitler's march into Russia in June, 1941.

Here a note is struck which in fact represents the theme song of modern dictatorships: war economy. *Wehrwirtschaft* became the commanding slogan of the Nazi economic order. Fascist Italy, more and more under the spell of the younger brother (grown up by now), soon followed suit. In the early days of Fascism and in theory even today, the concept of the *stato corporativo*, however, seemed to take the center of the stage.

The corporative idea in Fascist Italy grew from different sources: romantic and rational, nationalistic and syndicalist, totalitarian and autocratic. In fact, its vague character is partly due to these divergent motives. The *stato corporativo* could be used for the protection of capitalism just as well as for the introduction of a Socialistic society. It was a romantic attempt to recapture a medieval guild society; at the same time it was fashioned for modern patterns of the interventionist state.

As a nationalistic formula, corporativism derived from a rejection of the "class" organizations of the proletariat and the substitution of the nation for the class. Yet the concept of economic representation could also be attributed to a very different source of corporative ideas which find theoretical expression in the philosophy of syndicalism. Syndicalism, essentially opposed to organized action from a central agency, conceived instead of this the unit of the factory as the living center of political action. For this reason it favored a direct economic council instead of a political parliament based on geographic representation. Such ideas of economic representation could no doubt be found in democratic countries too; they were not incongruent with the democratic system as such, as long as the corporative council served only as an additional and advisory chamber to the continued political parliament. Such a supplementary economic parliament was the Reichswirtschaftsrat of the Weimar Republic which proved to be extremely valuable.

The primary aim of the Fascist *stato corporativo*, however, was the complete destruction of the political parliament. The latter's final replacement by the Chamber of Corporations did not even create an open forum of economic interest groups which in their diversity could have influenced the state machinery. On the contrary, the result of the complicated machinations of the new corporative setup was the complete conquest of the economic sphere by Fascism. This was the Italian answer to the problem of dictatorship and economics. There is no free interplay of economic forces in Fascism because the Italian dictatorship is above all totalitarian and autocratic; so is its economic system. Since the introduction of the Labor Charter in 1927, Fascism has systematically destroyed all autonomous groupings, especially the free associations of workers, and has supplanted them by a monopolistic, allembracing state organization. Even more significant than this totalitarian design is the autocratic intent of the regime as evidenced in the abolition of the political parliament. The corporative state easily lends itself to such absolutist purposes. None other than Bismarck had realized the usefulness of economic representation instead of political parties. The definitely expert character of occupational representatives limits their authority and naturally suggests the creation of a political apex which, beyond specific economic interests, claims to represent the whole of the nation.

This autocratic source of the *stato corporativo* intimates the more far-reaching impact of the *revolution of techniques* on political development in our time. The crisis of modern society has often been laid to the lag between technical development and social organization. This discrepancy, indeed, easily leads to the victory of machine over man. Instead of a tool, the machine becomes the driving force in society. An overgrown machine may destroy our civilization, which seems to be losing control over its own creation.

The astonishing success of mechanical inventions has affected the whole system of values held by modern man. The technical sciences have conquered the social sciences. The precision of mechanical equipment has made people desire to become a cog in a machine. To modern "efficient man," it seems almost sacrilege when Guy Stanton Ford suggests: "Our concern should be more soberly directed to finding the minimum price in inefficiency that we must always expect to pay if we are to preserve democracy."

In almost every country the motorcar has become the symbol of achievement, and everywhere young people can be found who would be ready to sell their souls for the right to pilot an airplane. It is almost an obsession with modern man to master such complex machines and thus liberate himself from his natural confinement. More than twenty years ago Oswald Spengler predicted that the age of the technician is arriving and that his rule spells the end of western civilization. Even if one does not accept his predictions, it is most significant that the great theorists who have been called the spiritual fathers of modern dictatorial systems arose in the intellectual climate of a world of techniques. Georges

Sorel, trained in the École des Chaussées (the M.I.T. of France), was an engineer by profession. Not until he was forty-five did he become a social scientist. This is true also of Vilfredo Pareto, who served as a railroad engineer until the same age. As a sociologist he has been rightly classified as belonging to the mechanistic school of thought. In the last analysis the irrational philosophy of Pareto is the translation of the devices of mechanics into the social world.

The *stato corporativo* is a technician's concept of politics. A council of experts by their essential limitations as experts necessitates dictatorship, i.e., the coordinating apex of the experts' pyramid. A "managerial revolution" can thus easily get out of the control of the great economic engineers and be diverted into the stream of those professional revolutionaries who have answered for themselves the query, "Revolution for What?"

That technology may furnish the pattern for acquiring and directing knowledge and no less for the control of the social organization itself was the dream of many social thinkers, such as Auguste Comte and Lester Ward, at a time when sociology was young.

The impact of techniques on the social order becomes especially obvious in wartime. New techniques in modern warfare give the technician a crucial position in national defense and in any dynamic scheme. Efficiency, the goddess of the technician, becomes the catchword in a society that has to make use of the machine if it wants to preserve a civilization outside of this Leviathan. Such a society has to be on guard. If there is any group that is immanently prepared to accept dictatorship, it is the technicians. There is an easy channel through techniques to the rise of dictatorship. Technical processes necessitate specialization. Specialization leads to coordination by way of planned guidance which not only is likely to develop dictatorial potentialities, but by the very limitation of the expert calls for such a controlling agency to put every cog in the machine into action.

Seen in its theoretical aspects and in its philosophical implications, the corporative idea certainly wins in complexity and, one may say, in danger also. The Italian reality, however, has hardly reached beyond paper manifestations. That it has been taken at all seriously in Italian Fascism is largely due to the syndicalist driving forces in early Fascism (and, for that, in Mussolini himself). These syndicalist elements led Mussolini to statements which made the *stato corporativo* appear an initial step toward Socialism.

Only the future can tell whether any basic changes in Italy's economic structure have been introduced by the corporate state. Almost all the Fascist proclamations on the subject—and they are now myriad—deal with forms, not with substance. In circumscribing its intricate and unreal character, one may say with Steiner that the *stato corporativo* represents "the institutional device for regimenting and controlling the agencies of national production in the interest of strong national policy." The few really decisive changes in Italian economy were made during the Italo-Ethiopian War and the Second World War. These steps were necessitated by the national policies in the war emergency; and since Fascism by its basic claim is a "government of the people in arms," the militant component of the Fascist economy becomes the policy-making factor in the whole economic setup. War preparation and warfare become the major objectives of economic planning in a military state.

Wehrwirtschaft is no doubt at the center of the German economic organization. It is, as officially stated, "the dynamic principle which embraces peace and war economics and stimulates their efficiency for the purpose of armed defense." The economics of the garrison state finds its classic illustration in the Third Reich and its Four-Year Plans.

Planning can have a multifarious meaning. Its basic purpose has to be sought out if its place in the whole system is rightly to be defined. One of the major mistakes in interpreting the dynamics and aims of National Socialism is to see its course in economic depression and its goal in economic recovery. Hitler is not merely a streamlined Keynes, promoting recovery. Useful though the suggestions of the British economist were, his Nazi "disciples" used them for their own purposes.

National Socialist planning was not simply a continuation of the interventionist social policy of the latter days of the Weimar Republic. No doubt governmental management of economic enterprises was always much more advanced in Germany than in any other western country. From its outset, German economics has even been called, with some justification, a "bureaucratic capitalism." When National Socialism came to power in Germany in January, 1933, the country's economy was under governmental control to a wider extent than ever before during peacetime. The preparatory steps toward a planned economy and especially the breakdown of a free economy under the impact of an economic depression certainly facilitated the rise of National Socialism; yet the victorious movement was prompted not by economic principles, but only by the desire for war preparation. True, National Socialism made ample use of the techniques of the preceding system it so much despised. The continuity of personnel in the civil service also assured preservation and systematization of acquired skills and tried management. Yet the policy-making party gave a completely different direction to state economics. "They wanted war," said Tolischus, one of the most circumspect observers of Nazi Germany, in commenting on their seven years' economic mobilization. They prepared for the "second world war." They knew that the new war of machines could be won only by a highly industrialized nation which, in getting a start on their potential enemies, could mobilize in a totalitarian effort the country's entire resources and man power.

Planning under the *Wehrwirtschaft* in effect became a relatively easy task as compared with complex peacetime production. War production is uniform and standardized. "In the beginning was the army," Werner Sombart, historian of economic development, once said, implying that production for the big consumer was the precondition for mass production and therewith for rising capitalism. Modern mass armies and production for total war multiplied the possibilities of this tremendous, well-known, and ever-expanding market. Such a background meant heaven for this kind of "planned economy," which in addition can free itself from any consideration of the "whims of the ultimate consumer" and direct him into channels of spending suitable to state necessities, or shut him out altogether.

What counted in this total conscription of the whole national economy under the *Wehrwirtschaft* was, above all, iron discipline and not economic acts. One may well go so far as to say with Douglas Miller, that "one characteristic of all totalitarian economics is essential unproductiveness."

An economic system which is tuned up for "economics of conflict" can afford to have a top-heavy economy with an ever-expanding bureaucracy and an exclusive interest in war production, if this economic mobilization finally bears fruit in a successful expansion in territory and therewith a possible exploit of other economics. In this sense, "Totalitarianism is by nature parasitic and predatory."

Before "the day" comes, internal sources have to be tapped: heavy taxation (including "voluntary winter help") of the country as a whole, special contributions and wholesale expropriation from unhappy minority groups, clever management of foreign trade and credit manipulation. Hoping for better days to come when the world's riches will be available, these dynamic governments can also order a high-speed exploitation of resources. In fact, measures may well contradict old-established economic laws as long as they serve the essential purpose of efficient armed defense. This total disregard for seemingly inviolable rules of economic teaching makes the Nazi economic warfare, internally and internationally, more mysterious and difficult to understand. Significantly enough, the "economics of the military state" has as its godfathers none of the academicians.

Just as peace in reversion of Clausewitz's classic formula becomes the continuation of war by other means in the Nazi ideology, so the traditional separation of war economy and peace economy is abolished. War economy changes from exceptional emergency into normalcy. Every economic activity is permeated with and subordinated to the permanent revolution. There is no need to wait for the outbreak of hostilities to shift and readjust economic policies. Traditional concepts of production and accumulation, of distribution and consumption are nullified in an economy "permanently geared to warfare." Overboard go rules for gold reserves and general fiscal policies, for limited utilization of national resources, for an established balance between agriculture and industrial production. Civilian consumption is no longer the final yardstick of production. In fact it has to take the largest reduction. War economy is an economy of scarcity, of "guns instead of butter," not of abundance. The limits of this maxim are set only at the danger point where deprivations may affect civilian morale in the totalitarian war effort. (According to economic experts, this limit is reached at about 70 per cent of "normal consumption.")

This economic mobilization undoubtedly had the effect of practically eliminating unemployment. This of course was of primary importance for the stabilization of the system. It compensated for loss of liberty with economic security, even if under reduced living standards. It also resulted in increased industrial production and national income. On this shrewd combination of rearmament and recovery largely rests the temporary success of Nazi economics; yet important as such a "crisis-proof economy" or "Socialism of the Labor front" may have been propagandistically, National Socialist economics centers around preparation for war. It is idle to ask whether the economic setup thus created should be called capitalist or Socialist, state capitalist or state Socialist (though such slogans could be usefully applied in manipulating public opinion). "War, if correctly understood, does not permit the establishment of a scientific system [of economics]. It requires the complete adjustment of science to its changing phenomena," says Lieutenant Colonel Hesse of Germany.

With this specific objective in mind, National Socialism significantly did not accept any definite "corporative ideology," though these ideas were generally identified with Fascist thinking. In fact, some of the economic romanticists, like the so-called organic school of Othmar Spann, who regarded themselves as spiritual forerunners of National Socialism, had the bitter experience of being completely discarded by the victorious movement. The few corporative schemers in the Nazi camp, such as von Renteln who attempted to create an estate of trades and handicraft, were soon pushed aside.

The only area in which the concept of "estates" found some realization was in the field of *agriculture*. Darré, a true representative of romantic economics, tried in the early days of the Nazi regime to change the agricultural structure of the Reich according to his ideas of "blood and soil." Yet even the two major laws promulgated under his control in 1933, the law establishing the *Nährstand* (Law on the Nutrition Estate) and the *Reichserbhofgesetz* (Hereditary Farm Law), were not exclusively derived from corporative ideas. In fact, the Nutrition Estate was primarily designed to stabilize prices of agricultural products and thus to remove agriculture as far as possible from the influence of general economic fluctuations. This guarantee of economic stability was the price victorious National Socialism had to pay to the peasants. In reality, their joining with the revolution was primarily due to realistic considerations. Significantly enough, the farmers seemed to be the only class which succeeded in collecting spoils from the permanent revolutionaries. Indeed, throughout all these years the National Socialist regime was careful thus to check discontent within the farmers' camp.

This rising unrest was based upon the farmers' sober realization that behind the screen of the protection and "liberation" of agriculture through autarchy and price regulation the Third Reich was progressively succeeding in "regimenting" and "collectivizing" the peasant economy—an essential part of its planning for total war.

The Hereditary Farm Law also had more than ideological significance. Making the land "sacred and inalienable" by decreeing the undivided passing of a farmer's estate upon his death to his eldest son and the restriction of the right to sell or mortgage his farm, this deprivation of fundamental property rights, this one-sided disruption of rural-urban migration was no doubt an essential aim of the whole agricultural legislation. As far as the farmers themselves were concerned, this measure was viewed with great reservations and many misgivings, since it definitely limited their freedom of action almost as much as did the law regulating the employment of agricultural laborers (May 15, 1934).

The Hereditary Farm Law was no less an attempt to create a new ruling class of small farmers. If this attempt aimed at the substitution of small farmers for the traditional ruling class of the Junkers, it certainly failed. Though National Socialism again and again proclaimed its enmity toward the remnants of the feudal aristocracy in East Elbia, it did even less than the Weimar Republic to break up the large estates of this old ruling class of the German Empire. The creation of the hereditary farms, however, had a political purpose too. It meant the settlement of East Elbia with German peasants and farms. At this stage of political strategy this new class was meant to serve as a living wall against the rising tide of the Polish population pressure. In short, the basic motives of agricultural legislation in the Third Reich were much more political than economic.

Such an intention became even more obvious in the field of *industry and labor*. Many of the most brilliant analysts of National Socialism have failed, particularly in this field, to recognize the basic nature of the National Socialist movement by picturing it as an "executive committee of Junkers and capitalists." Actually it was from the beginning a government by a new and revolutionary elite which tolerated industrialists and aristocrats only so long as they were content with a status that gave them no real influence over the determination of politics.

The first actions of victorious Fascism and National Socialism as such may have been most "encouraging" to those employers who wanted to rid themselves of free trade unions and who for this reason had financially supported the rising people's movement with right-wing radical tendencies. Yet the German labor unions, dramatically dissolved on May 2, 1933 (only one day after huge state-staged May Day demonstrations in honor of National Labor), were to be replaced only by the Nazi party-controlled Labor Front, the power and influence of which by far outweighed the Socialist and Catholic labor organizations. The destruction of the pre-Nazi labor organizations was an inescapable result of political defeat. Dr. Ley's newly created German labor front was just as much a political phenomenon. Modeled on the organization of the National Socialist party itself, including—at least on paper—practically all elements in the German economic structure, workers and employers alike, its main task was to "educate" the German masses in National Socialism. In other words, the party created in the Labor Front a political instrument to reach down to the people. Significantly enough, one of its most successful and best-advertised activities became the "Strength Through Joy" movement (*Kraft durch Freude*) which, following the Fascist Dopolavoro experiment, only reaffirmed this "educational" aim by also organizing and controlling the leisure-time activities of the working people.

The new social constitution regulating national labor that went into effect May 1, 1934, established the leadership principle in the factories. It made the employer the "leader of the plant." The workers and employees became the "followers" (represented in a "chosen" council); yet the real impact of their relationship could be evaluated only in terms of the actual direction that the whole economic process took. This ultimate decision was in the hands of neither capital nor labor, but at the party's will alone. All special legislation regulating national labor, such as the laws on "labor trustees" (*Treuhänder der Arbeit*) and the "honor courts" charged with the maintenance of social peace and social honor, represented mere trimmings on the new system. Such institutions no doubt could in concrete situations serve the useful purpose of supervising general policies, of regulating hours and wages, of adjusting personal injuries. They could and certainly did sometimes act as a buffer when human relationships were tense, but they could be just as easily degraded into paper legislation and shadow existence superseded by the centralized organization. The introduction of Goering's Four-Year Plan—a loan from Bolshevist arsenals—nullified the actuality of these ambitious social schemes. As for the true status of the economic order under National Socialism, practically nothing has been reported on these complex and much-advertised Nazi institutions since that time.

The actual position of capital and labor were redefined in terms of the *Wehrwirtschaft*. The substitution of Funk for Schacht was the official beginning of the war economy. It found its climax in the first days of the war in the flight of Thyssen, who once had claimed to have fathered the growing movement and its economic planning. Under the Four-Year Plan, it certainly took a far different turn.

The mechanics of this great economic transformation have often been described and need not concern this study. The dictatorial policies included a most intricate financial revolution such as control of currency expansion (inflation), labor-creating machinery, bilateral international commerce. Incidentally, it is in this field that the most revolutionary steps were taken—measures which apart from their political utility may be worth while examining. The fact that National Socialism completely discarded financial considerations as obstacles to its political ambitions gave rise to some bold thinking, the most original of which came largely from non-partisan experts. This reflects again the strange mixture of the political adventurer (who does not care or who feels himself beyond the law) and the daring scientific experimenter (who is ready to question his whole scientific theory). These strange combinations occur in twilight periods of political and social upheavals. "The Nazi explorers in effect have discovered and are making use of the fact that the financial world is round, while our financial geographers are still telling us that the heretics will sail off its edge."

Nazi fiscal policies have been a challenge to 19th-century ideas. Running into debt no doubt spelled certain ruin for a government because it indicated that the state was living beyond its means, i.e., its capacity to be taxed. In a period of expanding economy it had become axiomatic that it was private initiative which provided all the opportunity for the investment of savings and guaranteed the natural flow of capital. Twentieth-century economics soon realized the limitation of such an automatic self-regulation in a contracting society (transitory or permanent). It reconsidered, therefore, the essential place of the state in the direction of productive forces through active state interference. It commenced to view "national debt" in a different way. The real concern of modern capitalist society must be whether its total financial wealth, including the national debt, is large enough to permit the production of the national income that its fiscal capacity affords. Such considerations probably opened the way to some kind of financial double morality that conceived of different standards in individual household and state bookkeeping. The government can easily run into debt as long as it thus promotes business and creates labor. It may even control currency expansion if it succeeds in keeping the monetary circle closed by returning the profits of an expanded private industry to government sources. In other words, if the profits made by private industry are invested in government bonds, the state will thus finance its continuous expansion. Such an investment can easily be enforced by a policy of "suggestion" in a controlled and closed economy such as Germany represents. The "Vampire Economy" asks a "creative sacrifice" from industry and business to make possible the "creative efforts" of the Fuehrer. It can create miracles.

It is significant, however, that National Socialism in this field of economics, as well as in international politics, moved extremely cautiously during the first years of its control. Schacht and his ultra-conservative economic views ruled and checked the boldest plans of economic promotion. Not until 1937 did the Nazis feel sufficiently confident of themselves to let this wizard go. By this time they had also won a foothold in international economics. Capitalizing on a world depression that had filled the world's warehouses with stagnant surpluses, they suggested cleverly managed bilateral treaties to create barter trade.

Of course, the full picture of this essentially dynamic *Wehrwirtschaft* is perceived only in its international implications. War economics becomes a weapon, and a very essential one, in the Fascist strategy of world expansion, and must therefore be considered in connection with the concluding analysis of "Dictatorship in International Politics."

DICTATORSHIP AND THE ARMED FORCES

A system directed toward total war must make its peace with the armed forces. Especially in the Third Reich, most ambitious of all dictatorships, a precondition for success has been "the marriage" between the National Socialist party and the German army. Theirs has been a stormy relationship, laden with conflict from the beginning. In one sense, the military looked upon Hitler as a valuable force, the demagogue who could win over the masses in what they considered the unsoldierly Republic. On the other hand, they never trusted this self-made *condottiere* who became Chancellor only after long resistance by Hindenburg and his army clique.

The first open clash after Hitler's seizure of power came in 1934, when the army forced him to liquidate the rival Storm Troop leaders in the June purge. These concessions were necessary in view of rearmament and the expected death of President Hindenburg. The loyalty of the army was essential; it was literally bought by the sacrifice of the blood of old party veterans. Thus the army won the first round.

When Goering used this occasion to purge two generals as well, ex-Chancellor von Schleicher and his right-hand man General von Bredow, Hitler had to rehabilitate them with an honorable memory during a public demonstration in the Berlin Opera House.

Yet this army victory was only a strategic retreat of the Nazis which was reversed in 1938. In fact, during these four years there had been continuous tensions between the daring party leadership and the cautious army staff. The most important conflict centered around the remilitarization of the Rhineland in 1936. The military had warned against it, but Hitler triumphed and the "moderating influence" of the generals faded. Their counsel of prudence has been discredited again and again by the world appeasers' acquiescence in Hitler's daring moves. Thus the generals' prestige and power declined. Not even a Moscow trial was necessary to co-ordinate the leading personnel of the army with the National Socialist state. In February, 1938, a few weeks before Hitler started his Napoleonic march against the world—when he enforced the Austrian *Anschluss*—he could bluntly dismiss the generals who had built up the army and had become the focus of its loyalties. The leading figure among them, von Fritsch, came to his strange end in the Battle of Warsaw.

The shrewd strategy of Hitler's dealings with the army becomes obvious in this second round with the generals. He did not appoint the only outspoken National Socialist among the higher officers, General von Reichenau (suddenly departed in the Russian winter of 1942); von Brauchitsch and von Keitel, two career officers, members of the old-established military caste, were named to this supreme position. Victorious National Socialism filled the key positions of army and navy with reliable fighters who would at least not resist any Nazi order. Whenever one of the leading generals interfered with these plans, as did Colonel Beck, who was hesitant about bringing the Sudeten Germans "home" during the Czech crisis of 1938, he had to go.

Then the war started—the third act. The striking power of Hitler's military army was due especially to the exclusion of the "irregulars" from the commanding positions. Yet, after the Polish campaign was successfully concluded and the much-expected peace still did not follow, the conflict between Hitler and the generals was renewed. In January, 1940, Propaganda Minister Goebbels made a speech in Posen in which he cited Frederick the Great as saying to the generals who refused to follow him: "Then I will continue the war alone." It was a warning to the generals. Von Brauchitsch understood. Five days later he gave a definite answer in an article prominently displayed in the *Völkischer Beobachter*; he proclaimed the German army's determination to follow Frederick's example and his strategy of attack. This declaration seemed to indicate the final victory of the Nazi policies over the generals. Then came Norway, the Low Countries, and France —great military victories, laurels and honors for the generals bestowed upon them by the corporal, the upstart, the irrational. This was Hitler's hour of triumph. It looked like a *pax Hitleriana* over Europe and over the generals, too.

But the story was to be continued. And so was the war, because of Britain's unexpected resistance. The events of the year 1941 were not quite to Hitler's liking. In fact, he had good reason to suspect his generals. For years he had created a personal staff of military confidants, such as Generals Jodl and Varlimont, who became increasingly predominant in his councils. Significantly enough, they did not belong to the aristocratic ruling class. When the top commanders of his army—all proud veterans of Germany's military aristocracy—seemed to oppose his far-reaching schemes, Hitler himself took over. This happened in December, 1941.

The dismissal of Field Marshal von Brauchitsch as Commander-in-Chief of the German Army (an ample occasion for rumors and misleading speculations!) certainly did not mean that the long-predicted break between Hitler and the generals, between the party and the army, was here at last. Yet the change in command high-lighted the ever-present strains inherent in the nature of the system.

One may say that institutionally the army is deaf and dumb to politics. But within the controlling circles of the army there is a definite resentment against the irrational politics of the up-starts, because the modern army is to a large extent a rational institution. This quality only reflects the great changes that society has undergone since the Middle Ages. The changing structure of society transforms the character of the army, too. Though history books always tell about the feudal character of the Prussian state, it should be kept in mind that the founders of Prussianism, Frederick Wilhelm and even Frederick the Great, were deeply affected by the rising middle-class civilization. Not only was their whole cultural life largely shaped in terms of bourgeois virtues—industry, thrift, dutiful performance, domestic tranquillity—but their concept of the state was based upon state reason (*raison d'état*).

Absolutism's most obedient servants were bourgeois sons. Middle-class rationalism largely affected the bureaucracy, the court, and also the army. It has been from the beginning one of the yardsticks of efficient military performance. The personal orientation of an army officer is no different from that of an official in a governmental bureaucracy. He is "career-bound." This ambition provides the main motive for his work; promotion within a hierarchical order constitutes his chief reward. It is the skillful use of this demand for and expectation of advancement that becomes a powerful weapon for successful dictatorship in winning over a reluctant officers' corps. Since the expansive plans of Fascism promise a great military future, the new system becomes "respectable" in the eyes of many ambitious army professionals and acceptable to their rational life schemes.

In Prussia, the middle-class mentality among the military was strangely blended with a feudal concept of life which concedes to "civil society" a position secondary only to the "heroic military." Indeed, it was this tension between the feudal idea of personal loyalty and middle-class rationality that was so characteristic of the German army. This conflict remained latent only because the middle class in Germany did not succeed in winning political control and sufficient social prestige to challenge the contradictory Prussian formula. Yet the inaptitude of the Prussian officer to act in politics is largely due to this strange union of irreconcilable characteristics. With the growing claim of an urban and industrial middle class and an ambitious proletariat, the army felt unable to envisage a new political formula.

The First World War and especially the final breakdown of the regime brought the crisis to the fore. The immediate results seemed to be the complete defeat of the military elements. They were pushed into the background in the Weimar Republic, which had to pay dearly for not finding its own formula in relation to the military. Many of the returning soldiers lost themselves in Catilinian conspiracies against the hated Republic. Quite a few of them finally joined the new National Socialist movement.

The defeat, however, had a much deeper effect on some far-seeing military men. They took their lessons from the debacle and, as often happens in history, thus turned defeat into victory. While the Allied staffs rested on their laurels, the defeated German military officers revolutionized military thinking by simply developing the new tendencies that had become visible during World War I. Two major features had been brought forward especially during the last stages of that conflict: mechanized forces and the total character of war. Both elements were closely interrelated. The fact that the new weapons of mechanized warfare, the tank and the airplane, high-lighted industrial production gave new importance to the hinterland for the final outcome. No longer could the military say with Frederick the Great that "he did not wish his civilian subjects to care about the wars he was waging." Not only does modern mass war actually mobilize from 10 to 20 per cent of the total population, but the civil front also becomes an essential part of military warfare. It has been estimated that from ten to fifteen workers are necessary to equip one soldier in today's mechanized army. If one adds to this the fact that the airplane carries the actual fight into the hinterland, one must realize that this is a war in which no separation between combatants and noncombatants can be made. The morale of the hinterland thus becomes decisive.

The bitter experiences of the war since 1939 have slowly convinced the nations of the west of this basic transformation in military warfare. Yet it is significant that the German military had conceived the concept of "total war," long before. In fact, they blamed the military disaster of 1918 on the failure to organize the whole hinterland. The "stab in the back theory" not only served as an appropriate alibi for the "invincibility" of the military arm, but it also became the point of departure for far-reaching plans to prepare the country for war on a total basis.

This realization necessitated a complete shift in military thinking. A strong social basis in the nation became preconditional for the army whose generals now tried desperately to make contact with the people and even with the much-despised parliamentary representatives. This move was not simply a belated discovery of the social conscience among the military; it derived primarily from a realistic evaluation of modern wars which are largely won on the assembly line and are often decided long before the actual shooting starts.

The main attraction of National Socialism for the German army consisted in the movement's obvious hold on a large part of the populace, especially the young. To be sure, only a small number of the old army staff joined the party, and most of those who did so only played politics in the hope that they might use the revolutionary energies of this new dynamic movement to accomplish a revival of the militarist. The army was still regarded as "neutral ground" during the early years of the regime; people jokingly referred to the possibility of "emigrating to the army." But in the lower brackets and especially in the new fields of military expansion in the air force, the spirit of young National Socialism coincided with the ideas of the army corps. Fanaticism, dangerously uncontrollable though it might seem to the rational military, had become a necessary element in modern warfare. Toward the end of the last war the German army created a new military type: the shock troops. These modern gladiators and daredevils were to have no ties whatsoever with civil society. They were the forerunners of the National Socialist Storm Troopers, exquisite material for the blitzkrieg of the Second World War. The strange combination of highly developed mechanization and unleashed warrior brought about the miracles of the parachute and Panzer divisions. With so fanatical a machine at their service, the generals could conceive of a victorious campaign. They did not like National Socialism but they wanted to win the next war. The dictatorial party seemed to offer a mass backing, a total mobilization of the entire populace, and specialists in highly skilled violence. Thus the party triumphed.

The army in turn contributed extraordinarily to inner changes in the Third Reich. Students of the institutional structure of modern Fascism observed years ago that specific elements in the organization of the modern army were largely paralleled in highly developed capitalism and its rational process. It was in the military state that army and organized industry met. They had one aim in mind: to prepare for total war and to do it efficiently.

The most spectacular field of militarization in the Third Reich, the newly created air force, likewise showed its strength in masterful rational scheming. Goering, who first of all welded this revolutionary weapon together, was in a way the most bourgeois among Hitler's lieutenants. And what is more significant, he entrusted this gigantic job to experts: Erhard Milch, the proved organizer of commercial aeronautics, and the late Ernst Udet, the professional pilot of world fame. The latter, incidentally, as William Shirer rightly remarks, would probably never have won such a key position in any other political system. "Lacking in business experience" and living a "somewhat Bohemian life," he would have been too much of a risk. "People would hesitate to trust him with responsibility." He had the daring of the amateur, the secret of success in other fields of Nazi activity.

The striking power of Hitler's military arm was due not the least to the exclusion of the "irregulars" from commanding positions. Roehm and his Storm Troopers had demanded the recognition of the S.A. hierarchy on an equal footing. The army brusquely denied this claim. Even a Storm Troop general had to serve as a private. A trained staff of professionals was to organize the new army. Ironically enough, the Versailles Treaty had laid the groundwork for such an efficient organization. Limited by treaty stipulations to a standing army of 100,000 men, the German Reichswehr carefully selected its men and trained them fully to become officers of a future mass army. The spectacular reintroduction of general conscription in 1935 had only to fill out an organizational skeleton, completely perfected by that time.

In spite of this amazing technical accomplishment, the army was not a policy-making institution. Experts as such are politically blind. They can be directed and even defeated by the political powers in control. In fact, they normally expect the watchword to come from these quarters, and only if it does not happen to come forth do they seize the opportunity to play a dilettante's game in politics.

Military writers in our day have significantly stated that even war strategies have to be planned by civilians. Since modern warfare in its totalitarian aspect presupposes a coordination of extremely divergent forces, the perspective needed for effective planning cannot always be found among the specialists.

In fact, military efficiency seems to be increased by a strong political leadership that gives direction and purpose. The lack of this direction represented one basic weakness of the German army in the First World War. As long as the army accepts the political tenets of a dictatorship, the latter's preconceived solutions set "the believers" free for action and heighten their efficiency.

For this reason, the much-discussed institution of the *political commissars* in the Soviet army (abolished after the Finnish War and restored a month after the German invasion) does not at all spell a necessary weakening of the Red army's striking power. The opposite may be true. Incidentally, the introduction of these political commissars is not an absolutely new phenomenon. The *intendants* of French absolutism fulfilled similar functions (in a different political and social setup, to be sure). They were the eyes of the ruling system, carrying its control into the active centers of daily performance.

The strategy of "total war" emphasizes the military function of the political commissars. They become the organizers of guerilla warfare and "scorched earth" tactics. The political commissar is warrior, teacher, propagandist, and living example of the Soviet government and the Communist party at the front. A government statute defines the commissars' duties and powers. "They are instructed to report to the high command any commanders or political personnel whose actions discredit the army. They are charged with strengthening the prestige of the commanders and making certain that orders are carried out. They are ordered to inculcate in officers and men a contempt for death and to push forward for promotion men who render good services."

All commissars now have military training; they come from a military school or have served many years in the Red army. Party emissaries and military circles may also conform by training to a common "rational outlook." This fact does not exclude frequent tensions between the military commander, the head of the regiment, and its soul, the commissar. Understanding and collaboration largely depend not only on the political reliability of the military leader, but also on the tact of the political sentinel.

Experts have to be treated with respect. Their quasi-religious concept of efficiency must not be disturbed. Though they may not command ends, they are the masters of means and they want to be recognized as such. They have to be flattered by definite acknowledgment of their social prestige. A semblance of political independence has to be preserved. They do not want to be forced into a political camp. Only slowly can the "new spirit" infiltrate the military cadres. Tact is needed, careful procedure and even compromise. The political masters who never forget that military effectiveness always depends on the good will of the armed forces must duly respect those procedures. When army chaplains raise their voices against pagan tendencies, as they did in a telling memorandum early in 1938, even the Nazi party has to accept the reminder politely. If the political power does not strike a working formula with the military forces, the revolutionary state deprives itself of a good part of its military *Schlagkraft*. It may even lose the revolution altogether.

DICTATORSHIP AND THE ESTABLISHED CHURCHES

The restraint shown by modern dictatorship toward the army was not needed in respect to other agencies. Even the church experienced frontal attacks from the first days of dictatorships. The relation of state to church in dictatorships is a question of power politics and political strategy. Therefore, the fate which the church met varied accordingly. In Russia, where the church had been tied up with the czarist regime, it immediately became the personification of the enemy. In Italy, where Catholicism embraced the whole nation, clever tactics had to be adopted and were finally crowned in the Lateran Pact between the Holy See and the Fascist government.

Nazi Germany encountered a most complex situation in the religious field. The country since Reformation days had been divided between Protestantism and Catholicism. Religious factions could be played off against each other by shrewd tactics, a point which the church politicians in the Nazi party did not miss. Yet, what was more important, the strategic position of the two confessions was different. The dictatorship had to attack them in different ways. Catholicism represented more of an international issue, while the Protestant church, from its beginning closely tied together with the secular princes, was embedded in the national fate.

The concordat concluded in 1933 between the Holy See and the Reich was of special significance, for this first great international agreement was to prove the reliability of the new regime. It turned out to be an object lesson in the meaning of National Socialist treaty strategy, binding the other partner but never boundless National Socialism.

Innumerable incidents fully proved that there existed between the two powers a state of latent warfare. Undeclared though it was, and carefully kept from breaking into the open by far-sighted church diplomats and shrewd party tacticians, violations of the treaty provisions were the order of the day. Major issues centered around the conflict over Nazi education (finally resulting in an educational monopoly in the Hitler Youth), the systematic curtailment and suppression of Catholic organizations, and, last but not least, the clash with the Nazi *Weltanschauung* and its applications, particularly the racial legislation and the sterilization law. The government at the same time continuously tried to undermine the clergy's deeply rooted prestige and hold upon the common people. A lesson was taken from Bismarck's fateful *Kulturkampf* and his erroneous direct attack against and interference with religious worship. "No martyrs, just criminals," was the prescription handed out by party high officials. Thus disgraceful trials were staged for members of the church and religious orders for violation of exchange laws, for high treason (as in the case of Monsignor Bannasch for having given information detrimental to the state to representatives of foreign powers, i.e., the Papal Nuncio), and for "moral turpitude," all of which were intended to prove the utter decay of the church. Numerous warnings by church dignitaries, climaxing in the papal Encyclical of 1937, *Mit brennender Sorge,* pathetically illustrated the losing battle of the church—at least for the time being.

The fate of Catholicism was to an even greater degree the fate of other confessions which could not offer the former's close-knit organization and unified leadership. Small denominations and religious sects were hopelessly lost; they did not even present bargaining power to the political potentates.

The case of Protestantism was somehow different since it held a traditionally strong position in Prussia-Germany, especially among the crucial peasantry. In critical situations the church could also successfully appeal to army circles. Yet, powerful though the evangelical churches were numerically, they had lost in spiritual power long before dictatorship curtailed their actual domain. Often they were degraded to a taken-for-granted social institution of bourgeois respectability, with no real hold on the "enlightened" urbanized masses. Such a development indicates the more clearly the deep religious cataclysm when one recalls that the city had always been regarded as the site of religious piety outgrowing primitive superstition. (By no mere chance did early Christianity identify the pagan and the peasant [*paganus*], in this respect following similar traditions of post-prophetic Judaism.)

Protestantism not only had lost much of its vitality as a meaningful religion by the end of the 19th century, but since the days of Luther it had forfeited its political independence, preaching as it did unqualified obedience to "Caesar." The Protestant church became identified with a conservative patriotism that defended "Throne and Altar." Different from the Catholic church, the German evangelical church was never a free agent in political strategy. Such traditional ties also led to a rather outspoken enmity against the liberal Weimar Republic and therewith to a naïve acceptance of anti-republican forces. Many leaders of the church thus allied themselves with young National Socialism. The vague promise of "positive Christianity," though subject "to the moral feeling of the German race" according to the Nazi program, made these new patriots agreeable to the great majority of Protestant pastors.

It was only after the Third Reich had established itself that an increasing number of Protestant clergymen belatedly grasped the intransigency of victorious National Socialism (an experience similar to that of many conservatives in the political sphere). Their fight found a living symbol in gallant Pastor Niemoeller, submarine commander of World War I fame and National Socialist of the first hour, who now turned against the unbearable intolerance, totalitarian claim, and pagan tendencies of the Third Reich. His "Confessional Church Movement" (hastily organized against the official "Union of German Evangelical Churches") put up a heroic struggle. Yet it remained a dissident movement which, soon under the surveillance of the secret police, could not prevent the gradual acquiescence of the Protestant church to a Ministry of Church Affairs. These rebellious pastors may still attain lasting importance as symbols of resistance.

Dictatorship cannot be satisfied in coordinating the established churches. This task, incomplete though it still is, represents only a preliminary step in the farther-reaching aim of a national church that will epitomize National Socialism as the heir to all religions. Papist in outlook and rites, it simply substitutes Hitler for Christ and thus is carrying the process of de-Christianization to its final conclusion.

Romantic and artificial as this neo-paganism may seem, it fits to measure the ideology of the permanent revolutionaries, whereas in contrast a pious Christianity never has been acceptable to a martial world. "Concepts such as sin, redemption, and religious piety," Max Weber pointedly remarks, "are habitually foreign and painful indeed to all political ruling classes, first of all to a nobility of the sword."

The pagan "German Faith Movement," numerically weak

though it is today, has won powerful spokesmen in Hitler's inner circle, among them Alfred Rosenberg, Supreme Director of Cultural Activities and author of *The Myth of the 20th Century*. What may be even more important, this movement has found ardent and determined disciples in the Elite Guard of the Hitler Youth, spearheads of the intransigent movement.

Strategic considerations may sometimes push dictatorship's ambitious plans into the background; war in earnest in particular necessitates an appeal to the Lord whose help is conveniently invoked in an established clergy's prayers for victory. Yet such tactics will not prevent the careful observer from realizing that the basic attitude of dictatorship toward religion is defined by the very essence of dictatorship. The sweep of modern totalitarianism has to clash with the church. No compromise is possible. The dictatorial party in itself represents a church which competes for the souls of its adherents. Modern dictatorships are "political religions" (inner worldly religions, to be sure). In fact, their very survival depends on their final victory over religion. Because religion represents the supreme challenge to totalitarian rule, religious forces may be the last protection against totalitarian claims.

Aside from the specific doctrines, ceremonies, and institutional procedures, all religions are defined by human recognition of a transcendental power. Moral standards and individual responsibilities are thus confronted with a system of values beyond human reach. While salvation of souls for eternity may be regarded as the supreme task of the church, this transcendentalism serves at the same time as a guardian against human absolutism. But it is exactly this claim to absolute and total rule that characterizes the modern tribalism of dictatorships. They have therefore to fight religion, which presents an insurmountable barrier against their totalitarian rule.

William Hocking has pointed out that the rise of individualism is closely connected with the awakening of a religious conscience in the late Middle Ages. It is this religious basis that brings out "the lasting elements of individualism." No wonder that of all the fighters against the totalitarian regime, the churches—compromises though they may have made in order to preserve their institutions —have brought forward the most ardent and stiffest defense of human liberty. They represent the last vestiges of independent man.

The Family Under Totalitarianism

If dictatorship is to attack the last vestiges of independent man, totalitarianism cannot stop at the basic unit of man's social existence: the family. Though that "primary group" par excellence has undoubtedly changed and has even lost many of its earlier functions, it is still the chief force in building human personality. "Humanizing the animal drives," the family performs this greatest service to the group, thanks to its emotional ties, subconscious spontaneity, and preverbal intimacy. Unit cell of the social structure, it can make or break existing society.

The totalitarian state which claims the complete and all-embracing control of human existence must therefore seize power over this nucleus of all organizations. Modern dictatorships have from the beginning realized the necessity of subjugating this last free agency of social relations. Different techniques have been used because of the varying position of the family in different countries. But all dictatorships agree upon the fact that the family must be coordinated with the system, lest it serve as a crystallization of "counterrevolution."

The attack against the family in Soviet Russia had a twofold aim, similar to the Soviet endeavor in other fields. Here again westernization and radical social evolution found their expression in different, sometimes even divergent, policies pursued at the same time by the Soviet regime.

The new family policy meant in the first place the emancipation of women. There was a great distance between the pre-revolutionary attitude that "a chicken is not a bird and a woman is not a human being" and Lenin's idea that "every cook must learn to rule the state." In eastern Russia especially, westernization led to extraordinary transformations. It embodied a great crusade against prejudice and deeply entrenched traditions, against the wearing of the veil and the purchase and stealing of brides.

This modernization in giving women complete civil equality with men was only one part of the extensive Soviet legislation. Soviet Russia, the great laboratory of social experiments, also showed the same daring in regard to the family, for other and more revolutionary measures seemed to attack the very roots of the family itself. The changes were spectacular; the country went through a cycle of social legislation that completely reversed the status of the family within the life span of one generation.

In the early years of the regime, marriage and divorce were liberalized to an unheard-of degree. These initial steps led easily to a misunderstanding of the essential purposes of this legislation, and ignorant and malicious reports concerning the "nationalization of women" were widespread. That Soviet Russia was definitely not interested in the creation of a libertine attitude is manifest in the stern asceticism of its political leaders. The new regime was above all interested in destroying the power of the family; hence this "bourgeois" institution was to have no responsible place in public life, and all the laws that weakened it were directed toward its essential dissolution. Its resistance would be broken by making the family institution merely personal (i.e., by depriving it of all educational and social functions), which would automatically deprive it of all rights and authority, particularly as far as children were concerned. The family would lose its character and significance as a primary group; its function of molding human personality would be taken over by the community of the factory and the party organization. Thus everyone would be a trustworthy fighter for the Soviet regime.

When Soviet Russia came of age, the young generation of the *Konsomols* who had grown up under the regime was the first group to fight for the reestablishment of the family. This reversal of theories concerning marriage and the family which many foreign admirers called an ethical revolution had perhaps not so much to do with ethics as with tactics. Family life had been assailed earlier because it was tied up with bourgeois traditions.

Now the family life of the young revolutionaries could bolster up the Soviet regime and could thus become a weapon in the hands of the state.

Since the middle of the '30's, Soviet legislation has undone all the earlier regulations, including the much-discussed "post-card divorce." (Drop into the license bureau, declare incompatibility with your mate, and he or she will learn about the dissolved marriage by mail whenever the postman gets around.) Strict laws were passed to control easygoing "alimony jumpers" and to restrict divorces through graduated divorce taxes. What is more significant, extensive legislation was introduced to encourage an increase in the birth rate. These policies also included strong measures against abortion. "Soviet woman has gained equality with man, but she has not been released from that great and honorable duty of Nature—childbearing, and this is indisputably not her private business," said Solttz, member of the drafting committee of the New Family Legislation. As National Socialism had done earlier, the Soviet regime introduced large premiums for childbearing; the only difference was that in Russia no premium was paid until the eighth child was born, and the twelfth child meant an increased premium. All dictatorships want large armies. Moreover, all of them deny the right to a "private life." Everyone belongs to the community; the community has to decide upon the size of the family, the education of the children, and the daily activities of each member.

While both Fascist Italy and National Socialist Germany agree on the basic position of women in a dictatorship, the social status of women has a different meaning in the two systems. When Il Duce assailed the emancipated woman, when he praised the beauty of motherhood and the superior charm of the matronly figure, when he decreed that woman's place is in the home, he merely gave new expression to established customs and recognized relationships. This policy did not mean any digression from the prevailing trends in feminism and emancipation. The Italian mother had never really been away from home. The Catholic tradition of family life and the limited degree of industrialization had held back any tendency toward emancipation. Though no legal bounds to professional training were set, practically all the Italians were suspicious of career-bent women; the patriarchal family was still the prevailing pattern in Italy. Fascism did not have to make any major revolution in this field, and Mussolini merely stated a commonplace when he pompously declared in his talks with Emil Ludwig: "Woman must play a passive part. She is analytical, not synthetical. My notion of women's role in the state is utterly opposed to feminism. As far as political life is concerned, they do not count here."

The situation in Germany was different when Hitler's rule began. The position of women was much further advanced than was the case in Italy. In fact, the German Republic meant a great change, to women in particular. Not only did it bring the recognition of full civil equality with men in the granting of woman suffrage, but it also embodied a wide change in attitudes, especially as far as the family was concerned. Pre-war Germany was often called militaristic. This militarist attitude, of course, was not to be measured in numbers of soldiers; it meant a special set of values that typified social relationships in Germany. To express this attitude negatively, pre-war Germany was definitely no democracy. Heroic ideals, super- and sub-ordination, a militant attitude toward life infiltrated all institutions—the factory, the school, and the family. In the family it meant the definite establishment of the autocratic patriarchal family. One might even go so far as to say that the family was regarded as the father's "property" (a concept which, incidentally, made adultery robbery, apart from the possible violation of a deep affection). In return, such a family gave the housewife order and security. These essential features of German family life were broken by the war and post-war upheavals.

Incidentally, it is one of the major effects of war as such that this most "manly" business usually leads to the betterment of woman's status. It was a Punic war that broke the patriarchal family system of old Rome. It was the Civil War that liberated American women, in the words of Calhoun, from "ladylike futility." War necessarily brings such improvement because women are called upon to perform tasks unheard of in the traditional division of labor. To keep things going, they have to take over men's work during the war, and when peace comes they still know that they can do this work.

The emancipation, so-called, began in pre-war times. As a matter of fact, many leaders of this European movement were to be found in the German empire. Helene Lange, Marianne Weber, and Gertrude Bäumer became standard-bearers of women's emancipation, but they represented only a small number—the intelligentsia, the school teacher, the social worker. Not until after the war did the movement gain momentum as social conditions changed. A career became not simply a self-justification of proud womanhood, but an economic necessity. Women who wanted to marry found in these post-war years of inflation and depression that the men they knew could barely feed and clothe themselves; women who were married often had to support their families. The problem of women working was not reserved to the proletariat; it also embraced the middle classes. They all had to work. Many of these women, of course, did not enthusiastically exchange their function as housewife for that of shop assistant. They began to romanticize Home Sweet Home. They were weary of and disillusioned by freedom. When they thought of a housewife, they thought of security—and pre-war security at that. And when Hitler said that women have no place in politics, many of the women voters joined forces with him. The majority of the Hitler voters were women. They voted for a return to pre-war times and its values, security and property; but in reality they voted themselves out of political existence.

Kinder, Kirche, und Küche (children, church, and kitchen) became the slogan of National Socialism. It meant a setback to women's rights. Women with jobs were replaced by jobless men. Their admission to universities was restricted. Even their behavior patterns were dictated by a masculine world. Smoking was distinctly a male prerogative. Cosmetics were to be shunned as decadent. (Parenthetically, it may be said that here occurred the first battle which German National Socialism lost. This failure was not due solely to the fact that the late Captain Roehm, who made himself the spokesman for this movement, was not exactly an adequate representative of the customs of a healthy male.) Many of the ardent National Socialists even went so far as to say that women were to stop reading books that put ideas into their heads because men would now do the necessary thinking.

Motherhood became woman's noblest vocation. Special laws were introduced to encourage larger families. Whether loans were paid to newly married couples which would be reduced by one-quarter with every newborn child (children thus became payments on account), whether certain jobs were contingent on the holders being married, whether premiums were paid for the third child and every one thereafter—all these features hinted at the main concept, that family and children were not a private affair, but almost exclusively a concern of the state.

Significantly enough, these intensive attempts to increase the birth rate had only limited success. In spite of Mussolini's warlike speeches when he appealed to the national duty of Italian mothers to create a surplus population in an already overpopulated Italy the Italian birth rate has decreased from 32 to 25 per thousand since Fascism's rise to power. True, a careful check-up of German population statistics shows that the more systematic campaigns of the Nazi government were more successful in the beginning, for the birth rate rose from 14.9 to 17. Though the German experiment has not been in effect long enough to permit any definite generalizations, one may venture to say that all these policies may have only delayed the natural trend toward a declining birth rate in Europe. Even if such limited successes prove to be of some temporary significance in the struggle of power politics, these intensive drives definitely have not turned the prevalent tide.

The disintegration of the family, the most powerful unit for the domestication of man, is even more visible in the field of education and recreation. Here the dictatorships have succeeded in undermining the family to such an extent that practically nothing remains of the vital forces of this institution. What is left is the less enviable function of being the guardian of the new state. If the members of the family happen to agree on the dictatorial rule, they may all meet, as the often-told bootleg story reports, at the annual party meeting in Nuremberg; but if the parents still adhere to pre-revolutionary convictions, the children, trained in school and the dictator's youth organizations, have to watch and even report their parents' disloyalty. The psychological effects of such a procedure do not need to be described.

This development within the basic unit of social life is indicative of the definite dissolution of separate spheres for private and public life. There is no private existence left to the individual. Indeed, the absorption of the private sphere by the state may be regarded as one of the crucial elements of modern dictatorship.

EDUCATION IN UNIFORM

"He who has control of youth controls the future." This self-assured slogan of early National Socialism, commonplace though it is, points to the promise, claim, and secret success of modern dictatorships. They have made the first systematic attempts at the comprehensive political "education" of the oncoming generation. The psychological appeal to the youth of the right- or left-wing radical movements is obvious. The uncompromising fervor of these movements, their emotionalism, their call for action are natural attractions to youthful temperament. As long as the "revolution is on," it easily enthralls youthful recruits and can indeed lay claim to being a youth movement itself. But the test of the system's staying power comes after victory is won, when the fighters of the first hour grow old. Then the movement must carry on its violent thrust, increased in tempo and zeal, and thus hope to arouse a new generation by its promise of a permanent revolution. However, these children of the revolution are confronted with a far different situation. They must never question the victorious revolution. They cannot repeat their elders' radicalism. They have to accept "the new order."

In fact, it becomes a major concern of the dictatorships in power to safeguard the revolution against a new wave of revolutionaries who may not accept its basic tenets. In doing so, the "youth movement" has to take away from the rising generation the fundamental right of youth to doubt, dissent, and deny. Education in a dictatorship is not aimed at the awakening of the growing personality in all its unknown promise and startling surprise. On the contrary, its purpose is to guarantee perfect coordination with the system and "to prepare the rising generation for its set functions as the true representative of the nation." Rust, the Nazi Minister of Education, in thus defining the purpose of education, adds that it is "to make the young people racially sound, efficient, and ready for sacrifice." In this same guarded statement published in *Germany Speaks* (an effective propaganda symposium written for the Anglo-Saxon world in 1938), this minister, after praising Germany's leading part in the "19th-century educational program in the domain of intellectual refinement," proceeds to elaborate on two main weaknesses of this educational system: the "excessive importance attached to the individual as such, and the overestimation of intellectual capacities."

National Socialism—justly or not—has upheld these two criticisms and has postulated its guiding principles accordingly. Education in the Third Reich is above all anti-individualistic and anti-intellectual; its major precepts are directed at community life, physical stamina, and will power. According to the *Auslese Erlass* (Selective Decree) issued by the Department of Education in close collaboration with the *Rassenpolitisches Amt* (Racial Political Board), the demands made of young persons before they are admitted to high school are as follows: good physical health, capacity for endurance, high ethical standards, sense of community, increased intellectual achievements, and descent from pure German stock.

The center of Nazi education is the training of will and character, of bodily strength and skill. Germans who were once proud of being members of a "people of poets and thinkers" are now taught to regard such an epithet as a sign of national decay. There is no doubt that education under National Socialism has been very successful in building up physical stamina. The accent on physical education is a general feature of dictatorial upbring-ing. The test in courage that the average young National Socialist has to undergo is beyond the imagination of the western world. World War II is showing the results in the daring parachute and Panzer divisions. The whole educational system is earmarked for war. Discipline and obedience become the chief values for the maintenance of a war society even in peacetime. Spartanism has often been regarded as the underlying philosophy of German National Socialism. Such a formula summarizes the regimentation of the entire nation.

One may see elements of an exclusive orientation toward the state even in the early stages of the German educational develop-ment. In marked contrast to the Anglo-Saxon system which has grown from extremely divergent roots, Germany's system of edu-cation has been built up essentially by statesmen and legislators. This nation, coming of age belatedly, has always used education as a weapon for developing a spirit of nationalism. The defeat inflicted upon Prussia by Napoleon at Jena was the starting point of the "New Education" as formulated by Fichte's *Reden an die Deutsche Nation*, Humboldt's *Plans of the University of Berlin*, and Turnvater Jahn's *Sport Organizations*. (Konrad Hen-lein of Sudeten German repute is in this respect a disciple, though a poor one, of old Father Jahn.) Education in Prussia, like eco-nomics, has always been state-controlled and directed from above.

The great change which has come about with the rise of National Socialism is due to two factors: first, the complete shift in the political philosophy of the state shown in the abandon-ment of all the liberal elements of the preceding system, thus transforming the whole direction of education; and second, in consequence of this new philosophy, an all-embracing policy which leaves no free sphere of activity in the field of education and entirely eliminates self-administration, which is most essen-tial to higher education.

The curriculum of the schools under the Third Reich has been completely remodeled in order to fit "the education and instruc-tion of the German youth in the spirit of National Socialism."

The predominant fields—even in the lower grades—are biology and race study, anthropology and prehistory, political geography and national history, with special emphasis on the most recent development, and "defense" subjects—of course none of them taught detachedly. There is no truth for truth's sake. Every discipline is directed toward the "closest possible relationship with the national political needs of our people." In arithmetic the child no longer counts apples, but bullets; the military plane takes the place of the peaceful kite as the chief demonstrator of geometrical curves. What characterizes the new education is not only its orientation toward the pragmatic, but even more its prescription of prejudices and beliefs, of intimidation and indoctrination that permeate the exposition in every subject. This inculcation must make a deep impression on the plastic mind of the school youth; it has a no less deterrent effect on academic standards. Gone are the qualities that once made German universities the fountain of scholarship and science: freedom of inquiry and unimpaired search for truth, judicial temper and frank evaluation of controversial views, and the universality of intellectual intercourse in that great realm of science which recognizes no flags or frontiers.

This complete change in academic atmosphere is not adequately reflected in the numerical losses of the scholars who could not be "coordinated" and hence had to go. In fact, the percentage is somewhat smaller than is widely assumed. Careful statistical accounts put the total of dismissals at about 15 per cent of the academic teaching staff, although a disproportionate number of outstanding scientists are among them. More important is the general effect that this politicization had on the remaining academicians. Indeed, even in the provincialism of the new partisan endeavor the place granted to the universities is less glorious than in the old days. Their enrollment has been halved, which incidentally has the result of eliminating academic unemployment. "In one sense," as E. Y. Hartshorne conclusively shows in his circumspect analysis, *German Universities and National Socialism*, "the typical instrument of higher education in National Socialist Germany is not the university but the institute of technology and its close relative, the vocational school."

This great shift is due partly to the emphasis on the "practical versus the speculative," partly to the outspoken anti-intellectualism of the new system, and last but not least, to the transfer of the training of the "national elite" to the party's leadership schools.

The nine-year secondary school course in Germany has been shortened to eight; Saturday is set aside for *Wehrsport*, i.e., physical preparedness for military service. The newly created *Landjahr* camps—besides giving training in community life and political education—are intended to strengthen soldierly qualities and to develop a spirit of defense-mindedness (*Wehrhaftigheit*). The whole athletic program displays the same purposefulness, even in play. Roughly, two things are demanded of a game: it must develop the muscles and it must be a *Kampfsport*, i.e., it must give ample scope for the fighting spirit.

Such principles have been uniformly enforced throughout all the grades and in all the schools. The craving for uniformity has abolished private schools and denominational institutions, has guaranteed the extermination of every source of educational opposition (such as the family), and has taken complete control of the nation's youth. "We will not permit them to lapse into old ways of thinking, but will give them thorough training. We will take them when they are ten years old and train them in the spirit of the community until they are 18. They shall not escape us. They will join the party, the S.A., the S.S., or other formations"—thus goes the official version.

The emergence of a new generation of Nazi leaders is not left to chance. For this purpose special training schools, the Napolas (*Nationalpolitische Erziehungsanstalten*) were established early in 1933. A strange mixture of British public schools and the Prussian cadet schools of pre-war time, very selective in accordance with Nazi principles, these schools have in a way been a disappointment to the party. Five years later an additional group of fifteen *Fuehrerschulen* was established—a scheme that does honor to the frenzy of organization. The training of the future "political elite" begins at the age of twelve, continues for the select until they are eighteen; then they are taken into labor camp, army, university or professional school. Finally, when they are about twenty-five those selected are enrolled for a series of *Ordensburgen* which are to train the "chosen men" for the next four years and which lead to the "pinnacle of Nazi education"—a school which will be under the direction of Alfred Rosenberg, great mogul of Nazi *Kultur*. It will take seventeen years before the results of this gigantic scheme can be seen—if history allows such an experiment to develop.

It is altogether too early to make any definite appraisal of the effect of this "education in uniform." Undoubtedly dictatorships may feel confident in relying on the old Jesuit maxim: "Give us the first five years of a child's life and do with him as you like after that," especially since they are determined to hold him under their control all his life. Foes of these systems may be no less alarmed by the degree of indoctrination that has already been instilled into youth under dictatorship. Even its eventual defeat may not do away with the corruption of mind, the hatred and perversion, the aggressiveness and dream of power which have been systematically built up in a susceptible young generation. No better may fare youth which finds itself in bitter opposition to the system. Without any hope for decisive change, desperate young often regard utter cynicism as the only avenue of escape. Yet there may well be another side to this picture. Dictators may sense the paradox of an educational system that requires blind and unquestioning obedience and still expects to produce a new generation of great leaders. Democrats may pin their hope on the "ever-present creativeness of the human mind" and its natural vitality which has survived greater spiritual crises.

FEAR AS A POLITICAL WEAPON

The institutional framework, including the whole gamut of social and political organizations, is held together by a "system of interlocking fears." There are force and terror in every revolution, especially in its initial stages; but what differentiates the

20th-century pattern of world revolution from all earlier and more primitive models is the development of organized terror and its systematization into a strategy of frightfulness. This institutionalization somehow epitomizes the new type of full-grown revolution; it succeeds in prolonging the revolutionary spirit and channelizing the emotional outbreaks. It may thus preserve a continuous climax for the permanent revolution. It may even counteract a revolutionary cycle that threatens to lead to a Ninth Thermidor. Leading Bolshevists have often been said to be worried about these revolutionary prospects. In order to avoid the possibility that the terror created by the revolutionaries might finally catch up with its originators, modern dictatorships have institutionalized terror in the creation of the secret police. The two G's—the Gestapo and the G.P.U. (the relatively undeveloped Italian secret police may be omitted from a systematic consideration)—are no doubt the most powerful institutions guaranteeing the "preservation" of the system and the "loyalty" of its citizens.

The power of the omnipresent secret police and the efficiency of its machinery have often been described by eyewitnesses who escaped "out of the night." The systematic cruelty of its procedures has been movingly told "beyond tears." Hence no repetition is needed here. What should be stated in this connection, however, are a few basic principles that underlie fear as a political weapon. In the first place, modern dictatorships have discovered the time-honored principle that fear is one of the most essential guides for human behavior. It is fear, according to Hobbes, that forces the human being into the social contract. It makes him accept the coercion of the all-powerful absolute state. This pessimistic philosophy of mankind has found its optimistic counter in such social philosophers as Herbert Spencer, Gumplowicz, Ratzenhofer, Oppenheimer, and Lester Ward, who regard fear of enemies and war as the most important factor in social integration. Spencer even went so far as to translate the struggle for existence which involves "fear of living" and leads to civil and military organization and control, into the realm of the unknown where "fear of the dead" becomes the basis of religious control. Thus the importance of fear as an organizing principle in society is nothing new. But what dictatorships realize is that if a certain degree of horror is reached, man's physical resistance and moral personality vanish. Such a process can be advanced especially well in a time of unrest, the aftermath of a war, the breakdown of economic security, and the destruction of social institutions. A strategy of terror applied against the crisis strata of society may accomplish miracles, and has done so in the establishment and preservation of modern dictatorships.

While the exploitation of latent weaknesses represents a permanent threat to ordered society, the threat can be realized only if a group can be found within the community ready to use this weapon. For this reason one of the essential considerations in interpreting the strategy of terror must refer to the terrorists themselves and their basic motives. Modern abnormal psychology has analyzed most poignantly the effects of frustration and aggression. The rise of modern dictatorships no doubt can be well described in terms of such an interrelation. The origin of these movements is closely connected with specifically aggressive types that have grown up in a climate of world war and post-war unrest. Yet these irregulars, important as they are as the vanguard of revolutionary movements, do not represent the body of the revolutionary army. Large groups in society have to be dislodged in social status and frustrated in their major expectations in order to be ready to accept the promises of a "new order."

The pathological nature of the psychological make-up of leading dictators and their lieutenants has often been described by experts. Modern psychological methods certainly help to give depth to such pictures. There is a whole literature that explains contemporary dictatorships in terms of abnormal psychology: masterful biographical studies like Heiden's *Hitler*, comprehensive picturizations of the whole circle of post-war leaders by shrewd observers like John Gunther, and ingenious psychological analyses by such students as H. D. Lasswell. Studies of this kind often reveal the roots of personal motivations. Specific experiences in early childhood—isolation, loneliness, etc.—make a deep impression on a sensitive personality. It should be realized, however, that unless such illuminating details about personalities are used as skillfully as the above authors have used them, they may lead to unsound psychoanalytic notions. The German Empire, for instance, did not break down because William II had a short left arm and, because of it, an inferiority complex that had to be compensated for by power. Neither can post-war dictators be explained in terms of an Oedipus complex. Even liberal democratic leaders like Masaryk adore their mothers; dictators are not unique in this trait.

The rise of modern dictatorships is no doubt closely related to an abnormal climate of personal and social tensions that invites the liberation of frustration by aggression. This phenomenon has frequently been observed in the field of modern criminology. In fact, juvenile delinquency has often been explained, with some overemphasis, as the compensation of an inferiority complex by introverts. While delinquents can thus be dealt with through psychiatric treatment which reinstitutes them into social groups and rehabilitates them by providing prestige and a sense of belonging, unfortunately the marginal man in political society can sometimes engage the insecure marginal groups and thus exploit a revolutionary situation.

An interesting phenomenon in recent revolutions is the fact that these latent weapons are resorted to as a defense mechanism. The story of Fascism after the Matteotti affair is a perfect example of such a procedure. Matteotti, an outstanding leader of the Socialist opposition in the Italian parliament of 1924, in commenting on the pressure politics notoriously applied by Fascist militia in the recent election, said in his last speech: "Do you not remember that the government itself declared that the elections had only a relative value? The honorable Mussolini said that the government did not feel itself subject to the response of the elections and let it be understood that even in case of want of success he would keep the power by armed force." These words were received, according to the semi-official report of the *Corriere della Sera* (May 31, 1924), with an ovation from a large part of the House

and a confirming nod by the President of the Council. Matteotti
concluded his statement with the warning that he knew he would
not survive such a declaration. He was found murdered a few days
later, and even Mussolini soon had to admit that leading Fascist
agents, especially Philipelli (editor of the Fascist *Corriere Italiana*), had committed the crime. The Matteotti crisis created such
a devastating reaction all over the country that it almost spelled
the end of Fascist rule. It was in this critical situation that Fascism
really seized the power and became a totalitarian system. In order
to "survive," it had to secure the all-inclusive control of all agencies. Out of fear for their own survival, Fascist leaders systematized their terroristic tactics. The result was the creation of
an atmosphere which the Fascist *Epoca* described as one of "moral
hygiene" and which the then anti-Fascist *Tribuna* characterized as
"thick with violence and rancors." Similar reactions can be seen
clearly in other dictatorships. In fact, the purges in Nazi Germany
in June, 1934, and the mass trials in Soviet Russia in the late '30's
were no less the result of a consuming fear on the part of the
ruling elite.

One may follow the often-tried techniques of modern crimi-
nologists in analyzing the effects of terror on the terrorists themselves. It has often been said that force deteriorates the person
using it more than it does the victim. One can also observe specific
weaknesses "of the trade." The secret police has to cultivate mistrust and in doing so terror is automatically multiplied. The suspect is guilty. And who is not a potential suspect in a system that
is based more on constraint than on consent? Even the legal
machinery of most dictatorships follows this concept of making
"intended crime" punishable. The *Münchner Neueste Nachrichten*
of January 28, 1939, brought out a significant article on "The
Rising Generation of Police Leaders" which stated that "the way
of the security police [a mild expression for the Gestapo] leads
more often than not from the evildoer to the evil deed, whereas
the criminal police takes a crime as the point of departure to look
for the criminal." It is, therefore, the ideal procedure for a dictatorship to find definite scapegoat classes. But it cannot stop at

this. The totalitarian state, as such, has to develop an atmosphere "of vague though ever omnipresent terror." This fact faces the system with an obvious dilemma. While it has to impress the general public with its all-inclusive control and intimidating sternness, its efficiency depends on the creation of a cheerful readiness of seemingly free people. This obvious difficulty explains why the "scientific terror" of the modern dictatorship has to be much more subtle than the cruelty of earlier primitive types of revolutions, and more insidious than the present-day reports on open terrorism seem to indicate to the outside world. Every dictatorship is eager to create the impression of seeming normalcy essential not only to visitors from foreign countries but to its own citizens.

Yet the survival of the system depends on institutionalized terror. "If well-substantiated reports are to be believed, the Gestapo holds even Reich ministers and members of the inner party directorate under close watch. The state is controlled by the party, but the party is controlled by the Gestapo. The political police is today in Germany the innermost core of power." One may refer to the report of Miss Forbes, an English journalist, of her visit with Hitler and Goering a few years ago. When she flattered Goering in saying, "I am sure you are afraid of nobody, Your Excellency," Hitler smilingly asked, "What about Himmler?"

The strategy of terror is well known today in the field of international affairs, but it had been definitely blocked out in internal politics long before, and has developed through clear-cut stages. It starts with a threat which, of course, may often be a bluff that has not been called. The entire history of Italian Fascism is typified by these tactics. The war of nerves, the psychological terror, used with such great success in the conquest of other nations and showing the same clever mixture of intimidation and appeasement, had been applied in internal politics much earlier. The promise of a share in the profits and the exploitation of man's natural endeavor to be on the winning side are mixed with the threat of inescapable punishment for the stubborn opponent who does not conform with the victorious movement.

In the second stage, the threat is carried further to initial demonstration. This is a well-known tactic in international affairs today. Airplanes over the capitals of countries that are "to be coordinated" serve as a familiar warning, as did the castor-oil tactics of early Fascism.

The last stage is the "war in earnest." There is no doubt that dictatorships would like to avoid this stage if they could subdue the enemy with the softening tactics of the initial steps. Even if they have to apply this third degree of terror, they can often confine their activities to hostages. Threatened punishment has a tremendous effect. This policy is based upon the often-proved principle that the "man of today is ready to die, but he is deeply afraid of suffering." The result is that the political police can succeed in subduing a large country with relatively small effort, especially since its acts are outside the normal channels of legal procedure. While the essence of a police lies in the fact that it serves only as an executive organ for well-defined legal areas, the secret police is empowered "to uncover and combat all tendencies and developments inimical to the state and to take for this end all measures deemed necessary and expedient" (law of February, 1936).

Though the secret police might thus be regarded as the core of dictatorial power, it would be wrong to see in these activities the only attempt to control the nation as a whole. Dictatorships realized from the beginning that, in addition to such negative checks, a positive attempt had to be made to win over the country thus conquered because "you can do almost anything with bayonets, but you can't sit on them."

Chapter VII

THE CONTROL OF THE MASSES:
PUBLIC OPINION AND PROPAGANDA

_ _

PROPAGANDA: SOME MISCONCEPTIONS

Wherever human society exists there is propaganda, i.e., a "conscious attempt to control the attitudes of others and consequently to manage their actions." It has always played an important role in politics. Governments have invariably recognized their dependence upon public opinion, and have therefore realized the import of opinion leadership.

"It is on opinion only that governments are founded." This dictum of David Hume has been equally respected by democracies and dictatorships. We are living in an age of propaganda. Public opinion and propaganda undoubtedly represent vital issues of daily social and political life in democracies as well as in dictatorships. Numerous are the learned studies, more numerous are the popular treatises, and most prevalent, unfortunately, are the popular misconceptions concerning the nature of public opinion and propaganda. Among the last is the conviction that propaganda is the invention of modern dictatorial government and that there are no limits to its successful use by propaganda ministries. Such generalizations are wrong.

Another frequent misconception holds that public opinion, being defined as "the sum total of the popular reaction to any concrete problem at any given time," presupposes public discussions and for this reason is non-existent in dictatorship. Although public opinion cannot find free and unhampered expression under dictatorial government, dictators still have to reckon with public reaction. Modern autocracies cannot rely upon fear alone and upon a negative policy of repression. The victor's greatest feat is not to vanquish his enemies, but to make them sing his praises. Because modern dictatorships develop an atmosphere of stifled public opinion which does not give free expression to grievances, they must diagnose the "people's soul" with almost scientific precision. Ministries of propaganda have the twofold function of propagandizing the faith and serving as a listening post. With an ear to the ground, they must sense dissension before it grows to revolutionary dimensions.

Propaganda becomes a necessity for the survival of the dictatorial system. This, however, should not mislead public opinion in democracies, as it so often does, into regarding propaganda as a phenomenon of dictatorship alone. Such considerations erroneously associate the word "propaganda" with a necessarily insidious meaning: "All propaganda is lies," "He is just a propagandist," etc. As a matter of fact, slogans about the menace of demagogical propaganda contribute to the confusion and intensify the insecurities that threaten democratic government. Propaganda probably is often the clandestine dissemination of ideas and information for the purpose of helping or injuring a person or institution; but not all propaganda is vicious or unjustified.

This frequent identification of propaganda with "the bad cause" becomes especially dangerous if it is tied up with another conviction—that there are no limits to its success. It easily becomes a coward's counsel, thus leaving the field to the "enemy." The war of nerves—as spectacularly demonstrated in international exploits—is based not least upon this precipitous surrender to the master minds of mass seduction. No doubt, skill in propaganda has become one of the most effective roads to power in modern times. Yet in order to exert influence, this modern magician must answer (justly or not) grievances which people profoundly feel; at least, he must break down their resistance against his inducements.

In this respect, political propaganda is no more miraculous than commercial advertising, and in the long run depends for its success or failure on similar conditions. It has to supply a need (misleading though its solution may be). It has to find a market. It certainly does not have unlimited possibilities.

Equally dangerous and resulting from the same one-sided though convenient definition of propaganda, is another popular advice: to become propaganda-wise. In fact, the trade-mark of the enlightened, the mature, the sophisticated has become their ability not to "fall for" propagandist schemes.

Healthy criticism and training in critical ability are undoubtedly necessary tools for the growing and alert mind. Yet the modern American indoor sport—discovering one's neighbor's "propaganda," and especially the politician's real motives behind his actions—and finding them false, is based on the preconception that everyone is wearing a mask.

This prevalent belief, which makes propaganda nothing but deceit and a cynic's game, reflects a most serious trend of thought that has transformed a world of ideas into mere ideologies. What began and undoubtedly still serves as a fruitful technique of critical analysis (cutting through the surface of misleading formulas, derivations, pretenses—consciously or not—to the real motivations of actions and reactions) became, by the time Marx and Pareto were brought down to the common man's lingo, absolute mistrust in human sincerity and in a world of values.

Being "propaganda-wise," therefore, does not mean careful consideration of the worth-while findings of semantics and of recent research in public opinion techniques, or the recovery of time-honored logical thinking. It is the naïve belief that the "danger of propaganda" can be met by the clever application of six or seven simple devices, or, what is worse, that it may be nothing but a skeptic's credo. *Pilatus redivivus* falls easily into the hands of unscrupulous masters of modern propaganda machines.

It may be well to remember that the word propaganda in its original meaning derived from the College of Propaganda which was instituted by Urban VIII in the early 17th century to educate priests for missions, to propagate the faith. To stand on its convictions is no less the final test of effective propaganda today.

Propaganda as such is neither a modern invention of dictatorial machinations, nor is it invincible black magic. What is new (and therefore justifies an extraordinary interest in this phenomenon) is the scope and intensity of propaganda made possible by the spread of literacy and the miraculous improvements in the means of communication. Modern communication is characterized by its unheard-of ability to establish contacts. From the physical assembly in early times, in the church and the town meeting, in the pub and the country store, to the world-wide dimensions of modern means of communication, there has been a constant enlargement in the size of the audience. By now it is practically unlimited. About 2000 newspapers with a daily circulation of almost 40,000,000 copies are published in the United States; 100,000,000 people attend motion picture performances each week; the audience served by American broadcasting systems comprises about 20,000,000 families.

Not alone has the development of the means of communication in volume and under conditions hitherto unknown served to focus attention on the subject of propaganda; there is also the rise of modern mass democracy. In former times the opinions of relatively small publics were a prime force in political life. Now, for the first time in history, we are confronted nearly everywhere by mass opinion as the final determinant of political and economic action in democracies and even in "post-democratic" dictatorships.

The abundance of information and misinformation in itself demands an increasing degree of selectivity on the part of democracy's responsible citizens. Indeed, the constant need for forming opinions cannot keep pace with the supply of information on which opinions are demanded. The greater the supply, the more difficult it may easily become to form balanced opinions. Yet this is a vital problem for democracy, for its stability depends primarily on the development of a public opinion able to cope intelligently with the problems of our day. In fact, the pioneer farmer of a century ago was probably much better informed on the problems of his age than are many well-educated people nowadays on the issues that face our civilization.

But it is not only a complex society in which we are living. It is a society which because of war and post-war disturbances calls for a new orientation and for new methods of propaganda. Public opinion is raised to its highest intensity when old patterns of behavior are breaking down. People are ready to accept new ideas. They are open to suggestion; they are receptive to propaganda.

PROPAGANDA FOR WHOM?

Propaganda does not function in a social vacuum. It is always addressed to a specific public with specific needs. It has to be appropriate to specific conditions and, if successful, it may in turn influence its public specifically.

The study of propaganda, properly applied, may thus serve as a key toward an understanding not so much of the "trickeries of modern myth-makers" as of the vital forces that condition the success or failure of such propaganda.

The coordination of propaganda with the public to whom it is directed is somewhat shrouded by a purposeful ambiguity often commented upon by cognizant observers of modern mass movements. Says Lasswell: "A high degree of generality is essential to popular appeal. Symbols must be sufficiently vague to enable the individual to transfer his private loves and hates and hopes and fears to the slogans and catchwords of the movement."

The victorious revolutions in contemporary Europe give ample proof of such shrewd tactics. The great success of National Socialism largely rests upon its clever variations in propaganda appeal for different social groups. Most divergent, as a matter of course, were the images presented and the expectations aroused in the appeal to the Rhenish heavy industry and the proletarian masses of Berlin North, to the landed aristocracy in East Elbia and the small peasantry in southwestern Germany, to an idealistic youth movement and a hopeless unemployed. Similar variations may be observed in the Fascist beginnings in Italy in regard to the industrial Po Valley and the agrarian south.

In spite of such tactical maneuvers, there is no denying that modern dictatorships aimed their propaganda, above all, at the "conquest of the man in the street." In fact, an analysis of propaganda in dictatorship necessarily leads to an interpretation of the lowest stratum of dictatorial society, the basis of the dictatorial pyramid. The manipulators of dictatorial propaganda realize the differentiation between public enlightenment of the party members and "education" of the masses. In refuting the criticism of Papen, by then Vice Chancellor, concerning the "too enthusiastic young revolutionaries" (a speech which, incidentally, touched off the June purge of 1934), Goebbels himself said that "only members of the National Socialist party have the right to criticize. I deny the right to all others. Further, I do not consider it expedient that doubts arising in the controlling stratum [that of National Socialism] should be ventilated in public."

Dictatorial propaganda is addressed to the "mass" man especially, since he shifts the balance of decision in a mass state. National Socialist philippics against the stubborn intelligentsia have, above all, the function of devaluating the prestige that has been accepted even by the masses. Since "the people" become the master of political decision, the level of political argumentation has to be brought down to the marginal customer of political ideas. Since these masses, particularly according to the dictatorial interpretation presented above, are moved less by rational standards than by emotional drives, the character of the propaganda will be determined accordingly. Of course, the context of the social structure in different countries leads to differentiation, even within the masses, and thus to varied approaches for dictatorial propaganda. It has to fit itself into the social pattern prevalent at the time of its emergence. A country trained in militarist traditions lends itself to different patterns of dictatorial devices than those a clever demagoguery may employ in a nation of baseball fans and ice cream soda drinkers. There are great differences even in national gregariousness. Dictatorial attack, therefore, will use different devices in different social climates.

The short history of modern dictatorship, however, proves that this political system flourishes in an atmosphere of the amorphous masses. Dictatorship stands for equality—an equality of a sort that is revealed in the often-told story of the tyrant of Corinth. One day he asked the tyrant of Miletus, who was walking with him through the fields, to give him some advice concerning the art of government. The tyrant of Miletus vouchsafed no answer, but proceeded to strike off the ears of corn that had outtopped their fellows.

Equality is best stabilized at the *tabula rasa*, the point of illiteracy. As stratified society cannot be handled so easily, its traditions have to be destroyed. In this respect, the U.S.S.R. is in a unique position. Her people have begun to learn to read under the new regime, and hence they can learn the "right"—that is, the Communist—spelling.

Propaganda as a social phenomenon is one of the various devices designed to routinize and ritualize human behavior. The procedures of laws and customs, education and religious teaching are outstanding attempts to create in human society a frame of reference which guarantees specific standards of life and a degree of expectancy in social behavior. These attempts are necessary to bring order into the chaotic world of human beings. To put propaganda in such distinguished company may not be justified by the actual performances of what is usually classified as "propaganda," but it indicates the importance and the necessary function of its much-despised activities.

Numerous attempts have been made to find a clear-cut distinction between *education* and *propaganda*. The latter has been defined as the spread of controversial attitudes; the former, as the spread of axiomatic facts, accepted attitudes, and skills. (Such a definition, if accepted, clearly shows the historic context of propaganda and education. As time goes on, the two may change their conceptual boundaries). Furthermore, it has been said that education aims at independence of judgment, while propaganda offers ready-made opinions. In this sense the educator aims at a slow process of development, the propagandist at quick results. The educator tries to tell people *how* to think; the propagandist, *what* to think. The educator strives to develop individual responsibility;

the propagandist, to develop mass effects. The educator fails unless he achieves an open mind; the propagandist fails unless he achieves a closed mind. More careful analyses have circumscribed as the realm of education the fundamental molding of the human being, and as the endeavor of propaganda the direction of man toward particular action (or inaction). It has finally been stated that the function of the educator is to expand the jurisdiction of reason, and that of the propagandist is to rationalize emotional hungers.

Such descriptions are indeed very illuminating in respect to many modern developments. However, a distinction between education and propaganda cannot always be made in reality. What may be accepted as education in one country will be regarded as typical propaganda in another that has a different set of social values. Because of this fluidity it hardly matters whether management of public opinion is called education or propaganda.

More important, though equally difficult, seems to be the differentiation between *propaganda in dictatorships and in democracies*. The essential distinction centers around the monopoly of propaganda in dictatorships as compared with the competition of propagandists in democratic systems. Every propaganda undoubtedly attempts to create homogeneity among its followers. Democratic propaganda, however, has to reckon with the existence and interference of counterpropaganda and thus for propagandist reasons it has to adjust itself to the competitive scheme. Dictatorial propaganda not only may strive for uniformity, but can presuppose its unchallenged position before it attacks the human mind. True, in its revolutionary phase it has to stand up against other competitive agents. Yet even before the monopoly of propaganda is achieved in the established dictatorship, its patterns for managing public opinion are coined in a monolithic scheme. Just as the revolutionary party represents a state within the state, so its propaganda isolates the party adherents. It suppresses open discussions with the opponent and makes the party meeting nothing but the self-expression of the movement's will, a demonstration of the unity and unbroken warlike spirit of the party.

In a way every effective propaganda is aimed not so much at objective truth as at the advancement of a specific interest; therefore it approaches its victims dogmatically. But propaganda in democracies is confronted with competing systems in the free market of opinion dissemination. In fact, the trust in a final harmony that is almost automatically established through free competition in the body politic becomes as much of an axiom in democracy's propaganda as is the underlying belief in a liberal laissez-faire economy. There is no need to mention that in modern society definite limitations are met to unhampered competition and specifically to "freedom in the opinion industries" which presupposes equality of bargaining power. It may be advisable, for instance, to consider rules and even curbs against unfair propaganda practices in the new race for opinion control (so significant in modern psychological warfare). Yet, granted all shortcomings, democracy's public relations management insists upon the maximum opportunity for competitive schemes as the best guarantee for an enlightened public opinion. This policy, of course, presupposes another basic assumption underlying the whole philosophy of democracy—that of an essentially rational following open to reasonable argument and able to evaluate through sober consideration.

Dictatorship's concept of the masses, as analyzed above, runs counter to such expectations. It views human beings as undecided and uncertain, in bitter need of strong leadership that will force upon them uncompromising conclusions. And what is even more important, according to the modern dictator's vade mecum, the masses are moved not by reason but by sentiment alone. Primitive raw feelings—black or white, hate or love—must be evoked by dictatorial thought control. Truth is whatever intensifies passion. Propaganda becomes a master technique for collective hypnosis. Not accidentally does the age of the "organization of the masses" coincide with the discovery of the subconscious. Freud and

Adler gave useful weapons to the "editors" of the new totalitarian mind.

No less important for the success of dictatorial mass management is the actual transformation of society. The modern process of urbanization and mechanization led to the emergence of the masses; it destroyed organized groups and isolated the individual. The desire for a new security and group life could be answered by the promises of a new National Socialist community. While National Socialism thus appealed to an amorphous metropolitan population, it had to use different tactics in the rural areas where social groups were still intact. (The major appeal in these provinces, significantly enough, centered around concrete promises to raise the price of corn and cattle.)

The alarming loneliness of the individual in the modern machine age, overwhelmed and suffocated by the masses and degraded to a number in monster concerns and enterprises, is made an asset in the Fascist arsenal. In fact, it answers, though in a distorted manner, an essential desire of modern man. William Hocking has referred to the importance of what he calls the "commotive function," that is, the will to an active social unity in present-day society. This trend toward a stronger social unity and centralized authority is "not a temporary palliative for a passing disorder but a new stage which will remain." One may even be prepared to recognize the appeal that modern dictatorship possesses because of its commotive impulse making for national unity and action. But because of the recognition of the blind spot in the laissez-faire conception of a pre-dictatorial liberalism and hence the negative strength of the new dictatorial systems, one may also be able to point out the latter's fundamental blunders. "The perfect national and social unity of modern dictatorship is a unity of the drill squad, not of thinking beings. . . . A unity of individuals who do not think ceases to be a unity and tends to become a pure monologue and monodeed." The challenge of the modern state still persists in its attempts to create a strong social unity without mutilating the "incompressible individual." As long as modern democracy misled by an atomistic tradition does not succeed in creating this we-feeling, dictatorship's propaganda has a fertile ground. "Resocialization of adults" becomes a paramount function of modern society and a central task of its propaganda. Democracy no less than dictatorship can afford to disregard such a challenge, especially since democracy's opponent has the edge on it.

Propaganda in modern dictatorships is directed toward a complete homogeneity which finds its symbolic expression in putting its members into uniforms. It is not satisfied to create unanimity among the believers; it also strives to transform its adherents from spectators into participants. It is this call to action that appeals to a restless, dynamic young generation. It is this active belief that also creates the specific techniques of modern dictatorships.

TECHNIQUES OF TOTALITARIAN CONTROL

"Propaganda in itself," Goebbels says in his autobiographical *Struggle for Berlin*, "has no fundamental method. It has only a purpose—the conquest of the masses. Every means that serves this end is good." The master propagandist has certainly followed this rule. Such a statement also cautions against a common error: seeing in dictatorship's control of the masses a mere catalogue of tricky devices. It is amazing, however, to observe the degree of systematization that the rule of the modern soul engineers has achieved. Its power and unity derive not only from a definite evaluation of the masses and a dogmatic image of man, but also from the all-embracing organization of public relations management—secret of totalitarian success everywhere.

All dictatorial countries have organized an extensive *machinery* for public opinion control. This has been done most systematically by the German Ministry of Public Enlightenment and Propaganda. Other dictatorships developed similar agencies such as the Glaspolitprosvet of the U.S.S.R. (the main political education committee) and the Undersecretaryship for Propaganda in Italy.

The organization of Germany's cultural activities under Goebbels' leadership borrowed heavily from earlier Fascist attempts (i.e., the Roll of Journalists Decree, February 20, 1928). All cultural activities are organized by public law into a corporation of professions. Entry is strictly controlled by statute. Detailed legislation lays down codes of professional behavior, departure from which may lead to permanent exclusion from membership in the profession. This guarantees not only centralization of power but at the same time the mobilization of the whole field of national culture. A special order in March, 1933, to the German press on the aims of the Ministry of Public Enlightenment and Propaganda stated: "The modern leaders of the people must be the modern kings of the people. They must understand the masses. It is their task to make clear to the people what they desire and to see that they are understood." The decree of June 30, 1933, set up the new ministry in the following terms: "The Reich Ministry of Public Enlightenment and Propaganda is responsible for all factors influencing the mental life of the nation. It is responsible for winning allegiance to the state, its culture, and its economy, for the conduct of internal publicity, and for the administration of all institutions contributing to these ends." This definition of the new ministry's aims shows its all-inclusiveness and its virtually unlimited power over all agencies of communication and dissemination of opinion.

To illustrate specifically the control of the main channels of public opinion the Journalists Act of October 4, 1933, may be cited. According to its regulations, "Only German citizens, i.e., non-Jews, and only those who are friendly to the regime are eligible for membership in the national newspaper federation. All must be registered with the state organization, subject to a veto by the local officials and the Minister of Public Enlightenment and Propaganda. The director of the national association is appointed by Dr. Goebbels, as are the members of the professional courts. Registration may be cancelled and publication suspended for a variety of reasons, among which the following are especially significant: publication of anything which (1) confuses selfish with common interests in a manner misleading to the public, (2) is able to weaken the strength of the German nation, nationally or internationally, the will toward unity of the

German nation, German defensive ability, German culture, or German business, or that will hurt the religious feelings of others, (3) is offensive to the honor and dignity of a German, (4) illegally injures the honor or well-being of another person, hurts his reputation, or makes him ridiculous or despicable, (5) is for other reasons indecent." The interpretation of these vague phrases is left to the ruling hierarchy of the profession and the party under daily instructions from Berlin.

This complete control and censorship of the press has undoubtedly led not only to the end of "freedom of the press" but also to a decline of public interest in newspapers. The extraordinary drop in newspaper circulation is indicative of such a change. Even the official declaration of the Minister—"We want no opinionated nonsense. We want frank and honorable utterances. The press will now be monoform in will and polyform in the expression of that will"—has not made newspaper discussions alive, especially since the few papers which took this statement seriously had to pay dearly for their venture.

It may be mentioned that this complete control which has made no concessions at all to the journalists has not succeeded as well in other fields, such as motion picture production and the arts and literature. Stringent control leads to the drying up of the productive stream. There have been interesting examples of the circumvention of this all-powerful control by the use of vague terminology and symbolic intimidation. In general, however, the absence of any instrument of dissenting opinion makes it impossible to measure the amount of consent. The screen of compulsory acquiescence veils the actual status of the public mind.

The thorough and efficient organization of public opinion control, an extremely potent instrument in the hands of purposeful potentates, has been geared for quick action through painstaking and perfected propaganda *techniques*. The methods employed by modern dictatorships are not at all novel, as close students of propaganda have abundantly shown. Basic principles have been borrowed from centuries-old experiences of the Catholic church, from the more recent techniques in World War I, from Bolshevist arsenals, and, not least, from the treasury of American commercial advertising, revamped and systematized for use in politics. It may be worth while from time to time to take stock of prevalent expedients, as the Institute for Propaganda Analysis has done recently. Yet such a well-known catalogue of the seven principal devices of modern propagandists—name-calling, glittering generalities, transfer device, testimonials, plain-folk device, card-stacking, and band-wagon technique—may easily become a meaningless name-calling of glittering generalities. What concerns the analyst of public opinion beyond this preliminary classification is the query: where and why particular techniques succeed and what they stand for. The aim and addressee of propaganda, after all, are more significant in weighing public opinion than the methods applied, adroit and resourceful though they may be. Of course, means often reflect and indeed shape ends. In this sense, a study of techniques may well penetrate the surface of mass management, thus revealing the core of the body politic.

Dictatorship in the mass age is primarily directed at the masses. Its propaganda principles are shaped accordingly. Firmly established maxims of modern publicity serve as basic patterns—in particular, repetition and simplification.

The individual's social behavior, says Walter Lippmann, is conditioned by "the pictures in the head," most of which become highly stereotyped. *Repetition* is therefore one of the secrets of modern propaganda. Continuity and absolute uniformity of statement promise success in advertising. Popular autocracies simply apply this proved practice to their purpose. In the words of Hitler, "The masses with their inertia always need a certain time before they are ready even to notice a thing, and they will lend their memories only to the thousandfold repetition of the most simple ideas." From this follows the well-known Goebbels technique: "The intellectuals say that the more often a theme is presented, the less interested is the public. This is not true. When one possesses the talent for finding ever new forms of proof, ever more Draconic and sharper arguments, then the public will not lose interest. On the contrary, its interest will increase." Such a device parallels the familiar psychological formula of "flogging the dead horse." The solemn reiteration by the propagandist of what his listener already firmly believes is an effective method used in the daily newspapers. Even the introduction of new elements in public opinion development will be connected with familiar experiences of the reader in order to arouse his interest.

The appeal to the masses is no less visible in the second principle of dictatorial propaganda: *simplification*. The intelligentsia is not important; the average man is, because he holds the balance of power; hence the common man must understand. Demagogical agitation is based upon the conviction that the great masses' receptive ability is limited and their understanding is small. All effective propaganda, therefore, has to confine itself to a few points which must be repeated eternally.

Besides these general principles of repetition and simplification, there are of course more specific techniques of demagogical propaganda, among which is the *personification of politics*. Follow the leader, not an abstract program! Fight living individuals, not theoretical principles! The enemy is personified. A visible group that can be pointed at in the streets is singled out—the kulak, the Jew, the Trotskyist. Politics is thus simplified and made more appealing to the masses. Here is the place for "name-calling," the frequently mentioned device of successful propaganda. No less significant is concentration on the stirring up of hatred. It is, indeed, a most disturbing phenomenon (especially obvious in a society which has undergone war and civil war strife) that the spectacle of cruelty becomes an efficient instrument for mass agitation.

Pictures and human interest stories win the masses. The two great agencies of our democratic age, the newspapers and the movies, have prepared the way and developed the methods which have been applied so skillfully by modern demagogues. The big eye has to be caught, the great heart aroused; then the small mind will follow. The appeal to emotions is the expedient in the manipulation of the rootless masses.

The irrational approach may also be observed in the next

principle of demagogical propaganda. It may be called the law of the *psychological situation*. Modern demagogues take special care to build up a whole technique in this field. What is astonishing is the outspoken bluntness with which they advise their henchmen. They do not mind letting their followers look behind the curtain of demagogical domination. Such participation does not diminish its effectiveness. By revealing the secrets of their system they make its victims share in it and make them admire the efficiency of these methods. Some frank suggestions can be found in Hitler's *Mein Kampf*. "The hour of the day at which an address is delivered has a deciding influence on the effect of the address. Fine oratory by a dominant apostolic character will be more successful in the evening in inducing men whose power of resistance is by that late hour sensibly weakened than men who are in full possession of their energy of mind and volition."

Mass meetings guarantee this psychological effect by the simple fact of numbers. "Mass assemblies are necessary because while attending them the individual who feels on the point of joining a movement and takes alarm if left by himself receives his first impression of a large community. He submits himself to the magic influence of what we call mass suggestion."

The fact of increasing mass demonstrations has undoubtedly completely altered the character of political movements. Rational argumentation has lost ground and emotionalism has taken its place in the mass assembly. Far-sighted democratic party leaders have been aware of such changes in the political climate, yet have been able to make only haphazard adjustments at best.

The Great Rally—mass meetings, harvest festivals, and, greatest of all, the Nuremberg Party Congress—is a natural climate for demagogical dictatorship. Hadamovsky, a leading propaganda expert of the Third Reich, declares: "The most effective form of mass demonstration is the visible exhibition of power, i.e., the number of participants, the size of the meeting, and all that which demonstrates power, for instance, armed people, people in uniform, weapons of all kinds."

From such a statement, it takes only one step to conclude that "propaganda and force are never absolutely opposed to each other. The using of force can be part of the propaganda. Between them lie different grades of effectively influencing people and masses: from the sudden excitement, the attention, the friendly persuasion of the individual to incessant mass propaganda; from the loose organizing of convinced people to the creation of semi-official or official institutions; from individual terror to mass terror; from the authorized use of the force of the stronger one, i.e., the class or state, to the military enforcement of obedience and discipline through the death penalty."

"In the long run the average man is impressed only by force and discipline," says Goebbels.

This technique has become a familiar procedure in winning allies in international affairs. (The showing of the Nazi film, *Baptism of Fire*, has regularly preceded the successful conclusion of trade agreements and political treaties with foreign powers.) Long before, however, it was a proved method in internal politics as well, though the outside world has become aware of this "propaganda by force" only recently.

As long as arms cannot talk, the *spoken word* is respected as a powerful weapon for demagogical propaganda and, in fact, is much preferred to written propaganda. A hundred years ago Victor Hugo said: "Architecture is dead, dead forever. The printed book killed it. The great epos of mankind will not be written in stone, but in words." These predictions seemed to have come true in an age when knowledge was power and knowledge became almost identified with printed matter. He who wanted to make himself heard had to do it in print. But with the victory of the printed word, the mistrust against it rose. The printed word engendered criticism; criticism aroused mistrust. Furthermore, the printed word became effective in ever-widening circles, until the ideas underlying it were accepted as platitudes.

Thus the printed word itself is partly to blame for its own devaluation. In addition, the spoken word came to take its place. The popular orator with his direct and simplifying formulas pushed aside the printed word. Modern life has become so immense and incalculable, so complicated and differentiated that people are grateful to have it interpreted in a simple manner that does not involve too much intellectual exertion on their part. The possibilities of renouncing all intellectual ballast, all spiritual preconceptions brought about a new age of rhetoric. Rhetoric is a modern form of slavery. The masses—liberated in the last century to a literate existence—have remained intellectually illiterate. Motion pictures are their chief agent of entertainment. Even the books they read are written in a movie-like manner. Impressionistic and full of action, they appeal to the senses more than to the brain.

Demagogical propaganda has made good use of these psychological trends. Moreover, it requires such revolutionary changes of mind. Indeed, the printed word can be dangerous for demagogical propaganda. One can think about it when left alone. One may criticize it. It can even testify against its originator. It leaves an uncontrolled reaction with its reader. The word spoken in public, wisely directed, leaves a lasting impression. "The spoken word is the sole force capable of producing really great revolutions of sentiment." This statement of Hitler's is wrong as far as the great revolutions of history are concerned. The French Revolution would have been impossible without the Encyclopedists. The Russian Revolution would never have come about without Marx and Lenin. It is true, though, that demagogical revolutions are made by orators, and that even their journalists are orators. The effect of these spokesmen is multiplied by the new devices offered by the third great agency of our democratic age: the radio. It opens new possibilities for demagogical leadership which knows how to use its devices. It dramatizes the news. It kills every criticism. It reaches everyone, even and especially the illiterate. It is the last step in the long development of a "negative democracy." Communication has reached ever-widening circles from the "learned announcements" to the newspaper for the "educated classes" to today's tabloids, funny sheets, and the spoken newspaper of movie flashes—papers not only for people who cannot think but who also cannot read.

The spoken word unquestionably reaches a much larger group than does the written. It appeals in a more direct way to the emotions of the masses, and constitutes more effective propaganda. It is surpassed only by symbols as a weapon of mass emotionalism.

Symbols and Mass Management

Symbols are powerful instruments of emotional government. Here propaganda, the manipulating of collective attitudes, becomes practically synonymous with symbolism. Yet symbols are not a phenomenon of dictatorial government alone.

Symbols—as the neat definition puts it—always stand for something else. They are visible signs of something which is not shown but is realized by association—for instance, the group's essential ideas and intangible values. It is through this medium of stereotypes that the complexity of life is sufficiently simplified and the invisible is clearly materialized so as to bring them within the grasp of common man. Without such signposts social consensus and group loyalty could not be achieved. Language itself represents a generally accepted symbolization of thought processes. Writing is simply a means of communication by symbols. Education is charged with innumerable conventional abbreviations, and society's folkways create similar patterns of conformity. Symbols guarantee the solidarity of the community and define the situation for the individual. They create for him images of the supernatural, and they hold him in allegiance to his social group as well.

Of course, symbols in their ever-present crystallization are easily taken for granted, often underestimated in importance, and sometimes dismissed as childish and sentimental outbursts of emotions. This evaluation reflects a dangerous misapprehension of the nature of man and of the power of symbols. Besides, not all symbols are charged with emotions, nor are these "projected patterns of ideas" reserved for dictatorial systems. Democracies no less constantly depend on symbolic representation. The flag, the national anthem, the nation's heroes, the very existence of institutions symbolize and guarantee the stability of a prevailing value system. In fact, symbolic leadership, such as the institution of the monarchy, arouses the envy of many dynamic dictatorships. Such symbols are priceless. They stand outside the heated party controversy and thus epitomize the nation's unity and solidarity.

Important though symbols are for social integration, democratic governments have been reticent in invoking their appeal. This reserve is due to the historic tradition and the basic nature of democratic rule. In contrast to the medieval period in Europe when symbolism seemed to dominate man's imagination, the modern age does not constitute a favorable intellectual climate. The invention of the printing press, the discovery of the New World, the emergence of the individual, and the religious awakening of personal responsibility pushed symbols into the background. Rational man took the center of the stage. He was suspicious of emotional appeal; his analytical mind resented generalizing symbols and their evasive suggestions; above all, the emerging individual resisted the collective wave which symbolism as such engendered.

Established liberal democracy did not feel the urge to call upon dynamic symbols. State and society were sufficiently represented in unchallenged political institutions and in a generally recognized social order. Such stability, where it was achieved, allowed for the free competition of symbolic representations, an attitude that agreed with the tenor of democratic belief even though it often had a disintegrating effect on national unity. On the other hand, 19th-century nationalism—whose symbols captivated ever-widening circles—caused alarm among thinking democrats. This new political religion often reached a romantic "symbolization of symbols," doubly dangerous in its vague illusions and uncontrollable in its reactions. "The people," "patriotism," "freedom" became glittering and explosive slogans. On the other hand, they were easily degraded to colorless stereotypes by the pedestrian who deprived the erstwhile symbols of a victorious democracy of meaning. From symbols of aspirations and slogans of conflict for the daring fighters to signposts of victory and achievement for those who had arrived, their meaning and their symbolic reference had changed. In fulfilling their mission they had degenerated to frozen dogmas of etiquette whose dormant vitality might reawaken only if challenged.

It is human nature to perceive above all the symbol that challenges, just as in politics opposition to the existing order is the beginning of party organization. Therefore, revolutions calling for vigorous and extensive change in the composition and vocabulary of the ruling class seem to be laden with symbols. They appeal to the imagination of an aroused public that is shaken from its automatic acceptance of traditional patterns.

To the "personal leaders" the creation of symbols becomes a vital necessity. They serve as a substitute for institutions upon which the leaders can always fall back. In fact, the uprooting of long-established behavior patterns is one of the preconditions for a successful revolution. In order to break down the *status quo* attitude of governmentally-minded citizens, it has to recondition them. This twofold process of destruction and substitution is the main function of totalitarian opinion leadership.

Dictatorial movements have made full use of the findings of modern psychology. The creation of conditioned responses has been studied by experimental psychologists like Pavlov (and his salivating dogs) and Watson (in his experiments with emotional responses in infants). Frequent repetition of the conditioned stimulus evokes the desired response, and if successfully applied it allows the extinction of the original stimulus.

These principles have been applied by the modern soul technicians in their creation of a "political maze" that channelizes the public will. The swastika has been cleverly introduced as a means of creating a conditioned response. It has all the qualities of an effective symbol: it has simplicity and a stirring color scheme, and it is easy to reproduce (superseded in this respect only by the cross and the V for Victory). This Nazi emblem also represents an adroit adoption of established symbols to its own end, thus redirecting an available psychological attachment. The black swastika on a ball of white in a large field of red is a subtle combination of the black, white, and red of the imperial flag and the red banner of Socialism. Such symbolic borrowing from political opponents has been freely used by the rising movement. The May Day celebration is an example in question, although stripped by now of its original meaning in its adoption by National Socialism.

In fact, the choice of the party's name reveals the same proficient tactic of employing prevalent traditions in its appeal to the two outstanding dynamic forces of our day, Nationalism and Socialism, at the same time. It makes for strange companions, and in a disturbing strategy of glittering permutations the modern medicine men may even exploit and accentuate the utter confusion of political orientation and alignment among the general public of a twilight period. Propaganda flourishes in an atmosphere of disturbed equilibrium. What is more important, double-faced National Socialism has been successful in transmitting deep-seated loyalties of patriotism or Socialism to its own ranks, redirecting the newly won recruits in the name of old-established symbols that have been changed in meaning and redefined in "response" under the reinforcement of Nazi propagandists. The fate of Thyssen and Rauschning shows as well as that of the brothers Strasser how ambiguity and diversity in the meanings attached to specific symbols may be a useful aid to concerted action. Some day, however, these sincere adherents, emotionally bound to the ideas they spread, may suddenly find themselves outside the party line which in breath-taking changes is determined by the Fuehrer and his inner clique alone. Despite such continuous transformation, conformity to the movement will always be guaranteed by the indisputable fixation to the leader (the leader is always right!) and the passionate intensity of the faithful.

The lack of propagandist fervor in the democratic camp, on the other hand, may lead to oblivion for its taken-for-granted patterns under the pressure of the dynamic attack of dictatorship. There is a most suggestive line in Thomas Mann's short story, "Mario and the Magician." Says the magician, compelling a spectator to dance who earlier insisted that he would not do so: "The

will, merely directed to its own freedom, strikes into the void."
To which the author adds: "If I have understood correctly, the
gentleman was conquered because of the negative nature of his
stand."

Symbols of recruitment (the party emblem, the flag, uniforms,
the anthem, the party's martyrs, etc.) represent to the early revolutionary fighter the promise that they will be turned into successful symbols of identification and that they already bear the
mark of future institutions. But when they are finally accepted
as the mores of the new state they may lose their aggressive significance. They may even become emblems of safety behind
which the taciturn adversary hides for protection. The monopolistic enforcement of political symbols, at first glance the most
powerful weapon of totalitarianism, may turn out to be its actual
weakness. Free from any competitive challenge, the official symbol may easily be petrified into meaningless conformity, and new
symbols of an underground opposition may appeal to daring
fighters.

The renewed predominance of symbols in our time is the storm
sign of a period of transition whose revolutionary cycle is indicated by this succession of symbols. It is in times like these that
people feel the need of immediate orientation. Continuous change
fosters the urge for external symbols which as representations of
collectives help to identify friend and foe and thus to overcome
fear of isolation and insecurity. At the same time, an ardent
adherence to "the cause" is often a subtle method of being devoted
to oneself.

In times of stress every society naturally emphasizes representations of unity. The leadership symbol above all finds a renewed importance. Thus war Presidents have always stood out
in the history of American democracy as exciting symbolizations
of the nation as a whole.

The present-day dictator, however, represents more than a
rallying point; he *is* the nation. Its symbols are exclusively directed
toward the leader. This mystical elevation of the God-sent leader
to a godlike position is as much an essential of dictatorship's ex-

istence as is the active participation of the people. The modern
demagogue realizes that what the mass man longs for is an emotional outlet for active participation that the prevalent commercial entertainment does not offer (though football and baseball
games do!). The true demonstrations of dictatorships are no mere
spectacles; what is merely a good show misses the goal. To watch
the floats in a passing parade does not create an active sense of
belonging among the spectators. Yet action is all that counts with
a dynamic movement. Besides, fear increases in inactivity. To
overcome fear, active partnership becomes a necessity. The repression of fear is, in fact, the chief aim of dictatorial organization. The introduction of uniforms fulfills this purpose, as does
the observance of strict discipline.

Rituals are equally good outlets for anxiety feelings. People
who cannot make an appropriate response will be easily impressed
by ritual. The monstrous meetings of modern autocracies are
laden with rituals. They give security to the frightened masses.

These masses, as indicated above, are conceived by present-day
demagogues as being essentially irrational. To such childlike
masses symbols that appeal to the emotions become a need. Such
an approach is highly effective because democracies, following
the concept of rational masses, fall short of an emotional appeal.
In time of stress especially, the emotional behavior of the masses
can be easily excited; naturally prevalent inhibitions can be broken
down and all the fickleness, hysteria, and sadism of an unstable
crowd brought to the fore. The all-embracing modern agencies
of mass communication manipulated by a well-coordinated
propaganda machine can weld these restless masses into a powerful
weapon and, with unifying symbols before them, can send them
on the march. Bound together in an active crowd, every follower
can be reinforced in his reaction by the perception that others
are responding similarly. Mass meetings guarantee an irrational
psychological effect by the simple fact of numbers. Thus a multitude will be psychologically prepared by a whole set of rites
and specific symbols to become a unified mass. Military bands,
flags, parades, and the constant repetition of such rites intensify

the partisan feelings of individuals almost to the point of religious fervor. These well-staged mass meetings are not a fight over concrete issues in open discussion. They become a matter of the self-representation of the leader alone. Discussion and opposition are excluded. Only believers or those who want to be converted are welcome. This is the totalitarian scheme of dictatorial symbols.

Marching in particular becomes a value in itself. These men of unrest cannot rejoice in themselves, cannot stand still, cannot wait. They are deeply moved and fully absorbed by the mere consciousness of being on the march. For people on the march symbols are the substitute for institutions. These symbols stand for the extreme dynamics of demagogical dictatorships. Their driving force is expressed in the quasi-religious myth of a revolutionary world mission—the revival of a Roman Empire, the Proletarian World Revolution, the Third Reich's New Order.

The intense devotion and loyalty to one's group, crystallized in such Messianic symbols, creates self-exaltation and elation. It makes people reach for the stars. It puts them beyond reach on the road toward world domination. Dynamic symbols are the mark of modern totalitarianism—always on the march that never ends, incessantly at war with a world that it cannot possess.

Chapter VIII

THE IMPACT OF PERMANENT WAR

ROOTS OF TOTALITARIANISM

"War is the blessing of God, the eternal fount from which new generations of men are born. In this war lies the rebirth of our nation." This statement by Robert Ley, head of the German Labor Front (*Angriff*, March 27, 1941), points to the psychological roots of modern totalitarianism *in toto*. While the analysis of dictatorship's political pyramid—from the supreme leader down to the amorphous masses—has clearly shown that numerous factors have brought about the emergence of the total state, there has been one recurrent theme: boundless dynamics. The dictatorial regimes are governments at war, originating in war, aiming at war, thriving on war. Historically speaking, they emerged from the war, and their entire political order is shaped accordingly. The essential beliefs of their leaders and followers, their whole national climate, their racial ideologies, their plan in foreign affairs, their armaments, and their actual attacks show that Fascist dictatorships are bound for expansion; war is inseparable from their meaning.

The totalitarian philosophy of war is too obvious in the writings of Fascist leaders as well as in their deeds to need any further analysis. More important, however, is the recognition of permanent war as the mainspring of the whole totalitarian ideology. Dictatorship's *irrationalism* reflects the incalculability of armed conflict. War cancels causality. Force repudiates reason. Yet this irrationality of warfare has direction and meaning; if it is romantic, it is no less pragmatic. Victory for the community is all that counts; all standards, ideas, and actions are subordinated to this one end. It justifies all means. Good and true is what serves the nation at war. "War is the essence of everything," in the words of Nazi lawmaker Carl Schmitt; "the nature of the total war determines the nature and form of the totalitarian state." Politics is no longer an instrument to prevent war; it becomes a part of warfare, actual and potential.

This means the definite end of peace and international morality. In fact, thoroughgoing National Socialism theorizes on such a stand by decreeing that every race "is bound to have an intellectual and a moral standard peculiar to itself." There is no international science; even physics and mathematics have to accept their reinterpretation as being national and racial in character. This hypernationalism—again reflecting the psychology of war fever —that conceives sovereignty not only in its political aspects but as an economic and cultural phenomenon as well, is given added force by an uncritical acceptance of *social Darwinism*. The survival of the fittest in a continuous struggle for existence becomes the only maxim for action and the exclusive key to history. It is the application of Bagehot's collectivist interpretation that promises prosperity to the most homogeneous and best-disciplined band, and of Gumplowicz's inevitable struggle between races (in a low-brow version to be sure, and without any vision of the progressive concurrence of conqueror and conquered).

Social Darwinism is further hardened and fortified into an active creed by the concept of the racial superiority of the Nordic man—a doctrine of extremely doubtful scientific standing but extremely dynamic, especially in the hands of demagogical myth-makers. Now the rather thin though passionately presented theory of a Count Gobineau and a Houston Stewart Chamberlain becomes the cardinal feature of national policy and the moral justification for conquest and suppression. Permanent war has found its philosophical dressing.

While irrationality sets the tone and Social Darwinism gives direction to the militant philosophy, the idea of the *Männerbund* defines the structure of the military state. Society is no longer conceived as a peaceful organization in which the family represents the natural basic unit; it is seen as in a constant state of war. Consequently, an order of ardent fighters is made the center of the political and social community. This group of men, united by a common discipline, becomes the originator of the state, the ruling class in the established government, and the guarantor of the nation's future. The world of the perennial soldier is a society essentially without women, without civic order, without law. Justice becomes the function of the power that commands the political decision. The age of mass justice sets in. The masters of the sword no longer punish their enemies, they annihilate them. In 1881 six men and women had to pay with their lives for the assassination of Czar Alexander II. This produced a shattering effect on world opinion. Today, the morning's headlines, often reporting many more executions, leave the average man untouched. The world's capacity for horror has been dulled since 1914. Against that tragic precedent human life has lost its value. Four years of murderous war have prepared the social setting for the emergence of the garrison state.

The impact of the First World War on society was manifest. The nearer it approached total dimensions, the deeper it affected every sphere of social existence. War's supreme efforts necessitated swift action and firm integration, disciplined regimentation and tight centralization. Institutions had to be streamlined and individuals turned into robots. In the baptism of fire certain hitherto moral standards were tested anew and well-established social concepts redefined.

Of course, the dimensions and intensity of the effects of that war differed in every country according to national character and historic fate. Inscriptions on war memorials were revealing. *A tous ceux qui sont morts pour la civilisation* (To all those who died for civilization) said the monuments in every little French village. "They died for their nation" read English war inscriptions. The Vienna War Memorial commemorated not only a date from 1914 to 1918 but the passing of the Austrian army from the company of living institutions: *Dem Andenken der Ruhmreichen Kaiserlichen Armee* (In memory of the glorious Imperial

Army). The meaningful inscription on German tombs reads: *Sie werden auferstehen!* (They will rise from the dead).

Yet despite these variations in experience and meaning, the First World War had lasting effects everywhere. Any naïve return to pre-war times was impossible (though the great blunders of the Armistice period largely derived from the attempt at such forced forgetfulness). On the other hand, the war did not mean simply the complete crumbling of the pre-war order. While war no doubt quickens social change, often it only accelerates forces that otherwise might have emerged but slowly. The First World War was part of a much greater revolution, a climactic crystallization to be sure. It began long before the shooting started.

The *fin de siècle*, the "European malady" at the turn of the century, pointed at an impending crisis. It was reflected in politics and in economics, in religion and in morals, in the fine arts and in literature. One could easily view such an integral crisis as "the decline of the west." Yet differing from Spengler's sweeping formula and his fashionable talk of certain decadence, one might just as well not simply await the "inevitable end," but recognize in this great crisis a supreme challenge. Arnold Toynbee has thus formulated a basic law of human activity: "The greater the challenge, the greater the stimulus." It has been proved a thousandfold in the history of mankind. How the patient weathers a major crisis always depends on his will to live.

Seen in this greater historic perspective the impact of the First World War presents an extraordinary theme, doubly fascinating since it has evolved before our own eyes.

One may, for instance, compare the tremendous variations and constant shifts in the image of war as reflected in the war novels; he may relate the ideological turns during the 20th century to this upheaval; he may follow up the institutional transformations deriving from the First World War and foreshadowing the Second; he may outline the social change that has come about in post-war society. To give even a sketch of these and many other manifestations of the war is beyond the design of this study. Here the variant reactions of the conflicting generations con-

fronted by the war will be approached. This conflict of generations dramatizes and brings into bold relief an intricate social
process. It discloses the psychological roots of totalitarianism.
Besides, it calls attention to a crucial though strangely neglected
field of investigation. It may suggest some concrete illustration
of human motivations.

European politics from Versailles to Vichy can be largely explained in terms of a conflict of generations. To be sure, the
influence of the changing generations as such is not a phenomenon
of post-World War history alone. Plato and Aristotle had observed the importance of this conflict in politics and social life.
The contrast between father and son has always been a favorite
theme in literature, even before Turgenev's classic novel. Its increasing importance in our time, however, is due to several specific factors. No doubt youth today is more conscious of its
own value and independent existence. It no longer regards itself
as merely a transition stage. We are living in an age of self-
confident youth. In addition to that, the dynamics of change have
been more and more accelerated. The revolution in techniques
has brought about a transformation in living conditions in such
short periods that nowadays the cavalcade of thirty years includes
more changes than did three centuries in former times. Today
not only fathers and sons but older and younger brothers live
in a different world, speak a different language, have different
standards.

Such discrepancies are even more noticeable when the continuity of generations is suddenly broken—as happened at the
time of the First World War. The war not only clearly separated
the pre-war and post-war periods, but also meant the weakening,
if not the elimination, of an entire generation. The link was
broken. The normal succession of generations was disturbed.
The elders had to carry on. The younger generation did not grow
slowly and naturally into the existing institutions. There was no
apprenticeship because there were no apprentices. Yet the existence of the craft of modern statesmanship depends on a long
tradition always renewed and rejuvenated by a succeeding genera-

tion. The crisis in modern democratic institutions is largely due to this breach in the old link. This cleavage, of course, is less visible in the United States with her limited participation in World War I. However, a study of the after-effects of the Civil War would afford a striking illustration of similar difficulties in this country.

In Europe it was not only the destruction of the young war generation that was felt in post-war time, but also a restless youth which had lacked fatherly guidance in its childhood, had lost its normal connections with its elders and yet was eager to win its place in the world. Thus this youth was not ready to take a long training through normal channels and to wait for its culmination twenty years or so later. It looked for short cuts to power. This made the older men more suspicious of the youngsters; but in the latter's eyes the ruling generation was completely exposed too. Were they not responsible for the war and its outcome under which the new generation would have to suffer? The war had brought about a crisis in confidence in the political wisdom of the rulers.

What is a generation? What makes people members of the same age group? It is not simply coexistence in the same period. Different generations live together in the same chronological time. There is a Last Puritan in every period. The "contemporaneousness of the non-contemporary" is one of the most characteristic phenomena of the spiritual life of an epoch that makes it polyform and manifold. Contemporaries are not merely people born in the same year. Biological birth dates are only a starting point, an outward approximation, for a sociological differentiation. What identifies people as belonging to one generation is decided by their common experiences, the same decisive influences, similar historic problems.

Modern child psychology has shown that at seventeen or thereabouts the unqualified acceptance of environment ends. With the start of adolescence the child begins to reflect on his inheritance. But adolescents are at the same time plastic. They are "open to suggestions." They are ready for what lies ahead. This is the time for inspiring education; wisely developing youth's awakening resources, it may leave a deep impress on the growing personality. It is in these years that the young take their first decisive steps into the society of grown-ups, formulate their outlook on life, make lasting friendships, fall in love, lay the foundations of their future professions, and weigh their stake in society. It is not only melancholy and romanticism that make them, later in their lives, look back to high school and particularly college days, because this has been their life's commencement. Impressions received in these years are deep and persistent. Generations might be divided according to the essential impressions received toward the end of the teens.

This holds especially true of a generation of adolescents which has gone through weighty experiences. This gives them unity, a common style, a new approach to life. The First World War undoubtedly meant such a caesura in human life. It divided generations. There was a pre-war generation that included people born before 1890. Its education was finished, its life was formed before the war began. Not that this revolutionary upheaval did not disturb these older people. For a few it meant a career or business. For most of them it signified catastrophe, the destruction of their lives, work, and accomplishments. Those who survived this storm tried to return to the world in which they had lived before. They tried to forget the war and its experiences.

It was different with the younger age groups. To them the war meant a great formative experience. Admirable or brutal, it was in their blood. It could never leave them. These "children of the war" were called upon to make post-war history.

The Conflict of Generations in Germany

The influence of these experiences on youth was especially manifest in Germany. War events were more deeply felt there than elsewhere; the collapse was more complete; the post-war developments disturbed the country to the utmost. In addition to this, a unique pre-war youth movement had made Germany's younger generation alert to its specific position. A vanguard (born

between 1890 and 1900), it had the preconceived basic ideas of
the revolutionary post-war youth. It was a genuine movement to
fight the artificial and corrupt style of bourgeois society, to find
new contacts with the real sources of life in nature and society.
It was a burgher's secession of a middle-class youth, but it was
surprised and overtaken by the war. Though this movement spread
enormously after the war, its climax had been reached before the
world conflict. After the war this young revolt was disrupted
and deflated; its best representatives had been destroyed.

In the battle of Langemarck, to cite one instance, a thousand
volunteers, leaders of the German youth movement, were killed.
A skirmish around a little hill, although insignificant enough in
the panorama of major military operations, nevertheless might
signify the most decisive battle as far as human material was concerned. On October 22, 1914, in the bloodstained Flanders fields
of later campaigns, the prime of the Reich's elite was wiped out.
Post-war Germany never recovered from such losses. What was
left was a peakless pyramid, a truncated *young war generation.*

Those who returned, "even though they may have escaped its
shells, were destroyed by the war." Thus their spokesman, Erich
Maria Remarque, tersely opened his tense report, *All Quiet on the
Western Front.* They had lost connection with profession, with
family, with civil society. Unlike the generation only ten years
older, they had not found home and vocation before they were
called upon to fight in the war, or a place to return to when the
bloody strife was over. They had just left school, ready to carve
out lives of their own, enthusiastically receptive to a world to be
conquered. So they joined the army, these young volunteers. War
became their calling. When they were not sacrificed in the battlefields, they were hopelessly burned out by this great ordeal of
four long years. If the war had lasted only two years, they might
have created a new society out of their suffering and the strength
of their experiences in the trenches. When the end finally came
in an unexpected defeat, they went back bewildered, broken, and
without hope—erstwhile ardent idealists turned into cynics and
skeptics. "Wanderers between two worlds" they were called by

one of their number, Walter Flex, who himself became a victim
of the *danse macabre*. This war report was still full of promise
for this generation. Yet the young and romantic warriors seemed
to end up in a march to nowhere. Many of them were only too
grateful when they miraculously survived the deadly fire, and
only too happy to find a quiet escape for the rest of their lives.
Silent, impenetrable, shy dreamers, they distrusted the noisy petty
world of busy people to which they returned. The "citizens," in
turn, distrusted the strange fellows who had seen a no-man's-land,
had undergone experiences which they could exchange only with
their co-warriors. A civil world could not count on them. It did
not even ask them for active participation.

What Germany, and as a matter of fact the whole of Europe,
experienced in these post-war days was the rule of old people.
Even the revolution of 1918 was led by a generation grown up
in a pre-war world. The war had destroyed the flower of oncoming leadership. This is one of the many reasons why that revolution, born out of defeat, was doomed. A pre-war generation tried
to fill the gap. It made a sincere effort, but a fatal one nevertheless.
Its concepts came from another world. It was hard to make a new
start. The age distribution of the German Reichstag gives a
striking picture of the situation: as late as 1930 the average age
of the representatives was fifty-seven. Every attempt toward the
rejuvenation of the old parties failed.

Undoubtedly the party machines had a great responsibility for
this abnormal lack of mobility; the pre-war veterans felt themselves to be the only reliable standard-bearers of the old revolutionary concepts. They did not trust the handing over to inexperienced young fellows of even a part of the precious machine
that had been built up during the lifetime of a whole generation
in its hard fight against a hostile world. Georges Sorel, the great
French syndicalist, spoke sarcastically of these functionaries who
because of vested party interests forgot the revolution itself. Indeed, no longer did they represent a proletariat that had "nothing
to lose but its chains." They controlled big trade unions and

positions. They did not want to fight, not even to take chances in general strikes. They clung to their position. They had arrived.

Not so with the younger generation which was dispossessed. The persistent refusal to take in younger elements necessarily led to the blocking of forces. The revolution finally had to come, breaking the dam of unreleased energies which could not be directed into normal channels in time. This became the crucial question in the struggle between the generations.

Of course, the elders had good reasons for their suspicion. It was not merely the resistance of the "Haves" blocking the assault of the "Have-nots." It was the fear, justified or not, that these erratic youngsters were not reliable enough to administer and carry on the great heritage. This was especially felt in economics, for here more than anywhere else the gerontocracy kept the key positions after the war. The average age of the economic leaders in Germany in 1929-30 was sixty. The board of trustees of the large banking institutions reached an average age of the Biblical three-score years and ten.

Of course, this was partly due to the fact that in economic activities property was the key to power. The young soldiers had not made money while fighting the enemy. People who stayed home were more apt to succeed in controlling these worldly goods. But this was not the whole story. It did not explain why the younger generation could not slowly gain a foothold and infiltrate commerce and industry. Here a strange phenomenon of succession in generations may be observed. The history of the German captains of industry (and the life story of their colleagues in other countries) shows a typical sequence from the grandfathers who were the founders, to the sons who administered the heritage, to the grandsons who were not able or did not want to keep up their father's pursuit. They became "protectors" of the arts and sciences, or perhaps actors and musicians, or they saw their life's desire fulfilled in yachting and horse breeding—to use Thorstein Veblen's well-known formula, in conspicuous consumption. Heirs of a middle class whose virtues had been work and thrift, they became a leisure class of spendthrifts. Often they turned against the system whose product they were, or at least they played with the idea of doing so. In any case, they could not be trusted to hold positions. Just as the Merovingians once called their major-domo, the Carolinians, to administer the kingdom (since the royal children could not be trusted) and just as these *Hausmeiers* grew in power until they finally seized the crown, so the worried industrialists called upon their syndics to take care of their enterprises which could not be handed over to their own children. The trustees of the owners at first became their general managers; then they took over the job; finally they became the real bosses, eliminating the heirs from the enterprise and merely guaranteeing the latters' future through trust funds. Thus the family-owned enterprises were depersonalized, a fact which, incidentally, was well in line with the general tendencies of modern capitalism.

Responsibility for the tension rested upon both generations. Fathers had reason to be suspicious of sons who did not follow their path. Sons who had fought for their elders, who had protected their home and their property, who had endured and suffered for four years at the front called this cool reception ingratitude. They felt excluded from life. Thus the generation of young fighters became a tragic generation of outsiders.

One may wonder whether, behind the mask of cynicism and gloom, there was not actually a great readiness for social action among this young war generation. The simple fact of their living together through daily danger had blurred social demarcations, had brought about a greater mingling of classes than in any previous period, and had thus created a comradeship of the front. Though only vaguely felt by the soldiers and often unrealistically built up and exploited by ponderous writers on the home front, this "Socialism of the trenches" (*Schützengraben-Sozialismus*) was a sincere experience with many. It might have become a powerful force in post-war reconstruction if only it had been awakened fully and directed into positive channels. In fact, even in defeated Germany, there were hopeful beginnings that were giving meaning to the great carnage: a growing social consciousness throughout the nation and a novel feeling for international responsibility. The idea of the League of Nations had found ardent supporters in Germany, long before Stresemann made it the cornerstone of the Reich's foreign policy. Yet hardly any statesman had enough vision and vigor to activate such dormant strength. The few of them who at least tried to do this belonged, significantly, to an older war generation. The breach between the generations was too great in unhappy Germany.

The crucial young war generation remained outsiders of society. Either they had been put out of action, or they excluded themselves in their world weariness, or—and this comprised the small band of activists among them—they declared war on the "bourgeois world" of traders in which there was no room for warring heroes. Fighting was the only craft they really knew. So they joined the military cause, the Fighting Leagues. Wherever the drumbeat was sounded they followed the battle cry. They fought a hundred crusades, but they were crusaders without an aim. Their risings turned out to be irrelevant revolts. Such was Ehrhardt's Kapp *Putsch* in 1920 and Hitler's first beer-hall *Putsch* in 1923. This generation had had a most stirring experience at the front, but there its constructive flame had sputtered out. The future of Europe depended on her chances of postponing the necessary revolution for another fifteen years until a new and more fortunate generation was ready to take action and assume control.

It was already growing up, this generation of *war youth* (born between 1900 and 1910), and it did so under the suspicious eyes of its older brothers. These younger fellows had subconsciously experienced the war too. It may have made an even deeper impression on them because they lived through these years almost unaware of it. The war penetrated their minds and bodies without shattering them. Certainly they were bewildered youth; unguided by their fathers who were fighting at the front; but to this generation the war meant at the same time a great collective experience. It destroyed the pre-war isolation of the middle-class individual. The four years of tension had not injured the strength of the younger people but had built it up. All the suffering had made them vigorous and sturdy. Thus they met a post-war world with explosive energy. They felt sure of themselves, sure that some day they would build up a better society of their own. They could view the international scene with much less prejudice than could the soldiers' generation, stamped by hostilities. They had acquired much knowledge. They followed professions. It sometimes seemed to their elders that they took after their grandfathers. Indeed, they often locked hands with them over the heads of the preceding generation. This younger group too were idealists and reformers, but they were sober idealists and they could wait for their hour. The future belonged to them—at least they thought so. In the long run they would inherit the world that their elders could not master. They were the strongest generation, as far as actual numbers went. They had not been reduced by loss in battles as their older brothers had been, nor by the decline in birth rate that came in the succeeding generation. They felt no less superior to their younger brothers.

These younger brothers, the *post-war youth* (even if born before the war), were not at all impressed by this paramount event. They had no experience of the contrast between pre-war and post-war times. They were efficient, physically able, but poor in the substance of their inner life. They had no headaches. Economics, techniques, sports—these interested them. They had no problems. They did not want to reform the world. They wanted to live. The motorcycle was the embodiment of their ambitions. It was simpler than the luxurious automobile of the lazy, fat bourgeois. It matched the dynamic rhythm of their youth. In sports activities, which came into fashion only after the war, it was the games calling for motion—skiing, football, gymnastics—that became popular with them. If any great experience comparable to the war impressed this problemless generation, it was the inflation—to them a miracle world of fairy tales where one might lose a fortune of generations' standing and where one might just as well make it. It was a world lacking absolute bounds and preconceptions, where everything was possible and nothing impossible. This was not a generation of leaders; these youths were driftwood ready to break dams if thrown into a stream. They were material for any political revolution. Everything depended upon which generation would take up the challenge. The Nazi Revolution of 1933 decided it. This was no mere revolution of the young war generation. It was a strange alliance of the warriors with the pre-war technicians who thought they could tame the young revolutionaries. Victorious National Socialism was a hybrid, not only as far as name and program were concerned; it also united very different age groups.

Divergent as the human material of this movement was, it is important to note that almost all the active leaders of National Socialism were born between 1890 and 1900. The war was the decisive experience of this generation. Hitler, though born in 1889, had a somewhat retarded development and did not find himself before the war broke out. In fact, according to his own statement, the war meant to him the discovery of his place and mission in society. All his important lieutenants belonged to the young war generation—Goering (1893), Hess (1891), Goebbels (1897), Himmler (1900), Ley (1890), Otto Dietrich (1897), Alfred Rosenberg (1893), von Ribbentrop (1892), Amman (1891), Darré (1895), Funk (1890), etc. The few exceptions, like Lammers (1879) and Frick (1877), indicate the influx of an expert group which, desperately needed by the new movement, did not represent its main driving force.

It is no less significant that all the non-National Socialist Cabinet members belonged to an older generation, such as von Neurath (1873), von Papen (1879), Seldte (1882), Gürtner (1881), Hugenberg (1865), Meissner (1880), Schacht (1877), von Blomberg (1875), von Fritsch (1880), etc. The years following this national revolution brought the slow but constant elimination of these pre-war statesmen. The purges of the army, Foreign Office, and bureaucracy not only brought the Nazification of the more conservative institutions, but at the same time also gave the young war generation complete control of the old agencies. Thus the rule of National Socialism can almost be identified with that generation's political victory. All the basic concepts of the National Socialist government have been shaped by the experience of war. Politics itself has been defined by one of the Third Reich's belated partisans in terms of the "irreducible category of Friend and Foe." Fully militarized social relationships had been basically experienced on the battlefield. No concept of civic government was left. This explains the structure of the party as well as the idea of a permanent revolution in foreign affairs and internal politics. This militant climate was the fundamental justification for the totalitarian state.

Worth mentioning, however, is the fact that seizure of power in the Third Reich was accomplished almost exclusively by a younger war generation who, differing from their elder co-warriors, not only had a romantic concept of war but also lacked the balancing experience of a pre-war career. The few European statesmen of the older war generation—Bruening (1885), Beneš (1884), Daladier (1884)—showed striking differences from the younger war generation. The Third Reich was created by a capricious generation of young soldiers who, though they returned home, were broken by the war especially since they could not draw upon the reserve of stabilizing experiences from a peaceful pre-war world.

VARIATIONS OF THE THEME: FASCIST ITALY AND SOVIET RUSSIA

The problem of generations is by no means reserved for Germany alone, though there it certainly had the most sweeping effects and resulted in the most visible breaks. Strangely enough, however, the "revolt of the young people" found its first political expression in Italy, the country embodying classical Roman traditions. The Fascist revolution of 1922 had swept the country with its call for the rejuvenation of the nation. In spite of her great past, Italy had indeed been the Cinderella of the modern nations. United only in the second half of the 19th century and thus, like Germany, a late-comer in the concert of European nations, she suffered from an inferiority complex. Colonial conquests in Africa and even the victorious outcome of the First World War could not satisfy her pride. Her triumphs were merely the reflected glory of her allies. The Italian people showed only contempt for the returning officers of that war whenever they appeared in uniform. These officers were the first recruits of rising Fascism.

Fascism became the revolution of the war generation par excellence. But different from the leaders of German National Socialism more than ten years later, many leaders of the Fascist revolution had been shaped by decisive experiences in pre-war times. Though the war undoubtedly changed their basic attitudes, they had at least reached the age of maturity by that time. Mussolini had already made himself a name as an ardent and leading Socialist. His chief associates had formed their basic conceptions before 1914. Fascism was an attempt to amalgamate pre-war nationalism and syndicalism. The pre-war sources of Italian nationalism can be easily observed, especially in comparison with the younger German National Socialism. It is significant that it was Goering, who most resembled the pre-war nationalists in the Hitler movement, who made the first and most effective contacts with Mussolini.

While National Socialism is a typical post-war product, the real sources of Fascism go back to a vigorous reaction against the rationalism of the liberal parliamentarian bourgeoisie. Neo-idealism was developed in opposition to positivism. It found its way into the young generation's ideas in politics, art, literature, science, and philosophy. Fascism, although distorted, was nourished by these early sources and was carried along by the mightier waves of the irrationalism that swept over European nations in the first decade of the 20th century.

Young Mussolini, well aware of these intellectual currents in pre-war Europe, regarded himself as a perfect contemporary of Nietzsche's "new men who would live beyond good and evil." In fact, the emerging Fascist ideology—though it was more a state of mind than an elaborate and comprehensive theory of society—could claim a respectable list of philosophical forerunners who carried weight in the intellectual history of Italy and Europe: Vico and Machiavelli, Hegel and Nietzsche, Sorel and Pareto, among many others. True, such a roster could be easily construed *post festo*; every new movement naturally enforces itself with such traditional testimonials. Nazi Germany tried it in her use of Frederick the Great and Freiherrn vom Stein, of Herder and Hegel, of Schiller and Fichte, of Nietzsche and Spengler. Hardly any of these great spirits taught or intended to teach mankind to act as Mussolini or Hitler are doing. Their lives and their work testify against these modern exploiters of their ideas.

Yet granted these general reservations in respect to the incorporation of great philosophical systems into Fascist ideology and its arbitrary assemblage of the most divergent fragments of political thought, Fascism—as far as its intellectual foundations go—dates back to the pre-war period. This fact to some extent explains the more conservative outlook that an erstwhile independent Mussolinism showed as compared with the "younger" Hitlerism. In Italy it was much less a generation of disappointed cynics which seized power. This was also partly due to the fact that the Fascist revolution succeeded after only four years' preparation. It was not a delayed revolution, piling up disappointments and hatreds engendered by failure and long waiting. True, there was cruelty no less, with victorious Fascism dosing political enemies with castor oil, typifying human perfidy and turpitude. But such actions combined features of Italian buffoonery and burlesque.

One might say that the change in the character of Fascist Italy during the Italo-Ethiopian War was due less to the resistance she found unexpectedly in the western powers than to the necessity of allying herself with Hitler's Reich. From that time on, a process of radicalization could be observed in Fascist Italy, an acclimatization to the National Socialist ideology. The new racial policy was only the most visible phenomenon in these changes. This policy is no doubt inconceivable in terms of the Roman tradition that is so fundamental to the Fascist ideology. *Civis Romanus sum*—the pride of Rome had always been her power to absorb, to civilize whatever nationalities touched her soil or culture.

It would be most interesting to check this radicalization, which also found expression in economics and elsewhere, against the change of personnel in Fascist Italy. The growing importance of such people as young Ciano and Starace, and the comeback of Farinacci, all of them of the younger war generation, was a phenomenon worth watching. Long before the Second World War began, the Rome-Berlin axis was more than a tactical alliance. It has led toward the definite coordination of both systems, with Nazi Germany most certainly in the driver's seat and Italy now a mere province in Hitler's New Order.

The conflict of generations also throws some light on the dark continent of world politics: Soviet Russia. In his poignant study, *The Modern Theme*, Ortega y Gasset wrote: "In the most violent opposition of pros and antis it is easy to perceive a real union of interests. Both parties consist of men of their own time; and great as their differences may be, their mutual resemblances are still greater. The reactionary and the revolutionary of the nineteenth century are much nearer to one another than either is to any man of our own age."

When we have gained perspective, we may discover how much similarity can be found in the antipodes of the social and political struggle of today. Mussolini, critic though he was in the pre-war times, was himself a child of his period. This holds even more true of the revolutionaries ten years older than Mussolini who became the agitators for and the creators of Soviet Russia. In spite of their revolutionary attitude they were basically rooted in 19th-century rationalism, embedded in a belief in progress. Their godfathers might be Darwin or Bentham, Comte or Spencer. "Knowledge is might," the slogan of the natural sciences at the turn of the century, was also their guiding star. The *tabula rasa* of illiterate Russia seemed to offer a vast field for their educational schemes. The miraculous advancement of hygiene, the almost childlike admiration for technical achievements—all this was the 19th century at its best. Lenin became the Peter the Great of the

20th century. Communism and westernization seemed almost inextricably mixed in the twofold advances of Bolshevism. This connecting of Asiatic Russia with the western world was largely the byproduct of the work of revolutionaries who had spent their most impressionable years in Zurich, Paris, Leipzig, or London preparing the overthrow of capitalism and, incidentally, bringing home a century of European rational thinking. Indeed the progress made in revolutionary tactics by the Bolshevists as compared with their older cousins, the terroristic Narodniki, lay in just this step from a Utopian romantic Socialism to a scientific rational Socialism. In this sense Lenin, Trotsky, and the others only reflected the general trend of their time.

It might even be ventured that the unusual developments of the last ten years in Russia could find at least a partial explanation in the specific texture of a new generation. There are undoubtedly other elements—international implications, personality factors, etc. —which explain the spectacular changes. The U.S.S.R. may have come of age. A generation had grown up under the new regime that accepted life in a socialistic country as a natural condition. If its members called themselves revolutionary, their radicalism was surely far different from that for which their forefathers battled. They were rooted in the soil of their Socialist fatherland. They were nationalistic in a way, more conservative, more interested in constructive continuity than in the revolutionary wrecking of a hated system. They found a new interest in institutions, as the discussions on family problems in the Soviet youth movement showed. They began to speak a different language than their fathers did.

It seemed to be an essential technique of the man who inherited (or better, seized) Caesar's mantle that he began his rule in the name of the founder, but with the help of an oncoming generation and in staunch opposition to the remnants of the revolutionary period. Purges had become the standard method in a totalitarian state for coordinating the resistant party by wholesale liquidation. Trotsky, the Number Two Man of revolutionary days, died in exile, assassinated by the far-reaching efficacy of the

Third International. Zinoviev, Kamenev (next to Lenin during the last years of his illness), Tukhachevsky of Red army fame, the leading admirals Gervais, Orlov, and Viktorov—they were all put to death. Litvinov, with long experience as Commissar for Foreign Affairs, was superseded by Molotov, twenty years younger (only the developments of World War II—a bitter justification of Litvinov's consistent policies—brought him back into the political limelight). More and more key positions were taken by the post-revolutionary generation. Andreyev (1895- , the trade union specialist), Beria (1899- , Chief of the Soviet secret police), Malenkov (1902- , member of the State Defense Committee), Mikoyan (1895- , Commissar for Foreign Trade), Zhdanov (1896- , key man in the Communist party) were unknown men only a few years ago. Today they comprise the inner circle of the regime. The all-powerful Politbureau has completely changed its personnel; it has been filled with younger men born in the '90's and reared in the days of war and civil strife. The only leaders left from the old revolutionary days are President Kalinin (as powerless a representative of the system as Hindenburg or the King of Italy) and Voroshilov, political chief of the Red army. Since the beginning of the present war the latter's power has been definitely eclipsed; his prestige has been dimmed by the other marshals, Timoshenko and Budenny, and by the younger master-mind of the Red army, General Shaposhnikov, and his disciples of the Frunze Military Academy, such as General Zhukov.

The younger set among the Bolshevist leaders could for a time play with the idea of a completely new orientation of Soviet policies. The German-Russian *rapprochement* was organized and openly propagandized by the younger statesmen, Molotov and Zhdanov. It is even conceivable that this was not simply a tactical move of a desperate Soviet Union trying to stave off a threatening Nazi attack. Its underlying motivation on the part of these young Soviet politicians (though probably only vaguely conceived) may have been the conviction that a new generation of revolutionary realists—Red or Brown—could meet on common

ground. Such possibilities had been suggested since the emergence
of Hitler; moreover, the disappointing encounters with the older
western statesmen in the face of the rising danger of the Third
Reich could certainly fortify a united stand of "young revolutionaries."

The consequent life-and-death struggle of Soviet Russia against
the Nazi onslaught has overshadowed such incipient trends in
Soviet internal development. But some of the wavering tactics of
Soviet Russia in the '30's might be realized by an evaluation of the
changing intellectual climate during these crucial years, transitions
that found their visible expression in the succession of generations
in the U.S.S.R.

WESTERN DEMOCRACIES AND THE REVOLUTION OF WAR

In November, 1918, a German conservative, Moeller von den
Bruck—who a few years later christened "The Third Reich" in
a book of the same title—wrote an essay, "The Rights of Young
Nations" ("Das Recht der jungen Völker"). In essence it presented the philosophy of the "Have-not" nations which twenty
years later was to become the battle cry of the Axis powers. To
van den Bruck the prototype of a young nation was the Prussian,
and he saw no mere accident in the fact that the Piedmontese
were called the Prussians of Italy, the Japanese the Prussians of
the Orient, the Bulgarians the Prussians of the Balkans. He expected to find the self-assertion of these young peoples in rising
birth rates and a self-denying heroic attitude, in a natural will
to defeat Malthus and Bentham. The western powers to many
German interpreters became the incarnation of cowardly preservation, the petrification of human dynamics where young ideas
could never have a fair deal and where the fountain of perpetual
rejuvenation seemed to have dried up. Nations saturated with the
utter boredom of having "arrived" seemed to be an easy prey to
a young people which prided itself on "living dangerously."

At first glance such an analysis undoubtedly found some justification in the countries where a pre-war generation ran things.
Lloyd George (1863) and Clemenceau (1841) had made the

Peace of Versailles. Poincaré (1860) and Baldwin (1867), Briand (1862) and MacDonald (1866), Herriot (1872) and the Chamberlains (1863 and 1869 respectively) executed it—not exactly in patterns of a post-war world. As in the German Republic, the decision certainly was not a matter of their own choosing. They had to fill positions which should have been occupied by young men, lost in the World War and cheated of their share in making a new world. The honor rolls of Eton and Harrow, of Oxford and Cambridge, gave distressing testimony to the bloody sacrifice of the oncoming generation. "On the battlefields of France the British aristocracy perished as they perished in the Wars of the Roses; half the great families of England, heirs of large estates and wealth died without complaint," said Masterman.

The fact that the western powers did not follow the same scheme as Germany and Italy was due to a different historic fate and national traditions. Victorious as they were, the need for change did not seem so urgent. A flight back to pre-war days, the golden days of the Epsom Derby and the Boat Races, still seemed possible, and the numerous cynics among the young survivors of the war could "eat, drink, and be merry—for yesterday we died." "Debunkers-in-chief" though they were, they still had some reserves to fall back upon. Early post-war England soon found its way back from restlessness to normalcy. True, the compromised and hopelessly divided Liberals were superseded by the Labor party, which from then on became His Majesty's opposition and twice assumed the responsible position of the ruling party. Yet this change in personnel did not bring a "new deal" to England's internal politics.

All three parties in Great Britain felt equally the lack of a succeeding generation. This was especially apparent in the Labor party, which by tradition should take a progressive stand. However, an old group in control was largely responsible for its narrow trade union mentality. Intellectuals were mistrusted. The crisis of 1931 finally estranged many of the young war generation from the party. They either drifted away to aloof cynicism in politics or found a haven in literature or transferred their field of activities to the irresponsible intellectual dilettantism of a Communist party or a Mosley Fascism in Great Britain.

The fact of over-age was visible in every political party in Great Britain and France. A statistical study of democratic statesmen before and after the First World War in these two countries would be very revealing. For the leading actors on the British political stage, for instance, it could be shown that the average age at entry into Parliament before the war was twenty-nine; after the war, thirty-eight. If they succeeded in entering the Cabinet, it was at the age of forty-three and fifty respectively. If they attained the Premiership, it was at the age of fifty-seven and sixty-two respectively. Such delay certainly showed the lack of a war generation. It is significant that Mr. Baldwin resigned as "an old man" (in his own words) at the age of seventy in favor of Mr. Neville Chamberlain, aged sixty-eight.

A similar situation could be observed in France. Undoubtedly the shadow of Thiers, who was seventy-three when he became the first President of the Third Republic, was felt throughout its whole history. The Dreyfus affair, the exciting experience of French pre-war youth, certainly could not be compared with the youth movement in Germany. The Revolution of 1789 and its ideas were still valid for French radical Socialism and the French nation as a whole. Even French radicalism had the flavor of conservatism. Yet, granted such conservatism and, in consequence of the thoroughgoing belief in reason, a natural preference for the experienced and wise old men, the age distribution in French post-war politics was anomalous. The few statesmen who rose to political importance in these years were significantly enough men like Tardieu (1876) and Laval (1883). Moral redress and appeal could not be expected from such clever strategists.

The great unrest which increasingly seized the nation unfortunately did not find an adequate leadership to master it. The Popular Front—the answer to the rising Fascist danger—was still led by the sage and lonely Léon Blum, elder statesman of pre-war Socialism. It did not bring about the much-needed rejuvenation of French politics; furthermore, this "new deal" government was inextricably caught in the international web of the Italo-Ethiopian conflict, the Spanish Civil War, and the ever-increasing Nazi threat. This coincidence rendered somewhat ill timed the social reforms that were otherwise well justified and that in turn gave opposing circles an opening wedge for fostering disintegration and indecision, apathy and outright betrayal of French traditions of long standing. The formerly young and revolutionary nation retired behind a Maginot Line, actual and spiritual. Since pre-war days France had been weakened by a continuously declining birth rate and her man power had been thinned by tremendous war losses. She found no moral restitution in the years after the Armistice. When the zero hour of the French Republic came, the new youth had not yet received its call to united action. The "strongest power" on the Continent was easily overrun by an enemy whose greatest strength was the activation and inflammation of the young. Youth seemed to have a definite place in dictatorship; it apparently was itself a youth movement, marking for the very young a leading role in the new politics. Compared with such promising prospects, democracy did not look so attractive to the young.

The constitutional structure of the western democracies necessitated a longer career in statecraft. The rise to a responsible position in the government meant a long period on trial; even to become ministerial material ("ministrable") necessitated prolonged training in local government, in Parliament, and on committees. It certainly did not attract young men who were in a hurry. This fact is of extreme importance, not only for western democracies but for any evaluation of the "young generation in politics." Their reaction against parliamentarism was largely due to this fact of slow rise. They were more than ready, therefore, to follow any short cut to power. They became the champions of anti-parliamentarian movements.

In England and France this development was largely retarded by established traditions that exalted the great institutions. The rise of Stanley Baldwin began in his defense of institutions in his Carlton Club speech against Lloyd George, the demagogue.

Again at the end of his career good fortune gave him the function of preserving a great British institution in his handling of the monarchical crisis in 1936. The belief in institutions represented a most important reserve fund in British politics.

These factors, however, should not mislead the careful observer of contemporary Europe into believing that there was no problem of generations in the western democracies. The fact that the crisis could be still dormant led, indeed, to an extremely danger-ous development that dammed the normal flow of succeeding generations.

This conflict of generations became spectacular in world affairs with the crisis of Munich. In Hitler and Chamberlain, the leading actors in this cataclysm, there met two men who belonged not only to different nations adhering to different traditions and philoso-phies, but also to two different generations. The late-Victorian was confronted with a man twenty years younger whose awaken-ing experiences had been the First World War. Chamberlain and Hitler spoke a different language; one was reared in the civic virtues of the Victorian era, the other in a militant way of life. Chamberlain stood for the long tradition of the middle-class civilization of late Victorianism. He was characteristic of the pre-vailing type of British statesmen. Neither the neurotic nor the demagogue had any room in a political England which soon after the war dismissed the dynamic Lloyd George and never recalled him. Until the Second World War came in earnest, Great Britain was ruled by a pre-war generation of trustworthy business-men who believed that a contract is a contract and that money speaks.

But the "dynamics" of post-war politics spoke a different lan-guage. The still unwritten analysis of the momentous war genera-tion would be an important key toward understanding the "spirit of Munich" because Munich meant not only the liquidation of a peace treaty, but even more the result of a war that had trans-formed the people who lived through it and above all had killed off ten million young soldiers. It is this loss of a war generation that explains many of the blunders and great ills of post-war society.

The great gap left by the war could not be filled within one generation. Those who survived came back broken in body and spirit. And even those who returned home full of decision to build a better world where international chaos would be mastered by a world order of established institutions (such as the League of Nations and the World Court at the Hague) and by the renaissance of faith—even these activists among the younger generation reflected the weariness and nervousness of a war-shattered age.

The reconstruction of Europe in a way became a race against time. If the revolution which had been heralded by the fires of the First World War could only be delayed until the time was ripe for a new generation that had not been broken by the war and had outgrown the weary cynicism of the war shock! This young generation, born after the turn of the century, showed hopeful signs of physical stamina and balance of mind. Its promise was prematurely shattered in Germany when the preceding generation of perennial warriors took over. No happier was the fate of oncoming youth in France. Split into warring camps of undeclared but yet paralyzing civil strife, it was never put to action because it was never brought to a focus; France had lost her mission in Europe. Her final military defeat was foredoomed in her loss of imagination, of living tradition, and of will power.

In England, however, beneath seeming inactivity the young forces could be observed—emerging slowly, yet hopefully signalizing a courageous and positive new generation that might in the near future fill the positions held overtime by its elders.

The renewed war seems to shatter such feeble commencements in Europe and puts the heavy burden of future reconstruction upon the shoulders of a young America that is slowly awakening to this proud and inescapable responsibility. It is too early to make any statement as to the effect of the Second World War. Much will depend on its duration, more on the outcome, and everything on the moral status of the world when peace comes.

No two wars are alike. The beginnings of this latest total conflagration reflected a completely changed temper. War did not come as a sudden shock as it did in 1914 to a generation grown up in an atmosphere of undisturbed peace and startled by this great unknown adventure. For years after the Armistice, Europe had resigned herself to meet Armageddon again (many deemed it better to face an end in horror than horror without end). When war finally came, nowhere was there enthusiasm—no flowers, no singing troops marching into glorious battles—but everywhere there was set determination. The war did not begin with high-pitched expectations; it may not end in bitter cynicism. Despite its supreme sacrifices, it must not again paralyze the vital forces of the west which may thus find another chance to win the peace. It is this new war generation alone that can successfully take up the challenge of National Socialism, turning its glittering expedients into substantial solutions and in a truly youthful spirit finally winning the revolution.

Chapter IX

DEFINITION FROM WITHOUT: DICTATORSHIP IN INTERNATIONAL POLITICS

Background for Total War

The revolution of the First World War began long before the soldiers marched across the frontiers. It did not stop when the great guns were silenced after four years of continuous command. The Armistice began as promise and hope. When the postwar order should have come of age after twenty-one years of desperate attempts at a durable peace, the Second World War awoke the latent strife. The revolution of the World Wars has not yet ended.

In the lengthening shadow of war, dictatorships loom. They are the exploiters of world revolution. They are governments for war. The analysis of their inner structure, national differentiations notwithstanding, has proved conclusively that the permanent revolution of perpetual motion is the driving force of totalitarianism. Expansion is of its essence. The rise, development, and survival of modern dictatorship are inextricably tied up with continuous dynamics.

Foreign affairs thus becomes more than an outward description of the ingroup in its differentiation from the outgroup. Foreign affairs is the life line of modern dictatorship. Its structure is militant; its human material is soldierly; its driving force is limitless conquest; in fact, all its international politics represents nothing but preparation for "the day" and a general rehearsal of tactics soon to be used on a larger scale.

The strategy of international affairs, surprising though it

seems to an unprepared world, has been successfully tried out in the nation and is now merely applied to wider fields of activities in an "extended strategy." The mistakes made by western statesmen were only a repetition of the blunders of Thyssen and von Neurath, Schacht and von Schwerin-Krosigk. Some of these pathfinders later made a sincere attempt to redeem themselves; others were caught tragically in the net of their political error without hope of making atonement. They were all comrades-in-error who had expected to employ Hitler, the demagogue, as a useful tool in patriotic rallying and as a check against the "threat of Communism"; they realized too late that they in turn had become the instruments of his master plans.

Long before the effects of the fifth column became visible in international affairs—effects which led to the spectacular successes of the Third Reich all over Europe—the mixed strategy of promise and blackmail had been tried out in internal politics and had performed miracles. In fact, the victory and continuity of the Third Reich might well have been impossible without those involuntary godfathers. Their association with rising National Socialism in turn shrouded the real character of the movement to an outside world. It was defined as the "last stage of capitalism" by its leftist opponents; as a "bulwark against Bolshevism" by its rightist sympathizers. Complete misunderstanding of the real meaning of National Socialism led many elder western statesmen to believe that it could be appeased.

These failures to realize, to meet, and to check dynamic totalitarianism cannot be explained simply in terms of "utter stupidity" or "treason" on the part of those western statesmen. Such a convenient interpretation of the blunders of the Armistice period neglects two factors which are essential for a constructive evaluation of the crisis of our age.

Ambiguity, for one, is of the essence of modern totalitarianism. If Hitler has a secret weapon, this is it. To create confusion in their opponents' camp is a well-tried strategy of seekers of change because their greatest strength is often their enemies' weakness. To disguise their real aims, to say that "Fascism as an idea is indefinable; it is a fact that is taking place," or to retire behind the smoke screen of Goebbels' formulas such as "They do not understand us"—such vacillating tactics become useful weapons in the hands of dynamic potentates striving for power. Their programmatic ambiguity has blurred political fronts and has created a useful atmosphere of indecision, an intellectual vacuum which some idealists—within and without the dictatorial country—have hoped to fill with meaning. "Social reformers" in every nation were struck by the seeming novelty of a "social and national liberation"; the versatility of kaleidoscopic totalitarianism was full of promise.

Great is the number of European statesmen (a perfect match for their forerunners in Germany) who entered an alliance with the dynamic powers in order to win "freedom" for their own people or to avert threatening dangers to their cherished order. Prime Minister Imrédy fought for "justice for Hungary," a nation which had been the chief victim of the Paris Treaty System and thus was clamoring for the liberation of her irredenta. There were young national groups, the Slovaks, the Croats, etc., who had not found the expected national independence in the post-war world; and some of their ambitious leaders pinned their hope on the new map makers of Europe. Mussolini had solemnly pledged himself to rectify these bleeding frontiers and to support the claims of national minorities. A host of German writers had become the spokesmen of Europa irredenta.

There were ardent anti-Bolshevists, above all, Russian *emigrés* who for a whole generation had been desperately waiting for their hour to come, and who in the meantime had been eking out a miserable existence in European capitals. They put their trust in the Nazi cohorts; so did the enemies of Red Russia all over the world, encouraged by Alfred Rosenberg's wordy treatises and Mussolini's and Hitler's philippics and anti-Comintern pacts.

Yet it was not the master strategy of ambiguous promises alone that led to open partnership in or silent acquiescence to the bloodless victories of aggressive dictators. More important was the fact that the situation was ripe for such an attack. As in internal politics, propaganda had to fall on fertile ground in order to be acceptable. The emergence of dictatorships was the direct outcome of the *failure of democratic attempts* at the solution of crucial issues.

The crisis in international affairs was threefold: political, economic, spiritual. Integral nationalism, economic imperialism, and moral anarchy had created the latent tensions of the pre-war unrest. They had been raised to central importance as fundamental causes of the First World War. The following peace settlement had been a sincere attempt to solve these international perplexities. They were carried into the ensuing Armistice period and indeed presented its main themes. Failure of a definite solution finally led to the Second World War which in this sense is only a continuation of an old conflict.

The last three decades must be conceived of as an essential unit, perhaps as a second Thirty Years' War, in which latent issues of the preceding period have come to a climax and must eventually lead to a final answer. The emergence of modern dictatorships must likewise be seen in greater perspective if their challenge is to be rightly understood and fully answered.

The Paris Treaty System was the first attempt to answer the pre-war query, though an intellectual nihilism of the '20's and early '30's somewhat mistook its real intentions. Its whole setting was undoubtedly laden with conflicts, and in the light of the experiences of the Armistice period even its constructive formula proved to be wrong. Its basic principle of national self-determination was 19th century, carried to its conclusion. Such a formula emphasized national sovereignty at a time when its limitation was absolutely essential to the reconstruction of Europe. This principle likewise undermined the second beam of the world order erected by the Treaty System, the League of Nations.

This organization presupposed a new political morality and the adoption of a supra-national view. This the victorious nations failed to do. In fact, the tie-up of the League Covenant with the Treaty of Versailles made these new international institutions suspect in the eyes of the vanquished. Yet it was exactly this connection that had reconciled Wilson to the peace treaty. Did not Article 19 of the Covenant give promise of peaceful change and therewith justify the hope that the initial mistakes of peacemaking were not irreparable?

No doubt the impasse of Versailles became a reality only because of the blunders of post-war international politics which made no use of the dynamic elements of the Treaty System and did not live up to the promises of a new peace order.

The Armistice period may be adequately divided into four periods of almost equal length: the war after the war (1919-24), the period of stabilization and reconciliation (1924-29), the mounting crisis (1929-33), the march of the dictators (1933-39). The Second World War constitutes the final act in the great tragedy. While the last stages, as is true in any such tragedy, seem to lead toward the inevitable end, the beginnings were indeed full of hope and great expectations. This is forgotten today when history is so often written in relation to present-day dilemmas by prophets who look backward.

The first period, *the war after the war*, was full of contradictions. There was a genuine longing for lasting peace everywhere after the convulsions and losses of war; but from the first the air in both warring camps was also thick with revenge. The warrior had not returned home yet, and the hinterland especially had not settled down to peaceful reconstruction. After the terrifying war experiences this would perhaps have been too much to ask for. Years of readjustment were needed in order to make more lasting peace possible. In fact, considering the plight Europe was in, her post-war recovery was amazing. Great Britain, significantly, was the first to find her way back to normalcy. Even the hardest hit—France and Germany—soon succeeded in their thorny task of transforming a war economy into a peace economy. Yet in spite of such miraculous performances in the different nations, the international atmosphere was still laden with excitement. The war fever had not abated.

The idea of active resistance, of *levée en masse* was still very much alive in Germany; so was the idea of active intervention on the part of France. The withdrawal of the United States from Europe, her refusal to ratify the Treaty of Versailles and to participate actively in the peace settlement undoubtedly was a blow from which this feeble order never recovered. The World War had definitely changed the old balance between Europe and the U.S.A. and had shifted the weight toward the new creditor nation of the world. But the pre-war concept of two isolated continents still prevailed on both sides of the Atlantic at a time when new vistas of Europe and the world were needed.

The American withdrawal not only irreparably foiled the intentions of the new international institutions but also widened the breach between the victorious powers, France and Great Britain. It has been rightly emphasized in Arnold Wolfers' circumspect analysis, *Britain and France Between Two Wars*, that their conflict of aims and methods was at the base of the failure of the peace settlement. If Clemenceau had had his way, it would have led to a vindictive settlement (but a settlement, nevertheless). If British statesmen had succeeded, German grievances might have been met in time. Either way might have led to some kind of stabilization. Instead of that, throughout the whole post-war period the two powers checked each other to a stalemate, and thus finally made possible the emergence of National Socialism.

Both western powers returned to their historic role in regard to Europe—France, with her claim to hegemony, identifying French and European civilization; England, in her reassertion of the time-honored principle of the balance of power which now, in her fear of French continental supremacy, made her shift toward vanquished Germany. Yet Great Britain was no longer the neutral intermediary and interested outsider of Europe. Modern war techniques, particularly aerial attacks, had robbed her of insular security and had made her an integral part of the continent. On the other hand, the structure of the British Empire as a whole had also undergone decisive transformations. The Dominions, not least because of their considerable contributions in men and material during the war, demanded independence in international politics. They were especially eager to avoid any commitments on the European continent. Particularly in the first post-war period this issue was predominant since France, having failed at Versailles to safeguard what she regarded as her territorial security, insisted on legal guarantees from her former allies. The eventual failure of the guarantee pact (the Geneva Protocol of 1924) is a case in point. The Dominions, above all Canada, declined to accept any such commitment. British foreign affairs were no longer exclusively decided in Downing Street. This situation hampered Britain's political decisions and to some extent explains her wavering policies during the entire Armistice period.

The discord in the victorious camp was especially threatening because the whole continent was critically outbalanced by the revolutionary upheavals of the Armistice period. The challenge of Soviet Russia, vital through all these years, could not be put aside merely by an attempt to push her out of Europe. The new social order which had found a realization in Soviet Russian existence had become an integral part of all the European nations. But the attempt to isolate Russia from Europe constituted a major theme; it succeeded only twenty years later at Munich, ironically enough at the time when the support of the U.S.S.R. was badly needed in order to reestablish a European balance against Nazi Germany.

Italy also underwent a revolution that had disturbing effects on the European balance, especially since the Fascist revolution was full of ambitions for the restoration of the glory of the Roman Empire. Yet, despite the fact that Mussolini made himself the spokesman of the "Have-not" nations, primarily in the Danube basin, and that his love for the spectacular seemed to be leading him to an adventurous march on the world, Italy's claims could possibly have been adjusted within the framework of Europe and without a basic disturbance. After all, Italy adhered to European concepts, and even Mussolini was realistic and sober enough to know her definite limitations as a free agent in the international scene. It was only with the rise of National Socialism that Italy began to clamor for wider fields. In fact, Il Duce capitalized on the extreme unrest of the great powers. The utter confusion of the western powers as to what to do in view of the two centers of disturbance led to initial successes in Ethiopia; but history may prove that this seemingly adroit strategy meant not only the permanent estrangement of Italy from old European ties, but also with her entrance into the orbit of Nazi Germany the definite end of an independent Italy, the final outcome of the war notwithstanding. From the weak representation by Orlando in the Council of the Big Four at Versailles to the vain performances of Mussolini's son-in-law, Count Ciano, at Hitler's general headquarters, Italy has played a role only secondary to the great powers in world politics. Today it seems idle to raise the question of whether a different orientation as initiated in the early postwar years by such statesmen as the experienced and cultivated Count Sforza could have won for her the strategic position in the European balance which the true heir to classic civilization latently possessed. Her Axis alliance unquestionably threw Italy into the arms of another Europe which was not in her blood and which certainly would not be of her making. It is Nazi Germany's New Order and no one else's.

Germany's position in Europe presented the key problem for any post-war order. In this respect, Versailles had brought about a number of disastrous decisions, the consequences of which may not have been apparent to the peacemakers and which materialized fully only with the emerging Third Reich. The loss or political dismemberment of the western provinces (Alsace-Lorraine, the Saar Basin, the Rhineland) and the denial of Austria's *Anschluss* definitely shifted Germany's weight toward the east and withheld from her the balancing influence of the more Europeanized areas of German civilization. This happened, moreover, just at the time when the Weimar Republic was making a desperate attempt to bridge the gulf between west and east in Europe and within Germany herself.

Germany throughout her whole history has held a precarious position in regard to Europe. If Europe is conceived above all as a cultural concept resulting from a series of historic experiences (as it must be), the various nations regardless of their geographic position may well show a different gradation in Europeanization. Germany in this respect found herself in a peculiar and contradictory situation. She has been the heart of Europe, its bulwark against the east, and at the same time the great stranger in the midst of European civilization. This great northern power's dual role is largely the result of her geographic position at the periphery of historic Europe. The colonization and Christianization of the "barbarians" were accomplished only in stages and reached the outer provinces belatedly and superficially. This left its mark on Germany, whose provinces were thus divided by different degrees of participation in European traditions. The western and southern part of Germany (roughly speaking, west of the Elbe) became the central stage of European history and civilization, while East Elbia definitely remained European hinterland—outpost or even outsider of the continent.

The same split could be observed within the different social strata. In spite of the fact that few nations have given as many really great Europeans to the world as Germany has done—Lessing, Beethoven, Goethe, Kant, Ranke, to mention only a few of the thousands—there was hardly any significant country on the continent that, as a whole, stood so much apart from Europe. The German intelligentsia, symbol though it was to Europe and recognized by the whole world, lived essentially separated from the German people who did not understand their language, did not know their problems, and did not share their experiences. This tragic isolation—so different from the position of the French *hommes de lettres*—was partly due to the deep antagonism which has prevailed between the political powers and the cultural elite in German history, between *Macht und Geist*, a tension that the Weimar Republic tried in vain to eliminate.

National Socialism—the great revolt against the west and against all that historic Europe stands for—by no mere accident concentrated its major attacks on the intelligentsia, that is, on those forces which, by fate and tradition, had become the chief prototypes of this Europe. At the same time, the movement's strange turn toward a pagan pre-Christian empire was not only a whim of myth-maker Alfred Rosenberg; it also brought out deep-seated traditions still alive in the German people, forces present in no other civilized European nation. The stern and frightful consequences of this recovery of pagan influences became manifest only in the fifth act of the tragedy, yet it was a latent threat even in the first stages of the Armistice period.

Indeed, the eventual *stabilization* of the post-war world presupposed a recovery of a common European conscience. Such a miracle seemed to have come true in the second period of the great Armistice. This miraculous recovery—false though it proved to be in the end—could have been accomplished only after the first epoch had been brought to a climax by the conflict in the Ruhr. The French occupation had led to spectacular passive resistance, a united demonstration of the whole German people. Although this resistance soon collapsed (resulting in an inflation that soared to astronomical heights), the Ruhr adventure meant the failure of active French intervention just the same, and thus demonstrated to both countries the limits of direct action and of continued warfare. After this, international politics took a new turn.

The new era was clearly characterized in international affairs by the personalities of Briand, Stresemann, and Sir Austen Chamberlain. Essentially they belonged to the same world. They were representatives of the European burgher class, speaking the same language, holding the same social values, and adhering to a common human ideal. Upon this fact depended the entire policy for a true understanding between the erstwhile enemies; thus was created the so-called "Spirit of Locarno."

The Locarno Pact was not simply the result of a tactical maneuver (as a suspicious interpretation suggested in later years). Stresemann's policy of understanding raised the dispute of Versailles to another level and brought at least a temporary solution of the thorny reparations issue and of political conflicts.

This was the only period when the constructive ideas of Versailles were put to a test. These short five years meant Europe's chance to arrive at a peaceful solution. The eventual failure should not mislead the circumspect observer into underestimating the significance of the great trial and the actual influence of this temporary peace upon a whole generation.

Especially in Germany, the years 1924-1929, although in retrospect they seemed to be merely a surface boom, diffused an extraordinary amount of burgher philosophy even among the proletariat. This period of stabilization to a certain extent brought about a social readjustment by providing a rest period in which burgher values could revive. However, time was too short to bring about the longed-for peace. Furthermore, the suspicion and hatred of the first five years had not completely died down. The shadows of past memories could not be wiped out—particularly in France.

These difficulties became obvious in the fate of the League of Nations, which seemingly experienced its crowning success during this second period. No doubt it was the only time when Geneva took the center of the international stage. Germany, in consequence of Locarno, entered the League Council as a member with equal rights. This fact alone led to a transformation of the League and brought it nearer to the original intentions of its idealistic champions. Yet even in those years the discords between the major powers were evident. They derived in essence from divergent concepts of Europe.

Three interpretations of the League prevailed: reactionary, realistic, idealistic. They were irreconcilable. France had from the beginning conceived the League as an instrument to preserve and enforce the *status quo* of Versailles—a part of that system of security which she so emphatically strove for and which had been denied to her by her former allies. The "sanitary cordon" which she threw around Germany with the help of the succession states bordering Germany was another attempt at achieving peace of mind. Suspicion, natural to a nation of farmers and understandable for a country that had experienced three invasions in one century, did not create conditions favorable for the young institution.

One may say that Stresemann viewed the League in a different light. In his naturally liberal optimism he saw a silver lining where others scarcely perceived the first feeble rays. When one reads his maiden speech in the League Assembly, one easily perceives a concept of the League as a concert of the world's powers, an idea which, so different from France's monolithic concept of Europe, closely followed the "Europeans" among the German thinkers. At the same time this address showed a specific German interest in using the League machinery to better the German plight—thus making it an agency for a peaceful change in the order established at Versailles. In fact, Stresemann's concept of the League can be best summarized in realistic terms as a chessboard on which the great game of world diplomacy was being played. Such an interpretation came near to the reality. The League served as a meeting ground, and in this capacity it could and did perform minor miracles. The fact of meeting together instead of exchanging fiery notes between chancelleries often allowed a promising cooling-off period and frequently even brought success.

The British largely shared the German view. Yet, despite their realistic approach, they expected more from the League. In a way, Great Britain realized that her historic role as the great balancer was now beyond her power in view of the state of the British Empire and of the world. The *pax Britannica* was thus committed to the League. This typically British decision showed the strange mixture of selfish interests and the realization of the needs of the world at large. Furthermore, Great Britain could point proudly at the transformation that the British Empire itself was undergoing. The gradual change into a democratic and cooperative Commonwealth of Nations, finally legalized in the Statute of Westminster, could be presented as the forerunner of a League to be.

Such a concept of the League also approached the extremely idealistic thoughts conceived by Wilson and undoubtedly shared by many middle-class champions of Geneva. For them, behind this institution stood the great burgher ideal: the *world parliament*. It transferred into the sphere of international relations the internal methods and institutions of parliamentarism, the basis of which was reliance upon discussion and negotiation, instead of force and violence, to settle group conflicts. These free discussions in the political market place would finally result in generally recognized laws, as calculable and reasonable as the just price in economics and the one and only truth in philosophy.

One can easily perceive the difficulties of this idealistic conception if he recalls the fact that the League was organized at the time when the fundamental belief in a universally valid truth had been shattered by the World War and the post-war difficulties, and when the social basis of the European middle class had suffered a tremendous upheaval.

Those difficulties and failures most certainly give no grounds for a final judgment of the League as an institution of international order; if for no other reason, time did not permit an adequate test. It may take generations—as did the transition from feudal tribalism to the creation of the "Rechtsstaat"—before the definite contours of international order are guaranteed. Yet even this short experiment has brought out three fundamental preconditions for international organization—in fact, prerequisites for any legal system: universality, law enforcement, and peaceful change.

Universal acceptance of the law, or at least the unchallenged preponderance of its power, is the first precondition for any working legal system. A law that does not gain the moral sanction and full backing of public opinion cannot last in the long run. "Equality before the law" is one essential guarantee of this general approval. Even more important is a common set of values adhered to by all the members of the community. Such preconditions are no less basic for an international society. Failure to exterminate initial inequalities among the member states, especially in respect to armament and national sovereignty, and continuation of the strategy of great power politics has been a bad omen for the League.

There is also good reason to claim, as did little Switzerland in the discussion over Soviet Russia's entrance into the League, that the success of this institution is dependent upon a common political creed. In fact, differences of opinion often touched upon fundamentals. The acceptance of this prerequisite, however, would have defeated the principle of universality. A league of democratic nations alone would in reality have represented nothing but an alliance which by its very existence meant a challenge to the non-democratic powers, and thus would readily have invited preparation for war instead of organization for peace. This dilemma between universality and homogeneity—at the base of the crisis in international organization in the Armistice period—was simply the result of an ideological schism. Post-war Europe, even more than 19th-century Europe, was divided by ideologies that not only had found definite political representation but had also been raised to political religions. Thus they wore thin the bonds of cultural and moral unity which still held together the unstable peace of 19th-century Europe.

Collective security, which the League promised as an answer to pre-war anarchy, depended not so much on the necessary machinery for defining the lawbreaker (which the Covenant provided, at least in a framework) as on unquestioned unanimity among the member states as to the world order to be established. And here the split was wide open.

Codification could be the legal recognition of only an existing order; it could never, as such, establish a unified system which was not generally accepted. Basically the League's difficulties derived from a spiritual crisis. The fiasco of a modern Tower of Babel could be avoided only if the partners spoke the same language and adhered to the same values. This they did not do.

The second difficulty for the League derived from the need of law enforcement, which is essential for any established order. Here again, the young institution met barriers that were insurmountable, at least for the time being. The need to provide the League "with teeth" was generally recognized. In fact, there was an opportunity (so rare in history) to make use of a new and extremely powerful military weapon. If the new air force had been monopolized by the League, this step might have been as historic as the seizure of the invention of gunpowder by the rising monarchs. The new feudalism of modern tribalism might have been broken. But the statesmen of the Armistice period did not possess enough perspective and initiative to seize this occasion.

The real failure to achieve a well-functioning system of sanctions was due to deeper causes than the personal inadequacies of statesmen. The enforcement of the League's laws as a matter of course challenged the principle of national sovereignty. Yet this same principle seemed to have reached its climax in this post-war period with the general acceptance of national self-determination.

Significantly, the real resistance did not come primarily from the newly created smaller nations which soon realized that their only hope for survival rested with the League. Beneš of Czechoslovakia became the prototype of the new European statesmanship. The strongest defense of national sovereignty was made by the great powers. Wherever League policies touched upon their spheres of interest, the League had no chance.

The League had no armed force of its own; it had to appeal to the powers for law enforcement and even for police, such as were needed during the Saar plebiscite. In fact, its policies went only as far as the great powers allowed them to go. These powers in turn directed their actions exclusively in terms of national interest and were especially eager to counteract any curtailment of their sovereign rights. The central issue of any international order and of permanent peace, however, involved just such a renunciation and limitation of national sovereignty. This idea was too fully entrenched in the minds of the European peoples to be softened by the desire for international cooperation, sincere though it had become all over Europe. The crisis of national existence had not yet been carried far enough to break the concepts of a bygone narrow nationalism. The supreme crisis was soon to come.

That the League could not fulfill its third requirement, to serve as an agency for peaceful change, is not a matter for surprise, in view of the state of the world. The machinery for this essential function did exist. Equity could prevail if the nations so willed. But the responsible protagonists failed completely to realize that peace is a dynamic and continuous process and that any attempt to petrify it in a *status quo* is doomed. The second period showed the flaws in the existing international institutions and even more in the relations between the major powers. Such failures led directly to the third period of the Armistice years.

The *mounting crisis* brought to the fore the inner weakness in the premature peace order that had been conceived after the First World War and was slowly emerging in the second period. The third act in Europe's tragedy demonstrated how fragile was the basis of the preceding "stabilization and reconciliation." This was especially obvious in Germany, where the prosperity of 1924–1929 proved to be only apparent. But it was not until five years later that the social and political consequences of the inflation became evident. It meant the beginning of the end for the middle classes. It foreshadowed the rise of National Socialism.

In international affairs the crisis first appeared in international finance, with the breakdown of the Austrian Credit Institute (Oesterreichische Kredit Anstalt). It was not the first time that Austria had been the powder keg of world politics. In fact, the Austrian Republic was the battlefield of power politics; it echoed the great drama of post-war Europe. Its story was the history of European intervention. Here began the renewed world crisis of the '30's. Austria was also the first victim to fall before Hitler's march on the world.

Austria's position had been untenable from the beginning. Vienna had no hinterland; cut off from all international trade routes, there was no genuine solution for an isolated Vienna that had been the center of the life of the Danube monarchy and needed the entire Danube basin for her existence. But since the economic coordination of this natural unit seemed to be impossible in the midst of the high-pitched nationalism of the new succession states, nothing was left for Austria but to attempt a close economic understanding with her natural and greater partner in the north. The ill-fated tariff union with Germany in March, 1931, led to the first united intervention by the "guarantors" of the peace treaty. By appealing to Geneva and the Hague Court of International Justice, they succeeded in breaking this attempt by Austria to solve her economic stalemate. Significantly the Italian representative, Anzilotti, cast the decisive negative vote.

If these statesmen had only perceived that this act of theirs meant the factual end of Austrian independence and of near-peace for post-war Europe! In stopping the economic *Anschluss*, they seemingly succeeded in balancing German expansion, but in reality they released a much greater stream that soon engulfed the whole of Europe.

The breakdown of the leading banking institution, the Kredit Anstalt, first victim of the ensuing depression, was the official beginning of the world economic crisis. It had its international repercussions in the German banking crisis of July, 1931, and the break in the British pound in August, 1931. The Bank of England, which had heavily financed the Austrian institution, had to withstand a drain on its own resources. International power politics, especially French political pressure, played a great part in the economic crisis around Vienna. The effect of the European crisis was felt everywhere. The world's chief creditor was also thrown into this turmoil—the great American depression set in.

Of course, it would be utterly misleading to view this widespread crisis as an economic phenomenon alone. The major social threat—millions of unemployed—had unheard-of political implications. This was the hour of birth of a rootless radicalism. This fatal transformation brought the nations that had been worst hit close to civil war, with entrenched private armies and revolutions looming. Hitler's hour was near. In foreign affairs, understanding, compromise, and adjustment were gone. It was the period of a last hopeless attempt at new formulas; but faith in formulas had lost its spell, and they were presented without enthusiasm. Half-hearted measures and suggestions could not turn the tide. The Briand "Europa memorandum" of 1932 was such a belated attempt. It could not but fail.

One had only to observe the Briand-Laval visit to Berlin in 1931 (what an occasion this first visit of French statesmen to Germany after the war could have been!), or Bruening's desperate calls at the western capitals, to know that the Armistice had reached a point beyond which lay once again the valley of war.

During the last years of the breathing spell before the storm broke, when great vision and daring enterprise were needed, the countries that should have taken the initiative—France and England—were hopelessly split within and between themselves. Europe was still run by pre-war statesmen, sincere indeed, but unimaginative—and so tired! Soon even the last fighters of the second period died: Stresemann, Briand, Sir Austen Chamberlain. Those who were left were men like Baldwin and Laval. Theirs is a grave responsibility before history. It was not the institutions and the methods of international politics that made the great conferences of the early '30's a pathetic show; it was the men who failed.

It is needless to enumerate the blunders of the disarmament and reparations discussions and of the futile economic world conferences. Fear and fatalism ruled the minds of the great; the people without leaders were confused, desperate, and open to almost any suggestion. One must fully grasp the moral low of the early '30's in order to understand the relative ease with which the dictators seized power at home and entrenched themselves in a world without vigor and direction.

By 1933 the crisis reached its climax. Almost until the last minute the tide could doubtless have been turned. Such a chance might have been seized by courageous men. But the further the crisis progressed, the more it seemed that only a miracle could effect the salvation of Europe—a fatalistic Europe which took to the somber predictions of Spengler's *Decline of the West* and thus left the door wide open to the dictators. They marched in.

The *march of the dictators*, preparatory to their final concerted assault, was the theme of the fourth period. Their attack had a foreboding prelude in far-off Manchuria when Japan began her "undeclared war" in order to establish her new order, "The East Asia Co-Prosperity Sphere." This happened in 1931 while a confused Europe was fully occupied with the great economic depression. Ten years later, the Chinese incident engulfed all the powers around the Pacific in a world conflagration.

An analysis of this "first action" of larger dimensions in the post-war world might easily show amazing parallels with the methods and motivations which were later displayed by the European dictators. In fact, the "Prussians of the east" manifested the same underlying philosophy of a new tribalism that became the driving force of rising National Socialism. The Berlin-Tokyo axis was more than a tactical alliance. The concepts of these new comrades-in-arms were diametrically opposed to those of the peoples who respected responsible individualism and supra-nationalism as their basic tenets. Inevitable was the clash with the powers that lived by the standards of western civilization and, in this post-war period, made their first timid attempts at world-wide organization.

The Manchuria incident was the first clash of great power politics with the League of Nations and thus was the first test case for the young institution. China appealed to the League, and on December 10, 1931, the Council of the League appointed an international commission. Ten months later, this Lytton Commission reported to the League after careful investigation of the whole Sino-Japanese situation. The guardedly worded document recommended direct negotiations and at least nominal restoration of Manchuria to China. The League referred the report to a special December meeting of the League Assembly for action. In the meantime—in fact, seven days before the Lytton report was made public—Japan had signed a treaty with the state of Manchukuo (September 13, 1932), thus establishing a policy of *fait accompli* which became standard strategy for modern dictatorships. The League failed to act. On March 27, 1933, Japan informed Geneva of her intention to withdraw her membership.

Three days earlier, the Nazi dictatorship had been legalized by the passage of the "Enabling Act" in a well-staged demonstration by the newly elected Reichstag. The military aspect of the new revolution was made obvious in its hour of birth. It occurred at Potsdam, not at Weimar. In fact, by the clever manipulation of the master propagandist, the Third Reich looked like a renewal of Bismarck's empire—but with greater pomp and glory. Hitler bowing before Hindenburg seemed to symbolize to a confused middle class and to a no less stunned outside world the fact that the ill-considered outbursts of early revolutionaries from then on would be directed into the channels of a well-balanced foreign policy. In the same way that Bismarck's "art of the possible," after rectifying the *injuria temporum*, served as a force for peace in Europe, German conservatives and many European statesmen expected from the victorious Fuehrer a turn toward statesmanlike responsibility.

But the international climate had changed and the Japanese action was the first crystallization of the transformation. The United States was the only power which fully recognized the world-wide implications of the "Manchukuo crisis." She established in the Stimson doctrine and her non-recognition of forcibly seized territory a declaration of principle which gave her Far Eastern policy the consistency and backbone so badly lacking in the attitude of the other western powers. Britain's failure to support the United States in her strong stand led to coolness between the Anglo-American powers.

More far-reaching was the effect on Europe of the Manchukuo incident and the blunders of the League. Japan's unchallenged success encouraged imitation. Mussolini was the first to learn the Far Eastern lesson. The Italo-Ethiopian War was the next great attack that brought the issue much closer to Europe. Again two member states of the Geneva Assembly were involved. Ethiopia, in fact, had been sponsored in the League by Italy herself, who now denounced her as unworthy of independent existence. Italy declared herself ready to take over the "white man's burden" in the last free spot in Africa and—with the help of machine guns and airplanes to be sure—to bring European civilization to a savage people.

Population pressure figured high as an argument for direct action. (Ethiopia, incidentally, held out no promises in this respect.) More important was the drive for power and prestige to revenge the defeat of Adowa forty years earlier and to fulfill the great dreams of expansion and the creation of Mare Nostrum.

The importance of the Italo-Ethiopian War lay not so much in the actual conquest. (Italy certainly did not reap any fruits from her African Empire during the short time it lasted.) Not even the new possession's strategic threat against Egypt and the British Empire's life line was decisive. Much more significant in the pattern of European politics were the after-effects and above all the failure of the League to enforce its laws. This held especially true now, when the League really tried to make its authority felt by applying sanctions against the aggressor—and failed.

"Italy against the world" had succeeded. The defeat of the League was undoubtedly due to the half-hearted measures taken against Fascist Italy. When Mussolini threatened to regard the oil sanctions as a *casus belli*, Geneva avoided the application of this, her only effective weapon. This soft-pedaling was partly the result of a genuine desire for peace among the western peoples who wanted sanctions, as the 1935 "peace ballot" in England had shown, but at the same time dreaded the possible consequence: war. A strong and courageous political leadership might have directed a well-meaning though confused public, but such leaders were missing. The responsible statesmen were wavering. Some of them, even among the military, were afraid to call the bluff of an Italian navy and air force whose strength was unknown. Others were concerned about the possible breakdown of Fascist Italy (if she failed in international affairs) and, in this case, could picture as Mussolini's successor only a much dreaded radical, perhaps Bolshevist, regime. This nightmare of numerous western conservatives became useful in Fascist strategy. Many other thoughtful diplomats were eager to avoid estranging Italy in view of a much greater danger: the Third Reich. They were therefore ready to compromise and to satisfy some of Italy's ambitions even though such "understanding" looked much like blackmail. After all, the Stresa front erected in January, 1935, between Great Britain, France, and Italy against the German threat had been regarded as a basis of European peace. Even Mussolini had prided himself on his role of great arbiter in the Four-Power Pact. This guarantee would be at stake with an outright attack against Italy.

There were numerous European statesmen like Pierre Laval who hoped for the erection of a Latin bloc against Nazi Germany. The compromise suggestion of the Hoare-Laval plan during the Italo-Ethiopian conflict was the result of such considerations. (This idea was not completely dismissed even after the Second World War began. It was reflected in an undecided attitude toward Fascist Italy until her entrance into the war just before France collapsed.) There is no doubt that the chief winner in the Italo-Ethiopian War was Nazi Germany. The simple fact of non-participation in the League sanctions (which, incidentally, meant good business for Germany) indebted Italy to the Third Reich to such an extent that the erstwhile greatest opponent to Hitler's ambitions in the Danube basin became his staunchest supporter and soon his vassal.

How the strategic position of Italy had changed! In July, 1934, Hitler's hope of seizing Austria by a dilettante *Putsch* had been shattered by Mussolini's stern warning that the Fascist cohorts were ready at the Brenner Pass to march against a Nazi invasion of Austria. Only two years later, Il Duce had to advise his Austrian protégé, Schuschnigg, successor of the assassinated Chancellor Dollfuss, that he had better accept a German "Treaty of Friendship." This surrender to the Nazis was somewhat sweetened by an additional eighteen months granted Austria in which to adjust her internal structure to that of her big brother in the north. A vain hope it was for little Austria to expect any turn of the tide. When the time ran short, Schuschnigg was ordered to appear before the Fuehrer at Berchtesgaden to undergo a humiliating ordeal.

The choice before Schuschnigg was clear: surrender or destruction of Austria. The only thing left for this tragic marionette of the last act was a great gesture: the calling of a plebiscite in order to show the outside world that the final *Anschluss* was not a voluntary homecoming of the Austrians to the Reich. But the fate of Austria and that of central Europe had been decided long before on the far-off battlefields of Ethiopia.

This African campaign opened the way for another even more decisive step of Hitler's Germany, perhaps the most important one before the Third Reich launched its march against Europe and the world. While the western powers were fully occupied with Italy's moves, Hitler seized the strategic opportunity to march into the Rhineland. This remilitarization of the Rhineland (March 7, 1936)—an open breach of the stipulations of Versailles and of the Locarno Treaty—was the real defense line between two political continents. By erecting the West Wall fortifications, Germany definitely blocked French military aid for southeastern Europe, help on which the succession states had counted for their survival. France's allies in the Danube basin whom she had regarded as a "sanitary cordon" around defeated Germany now had to work for a new political orientation.

Since the rise of Hitler, the small succession states had become feverishly active. Traveling statesmen were a daily sight, and the ubiquitous and ambitious Polish foreign minister, Colonel Beck, was everywhere. His master scheme called for a "Third Europe" extending from the Baltic to the Black Sea. It might have kept the balance between the German and Russian dictatorships; it might have served as a buffer and a neutralizing strip. But his plan could not conceal his design of great power politics. Suspicion killed these ambitious projects.

Other plans, however, crystallized in this period. An important instrument and diplomatic high light in the front against the German advance might have been the Franco-Soviet treaty of May 2, 1935, following Russia's entrance into the League in September, 1934. The Czech mutual aid treaty with the U.S.S.R. of May 17, 1935, was a further result of this defensive coalition.

Even more significant might have become the Balkan Entente of February 9, 1934 (including Yugoslavia, Greece, Rumania, and Turkey). Primarily meant as an insurance against Bulgaria, it represented the first crystallization of an awakening consciousness on the part of the small nations—"the Balkans for the Balkan people." These understandings, while removing long-standing sources of friction and certainly leading to a general *rapprochement* among neighbors, were even more indicative of the nervous tension. A policy of reservation, of counter assurances, and of double plays from then on characterized the dealings of the southern European nations. The shadow of the increasing might of Hitler's Reich grew longer and longer.

Throughout all these years Hitler's objectives had been clear and unchanged. To the astute observer they were twofold: the first was to bring all the German minorities under the sway of the Third Reich. This objective was inseparably linked with the revival of the old *Drang nach dem Osten*. To accomplish this purpose National Socialist "diplomacy" tried to bring the internal government of the various states under German influence, either directly, as was done in Austria, or by encouraging and financing Nazi movements in southern European countries.

Hitler's second objective was his determination to destroy or at least to split up the existing international blocs. In this attempt Germany had hearty cooperation from Italy, especially after the accord of Berchtesgaden on October 25, 1936, the beginning of the Rome-Berlin axis.

Germany's political ambitions were well supported by her economic infiltration into the southeastern countries. Dr. Hjalmar Schacht went out to capture the Balkans for German trade and to exchange German industrial products for urgently needed raw materials, thus guaranteeing economic autarchy, the dream of Nazi economics. Ingenious barter treaties were introduced. They were sweetened for the consumption of the not-too-willing Danubian countries by an offer to reduce their frozen credits in the Reich. This successful trade offensive was a political asset in Hitler's hands. Included in the German economic orbit, the

Danubian countries became more and more dependent on Germany's grace. Her exports to Rumania, Hungary, Yugoslavia, Bulgaria, and Greece increased by 260 per cent in the first four years of the Nazi rule; imports in the same period increased by 190 per cent. With further drives during 1938 and particularly with Austria's inclusion in the Reich, these figures increased considerably. An interesting feature in this respect is the fact that a large part of Germany's manufactured exports included armaments, thus automatically binding these nations to the German source in "case of emergency."

This "unarmed" conquest, however, was not Germany's only attempt to direct the international orientation of the southeastern nations. It was accompanied by a systematic propaganda drive to shape the internal policies of the countries concerned. Anti-Semitism always found a fruitful soil in the Balkans. National Socialist parties, with the Reich's financial backing, grew up in every country. These attempts had varying results in the different states. The nations wavered between semi-democratic and more overtly Fascist governments. Their internal policies were nothing but the reflection of the changing constellations in international affairs—a repetition of the world powers' struggle for dominance in every country. In the last analysis, the fate of southeastern Europe always depended on the political and economic relations between the world powers. The weakening influence of the western democracies and the increasing power of the Fascist bloc became the definite trend. An ideological assimilation went on steadily over a period of years. True, there were ups and downs in this ideological infiltration. The frequent changes in the internal political fronts were undoubtedly significant for the uncertainty of the European situation. The prestige of the western powers was still great until September, 1938.

STRATEGIES OF CONQUEST

The first period of the Third Reich's undercover expansion was characterized by a number of specific strategies. *Bilateral treaties* were the first weapon of National Socialist foreign politics. The Hitler-Pilsudski treaty of January, 1934, was the first evidence of this strategy. It was also the first example of what these new treaties of friendship (concluded for ten years) really meant in the policy of permanent conspiracy. Pilsudski did not accept the treaty until he had assured himself that the western powers would not be ready for "preventive action" against Hitler. "Make peace with the dictators" and *Sauve qui peut* became the slogan of the small powers. This was a clear indication of the decline of confidence in the League of Nations and in collective security. To Hitler, bilateral treaties were a definite means of isolating the enemy one by one. Hitler continued this policy in Norway, Holland, Belgium, and France, and southeastern Europe even after World War II began. There is no doubt that it was also his intention to use this strategy when he attacked Russia. But here, for the first time, the strategy failed.

Bilateral treaties and isolation of the enemy were the background of Hitler's second strategy, the *piecemeal policy*. "The shrewd victor will, when possible, present his demands to the conquered piecemeal," he says in *Mein Kampf*. He continues: "A people without character—and such will be any people that voluntarily submits—will see no sufficient reason for again going to war over any one of his several encroachments. The more extortions of this kind are docilely accepted, the more unjustified will it seem to people finally to go to war over a new act of oppression . . . especially since they all in all have already put up with so many more and greater abuses in patient silence." This policy of erosion and of the crippling of the enemy's will became a major strategy in his conquests.

The third element in Hitler's strategy was his clever use of the *fear of Bolshevism*. By presenting himself as the savior from the Red peril, he won over many among the reluctant middle class on the internal front. The same policy was simply repeated in international affairs when Fascism felt strong enough to march against the world.

This policy of confusion no doubt met with appreciable success among the aristocratic classes in Great Britain and France who lived under the shadow of the great fear: social revolution from below. The U.S.S.R. and the Comintern, their argument went, represented the most menacing of all threats to their values and their way of life. Hence they supported the anti-Comintern crusaders who were arming and who should be strengthened for a final attack against Soviet Russia—a conflict in which the western powers should remain neutral. This hope of finding in the Fascist triplice a militant check against the threatening world revolution made the preservation of such a protective power essential for the survival of western capitalism. The breakdown of Fascism, especially since it was identified with the succession of Communism, had to be prevented at any price. This consideration prevented the application of oil sanctions during the Italo-Ethiopian War and was most influential in the acceptance of the Munich Accord by conservative circles. Incidentally, the diversion of dynamic nationalism toward southeastern and eastern Europe was viewed as clever strategy. Did it not offer a safety valve for an otherwise threatening explosion of bottled-up Germany, thus preserving the *status quo* of the old colonial empires? It looked like a splendid proposition, particularly since the price would still be paid out of a margin of safety by concessions from a third party, i.e., one of the weak European succession states.

Needless to say, this interpretation of the role of Fascist dictatorship in international affairs was most erroneous and unquestionably embodied great risks for any capitalist oligarchy which apparently adopted it. Moscow might win the conflict and thus inevitably spread Communism over the world. Victorious Fascism might achieve invincibility and then turn against the west, or it might utilize its power to attack not the U.S.S.R. but the western powers instead. It was this course that National Socialism finally chose after assuring itself, for the time being at least, of Russia's neutrality by the German-Russian treaty of August, 1939.

This analysis of Fascist dictatorship may seem incomprehensible in view of subsequent events, especially since the outcome could easily have been foreseen if the lesson of dictatorship's previous internal development had only been learned.

Yet the Fascist success was not due simply to the "utter stupidity" or the "capitalist intrigues" of "senile and tricky" western statesmen. Democracy found itself in a dilemma which derived from the tripartite division of the post-war world into Democracy, Bolshevism, and Fascism. The existence of this triangle is responsible for a good deal of the confusion in the ensuing ideological war. The fight on two ideological fronts has proved as fatal as the opening of two military fronts in actual warfare.

It did not help (though it seemed to simplify matters) to pretend that there were only two parties—friend and enemy, insiders and outsiders—and that, for instance, a common enmity against Communism identified Tory democracy with Fascism. They were still worlds apart. It was even more fatal not to recognize the supreme challenger in a world of power politics. Indecision as to whom to regard as the primary and more dangerous enemy led, in the Italo-Ethiopian War for example, to democracy's twofold defeat at the hands of Italy and Germany. Not until 1941 did the British—and only then because of the realist Churchill—learn the lesson that any good history text could have taught them, that the strongest military force could be checked in its aggression only by a coalition of the other powers and that therefore the most promising policy for a hegemonic power would be to counteract the establishment of such a combination. *Divide et impera* is a time-honored strategy; but the western statesmen, and at times Soviet Russia as well, were maneuvered into an impasse that gave the Axis strategists the decisive upper hand.

That this triangular policy was well planned and shrewdly administered by the Fascist powers is evidenced by an analysis of the Spanish Civil War. This war seemed to be only a side show; in fact it somewhat sidetracked the western powers (a fact which in itself was clever strategy on the part of the Brown International) by focusing their interest on the periphery of Europe instead of concentrating it on the center of peril—the Danube basin, Czechoslovakia above all. Yet this three-year struggle in Spain was an important prelude to the Second World War and in a sense its first battle. Its outcome had strategic significance for Republican France, which now had to face a three-front threat with the rise of a third Fascist power on her frontiers. The Franco victory was of even greater importance to the British Empire because Nationalist Spain would certainly endanger Gibraltar and the British life line in the Mediterranean. That both countries, France and England, did not act in view of these obvious dangers is due to the ideological confusion which had been largely created by the Fascist intervention on the side of General Franco against the "Bolshevist" government of Republican Spain. Notwithstanding the justification of this accusation against a plotting Third International (if Moscow actually had serious intentions of this kind, she certainly chose a poor time and place, and no doubt gave not much material support to such a policy), the fact remains that the Fascist powers succeeded in raising the inner Spanish revolution to an international civil war. The monster of Bolshevism was haunting a frightened bourgeoisie. The battlefront went right through the western democracies, splitting them wide open. Great Britain experienced such divisions both at home and throughout the Empire.

The Popular Front government of Léon Blum found itself in an even more precarious position. While it naturally sympathized with the Republican government, it could not push the issue without risking the open civil war that had been a latent threat in France since the early '30's. Furthermore, Blum was dependent on British support for a positive policy toward Spain. This support, however, could not be expected from the British "National Government." Too many of its members viewed Fascism and National Socialism as the protectors of the west against the "Bolshevist hordes." The result of this ideological confusion was the fatal non-intervention policy—a tragicomedy of errors. Spain was a general rehearsal of the strategy of the triangle. It was a complete success for the Fascist powers.

The Spanish Civil War served no less as an experimental laboratory for military strategies. Indeed, it was a godsend for the untried armed forces of Nazi Germany which thus secured experience in actual combat, tested her new weapons for the mechanized forces and the young Luftwaffe, and won confidence for her invincibility.

From Manchukuo to Ethiopia to Spain the march of the dictators with their policy of direct action moved closer and closer to the main battlefield of European politics until it finally struck center in the Czechoslovakian crisis.

The attack against Czechoslovakia was begun with the help of a fourth weapon of strategy taken directly from the arsenals of victorious democracies. In fact, it was *the* basis of their postwar order that National Socialism now usurped for its own policy: the principle of *national self-determination*. What else was the idea of Greater Germany that Hitler made the keystone of his foreign policy? In the name of this principle he made his initial conquests and his further claims for the rectification of Versailles. The first round was won in the Saar plebiscite which had been set by the treaty and only incidentally occurred in the early days of the Third Reich. This plebiscite was still being propagandistically built up as a Nazi victory. Then followed the reintroduction of military conscription, the remilitarization of the Rhineland, and Germany's liberation from Allied river control. These measures, though unilaterally enforced by the Third Reich, could still be interpreted in terms of national self-determination. This interpretation was also possible for the first move beyond Germany's frontiers: the *Anschluss* of Austria. The western powers, particularly Great Britain, felt unable to resist such a step which, after all, could be construed as identical with the spirit of the Paris Treaty System.

The systematic erosion of the Treaty System soon showed results; in fact it morally disarmed especially those western statesmen who were suffering from a guilty conscience because of Versailles and who in fairness recognized Germany's grievances.

Tied up with the piecemeal policy, the strategy of *fait accompli*, and the constant threat of war in earnest to a world that wanted peace at almost any price, Hitler's policies of bloodless conquest performed miracles. They strengthened his hold on the

German people and even more his strategic position in a world of power politics.

While Hitler seemed to care only for the protection of "those fellow Germans who live beyond our frontiers," as he emphatically stated in his speech on February 20, 1938, which opened the Austrian action, the *Anschluss* was no less a move in a war strategy. With Austria a part of Greater Germany, Czechoslovakia was caught in a pincers and was hopelessly lost whenever Germany was ready to attack.

The assault soon followed. Again it was shrouded by the national minorities issue. Sudeten Germany was presented as "the last territorial claim" the Third Reich had on a world that was organized according to the principle of national self-determination and thus could not possibly resist such a proper claim. In fact, national self-determination was made the main strategy in this last unchallenged major campaign. It is the irony of history that Versailles was destroyed by its own principle.

The day after the Munich Pact was signed, the semi-official *Deutsche Diplomatische Korrespondenz* said sarcastically that the new accord represented the first application of a peaceful revision following Article 19 of the League Covenant and that it was based upon the core of Wilson's Fourteen Points. The Sudeten German issue certainly would have been poor justification for a renewed world war in a post-Versailles world.

If one is to believe Neville Chamberlain's own interpretation, Munich should have been the beginning of a new era—"Peace in our time"—after all possible frictions and injustices had been formally removed by this last sacrifice, the secession of Sudetenland. Undoubtedly the complete record of the crisis year would give definite indications that there had been deliberate planning on the part of the western powers to "sell out" Czechoslovakia.

As early as May 5, 1938, on the basis of statements by the highest authority, the dispatches of Joseph Driscoll, London correspondent of the *Herald Tribune*, indicated the British unwillingness to fight, and hinted at partition as the solution. One may add to this the strange role of Bonnet throughout the crisis, the

Runciman mission including its report and far-reaching proposals, and finally the historic *London Times* editorial of September 7 suggesting the secession of Sudetenland. All these facts give color to such an analysis.

Yet all these moves, questionable though they were in respect to Czechoslovakia, especially on the part of France which had a full-fledged alliance with the Czechs and had repeatedly guaranteed armed support in case of aggression, were interpreted by Chamberlain as a great house-cleaning. For a while he really believed that he had brought home a "peace with honor" after having thrice flown to Germany. He had been partly flattered into this belief by the spontaneous and sincere ovation given him by the frightened people of Munich.

Long before Chamberlain made his *tour de force*, which was not without personal sacrifice of prestige and precedence, he had officially abandoned the basis of the post-war settlement. It was he who, on June 10, 1936, declared that the "midsummer madness" of sanctions was dead. Half-brother of Sir Austen, the great champion of the League, he sought a new realism free of the "League romanticism of early post-war idealists." At the outset of the crisis (February 22, 1938) he said: "The League is unable to provide collective security." A European concert of powers— a renewal of Mussolini's stillborn Four Power Pact of 1933—was to take its place. How unreal this realist's dream looks in view of post-Munich history!

A careful analysis of Munich would prove that it could not be explained merely in terms of one motive—high or low, "peace in our time" or "treason"—but that its acceptance by the western powers was due to numerous motives.

The most inclusive interpretation and the one most closely following the factual analysis of the crisis sees in its outcome no finality, no definite decision, but an armistice, perhaps only a postponement of a hardly avoidable clash between two worlds. International affairs reflected not only a clash between imperialisms but a new religious war of conflicting ideologies. Democracy and dictatorship had a different concept of life; even if they used the same vocabulary, it had a different meaning. How was any real, not merely tactical, understanding possible between such uncompromising doctrines? Their clashing interests and concepts could not be reconciled. Munich could serve as a case study. Carefully evaluating all the essential moves and conflicting statements, one sees the complexity of the motives that explain the final surrender by the western democracies. Universal rejection of war as a useful instrument of policy; military unpreparedness; fear on the part of the propertied group that a conflict would result in final economic disintegration and Communist chaos; and last but not least physical fear—these were the chief factors in the Anglo-French capitulation.

Czechoslovakia was only the front for a much greater drama. Indeed, it may be well to remember that "the organic inconsistency of the mosaic state" and its necessary dismemberment did not appear on the European agenda until 1938. As late as March of that year Germany made the explicit declaration that she would respect the Czechoslovak frontiers. Autarchy for the Sudeten Germans within the Czechoslovak state was the only claim made even by the extremely radical Henlein movement.

Czechoslovakia was not just a caprice of the peacemakers. She had a specific function in the post-war world; her significance was twofold. She was the bulwark of France's system of alliances, a part of the "sanitary cordon" around Germany. Prague was the key to that system, as was also the Little Entente, organized above all to preserve the *status quo* of the succession states. In addition to this, however, Czechoslovakia stood for a synthetic state. She might have symbolized a synthetic process which in central Europe was the only alternative to German domination. Even if the principle of national self-determination had been applied in a more just and equitable manner, it could not have solved the intricate problem of the national minorities so inextricably mingled in the Danube basin. The atomization of the Hapsburg monarchy led of necessity to the creation of several little Austrias. Czechoslovakia, one of them, was called upon to fulfill the task at which the Hapsburg monarchy had failed. She might have served as a dam against the centrifugal forces of modern dynamic nationalism. It was not the sheer tactical consideration of a small nation's possibilities that made Beneš the champion of a democratic League of Nations calling for supernational cooperation.

There was also a strategic reason for keeping Bohemia, the gateway to the south and southeast, in the hands of a small nation. Bismarck had said, "The master of Bohemia is veritably the master of Europe." It was this strategic importance of Bohemia, and not so much the Sudeten German issue, that decided the German drive to destroy the military and political "outpost of Bolshevism in central Europe." This has been definitely proved by the aftermath of Munich. "Munich was a dike; it was an experiment in canalizing an immeasurable tide." Such was the hope of western statesmen, as expressed by Sir Nevile Henderson, Great Britain's last Ambassador to Germany and chief proponent in the appeasement policy.

Immediately after Munich it became evident that the dam could not hold, that dictatorial dynamics was not satisfied because a permanent revolution never is. Hitler's speech in Saarbrücken, a week after he signed a treaty of friendship with Great Britain, gave the watchword.

On March 15, 1939, less than half a year later, Hitler marched into Prague. This was the opening of the fifth period in the European tragedy and the actual beginning of the *Second World War*. During these few months, from Munich to Prague, the whole strategy of the Third Reich changed completely. The concepts of geopolitics and the master race, the tactics of the fifth column, the threat of frightfulness, and the surprise attack of war in earnest, became the basis of the new totalitarian strategy.

At the height of the Sudeten crisis Hitler had proudly pronounced: "We want no Czechs." His only declared aim was the German *Volkstaat*, e.g., the inclusion in Greater Germany of all compact groups of German nationality within the reach of the fatherland. As soon as this aim was practically achieved, however, new dynamic concepts were needed for further expansion, and the school of *Geopolitik* took the reins. This school was by no means the invention of Professor-General Karl Haushofer. It had a long line of intellectual forerunners. Heinrich von Treitschke, dynamic historian of the Bismarckian era; Otto Hintze, master of German history; Friedrich Ratzel, professor of geography at Munich in the late 19th century; and Rudolf Kjellen, Swedish author of *The State as Living Space*—these men and many others laid the foundation of the new science of geopolitics. But it was Haushofer who gave political meaning to these theoretical concepts, who organized a school of fanatic disciples around him, who created a dynamic style and impressive vocabulary, and who finally raised geopolitics to a *Weltanschauung* with the all-embracing claim typical of a newly discovered science.

Son of a professor of political economy, Haushofer had originally planned an academic career, but during his year of compulsory military service his interest changed and he went on to study at the military college, from which he graduated with "all highest commendation." On the basis of this rare qualification, he entered the German war academy at an early age and soon became a general staff officer. In this capacity he was sent on a military mission to Japan. During his two years in the Far East, traveling in India and Australia, North China and Korea, he developed a great interest in the Indo-Pacific area. His observations awakened in him political concepts which later led to his dynamic political theory and finally found practical expression in the German-Japanese alliance. It was as early as 1912 that he conceived the idea: "Whoever could make an alliance with that part of the globe [the Indo-Pacific area], with its rich resources and superabundant population, could rule the rest of the world." His book, *Greater Japan* (1912), reflected all these observations, and also noted "the relaxation of the British Empire's grip and the immensely increased will to dominate which Japan had acquired with its victory over Russia." His conclusion that Germany should cooperate closely with Japan in controlling these areas was not shared by the imperial government. A generation later his ideas bore fruit in the reorientation of the National Socialist foreign policy.

Haushofer became the chief adviser on National Socialist policy, though he himself was not a party member, if only on account of his Jewish wife. (His two sons, however, were later made "honorary Aryans"—a fact of special significance because one son, Albrecht, has now become his real successor in formulating the important policies of the Third Reich.) Haushofer came in contact with the National Socialist party through Rudolf Hess, who had sat in his classes and was deeply impressed by his teachings. It was Hess who brought him and Hitler together. There are reports that at the time Hitler was a prisoner at the fortress of Landsberg, the professor went to visit him every Wednesday and taught him the fundamentals of geopolitics. This collaboration no doubt was intensified in the years that followed. It was due to Haushofer's influence that the whole concept of the Nazi foreign policy was completely reversed after Munich. Haushofer formulated the "natural right of the capable peoples to living space as against that of the possessors of territory who were unable to develop it." He postulated the right of the stronger over the weaker, a return to the old right of nature. "To suffer from undeserved restriction of space is the strongest world political motive."

The advantage of this concept of living space (*Lebensraum*) consisted in the fact that it gave practically unlimited possibilities to an ambitious people. Everyone had a right to as much living space as he could control; as soon as one's ambition was aroused, there was no limit to further expansion. People who live happily in two rooms will soon feel crowded and will gladly move into a three-room apartment if they can afford it. Their drive toward more spacious living quarters will be limited only by their budget. But while such an ambition may be the principle underlying many human actions, it is not the organizing principle of human society. Actual need and social status are continuously adjusted to and limited by the social whole. The same principle must be and is prevalent in international affairs under normal conditions. The nations represent the political units in a world structure which must guarantee their mutual right to existence and equality. The concept of living space, however, not only carries in itself the seed of unlimited dynamics, but fails to recognize the neighbor's equal right to living space. The complete absence of any sense or feeling of reciprocity, a characteristic of National Socialist thinking, has often been commented upon by careful observers of the Third Reich.

It is most significant that population pressure has been presented by the dictatorial nations as one of the major incentives for dynamic foreign policies. "A nation with a declining birth rate," says Mussolini, "has no right to imperialism." For this reason, Italy, Germany, and Japan alike made an intensive drive for an increase in the birth rate. The population pressure was consequently used as justification for an expansive foreign policy leading to greater living space. But it did not occur to these dynamic nations that the neighboring countries—such as Poland in regard to Germany, or China in regard to Japan—had an even higher birth rate and hence equal justification for *Lebensraum*.

Volk ohne Raum—thus Hans Grimm's best-seller novel had vividly phrased the plight of Germany in the Armistice period. No wonder that geopolitics found ardent supporters and a natural climate in that country. To the young officers who filled the lecture halls of the soldierly academician it was more than an academic science; it gave promise and direction.

Geopolitics pointed at the weaknesses of the Paris Treaty System which, dictated by the great sea powers, had neglected the potentialities of the compact land powers, the great world island of Europe-Asia-Africa. Sir Halford Mackinder had in vain warned the Peace Conference against the emergence of a land block that would find its center in the "heartland" stretching from the Arctic to the Himalaya Mountains and from the Volga to the Yangtze River. These land masses would be invulnerable to sea power. From Napoleon's time to Hitler's, they represented the graveyard of daring invaders.

Haushofer accepted the great Englishman's theory. In a realistic evaluation he recognized Germany's strategic position as the key to the wide open spaces of Eurasia and formulated his geopolitical strategies accordingly. Orientation in international affairs, so he taught, should be directed not by political ideologies but by the iron laws of the great spaces alone. A transcontinental block including Germany, Russia, and Japan would represent a natural and undefeatable alliance. A German-Russian understanding seemed to be the way out from Versailles. In fact, long before Haushofer's star was rising, the German Republic had accepted such maxims. The rise of National Socialism led to a complete turn in German-Russian relations in the direction of unavoidable conflict. Yet the German-Russian treaty of 1939 seemed to give final victory to the Haushofer school, which greeted the reversed stand with enthusiasm. There is no record available on Haushofer's attitude toward Germany's attack on the U.S.S.R. in the summer of 1941, but one may well be reminded of his warning in an earlier article, "Space as a Weapon."

While Haushofer's actual influence on National Socialist policies remains a matter of conjecture (though a flashy journalism soon raised the newly discovered master mind to the position of being the "man behind Hitler"), his school has undoubtedly shaped such major decisions as the Berlin-Tokyo Pact and has made a deep impress on a whole generation of young Germans. It taught them to think in terms of continents; it gave room for ambitious scheming; it also could lead to liberation from provincial nationalism. The division of the earth into great spheres of interest certainly meant the end of small nations. But this fate followed equally from the military considerations of mechanized warfare and the economic realities of a shrinking planet. The age of the great empires seemed to be in the offing. Geopolitics gave a fashionable lead. The law of the territorial growth of states and the movement toward continually greater areas (which had been formulated by Ratzel long before) made the whole trend toward the new empire-building look scientific and irresistible.

It is true that "space" had been a neglected factor in the dynamics of power politics during the period of awakened social and economic forces. Marxian philosophy had penetrated the minds of friend and foe of the Socialist doctrine. Geopolitics must be considered as a reaction against Marxism, or better its counterpart, bourgeois Marxism. It was greeted as such by its followers; but its new and ardent adherents made the same mistakes as their opponents. Now, instead of economics, it was space that became the absolute and exclusive yardstick. Geopolitics was raised to an all-embracing *Weltanschauung*. It preached a geopolitical materialism void of any moral evaluation and restraint. Independent man was replaced by space and soil.

Geopolitics became an ideal weapon in the hands of those who were striving for unlimited power and dynamic nihilism. *Lebensraum* could be granted or denied the nations that were on their good behavior before the court of geopolitical potentates. If the British Empire would play the game with the "renovating powers," she might keep a sphere of interest of her own. If not, then the "declining empire" would have to abdicate, and the spoils would be redistributed among the rising world powers. The final outcome was obvious: a world empire for one supreme power dominating the entire globe.

This dangerous turn became evident in the substitution of the even more flexible *Befehlsraum* for the concept of *Lebensraum*. The living space which, according to the Haushofer school, included especially southeastern Europe in the sphere of German interest was soon enlarged into the German *Befehlsraum*. This larger space added to Nazi control all the areas in which Germany was "to give orders." At the time when this idea was conceived, it included, according to its intellectual originators, all the nations of the Oslo bloc and France too—roughly, all the countries which by 1942 were under the control of the Third Reich. The idea of *Befehlsraum* has an even more dynamic feature. As long as another *Befehlsraum* exists, the New Order is endangered. This fact shows that the concept of *Befehlsraum* not only is a glorification of the well-known idea, "might is right," but also carries in itself an unlimited dynamism. From the concept of Greater

Germany to *Lebensraum* to *Befehlsraum*, a direct way leads to modern dictatorships' unlimited drive toward world control.

The ideals of geopolitics became explosive dynamics in the hands of the National Socialists, who tied them in with their basic concept of the *master race*. The idea of the race, most essential weapon in the ideological arsenal of German National Socialism, is no doubt a political concept and not a scientific notion. Modern anthropology has proved that absolutely "pure races" do not exist, most certainly not in modern Europe. Germany in particular represents the worst example of racial purity. Because of her historic development and geographic position she has always brought together different racial streams and thus represents an essentially mixed nation. The Junkers, Prussia's ruling class for many centuries, have gone through a process of intermingling with the Slavic people. The physiognomy of many famous Germans, such as Bismarck, Luther, Beethoven, is sufficient proof that the greatest contributions were not made exclusively, if at all, by purely Nordic types in Germany. In fact, recent theories make well-established suggestions that it is particularly in racially mixed areas that the greatest civilization flourishes.

The idea of the Nordic race was first presented by the French Count Gobineau and the originally British Houston Stewart Chamberlain. As far as this theory found acceptance in Germany, it was largely a defense mechanism. Just as late-comers in the field of international economics are ready to build protective tariff walls in order to stand up in international competition, so a parallel development could be observed in the field of cultural and racial penetration. The intense nationalism that arose in the 20th century in Germany and Italy is largely due to a similar experience. This nationalistic feeling which did not recognize equal rights for other nationalities and which certainly was not ready to accept a free trade of cultural relations—such an attitude was not least an expression of inner weakness. Only those who are strong and self-reliant feel free to accept, to absorb, and to assimilate external forces. The fate which the stranger met in the various European nations thus became the shibboleth of different types of nationalism. Western democracies of long standing could allow themselves to accept the constant infiltration of new forces; they could even make these newcomers constructive and creative participants in the ever-growing dynamics of their national civilization. The young nations of central Europe, on the other hand, developed a static concept of nationalism that was not due to inner strength. Its exclusiveness and intolerance were signs of inner weakness.

This is likewise true of the concept of race that has recently been brought forward. This race consciousness, as far as it infiltrated the country as a whole, was not the expression of a strong and pure race, sure of itself and self-assertive. It had all the earmarks of a definite feeling of inferiority. The major appeal of racial theories in modern society is due not only to national insecurity but even more to personal instability. In a world which seems to have lost all the basic values, the yearning for stable concepts has to be satisfied. The attractiveness of these new theories rests, above all, in their concreteness and "scientific" absoluteness. Like space, race seems to be a most tangible and concrete manifestation of human life.

Post-war Germany found specific relief in the theory of the *Herrenvolk* (master race). This released the high-pitched emotions of a proud nation which had suffered defeat and somehow hoped to overcome this national low with an uplifting myth. The two most outstanding German myths—the saga of the Kyffhaeuser cave and the story of Wieland, the smith—significantly enough illustrate such dreams of ultimate victory for a country haunted by fear and defeat.

The rise of anti-Semitism, which had some hold especially among the lower middle classes even in the Bismarckian Empire, was no less a similar compensating move of a humiliated people. In fact, post-war Germany not only did not fit into the Versailles world, but her place in Europe as a whole could be questioned. Her whole history, as was shown above, was characterized by constant tension between a highly Europeanized vanguard, particularly her intelligentsia, and a pre-European people who only superficially had participated in the European experiences. The Jew, on the other hand—not least because of his belated entrance into German civilization under the impress of the enlightenment and the French Revolution—had become the champion of the European conscience and thus of a supra-national concept and tradition. The emergence of an anti-European pattern with National Socialism hit this vanguard first. It is one of the paradoxes of this race-conscious movement that in the Jew it attacked perhaps the only group in European civilization who can claim relative racial purity. One need only be reminded in this connection of what Nietzsche (who today has been made the intellectual forerunner of National Socialism) said about the Jews who as a race, according to him, possessed precisely the qualities which the *Voelkische* doctrine of National Socialism was to claim for the Aryans: "The Jews are beyond all doubt the strongest, toughest, and purest race now living in Europe."

Representing a small minority without any support from a powerful motherland, the Jew was an easy scapegoat. He became the "personified enemy" who presumably could be spotted without difficulty. Anti-Semitism became a symbol of unity in an otherwise mixed Nazi camp. It also served as a good article for export to the traditionally anti-Semitic Danubian countries. But what was more important, the cruel treatment of the Jews in Germany, especially in its legalized practice, was only a general rehearsal of a basic attitude toward minorities and a systematic training in the art of violence.

It is no mere accident that Fascist Italy belatedly accepted these racial concepts of National Socialism. Yet this discovery of the racial foundations of Fascism is not genuine with the Italian nation or, for that, with Fascism itself. The new racial legislation was only an ideological adjustment to the political Rome-Berlin axis. In reality, the extraordinary mixture of races and the successive invasions that were so significant for the Italian peninsula made a racial theory of an Italian nationality practically impossible. The physical make-up of the Italian people differed widely from north to south. Italian civilization represented above all a "heritage and an enterprise." It had always been the pride of the Roman Empire that it had the power to absorb or, as classical Rome put it, to "civilize" whatever nationalities touched its soil or culture. The restoration of the Roman Empire was the inspiring myth of young Fascism.

Even in the early days of modest expansion, Fascism could never make use of unredeemed minorities—a weapon that was so useful in the hands of National Socialism. Italy had practically no irredenta to be liberated in the post-Versailles world. She had won her minorities as a result of World War I. Fascism therefore directed its expansive moves not toward national and racial aims but toward the restoration of the supra-national Roman Empire. The belated acceptance of anti-Semitism by Fascist Italy not only was an artificial coordination with Nazi Germany but also represented a renunciation of the Fascist myth. It took away from Mussolini his historic justification for a drive toward Mediterranean rule and deprived his moves of any other claims but that of naked power. In fact, every Fascist conquest was nothing but a present handed to the minor partner by his big brother in the north. The creation of Croatia for the Duke of Spoleto was definitely not an absorption into the coming Roman empire. This policy of empire-building definitely followed the patterns of the Nazi conquest. It made Fascist Italy at best only the proconsul of her northern master, a participant in and recipient of the Nazi New Order.

The ill treatment of minorities becomes a cornerstone in this new organization of the world. Lawrence Dennis, one of the few spokesmen for Fascism in the United States, says significantly in his recent *The Dynamics of War and Revolution*: "Democracy may be identified by phrases, 'parliamentary government,' 'liberalism,' 'government of checks and balances'—all of these terms meaning, among other things, a governmental system in which the right of the minority to oppose the majority in certain approved ways is respected."

Anti-Semitism is the preparation for the New Order. Evidence of this is given by the close relationship between the treatment of the Jews in Germany "at peace" and the methods with which the Third Reich exploits the peoples conquered by its armies.

The first practice drill of "the spoil of Europe" was the seizure of Czechoslovakia; this was the first step toward the emergence of the New Order. The partition of Czechoslovakia followed strict racial lines. Germanic Sudetenland was incorporated into the Reich; for obvious reasons the ethnically distinct Slovakia was granted a seeming independence; the core of the former republic, Bohemia and Moravia, was organized as a Reich protectorate.

The Organic Law of the Czech Protectorate of March 16, 1939, preconceives the entire pattern of the New Order, a scheme which since that time has been repeated in the government-general of Poland and elsewhere. It is frank and unambiguous. It is the codification of the rule of the master race.

The idea of a "blood hierarchy," the fantastic scheme for a master-slave society suggested in National Socialist literature, acquires weight and contour in the Nazi conquests of the Second World War and the subsequent organization of the vanquished nations. In this Nazified world the people of Europe are divided into four distinct castes. The first represents the master race of *Reichsdeutsche* or *Volksdeutsche*, the Brahmins of the New Order. The second group consists of the clansmen of the Third Reich, who, though often not even members of the Nordic race, are aligned with National Socialism. The Italian people, "the Nordics of the South," and the Japanese, "the yellow Aryans," the Quislings, and the Lavals may be included in this stratum. The third caste includes the defeated nations. The lowest stratum is left to the pariahs of Nazi society, the Jews.

National Socialism did not wait to put its reorganization of the world into practice until victory was guaranteed. The policy of *fait accompli*, often successfully applied in internal and international politics, was tried in this supreme thrust for the Thousand Years' Reich.

The blueprints for the new *Herrenvolk* are no longer a matter of conjecture. Within the Nazi ranks there are men with different and competing schemes for achieving this peace which, according to Hitler's *Mein Kampf*, is "guaranteed by the triumphant sword of a people endowed with a power to master the world." There is first the much-advertised Schacht plan for a German *Grossraumwirtschaft*, an economic federation of central Europe under German leadership. It is not lacking in some sound economic principles, but it has been long discarded. It is far too modest for present-day designs and, above all, it is contradictory to basic Nazi concepts: the primacy of politics over economics and the ideology of the master race. Not much has been heard recently of Dr. Schacht.

His successor, Dr. Funk, in collaboration with Goering, has conceived, and by now partly put into practice, a much farther-reaching scheme for industrial monopoly. "He who controls the means of production is the political master." This lesson from the Marxian textbooks has been taken seriously by the anti-Cominterns of the 20th century.

In modern industrial society, so the *Völkischer Beobachter* stated on August 20, 1940, "Germany will become Europe's tool forge" and will thus be the foundation pillar of the European-African economic area. In order to guarantee the permanent supremacy of Germany, the entire economic map of Europe is to be changed. The industries of France and the Low Countries are to be systematically dismantled and transferred to south-eastern and eastern Europe, and the erstwhile industrial areas are from now on to serve as the farmland for dominant Germany. This transplantation (cleverly tied up with a back-to-the-land movement in France herself) is not due merely to the good soil and even climate of the west; it is above all a political scheme. The industrialization of Slovakia and of Poland—removing key industries farther from the reach of the R.A.F.—transfers heavy industry from highly developed cultures to semi-civilized Europe which can be much better controlled by the Third Reich.

This transformation also serves a second scheme pursued by National Socialism for strategic reasons: the strengthening of artificially created vassal states. This plan largely derives from military considerations. It is not original with the Nazis; Napoleon and Clemenceau tried similar schemes. Military supremacy cannot be preserved forever; this the Nazis know well from their own experiences. Though they cannot picture today the specific techniques which the vanquished will use in order to regain military power, their recovery must be prevented. The creation of vassal states is the Nazi answer.

National Socialism has applied to its master plans two lessons learned from past mistakes. In the first place, the new vassal states must never be too large. This was the "weakness" of the succession states in post-Versailles Europe; they were strong enough to develop an independent foreign policy. Second, these newly created states must never be expected to serve as colonies for exploitation. They are definitely not an economic asset; they are a liability. Their creators have been forced to recognize this. These states must be financed. They should even share the spoils of victory; but these spoils will bind them close to victorious Germany. This is the price the Third Reich is ready to pay for having all over Europe guarantors of its *status quo*, guarantors whose whole existence depends on the New Order. Slovakia and Croatia are the results of this scheming. So are the ambitious plans for a Flemish state and a new Brittany (and, one day, even Ireland in part), which will serve as political centers in the midst of the enemy states.

Yet even this systematic economic and political transformation of the map of Europe does not suffice to guarantee the coming of the New Order. A moral erosion is also needed. Goebbels and Himmler are the masters of this technique. What must be prevented in the conquered countries is the awakening of such dynamic nationalist movements as National Socialism is itself. The danger of a Red imperialism or the creation of a Latin bloc (the old dream of Monsieur Laval) is clearly visualized by the professional revolutionaries. This fear gives meaning to Mussolini's early and often-repeated statement, "Fascism is no article of exportation." In a way the dictators' reaction reflects the same attitude that Léon Daudet (spokesman of the monarchist *L'Action française*) drastically expressed immediately after the First World

War, "I wish Germany to be a republic, because I wish Germany hell." And while the strategists of the permanent revolution were most eager to build up National Socialist parties in the neighboring states before the invasion began—thus forging useful weapons in a fifth column—they certainly shifted their policies as soon as they entered the stormed citadel. Quisling in Norway, Mussert in Holland, and the Iron Front in Rumania suddenly discovered that their dream of an independent nationalist state would have hard going under German occupation. To the Nazi conquerors, the ideal setup in the occupied zones is a puppet government to be run by timid routine administrators and definitely unpopular old-timers. Just as Japan tried to demoralize China by spreading the opium habit, the revolutionary bosses tried to create in Czechoslovakia, Holland, Norway, France, Greece, Yugoslavia, etc., political organizations which at best were administrative units subservient to victorious Germany. Such a structure, the Goebbels Incorporated think, will have a tremendous moral effect on the conquered nations. It will create a definite inferiority complex within them. Looking at the strutting National Socialist conquerors and comparing them with their own drab and colorless bureaucrats, the vanquished will definitely accept history's verdict that the master race should rule the world.

Aldous Huxley in his *Brave New World* imagines a world in which human beings are produced scientifically and graded into Alphas, Betas, and Gammas. The Alphas are the aristocracy and the Gammas are the serfs. In order to insure that the Gammas will not suddenly become a bit "uppish" and try to usurp power, a kind of loud-speaker which speaks to their subconscious selves is put in their bedroom when they are young. It tells them unceasingly through the night that they are miserable little Gammas, the scum of the earth, whose business is to serve everyone else. The result is that any Gamma who on the previous day was suffering from a swelled head wakes up the next morning appropriately subdued. In the same way the Alphas are made to realize that they are the leaders of the world and must not be allowed to fall from their lofty pedestals. Huxley calls this form of education "hypnopedia." It certainly has a lot in common with the intentions of the fabricated New Order of the Third Reich. National Socialism, above all, believes man to be manageable.

The New Order is nothing but the perpetuation of the rule of a warrior caste. Its achievement, of course, presupposes complete victory for Nazi Germany. Hitler hoped, and probably could only hope, to win this decisive victory by a surprise attack. The *Blitzkrieg*—much-advertised strategy of the Second World War—is, however, not his invention. Considering recent history alone, one may be reminded of Hitler's Far-Eastern ally and the opening of the Russo-Japanese War, when the Nipponese surprise attack on the Russian navy at Port Arthur gave Russia a blow from which she never recovered. Pearl Harbor was a similar attempt to knock out the United States Navy before the war began in earnest.

The certain advantage of the aggressor who can choose the time and place for his attack may well, however, be wiped out by the victim after the first shock is met. Hence, in order to counteract their enemy's recovery of strength, modern dictators have concentrated on a war of nerves. Again it would be a mistake to regard this "psychological warfare" as their own invention. The war of nerves is as old as Joshua and the collapse of the Walls of Jericho. The fifth column has numerous predecessors in the mythical wars of classical periods; the much-publicized "Trojan Horse" has undoubtedly been borrowed from ancient war tactics. In fact, it may be suggested that the fifth column and the Trojan Horse were not so much real weapons of the victorious National Socialists as they were tactical devices used to disturb the security of the enemy's country. Such traitors to their own nation do not have actually to exist as long as the threat of their existence can destroy taken-for-granted confidence among its citizens. True, the psychological laboratories of the German War Office have developed amazing techniques of intimidation, e.g., the "professional weepers," the black-clad veiled ladies who walked up and down the Paris boulevards in the spring of 1940, pretending deep sorrow over the loss of their loved ones.

Yet in a way such tactics are only refinements of those of an Attila, whose troops' reputation for bravery and cruelty won their battles before they started. The German horror picture, *Baptism of Fire*, found its historic forerunner in the Assyrians' ferocious inscriptions on stone tablets: No quarter given on the battlefield, the cities of their enemies destroyed, the inhabitants sold into slavery. The Assyrians regarded such warnings as excellent publicity, for great fear was thus instilled in their opponents before any actual fighting took place; many times the enemy would take to flight rather than face the Assyrian army.

This borrowed strategy of conquest has played an extraordinary part in dictatorial foreign policies in peace as well as war. There have been shrewd timing, astute estimates of political and social forces, able camouflage of the issues at stake, censorship at home, and blackmail abroad, each time raising the ante. Above all, fear has been used as a powerful weapon with the same success as in domestic politics. This is also true of the insurrectionary technique which was borrowed from the Bolshevik arsenal. Long before any frontal attack was made on the class or national enemy, the foe's position was undermined by underground activities and by boring from within. The disciple proved to be far more successful than the Third International.

To replace the preliminary artillery bombardment, to break down the enemy psychologically before the armies begin to march, to destroy the enemy from within—this invisible war is a major strategy of a conflagration that is a civil war on an international scale.

This psychological war has, no doubt, contributed to the amazing successes of the dictatorial campaigns in Norway, in the Low Countries, and even more in France. Yet the defeat of these nations was above all a military disaster, undoubtedly due to the crushing technical superiority of German armament. What counts in this modern mechanized war are airplanes and tanks, the coordination between the military services, and the striking power of the revived mobile warfare of the early part of World War I.

Like Napoleon, Hitler found his best ally in his opponents'

antiquated method of waging war. One may be reminded of a historian's statement in respect to the defeated Prussian army in the Battle of Jena: "It was indeed the army of Frederick the Great—twenty years older." Substitute Foch for Frederick and this can be said of the Battle of France.

In the new patterns of warfare the small nations are hopelessly lost. Only highly industrialized countries can resist, and only those which are prepared. Dictators are ready, because war is what they have been preparing for. Democracies are governments for peace, which is their political virtue. Yet they have not realized that there is no less a price to be paid for peace and that the war against war is "no holiday excursion or camping party," but can only be won, in the words of the great pre-war sage, William James, by a "moral equivalent of war."

In the last analysis, the breakdown of France, as shown above, and the temporary weakness of other democracies were the result of a moral crisis. The morale of the nation becomes of paramount import in a total war such as ours, because it is fought not exclusively at the front but in the hinterland as well. Even its decisive battles are fought not by soldiers but by civilians. The morale of London saved England in 1940; the surprising stamina and staying power of the U.S.S.R. in 1941 were due not only to her generally underestimated military preparedness, but even more to the morale of her people. It excluded any fifth column activity and made possible new tactics of guerrilla warfare on a large scale. The stubborn and heroic resistance of millions in the occupied areas has thus far prevented the establishment of the New Order in Europe. The battle of production may decide the final outcome of the war.

THE CHALLENGE TO DEMOCRACY

This is a triple war: the military war on an international scale, the civil war in every country, and a war going on within each person. The military war, though fought on many fronts on land and sea, is one and undivided. The democracies have slowly **awakened to this fact.** This awakening constitutes the first defeat of the dictators, whose whole strategy is coined for separate campaigns, one after the other, but with one final aim: the subjugation of all opponents to the New Order. They are waging a total war which can end only in total victory or total defeat. After more than two years the conflagration has now spread to a war of the entire world, but the dictators are farther from their aim than ever. Their failure largely results from their defeats on the civil front. The initial successes of international Fascism made the dictators completely misjudge the inner strength of the democracies.

One of the major difficulties of democracies in foreign affairs can be traced to the fact that the concept of democracy was originally formulated in an internal struggle to fight the sovereigns and to establish the rule of the people. Efficient foreign policy, however, presupposes national unity and continuity. Open discussion, the essence of democratic government, necessarily leads to divided loyalties which weaken any united front against the other nations. Thus the partisan struggle may produce a dangerous split at the brink of war, easily played up by shrewd dictatorial diplomacy. Such division was no doubt influential in the final outcome of the Munich crisis. It threw its shadows on internal discussions in the United States before Pearl Harbor.

Dictatorships are more cunning than democracies in the game of bluff. Not that they have "stronger nerves," but they can disregard peace sentiment (though it is undoubtedly as strong in their own nation as anywhere else). Totalitarian dictatorships, as repeatedly shown, prosper in warlike situations. If, however, war really comes, dictatorships' enforced unity is put to the test. History certainly proves that they cannot stand defeats; they may not even take continuous aerial attacks very well.

Democracies, on the other hand, always underestimating their own strength on account of their internal partisan struggle, rally to united action in emergencies. This is their surprise for the dictators, who do not understand and thus underestimate the vitality of the democratic spirit.

The transfer of domestic strategies to foreign affairs, despite some initial successes, shows the mortal weakness of Nazi propaganda. While in internal politics the dictators command a monopoly on the management of opinion, in international affairs they are for the first time confronted with the competition of counter-propaganda. The autocrats' monolithic techniques are not ready to meet this challenge, nor are they flexible enough to adjust themselves to new media. Dictators do not understand the outer world. The spiritual autarchy of totalitarianism must defeat itself. Furthermore, German propaganda was never strong in recognizing the different value patterns of other nations. Ribbentrop convinced Hitler that the western powers were decadent and would never fight. Yet they accepted the challenge.

The total attack by dictatorship leads to the real awakening of democracy. This constitutes, in addition to the military warfare and the different phases of civil war, the third, inner battle front of this war, probably the most decisive one in the end. Only a democracy that has an unshaken belief in its own way of life can defeat the new way of life of the dictators. Only a democracy that can give a constructive answer to the burning problems of our age will survive the onslaught.

This war is a world revolution which began long before the fighting started. It must be seen in its long-range development. The war is only a phase of it—possibly its climax. The total war will lead to total transformations in the whole structure of society. There will be no return to pre-war times. The implications of these changes are already visible in Europe, but they will be felt everywhere in a world which is no longer divisible.

Gone are a world at ease and the softness of those who have "arrived." To win the war will demand all the energies of society. Whatever the outcome, it will be a gigantic task of an entire generation to resolve the chaos. All the concepts we have lived by will have to be reconsidered and redefined in this period of world transition.

The dictatorships' temporary success is largely due to the vacuum left by the destruction of the 19th-century world. But they have tried only expedients; they have blocked the real solutions, which democracies must work out. Democracies pushed into the defensive by a totalitarian aggressor have to become more than the defenders of the *status quo*. They must seize the initiative, must accept the challenge of the 20th century, and must strike a new balance on all three planes: international, national, and personal. The United States will have a great contribution to make in all three planes.

In world politics it is nationalism that is on trial as the organizing principle of a world order just as religion was three hundred years ago. At the end of this second Thirty Years' War, nationalism—like religion after the first one—will not disappear but will have to find its definite place in an international society.

Within the nations the political institutions must be tested anew, the relations between leaders and followers must be reconsidered, the social question must be courageously met; because wherever democracy has failed in providing adequate leadership and social equilibrium, crises strata have become an easy prey of the dictatorial exploiters of the revolutionary situation. A new social vision will be needed.

It is the individual who will have to redefine his position in the community. The social individual in a reintegrated society must reject both the laissez-faire concepts of the 19th century and the Leviathan order of totalitarian world power. He must find a new adjustment between individual freedom and planned society. This task will demand vigor and perspective, passion and perseverance, bold daring and a dynamic faith.

Democracies in their life-and-death struggle must teach their citizens the fundamental fact that the community demands service and devotion as well as offering privileges and rights. This twofold relation democratic society has failed to recognize in internal politics and no less in foreign affairs. There is a price to be paid for freedom and peace.

While democracies by their essence not only respect minorities but live by a pluralistic concept of competing forces, their staying power will lastly depend on their continuous ability to impose upon themselves the limitations which are necessary for the preservation of group unity.

This fight against moral anarchy, however, should never obscure the basis of human existence: individual responsibility. It is an inalienable right. Dictators attack it. They must be defied. No compromise is possible because this personal responsibility is the fountain of life. Nobody shall take it away from us, for on this responsibility rest the pride and dignity of man.

BIBLIOGRAPHY

Chapter I

MODERN DICTATORSHIP DEFINED

THE HISTORIC SETTING

Among the innumerable studies on modern dictatorship, the following contributions are of special value:

Armstrong, Hamilton Fish, *We or They; Two Worlds in Conflict.* New York: Macmillan, 1936.

Barthélemy, Joseph, *La crise de la démocratie contemporaine.* Paris: Librairie du Recueil Sirey, 1931.

Brooks, Robert C., *Deliver Us from Dictators.* Philadelphia: University of Pennsylvania Press, 1935.

Cambo, Francisco, *Las Dictaduras.* Tercera edicion. Madrid: Espasa-Calpe, 1929. French translation, *Les Dictatures.* Paris: Alcan, 1930.

Cobban, Alfred, *Dictatorship; Its History and Theory.* New York: Scribner, 1939.

Drabovitch, W., *Fragilité de la liberté et séduction des dictures.* Paris: Mercure de France, 1934.

Ford, Guy Stanton (ed.), *Dictatorship in the Modern World.* 2nd ed. Minneapolis: University of Minnesota Press, 1939.

Forst de Battaglia, Otto, *Dictatorship on Trial.* New York: Harcourt, Brace, 1931.

Gooch, G. P., *Dictatorship in Theory and Practice.* London: Watts and Co., 1939.

Halévy, Elie, "The Age of Tyrannies," *Economica,* 8 (N.S.):77-93 (1941). (Translation of the article: "L'Eve des Tyrannies" published in E. Halévy's posthumous volume of essays, 1938.)

Hoover, Calvin B., *Dictators and Democracies.* New York: Macmillan, 1937.

Kantorowicz, Hermann, *Dictatorships.* With a bibliography by A. Elkin. Cambridge, England: W. Heffer and Sons, 1935.

Kelsen, Hans, "The Party Dictatorship," *Politica,* 2:19-32 (London, 1936).

Kohn, Hans, *Force or Reason: Issues of the Twentieth Century.* Cambridge, Mass.: Harvard University Press, 1937.

Loewenstein, Karl, "Autocracy versus Democracy in Contemporary Europe," *American Political Science Review,* 29:571-593, 755-784, (1935).

Marriott, Sir John Arthur Ransome, *Dictatorship and Democracy.* Oxford: Clarendon Press, 1935.

Merriam, Charles E., *The New Democracy and the New Despotism.* New York: Whittlesey House, 1939.

Rogers, Lindsay, *Crisis Government.* New York: Norton, 1934.

Schmitt, Carl, *Die Diktatur. Von den Anfängen des modernen Souveränitätsgedanken bis zum proletarischen Klassenkampf.* 2nd ed. Munich: Duncker und Humbolt, 1928.

Spearman, Diana, *Modern Dictatorship.* London: J. Cape, 1939.

Spencer, Henry R., "Dictatorship," *Encyclopaedia of the Social Sciences,* 5:133-136. New York: Macmillan, 1931.

Wittke, Carl F. and others, *Democracy Is Different.* New York: Harper, 1941.

On Latin-American dictatorship, see:

Chapman, Charles E., "The Age of the Caudillos," *Hispanic American Historical Review,* 12:281-300 (1932). Bibliography, *ibid.,* 13:143-146 (1933).

Garcia Calderón, F., "Dictatorship and Democracy in Latin America," *Foreign Affairs,* 3:459-477 (1924-1925).

Wilgus, A. Curtis (ed.), *South American Dictators During the First Century of Independence.* Washington, D.C.: George Washington University Press, 1937.

For historical comparisons, see:

Bainville, Jacques, *Dictators.* London: J. Cape, 1940.

Carr, Albert, *Juggernaut, the Path of Dictatorship.* New York: Viking, 1939.

Kellett, E. E., *The Story of Dictatorship from the Earliest Times till Today.* London: Nicholson and Watson, 1937.

On classic dictatorship, see:

Johnson, A. C., and others, *The Greek Political Experience.* Princeton: Princeton University Press, 1941.

Mommsen, Theodor, *Römisches Staatsrecht.* Vol. II, pp. 125 ff. Berlin: Weidmann, 1881.

Syme, Ronald, *The Roman Revolution.* Oxford: Clarendon Press, 1939.

For the era of the French Revolution, see:

Constant de Rebecque, Benjamin, *Prophecy from the Past.* New York: Reynal, 1941. Edited and translated by Helen Byrne Lippmann. On the conquest and usurpation.

Loewenstein, Karl, "The Dictatorship of Napoleon the First," *South*

Atlantic Quarterly, 35:298-318 (July, 1936), and also his "Die Diktatur Napoleons des Ersten," *Zeitschrift für Öffentliches Recht,* 16: 619-651 (Vienna, 1935).

Palmer, R. R., *Twelve Who Ruled; the Committee of Public Safety During the Terror.* Princeton: Princeton University Press, 1941.

Valuable historical comparisons can also be derived from numerous studies on the sociology of revolutions, although one must be cautioned against far-reaching generalizations. For challenging attempts, see:

Brinton, Crane, *The Anatomy of Revolution.* New York: Norton, 1938.

Edwards, L. P., *The Natural History of Revolutions.* Chicago: University of Chicago Press, 1927.

Hertzler, J. O., "Crises and Dictatorships," *American Sociological Review,* 5:157-170 (1940).

Merriman, R. B., *Six Contemporaneous Revolutions, 1640-1660.* Oxford: Clarendon Press, 1938.

Pareto, Vilfredo, *The Mind and Society.* (Trattato di sociologia generale). 4 vols. New York: Harcourt, Brace, 1935.

Pettee, George S., *The Process of Revolution.* New York: Harper, 1938.

Rosenstock Huessy, E., *Die Europäischen Revolutionen.* Jena: Diederichs, 1931. English version, *Out of Revolution.* New York: Morrow, 1938.

Sorokin, Pitirim, *The Sociology of Revolutions.* Philadelphia: Lippincott, 1925.

Soule, George, *The Coming American Revolution.* New York: Macmillan, 1934. Especially Part I, "The Nature of Revolution."

On constitutional dictatorship, see:

Friedrich, Carl J., *Constitutional Government and Democracy.* Boston: Little, Brown, 1941. Chap. 13, "Constitutional Dictatorship and Emergency Powers." Bibliography, *ibid.,* pp. 627-629.

Watkins, F. M., "The Problem of Constitutional Dictatorship," *Public Policy.* Cambridge, Mass.: Harvard University Press, 1940. Vol. I.

For the German development, see:

Anschütz, Gerhard, *Die Verfassung des Deutschen Reiches.* 14th ed. Berlin: Stilke, 1933.

"Diktatur des Reichspräsidenten" (Symposium). *Verhandlungen der Vereinigung der Deutschen Staatsrechtslehrer,* Berlin: De Gruyter, 1924. Vol. I.

Grau, R., "Die Diktaturgewalt des Reichspräsidenten" in G. Anschütz and R. Thoma, (eds.), *Handbuch des Deutschen Staatsrechts*, 2: 274-295. Tübingen: Mohr, 1932.

Henemen, H. J., *The Growth of Executive Power in Germany: A Study of the German Presidency*. Minneapolis: Voyageur Press, 1934.

Muhr, Fritz, "Die Wirtschaftliche Diktatur des Reichspräsidenten," *Zeitschrift für Politik*, 13:483 ff. (1923).

Preuss, Hugo, "Reichsverfassungsmässige Diktatur," *Zeitschrift für Politik*, 13:97 ff. (1923).

Rogers, L., Schwarz, S., and Kaltschas, N., "German Political Institutions: Article 48," *Political Science Quarterly*, 47:576 ff. (1932).

Watkins, F. M., *The Failure of Constitutional Emergency Powers Under the German Republic*. Cambridge, Mass.: Harvard University Press, 1939.

THE ORIGIN OF MODERN DICTATORSHIP

Soviet Russia

Among the general treatises, the following studies are especially valuable:

Chamberlin, William Henry, *Soviet Russia*. Boston: Little, Brown, 1930.

Chamberlin, William Henry, *The Russian Revolution, 1917-1921*. 2 vols. New York: Macmillan, 1935.

Dean, Vera M., "The Political Structure of the Soviet State," in R. L. Buell (ed.), *New Governments in Europe*. Rev. ed. New York: Nelson, 1937.

Florinsky, Michael T., "Russia—The U.S.S.R.," in James T. Shotwell, (ed.), *Governments of Continental Europe*. New York: Macmillan, 1940. Pp. 755-936.

Harper, Samuel N., *The Government of the Soviet Union*. New York: Van Nostrand, 1938.

Johnson, The Very Reverend Hewlett (Dean of Canterbury): *The Soviet Power*. New York: Modern Age Books, 1941.

Maxwell, B. W., *The Soviet State; a Study of Bolshevik Rule*. Topeka: Steves and Wayburn, 1933.

Williams, A. R., *The Soviets*. New York: Harcourt, Brace, 1937.

For the historical background, see standard books such as:

Florinsky, M. T., *The End of the Russian Empire*. New Haven: Yale University Press, 1931.

Gronsky, P., and Astrov, J. J., *The War and the Russian Government*. New Haven: Yale University Press, 1929.

Kliuchevskii, V. O., *A History of Russia*. 5 vols. London: Dutton, 1927-1931.

Malaparte, C., *Coup d'état*. New York: Dutton, 1932. Chaps. 1-2.

Mavor, J., *The Russian Revolution*. New York: Macmillan, 1928.

Pares, B., *A History of Russia*. 3rd ed. New York: Knopf, 1937.

Pokrovsky, M. N., *Brief History of Russia*. Translated by Dimitry S. Mirsky. New York: International Publishers, 1933. An official "Marxist" interpretation.

Vernadskii, G., *The Russian Revolution, 1917-1931*. New York: Holt, 1932.

Vernadskii, G., *Political and Diplomatic History of Russia*. Boston: Little, Brown, 1936.

Accounts by active participants pro and con:

Kerensky, A., *The Catastrophe*. New York: Appleton-Century, 1927.

Lenin, V. I., *The Revolution of 1917*. 2 vols. New York: International Publishers, 1932.

Lenin, V. I., *Readings in Leninism*. New York: International Publishers, 1936.

Trotsky, L., *History of the Russian Revolution*. 3 vols. New York: Simon and Schuster, 1932.

Fascist Italy

Informative analyses of emerging Fascism, pro and con, will be found in:

Ascoli, Max, and Feiler, Arthur, *Fascism for Whom?* New York: Norton, 1938.

Borgese, G. A., *Goliath, the March of Fascism*. New York: Viking, 1938.

Ebenstein, William, *Fascist Italy*. New York: American Book, 1939.

Finer, Herman, *Mussolini's Italy*. New York: Holt, 1935.

Gorgolini, Pietro, *The Fascist Movement in Italian Life*, with a preface by Mussolini. Boston: Little, Brown, 1923.

Malaparte, C., *Coup d'état*. New York: Dutton, 1932. Chap. 7. On the technique of the Fascist revolution.

Prezzolini, Giuseppe, *Fascism*. New York: Dutton, 1927.

Rossi, A., *The Rise of Italian Fascism, 1918-1922*, with a preface by Herman Finer. London: Methuen, 1938.

Schneider, Herbert W., *The Fascist Government in Italy*. New York: Van Nostrand, 1936.

Spencer, H. R., *Government and Politics of Italy*. Yonkers: World Book, 1932.

Steiner, H. Arthur, *Government in Fascist Italy*. New York: McGraw-Hill, 1938.

Sturzo, Don Luigi, *Italy and Fascismo*. New York: Harcourt, Brace, 1926. The account of the leader of the Popolari.

Villari, Luigi, *The Awakening of Italy! Fascista Regeneration.* London: Doran, 1924.

Zurcher, Arnold J., "The Government and Politics of Italy" in James T. Shotwell (ed.), *Governments of Continental Europe.* New York: Macmillan, 1940.

For the social and cultural background, see:

Croce, Benedetto, *A History of Italy, 1871-1915.* Oxford: Clarendon Press, 1929.

Michels, Roberto, *Sozialismus und Faschismus als politische Strömungen in Italien.* 2 vols. Karlsruhe: Braun, 1925.

Michels, Roberto, *Italien von Heute, Politische und Wirtschaftliche Kulturgeschichte 1860-1930.* Zürich: Orell Füssli, 1930.

Valsecchi, Franco, *Das Moderne Italien. Politische Geistesgeschichte seit 1900.* Hamburg: Hanseatische Verlags-Anstalt, 1935.

National Socialist Germany

The history of the Weimar Republic is still unwritten; for preliminary background studies, see:

Clark, R. T., *The Fall of the German Republic.* London: Allen and Unwin, 1935.

Emerson, R. E., *State and Sovereignty in Modern Germany.* New Haven: Yale University Press, 1928.

Heiden, Konrad, *A History of National Socialism.* London: Methuen, 1934.

Kosok, Paul, *Modern Germany.* Chicago: University of Chicago Press, 1933.

Lichtenberger, Henri, *The Third Reich.* New York: Greystone, 1937.

Loewenstein, Karl, "Government and Politics in Germany," in James T. Shotwell (ed.), *Governments of Continental Europe.* New York: Macmillan, 1940. Especially pp. 339-404.

Marx, Fritz M., *Government in the Third Reich.* 2nd ed. New York: McGraw-Hill, 1937.

Mattern, J., *Principles of Constitutional Jurisprudence of the German National Republic.* Baltimore: Johns Hopkins Press, 1928.

Mowrer, E. A., *Germany Puts the Clock Back.* New ed. New York: Morrow, 1939.

Neumann, Sigmund, "Die Bedeutung des gesellschaftlichen Aufbaus für die Verfassungsstruktur in Deutschland," *Jahrbuch für Politische Forschung.* Berlin: Junker und Dünnhaupt, 1933.

Neumann, Sigmund, "Germany: Battlefield of the Middle Class," *Foreign Affairs,* 13:271-283 (1935).

Ogg, F. A., *European Governments and Politics*. 2nd ed. New York: Macmillan, 1939.

Olden, Rudolf, *Stresemann*. New York: Dutton, 1930.

Pollock, James K., *The Government of Greater Germany*. New York: Van Nostrand, 1938.

Quigley, H., and Clark, R. T., *Republican Germany*. New York: Dodd, Mead, 1928.

Rosenberg, Arthur, *The Birth of the German Republic*. London: Methuen, 1931.

Rosenberg, Arthur, *The History of the German Republic*. London: Methuen, 1936.

Schuman, Frederick L., *The Nazi Dictatorship*. 2nd ed. New York: Knopf, 1936.

Shotwell, James T., *What Germany Forgot*. New York: Macmillan, 1940.

Sutton, Eric (ed.), *Gustav Stresemann, His Diaries, Letters and Papers*. 2 vols. New York: Macmillan, 1935-1937.

Vallentin-Luchaire, Antonina, *Stresemann*. New York: R. R. Smith, 1931.

Vienot, Pierre, *Ungewisses Deutschland; zur Krise seiner Bürgerlichen Kultur*. Frankfurt a.M.: Societäts Verlag, 1931.

Watkins, F. M., *The Failure of Constitutional Emergency Powers Under the German Republic*. Cambridge: Harvard University Press, 1939.

Wertheimer, Mildred, "The Third Reich," in R. L. Buell and others, *New Governments in Europe*. New ed. New York: Nelson, 1938.

Wheeler-Bennett, J. H., *The Wooden Titan; Hindenburg in Twenty Years of German History, 1914-1934*. New York: Morrow, 1936.

Chapter II

THE LEADER

Definition by Contrast: Institutional Representation

On democratic statesmanship and common qualities of political leaders, see:

Allport, Floyd H., *Social Psychology*. Boston: Houghton Mifflin, 1924.

Babbitt, Irving, *Democracy and Leadership*. Boston: Houghton Mifflin, 1927.

Barnard, Chester J., *Dilemmas of Leadership in the Democratic Process*. Princeton: Princeton University Press, 1939.

Benes, Eduard, *Gedanke und Tat*. Prague: Orbis Verlag, 1937. Vol. II, pp. 15-99.

Benes, Eduard, *Democracy Today and Tomorrow*. New York: Macmillan, 1939.

Bernays, E. L., "Group Leaders of Democracy," *American Mercury*, 44:437-444 (1938).

Brown, A., *Democratic Leadership* (Swarthmore Lectures). London: Allen and Unwin, 1938.

Carmichael, O. C., "Leadership and the Present Crisis," *Vital Speeches*, 8:139-142 (December 15, 1941).

Cowley, W. H., "The Traits of Face-to-Face Leaders," *Journal of Abnormal and Social Psychology*, 23:137-143 (1928).

Gosnell, Harold F., *Boss Platt*. Chicago: University of Chicago Press, 1924.

Merriam, Charles E., *Political Power*. New York: McGraw-Hill, 1934.

Merriam, Charles E., and Gosnell, Harold F., *The American Party System*, 3rd ed. New York: Macmillan, 1940.

Mumford, E., "The Origins of Leadership," *American Journal of Sociology*, 12:216-240 (1906-1907).

Munro, W. B., *Personality in Politics*. New York: Macmillan, 1925.

Pigors, P. J. W., *Leadership or Domination*. Boston: Houghton Mifflin, 1935.

Reyburn, S. W., "Discourse on Leadership," *Vital Speeches*, 5:77-83 (November 15, 1938).

Salomon, Albert, "Leadership in Democracy," in Max Ascoli and F. Lehmann (eds.), *Political and Economic Democracy*. New York: Norton, 1937.

Tead, O., *The Art of Leadership*. New York: McGraw-Hill, 1935.

Weber, Max, *Gesammelte politische Schriften*. Munich: Drei Masken Verlag, 1921.

Whitehead, Thomas North, *Leadership in a Free Society*. Cambridge, Mass.: Harvard University Press, 1936.

For the British Prime Minister, see:

Finer, Herman, *The Theory and Practice of Government*. New York: Dial, 1934.

Jennings, W. Ivor, *Cabinet Government*. Cambridge: Cambridge University Press, 1937; New York: Macmillan.

Jennings, W. Ivor, *Parliament*. Cambridge: Cambridge University Press, 1940; New York: Macmillan.

Jennings, W. Ivor, *The British Constitution*. Cambridge: Cambridge University Press, 1941. New York: Macmillan, 1941.

Laski, Harold J., *The Parliamentary Government of England*. New York: Viking, 1938.

On the President of the French Council, see:

Gooch, R. K., "The Government and Politics of France," in James T. Shotwell (ed.), *Governments of Continental Europe*. New York: Macmillan, 1940.

Moutafoff, Leon, *Le président du conseil des ministres en France*. Bordeaux: Imprimerie Bière, 1940.

Sharp, W. R., *The Government of the French Republic*. New York: Van Nostrand, 1938.

Valeur, R., "French Government and Politics," in R. L. Buell (ed.), *Democratic Governments in Europe*. New York: Nelson, 1939.

Vizetelly, E. A., *Republican France, 1870-1912: Her Presidents, Statesmen, Policy*. London: Holden and Hardingham, 1912.

For the American President, see:

Beard, Charles A., *American Government and Politics*. New York: Macmillan, 1938. Chap. 7, "The Office of President."

Corwin, E. S., *The President: Office and Powers*. New York: New York University Press, 1940.

Herring, E. Pendleton, *Presidential Leadership*. New York: Farrar and Rinehart, 1940.

Johnson, G. W., *Roosevelt: Dictator or Democrat*. New York: Harper, 1941.

Laski, Harold J., *The American Presidency*. New York: Harper, 1940.

Odegard, Peter H., and E. A. Helms, *American Politics*. New York: Harper, 1939.

On democratic leadership in wartime, see:

Berdahl, Clarence A., *War Powers of the Executive in the United States*. Urbana: University of Illinois, 1921.

Dawson, R. MacGregor, "The Cabinet Minister and Administration; Asquith, Lloyd George, Curzon," *Political Science Quarterly*, 55:348-377 (1940).

Finer, Herman, "The British Cabinet, the House of Commons and the War," *Political Science Quarterly*, 56:321-360 (1941).

Herring, E. Pendleton, *The Impact of War*. New York: Farrar and Rinehart, 1941. Especially pp. 140-163.

Jennings, W. Ivor, *The British Constitution*. Cambridge: Cambridge University Press, 1940. Chap. 8, "Government in War Time."

Rogers, Lindsay, "Presidential Dictatorship in the United States," *Quarterly Review*, 231:127-148 (1919).

On Churchill, see:

Begbie, Harold, *The Mirrors of Downing Street.* London: Mills and Boon, 1920.

Guedalla, Philip, *Mr. Churchill.* New York: Reynal and Hitchcock, 1942.

Kraus, René, *Winston Churchill.* Philadelphia: Lippincott, 1941. See also Churchill's own writings, especially the collections of his recent speeches: *While England Slept* (New York: Putnam, 1938); *Step by Step* (New York: Putnam, 1940); *Blood, Sweat and Tears* (New York: Putnam, 1941).

DICTATORIAL LEADERSHIP

The Demagogue

The concept as applied here does not follow the derogative usage of everyday language. The demagogue is not simply "the man who promises everything, knowing that he cannot keep his promise," i.e., the man who covers his egoistic aims under shining phrases and the expression of splendid ideas, who betrays the loyalty of his followers for personal ends and wins adherence through cheap trickery, the man whose dealings are characterized by dishonesty and complete disregard for morality. Such a description of the demagogue as the "bad man" in politics is too simple to be true. The phenomenon of the modern demagogue cannot be coped with in terms of moral indignation. Even if it is useful to characterize such fanatics in our daily life as demagogical, this description does not always fit extremely powerful demagogues like Hitler who are no doubt fanatic but, like most fanatics, are sincere in their belief in their mission and their capacity to be the savior of their people. Indeed, this self-belief is one of the characteristics of modern messiahs who are not tortured by skepticism. It is this defect in self-evaluation that makes them the heroes of masses harassed by uncertainties. The real demagogue gives them faith and security because he is so sure of himself. He regards himself as a godsend, as always godlike.

Since the time of Aristotle the demagogue has been, above all, the "leader of the people" who really succeeds in winning the masses and must utilize some bit of demagoguery. Thus a democratic climate may well breed "demagogues."

An example is David Lloyd George, a forerunner of the dynamic post-war demagogues; see J. H. Edwards, *Lloyd George, the Man and Statesman,* 2 vols. (New York: Sears, 1929); Sir Charles E. Mallet, *Mr. Lloyd George, a Study* (New York: Dutton, 1930); and Lord Riddell, *Intimate Diary of the Peace Conference and After* (New York: Reynal, 1934). Baldwin's famous Carlton Club speech was a declaration of war against Lloyd George, the demagogue, by Baldwin, the defender of institutional politics. Without the institutional traditions and safeguards of Great Britain, the rise of Lloyd George to power might have brought about the emergence of leadership of the by now familiar type.

The most outstanding demagogues among present-day dictators are Mussolini and Hitler. For Mussolini, see the following studies and also the general studies on Fascist Italy listed above:

Ludwig, Emil, *Talks with Mussolini*. Boston: Little, Brown, 1933.

Megaro, Gaudens, *Mussolini in the Making*. Boston: Houghton Mifflin, 1938.

Petrie, Sir Charles A., *Mussolini*. London: Home Press, 1931.

Sarfatti, Margherita, *The Life of Benito Mussolini*. New York: Stokes, 1925. The story of Mussolini's erstwhile private secretary, obviously biased, yet very revealing.

Less informative are other appraisals by enthusiastic admirers, as well as Mussolini's own writings. See:

Autobiography, translated by R. W. Child. New York: Scribner, 1928.

Diels, Louise, *La generazione di Mussolini*. Milan: A. Mondadori, 1936.

Kemechey, L., *Il Duce*. New York: Richard R. Smith, 1930.

Quaranta di San Severino, Bernardo, *Mussolini as Revealed in His Political Speeches*. New York: Dutton, 1923.

Among the numerous studies by opponents of Fascism, see:

Lussu, Emilio, *Enter Mussolini*. London: Methuen, 1936.

Seldes, George, *Sawdust Caesar*. New York: Harper, 1935.

Hitler's autobiographical material includes:

Mein Kampf. New York: Reynal and Hitchcock, 1939. This English edition is complete and unabridged, and is fully annotated.

My New Order. New York: Reynal and Hitchcock, 1941. A collection of Hitler's speeches, and a running commentary, edited by Raoul de Roussy de Sales.

Official biographies include:

Bouhler, Philipp, *Adolf Hitler*. Lubeck: Coleman, 1937.

Czech-Jochberg, E., *Hitler*. Oldenburg: Stalling, 1930.

Hinkel, Hans, *Einer unter Hunderttausend*. Munich: Knorr und Hirth, 1938.

Schott, Georg, *Das Volksbuch vom Hitler*. Munich: Eher, 1938.

Careful analyses, although by ardent opponents, will be found in:

Heiden, Konrad, *Hitler; a Biography*. New York: Knopf, 1936.

Olden, Rudolf, *Hitler*. New York: Covici, Friede, 1936.

The Master of the Machine
Stalin remains a human enigma despite the numerous books written about the U.S.S.R.'s Number One Man. Among them are:

Barbusse, Henri, *Stalin; a New World Seen Through One Man*. New York: Macmillan, 1935.

Eastman, Max, *Stalin's Russia and the Crisis in Socialism*. New York: Norton, 1940.

Essad, Bey, *Stalin; the Career of a Fanatic*. New York: Viking, 1932.

Levine, I. D., *Stalin*. New York: Blue Ribbon, 1931.

Lyons, Eugene, *Stalin, Czar of All the Russias*. Philadelphia: Lippincott, 1940.

Souvarine, Boris, *Stalin, a Critical Survey of Bolshevism*. New York: Alliance, 1939.

Stalin's own writings should also be consulted:

Leninism. New York: International Publishers, 1938.

Marxism and the National and Colonial Question. New York: International Publishers, 1936.

Werner, M. R. (ed.), *Stalin's Kampf; Joseph Stalin's Credo*. New York: Howell, Soskin, 1940.

The Marginal Men: Gabriele d'Annunzio

Antongini, Tommaso, *D'Annunzio*. London: Heinemann, 1938.

Antongini, Tommaso, "Portrait of Extravagance," *Readers' Digest*, 33: 41-44 (1938).

Ascoli, Max, and Feiler, Arthur, *Fascism for Whom?* New York: Norton, 1938.

Borgese, G. A., *Goliath, the March of Fascism*. New York: Viking, 1938. Pp. 150-168.

Crespi, A., "Significance of Gabriele d'Annunzio," *Contemporary Review*, 153:427-433 (1938).

Giannantoni, Mario, *La vita di Gabriele d'Annunzio*. Milan: Mondadori, 1933.

Griffin, Gerald, *Gabriele d'Annunzio; the Warrior Bard*. London: Long, 1935.

Sprigge, C. J. S., "D'Annunzio's Italy and England," *Fortnightly*, 149 (N.S. 143):459-466 (1938).

Franz von Papen

Ebbutt, N., "Franz von Papen. Nazi," *Fortnightly*, 156 (N.S. 150):33-42 (1941).

Koeves, T., *Satan in Top Hat*. New York: Alliance, 1941.

Papen, Franz von, *Appell an das deutsche Gewissen. Reden zur na-*

tionalen Revolution. Oldenburg: Stalling Bücherei, 1933. Neue Reihe No. 32/33 and No. 51/52.

Solon, S. L., "Hitler's Gentleman of Intrigue," *American Mercury*, 52: 475-482 (1941).

The Condottiere

For the concept of the *condottiere* and his appearance in the Renaissance, see:

Burckhardt, Jakob, *The Civilization of the Renaissance in Italy.* New York: Oxford University Press, 1937.

Semerau, Alfred, *Die Condottieri.* Jena: Diederichs, 1909.

For the modern *condottiere*, see:

Buell, R. L., *Poland: Key to Europe.* New York: Knopf, 1939.

Chernov, F., "Joseph Pilsudski: From Socialist to Autocrat," *Foreign Affairs*, 14:146-155 (1935).

Machray, R., *The Poland of Pilsudski 1914-1936.* New York: Dutton, 1937.

Oertzen, F. W. von, *Marcshall Pilsudski.* Berlin: Mittler, 1935.

Pilsudski, Joseph, *The Memoirs of a Polish Revolutionary and Soldier.* London: Faber, 1931.

Pilsudski, Joseph, *Erinnerungen und Dokumente.* 3 vols. Essen: Essener Verlagsanstalt, 1935.

Allen, H. E., *The Turkish Transformation.* Chicago: University of Chicago Press, 1935.

Armstrong, H. C., *Gray Wolf, Mustapha Kemal.* New York: Minton, Balch, 1933.

Froembgen, H., *Kemal Attatürk, Soldat und Führer.* Stuttgart: Frankh, 1935.

Gilman, W., "Turkey Offers Her Own Ism," *South Atlantic Quarterly*, 33:377-391 (1939).

Jones, D. D., and Johnston, H., "Mustapha Kemal and Peter the Great; a Study in Parallelism," *Sociology and Social Research*, 22:212-222 (1938).

Kemal Pasha, *A Speech Delivered by Ghazi Mustapha Kemal.* Leipzig: Koehler, 1927.

Mikusch, D. von, *Mustapha Kemal; Between Europe and Asia.* New York: Doubleday, Doran, 1931.

Roger, N., "La Turquie de Kemal Ataturk," *Revue de deux Mondes*, 48:601-623 (1938).

Webster, D. E., *The Turkey of Ataturk.* Philadelphia: American Academy of Political and Social Science, 1939.

Wortham, H. E., *Mustapha Kemal of Turkey*. Boston: Little, Brown, 1931.

Chapter III

THE POLITICAL LIEUTENANT

THE NUMBER TWO MEN, NATURE AND VARIANTS

Most of the abundant publications, especially in popular magazines dealing with "personalities in politics," are trite and at best serve only as an appetizer. For a scientific investigation of the phenomenon of the subleader, they can be disregarded. Among the better-informed books, the following should be mentioned:

Bayles, William D., *Caesars in Goose Step*. New York: Harper, 1940.
Dutch, Oswald, *Hitler's 12 Apostles*. New York: McBride, 1940.
Gunther, John, *Inside Europe*. New York: Harper, 1940.

Cf. also the vivid descriptions in general treatments of modern dictatorships, such as:

Davies, Joseph Edward, *Mission to Moscow*. New York: Simon and Schuster, 1941.
Dodd, Martha, *Through Embassy Eyes*. New York: Harcourt, Brace, 1939.
Dodd, W. E., Jr., and Martha (eds.), *Ambassador Dodd's Diary*. New York: Harcourt, Brace, 1941.
Fischer, Louis, *Men and Politics*. New York: Duell, Sloan, and Pearce, 1941.
Huss, Pierre J., *The Foe We Face*. New York: Doubleday, Doran, 1942. A most readable account of the Nazi leaders by the former head of the Berlin bureau of the International News Service.
Luedecke, K. G. W., *I Knew Hitler*. New York: Scribner, 1937. Although this book is written by a disappointed Nazi, it contains valuable characterizations of some of the subleaders such as Goering, Rosenberg, Goebbels, and Himmler.
Rauschning, H., *The Voice of Destruction*. New York: Putnam, 1940.
Roberts, Stephen, *The House That Hitler Built*. New York: Harper, 1938.
Shirer, William, *Berlin Diary*. New York: Knopf, 1941.

The following lists some of the autobiographies and collected writings of the lieutenants themselves:

Goebbels, Joseph, *Der Angriff, Aufsätze aus der Kampfzeit*. Zusammengestellt und eingeleitet von Hans Schwarz van Berk. 6th ed. Munich: Eher, 1937.

Goebbels, Joseph, *Kampf um Berlin. Der Anfang. Zeichnungen von Mjölnir.* Munich: Eher, 1938.

Goebbels, Joseph, *Vom Kaiserhof zur Reichskanzlei. Eine historische Darstellung in Tagebuchblättern* (Vom 1. Januar 1932 bis zum 1. Mai 1933). Munich: Eher, 1934. Translation: *My Part in Germany's Fight.* London: Hurst and Blackett, 1938.

Goering, Hermann, *Aufbau Einer Nation.* Berlin: Mittler, 1934.

Goering, Hermann. *Germany Reborn.* London: Mathews and Marrot, 1934.

Hess, Rudolf, *Reden.* Munich: Eher, 1938.

Roehm, Ernst, *Die Geschichte eines Hochverräters.* Munich: Eher, 1933.

See also the semi-official biographies by "court" scribes, such as:

Fabricius, Hans, *Frick, der revolutionäre Staatsmann.* Berlin: Kameradschaftsbund deutscher Polizeibeamten, 1935.

Gritzbach, Erich. *Hermann Göring—Reden und Aufsätze.* Munich: Eher, 1938.

Kiehl, Walter, *Der Mann an Der Fahne. Kameraden Erzählen von Dr. Ley.* Munich: Eher, 1938.

Pfundtner, Staatssekr Hans (ed.), *Dr. Wilhelm Frick und sein Ministerium.* Munich: Eher, 1937.

Sommerfeldt, Martin H., *Hermann Göring.* Berlin: E. G. Mittler and Son, 1932.

The inner circle of modern autocracies is by no means as stable as the popular myth of the "continuity in leadership" seems to assume for dictatorial governments. The great shifts in the personnel of the Polit-bureau are proof to the contrary. With the exception of Stalin, Kalinin, and Molotov, none of the present members of the Polit-bureau belonged to it ten years ago. "Changing the guards" is a well-known fact and a regular feature of the Fascist regime, as witness the continuous succession in the Fascist party secretaryship, a vital office that represents the unity and continuity of the movement. Farinacci, Turati, Giuriati, Starace, Muti, Serena, Vidussoni have all held this office in comparatively rapid succession.

A similar change in personnel can be observed in the Third Reich. The only constant figure in the shifting composition of the ruling elite is Hermann Goering. Leaving aside the turbulent times of the early days (gone are the "founders"—Harrer, Drexler, etc.), of the beer-hall *Putsch* of 1923 and its aftermath, and beginning the chronology only after the movement was stabilized under the unchallenged leadership of Hitler, one draws up the following list (in five-year intervals) of powerful henchmen:

> 1925—Gregor Strasser, Goering, Streicher, Feder, Rosenberg.
> 1930—Gregor Strasser, Goering, Goebbels, Roehm, Frick.
> 1935—Goering, Goebbels, Himmler, Schacht, Hess.
> 1940—Goering, Himmler, Ribbentrop, Brauchitsch, Hess.

In the meantime, Hess and Brauchitsch have already experienced their eclipse and the pitiless process of elimination continues. In contrast to the reshuffling of democratic leaders, Fascist lieutenants, once they have lost their place in the dictator's sun, rarely regain it.

THE COMPOSITE STRUCTURE OF THE ELITE

The phenomenon of the political lieutenant must be studied in connection with modern dictatorship's underlying theories of the ruling class (*classe dirigente*). Consult the following much-discussed books:

Mosca, Gaetano, *The Ruling Class*. New York: McGraw-Hill, 1939. A translation of his early study under the more adequate title, *Elementi di scienze politica*. 1st ed., 1895; 2nd ed., 1923. Torino: Bocca.

Pareto, Vilfredo, *The Mind and Society*. 4 vols. New York: Harcourt, Brace, 1935. A translation of *Traité de sociologie générale*. Paris: Payot, 1917-1919.

Pellizzi, Camillo, *Fascismo e aristocrazia*. Milan: Casa edit. Alpes, 1925.

For a clear exposition of the recent doctrines of anti-democratic movements, see:

Coker, Francis W., *Recent Political Thought*. New York: Appleton-Century, 1934. Chaps. 11, 12.

Lasswell, Harold D., *Politics; Who Gets What, When, How?* New York: Whittlesey House, 1936.

Merriam, Charles E., *The New Democracy and the New Despotism*. New York: Whittlesey House, 1939.

Valuable material for a systematic and historical analysis will be found in:

Michels, Robert, *Umschichtungen in den herrschenden Klassen nach dem Kriege*. Stuttgart: Kohlhammer, 1934.

Sorokin, Pitirim, *Social Mobility*. New York: Harper, 1927.

Weber, Max, *Wirtschaft und Gesellschaft*. Tübingen: Mohr, 1922. Especially pp. 122-180, 603-817.

A comparison with the democratic subleader will clarify the lieutenant's place in the dictatorial system. The following deal with the American scene:

Herring, E. Pendleton, *The Politics of Democracy*. New York: Norton. 1940.

Holcombe, Arthur N., *The New Party Politics*. New York: Norton, 1933.

Logan, Edward B. (ed.), *The American Political Scene*. New York: Harper, 1936.

Merriam, C. E., and Gosnell, H. J., *The American Party System*, 3rd ed. New York: Macmillan, 1940.

Munro, W. B., *Personality in Politics*. New York: Macmillan, 1924.

Odegard, Peter H., and Helms, E. A., *American Politics*. New York: Harper, 1938.

Salter, John T., *Boss Rule*. New York: Whittlesey House, 1935.

Salter, John T., *The Pattern of Politics; the Folkways of a Democratic People*. New York: Macmillan, 1940.

Salter, John T. (ed.), *The American Politician*. Chapel Hill: University of North Carolina Press, 1938.

Schattschneider, E. E., *Party Government*. New York: Farrar and Rinehart, 1942.

Zink, Harold, *City Bosses in the United States*. Durham: Duke University Press, 1930.

TRAINING AND SUCCESSION IN LEADERSHIP

For the selection of democratic leaders, see:

Heinberg, J. G., "The Personnel of French Cabinets, 1871-1930," *American Political Science Review*, 25:389-396 (1931), and a supplementary study: "The Personnel Structure of French Cabinets," *ibid.*, 33:267-279 (1939).

Kamm, Walter, *Abgeordnetenberufe und Parlament*. Leipzig: Buske, 1927.

Lambach, Walter, *Die Herrschaft der Fünfhundert*. Hamburg: Hanseatische Verlags-anst, 1926.

Véran, Jules, *Comment on devient Deputé, Senateur, Ministre*. Paris: Editions Bassard, 1924.

For the historical background, see:

Laski, Harold J., "The British Cabinet, 1801-1924," Fabian Tract No. 223. London: The Fabian Society, 1928.

MacDonagh, M., *The Pageant of Parliament*. London: Benn, 1921. Vol. I, pp. 141-150.

Namier, L. B., *The Structure of Politics at the Succession of George III*. London: Macmillan, 1929.

On the "class" character of the national government in Great Britain, see the material collected by the Labour Research Department, London, and reprinted in N. L. Hill and H. W. Stoke, *The Background of European Governments* (New York: Farrar and Rinehart, 1940, 2nd ed., pp. 57-60). See also:

Hartman, D. A., "British and American Ambassadors," *Economica*, 11: 328-341 (1931).

Macmahon, A. W., "Selection and Tenure of Bureau Chiefs in the National Administration of the United States," *American Political Science Review*, 20:548-582, 770-811 (1926), and "Changes of Bureau Chiefs in the National Administration," *ibid.*, 29:383-403 (1929).

Nightingale, R. T., "Personnel of the British Foreign Office and Diplomatic Service," *American Political Science Review*, 24:310-331 (1930).

For dictatorships, see the following titles, and also those listed under "Education in Uniform" in the Bibliography for Chapter VI.

Binzer, M. von, *Die Fuehrerauslese im Faschismus*, Langensalza: Mann's Magazine, 1929.

Gerth, Hans, "The Nazi Party: Its Leadership and Composition," *American Journal of Sociology*, 45:517-541 (1940).

Harper, S. N., *Making Bolsheviks*. Chicago: University of Chicago Press, 1931.

Lasswell, H. D., and Sereno, Renzo, "Governmental and Party Leaders in Fascist Italy," *American Political Science Review*, 31:914 ff. (1937).

Rowan-Robinson, I. A., "The Training of the Nazi Leaders of the Future," *International Affairs*, 17:233-250 (London, 1938).

Schneider, Herbert W., and Clough, S. B., *Making Fascists*. Chicago: University of Chicago Press, 1929.

Steinbömer, J., "La formation des élites en Allemagne," *Sciences Politiques*, 52:315-318 (1937).

Chapter IV

THE AMORPHOUS MASSES EMERGE

THE REVOLT OF THE MASSES

It is beyond the limited purpose of this bibliography even to enumerate the students of the 19th and 20th centuries who have given thought to the disturbing phenomenon of the emerging masses. Such a catalogue would have to consider such diversified schools of thought as those represented by Burckhardt and Bagehot, Marx and Mereshkovsky, Dostoevsky and Tocqueville, Nietzsche and Dilthey, Ruskin and Spengler. In fact, it would have to include the inexhaustible list of critics of "modern society."

Mention will be made of only a few studies that give an insight into and a challenging view of this crucial process of western civilization. See, for example:

Briefs, Goetz, "Mass Age in Agony," *Review of Politics*, 3:83-99 (1941).

Lippincott, Benjamin E., *Victorian Critics of Democracy*. Minneapolis: University of Minnesota Press, 1938.

Loewith, Karl, *Von Hegel bis Nietzsche*. Zurich: Europa Verlag, 1941.

Maritain, Jacques, *Le crépuscule de la civilisation*. Paris, Éditions des Nouvelles Lettres, 1939.

For the concept of the masses, consult the following titles. The first one is the "early classic;" the others are even older.

LeBon, Gustave, *The Crowd: A Study of the Popular Mind*. London: T. R. Unwin, 1897.

Moede, Walter, *Experimentelle Massenpsychologie*. Leipzig: Hirzel, 1920. This gives a comparison of LeBon and Sighele.

Sighele, Scipio, *Psychologie des Auflaufs und der Massenverbrechen*. Dresden, Reissner, 1897. A translation from the Italian *La folla delinquente* (1893).

Tarde, Gabriele, *Les crimes des foules*. Lyon: Storck, 1892.

Among the recent contributions the following should be consulted:

Cantril, Hadley, *The Psychology of Social Movements*. New York: Wiley, 1941.

Chakotin, Serge, *The Rape of the Masses*. New York: Alliance, 1940.

Freud, Sigmund, *Group Psychology and the Analysis of the Ego*. London: International Psycho-Analytical Press, 1922.

Geiger, Theodor, *Die Masse und ihre Aktion*. Stuttgart: Enke, 1926.

Jung, Carl G., *Psychological Types*. New York: Harcourt, Brace, 1924.

La Piere, Richard T., *Collective Behavior*. New York: McGraw-Hill, 1938.

Lasswell, H. D., *Psychopathology and Politics*. Chicago: University of Chicago Press, 1930.

Lasswell, H. D., *World Politics and Personal Insecurity*. New York: Whittlesey House, 1935.

Lederer, Emil, *State of the Masses. The Threat of the Classless Society*. New York: Norton, 1940.

Man, H. de, *Massen und Fuehrer*. Potsdam: Protte, 1932.

Mannheim, Karl, *Man and Society in an Age of Reconstruction*. New York: Harcourt, Brace, 1940. An excellent bibliography by E. A. Shils.

Ortega y Gasset, José, *The Revolt of the Masses*. New York: Norton, 1932.

Rougement, Denis de, "Passion and the Origin of Hitlerism," *Review of Politics*, 3:65-82 (1941).

Sherif, M., *Psychology of Social Norms.* New York: Harper, 1936.

Stieler, G., *Person und Masse; Untersuchungen zur Grundlegung einer Massenpsychologie.* Leipzig: Meiner, 1929.

Vleugels, W., *Die Masse.* Munich: Duncker und Humblot, 1930.

THE INDUSTRIAL REVOLUTION

[The statement on the specific repercussions in France is taken from the excellent study by W. L. Middleton, *The French Political System,* pp. 15-16, and is reprinted by kind permission of the publisher, E. P. Dutton and Co., Inc., New York, copyright 1933.]

The concurrence in time of political revolution and major social change explains many of the intricate tensions within practically all European nations.

A substantial analysis of the respective positions of the agricultural and industrial classes in modern politics presupposes a careful comparison of rural and urban society. The following are valuable in this connection:

Holcombe, Arthur N., *The New Party Politics.* New York: Norton, 1933. An outstanding contribution on the changing structure of political parties under the impact of urbanization.

MacIver, R. M., *Society.* New York: Farrar and Rinehart, 1937. Chap. 7, pp. 114-139.

Mumford, Lewis (ed.), *The Culture of Cities.* New York: Harcourt, Brace, 1938.

Simmel, Georg, "Die Grossstädte und das Geistesleben," in Theodor Petermann (ed.), *Die Grossstadt.* Dresden: Zahn, 1903, pp. 187-206.

Sorokin, Pitirim, and Zimmerman, C. C., *Principles of Rural-Urban Sociology.* New York: Holt, 1931.

Weber, Max, *Wirtschaft und Gesellschaft.* Tübingen: Mohr, 1922.

Wirth, Louis, "Urbanism as a Way of Life," *American Journal of Sociology,* 44:1-24 (1938).

For the present-day controversy over dictatorship and agriculture, consult:

Friedrich, C. J., "The Agricultural Basis of Emotional Nationalism," *Public Opinion Quarterly* (1937), 1:50-61, and "The Peasant as Evil Genius of Dictatorship," *Yale Review,* 26:724-740 (1937).

Marr, Heinz, "Die Grossstadt als politische Lebensform," *Grossstadt und Volkstum.* Hamburg: Hanseatische Verlags-Anstalt, 1927.

Neumann, Sigmund, "Die Bedeutung des gesellschaftl. Aufbaus für die Verfassungsstruktur in Deutschland," *Jahrbuch für Pol. Forschung.* Berlin: Junker und Dünnhaupt, 1933.

Topf, Erwin, *Die Grüne Front.* Berlin: Rowohlt, 1933.

Extremely valuable material on the actual reaction of the rural sections toward rising dictatorship can be found in German fiction before 1933. See also:
Salomon, Ernst von, *Die Stadt*. Berlin: Rowohlt, 1932.

For the social effects of the machine age, see:
Holzer, Martin, *Technik und Zivilisation*. Jena: Diederichs, 1932.
Klatt, Fritz, *Die geistige Wendung des Maschinenzeitalters*. Berlin: Protte, 1932.
McKee, S., and Rosen, Laura, *Technology and Society*. New York: Macmillan, 1941.
Man, Hendrik de, *Der Kampf um die Arbeitsfreude*. Jena: Diederichs, 1927.
Mumford, Lewis, *Technics and Civilization*. New York: Harcourt, Brace, 1934. See also the extensive bibliography, pp. 447-474.
Odum, Howard W., "Notes on the Technicways in Contemporary Society," *American Sociological Review*, 2:336-346 (1937).
Ogburn, W. F., "Technology and Society," *Social Forces*, 17:1-8 (1938).
Rathenau, Walter, *In Days to Come*. London: Allen and Unwin, 1921.
Rathenau, Walter, *The New Society*. New York: Harcourt, Brace, 1921.
Salter, J. A., *Modern Mechanization and Its Effects on the Structure of Society*. London: Oxford University Press, 1933.
Veblen, T. B., *The Instinct of Workmanship*. New York: Huebsch, 1914.

On the industrial proletariat, especially its social conditions and discrepancies, valuable material will be found in the following studies, in addition to the well-known Marxian analyses:
Briefs, Goetz A., *The Proletariat, a Challenge to Western Civilization*. New York: McGraw-Hill, 1937.
Hermes, Gertrud, *Die geistige Gestalt des marxistischen Arbeiters*. Tübingen: Mohr, 1926.
Man, Hendrik de, *Psychology of Socialism*. New York: Holt, 1928.
Michels, R., "Psychologie der antikapitalist Massenbewegungen," *Grundriss der Sozialökonomik*. Tübingen: Mohr, 1926. Vol. IX, Part I, pp. 241-359.
Woldt, D., *Die Lebenswelt des Industriearbeiters*. Leipzig: Quelle and Meyer, 1926.

On the significance of work and profession in modern society, see:
Carr-Saunders, A. M., and Wilson, P. A., *The Professions*. London: Oxford University Press, 1933.
Dunkmann, Karl, *Soziologie der Arbeit*. Halle: Carl Marhold, 1933.

Dunkmann, Karl, *Die Lehre vom Beruf.* Berlin: Trowitzsch und Sohn, 1922.

Mann, F. K., "Zur Soziologie des Berufs," *Jahrb. f. Nationaloekonomie und Statistik,* 138:481-500 (1933).

Parsons, T., "The Professions and Social Structure," *Social Forces,* 17: 457-467 (1939).

The Social Basis of Fascism

Special emphasis on the social causations of emerging National Socialism and Italian Fascism has been given in general analyses, such as:

Ascoli, Max, and Feiler, Arthur, *Fascism for Whom?* New York: Norton, 1938.

Borgese, G. A., *Goliath: The March of Fascism.* New York: Viking, 1938.

Brady, Robert A., *The Spirit and Structure of German Fascism.* New York: Viking, 1937.

Drucker, Peter F., *The End of Economic Man.* New York: Day, 1939.

Heimann, Eduard, *Communism, Fascism and Democracy,* New York: Norton, 1938.

Lederer, Emil, *State of the Masses: The Threat of the Classless Society.* New York: Norton, 1940. An extremely challenging study.

Raushenbusch, Stephen, *The March of Fascism.* New Haven: Yale University Press, 1939.

Schuman, Frederick L., *The Nazi Dictatorship.* 2nd ed. New York: Knopf, 1937.

For the salaried employee, see:

Gablentz, Otto von der, and Mennicke, C., *Deutsche Berufskunde.* Leipzig: Bibliographisches Institut, 1930.

Geiger, Theodor, *Die soziale Schichtung des deutschen Volkes.* Stuttgart: Enke, 1932.

Lederer, Emil, and Marschak, J., "Der neue Mittelstand," *Grundriss der Sozialökonomik.* Tübingen: Mohr, 1926. Vol. IX, Part I, pp. 120-141.

Speier, Hans, "The Salaried Employee in Modern Society," *Social Research,* 1:111-133 (1934).

For the controversial discussion concerning the future of the "new middle class" or "the new proletariat," see:

Bingham, Alfred, *Insurgent America.* New York: Harper, 1935.

Corey, Lewis, *The Crisis of the Middle Class.* New York: Viking, 1935.

Kracauer, S., *Die Angestellten.* Frankfurt a.M.: Sozietäts-Verlag, 1930.

Palm, F. C., *The Middle Classes Then and Now.* New York: Macmillan, 1936.

In the early thirties, a number of German periodicals such as *Die Tat* and *Deutsches Volkstum* gave significant expression to the restlessness of a German youth which, though most sincere in its reactions, was soon to be absorbed and pushed into directions not of its own choosing by victorious National Socialism. In addition to these periodicals, the following are pertinent here:

Dingräve, Leopold, *Wo steht die junge Generation?* Jena: Diederichs, 1932.

Freyer, Hans, *Revolution von Rechts.* Jena: Diederichs, 1931.

Fried, Ferdinand, *Das Ende des Kapitalismus.* Jena: Diederichs, 1931.

On unemployment, see:

Bakke, E. W., *The Unemployed Man; a Social Study.* New York: Dutton, 1934.

Bakke, E. W., *Citizens Without Work; a Study of the Effects of Unemployment.* New Haven: Yale University Press, 1940.

Beales, H. L., and Lambert, R. S., *Memoirs of the Unemployed.* London: Gollancz, 1934.

Children, Young People and Unemployment. A Series of Inquiries into the Effect of Unemployment on Young Children. Geneva: Save the Children International Union, 1933.

Komarovsky, Mirra. *The Unemployed Man and His Family,* New York: Dryden Press, 1940.

Lazarsfeld, Marie, and Zeisl, Hans, *Die Arbeitslosen von Marienthal.* Leipzig: Hirzel, 1933.

Wunderlich, Frieda, "New Aspects of Unemployment in Germany," *Social Research,* 1:97-110 (1934).

No systematic attempt has been made to analyze the social pattern and political significance of the militia of irregulars in 20th-century Europe. Abundant material, however, can be found in numerous autobiographical and semi-fictional books.

Posse, Ernst H., *Die politischen Kampfbünde Deutschlands.* Berlin: Junker und Dünnhaupt, 1931. For an early description of the semimilitary organizations in the German Republic.

Roehm, Ernst, *Die Geschichte eines Hochverräters.* Munich: Eher, 1928.

Salomon, Ernst von, *Die Geächteten.* Berlin: Rowohlt, 1933. The story of the Rathenau murder.

Chapter V

THE ONE-PARTY STATE

BREAKDOWN OF THE DEMOCRATIC PARTY SYSTEM

On the nature of the modern party systems, see:

Ascoli, Max, "Political Parties" in Max Ascoli and F. Lehmann (eds.), *Political and Economic Democracy*. New York: Norton, 1937.

MacIver, R. M., *Leviathan and the People*. Baton Rouge: Louisiana State University Press, 1939. Especially his commentary on "Democracy and Political Parties," pp. 155-157.

Merriam, C. E., and Gosnell, H. F., *The American Party System*. 3rd ed. New York: Macmillan, 1940.

"Political Parties" in the *Encyclopaedia of the Social Sciences*. Vol. XI.

A very extensive discussion of the essence and character of modern parties appeared in pre-Nazi German literature. Consult:

Calker, Fritz van, *Wesen und Sinn der politischen Parteien*. 2nd ed. Tübingen: Mohr, 1930.

Koellreutter, Otto, *Die politischen Parteien im modernen Staate*. Breslau: Hirt, 1926.

Marr, Heinz, *Klasse und Partei in der modernen Demokratie*. Frankfurt a.M.: Englert and Schlosser, 1925.

Nawiasky, Hans, *Die Zukunft der politischen Parteien*. Munich: Pfeiffer and Co., 1924.

Neumann, Sigmund, *Die deutschen Parteien*. 2nd ed. Berlin: Junker und Dünnhaupt, 1932. This contains an extensive bibliography.

Sulzbach, Walter, *Die Grundlagen der politischen Parteibildung*. Tübingen: Mohr, 1921.

Triepel, H., *Die Staatsverfassung und die politischen Parteien*. Berlin: Liebmann, 1930.

Weber, Max, "Parlament und Regierung im neugeordneten Deutschland, 1918," and "Politik als Beruf," *Gesammelte politische Schriften*. Munich: Drei Masken Verlag, 1921.

Weber, Max, *Wirtschaft und Gesellschaft*. Tübingen: Mohr, 1922.

Unfortunately, the discussion of the sociology of political parties has not outgrown its early stages; it still follows the prevalent patterns of such books as:

Michels, Roberto, *The Political Parties: A Sociological Study of the*

Oligarchical Tendencies of Modern Parties. New York: Hearst's International Library, 1915. See also his "Some Reflections on the Sociological Character of Political Parties," *American Political Science Review,* 21:753-772 (1927).

Ostrogorski, M., *Democracy and the Organization of Political Parties.* 2 vols. New York: Macmillan, 1908.

Valuable material can be found in the numerous descriptive studies of the machinery of modern political parties, such as the titles listed below. See also the Bibliography for Chapter III above.

Brooks, R. C., *Political Parties and Electoral Problems.* 3rd ed. New York: Harper, 1933.

Key, V. O., Jr., *Politics, Parties and Pressure Groups.* New York: Crowell, 1942.

Long, Norton, "Party and Constitution," *Journal of Politics,* 3:198-209 (1941).

Odegard, Peter, and Helms, E. H., *American Politics.* New York: Harper, 1938.

Rohden, P. R. (ed.), *Demokratie und Partei.* Wien: Seidel und sohn, 1932.

Sait, E. M., *American Parties and Elections.* 3rd ed. New York: Appleton-Century, 1942.

Sultan, Herbert, "Zur Soziologie des modernen Parteisystems," *Archiv für Sozial-Wiss. und Soz.-Pol.,* 55:91 ff. (1926).

CHARACTER OF THE TOTALITARIAN PARTY

The Soviet Party

For the theoretical background, early development, and basic conflicts in the Soviet party system, consult Lenin's writings (especially *The State and Revolution, What Is Leninism?* etc.), the historical and critical studies by Trotsky (*The Russian Revolution, The Revolution Betrayed, Stalin,* etc.), and the books by Stalin (*The Problems of Leninism,* etc.). See also:

Dean, Vera M., "The Political Structure of the Soviet State: The Communist Party," in R. L. Buell, *et al., New Governments in Europe.* New ed. New York: Nelson, 1938.

Gurian, Waldemar, *Bolshevism: Theory and Practice.* London: Sheed, 1933.

Maxwell, B. W., *The Soviet State.* Topeka, Kansas: Steves and Wayburn, 1934.

Popov, N., *Outline History of the Communist Party of the Soviet Union,* New York: International Publishers, 1934.

Seibert, Theodor, *Das Rote Russland.* Munich: Knorr and Hirth, 1931. Pp. 64 ff. This contains significant material on the changing social composition of the party.

Yaroslavski, Emeljan, *Aus der Geschichte der kommunistischen Partei der Sowjetunion.* Berlin: C. Hoym, 1930.

Zinoviev, Gregorii, *Geschichte der kommunistischen Partei Russlands.* Hamburg: Hoym, 1923.

For the international aspects of Russian Communism, see:

Borkenau, Franz, *World Communism—a History of the Communist International.* New York: Norton, 1938.

Commission of the Central Committee of the C.P.S.U. *History of the Communist Party of the Soviet Union.* New York: International Publishers, 1939.

Rosenberg, Arthur, *A History of Bolshevism.* London: Oxford University Press, 1934.

The Fascist Party

Ashton, E. B., *The Fascist, His State and His Mind,* New York: Morrow, 1937. Chap. 3, pp. 46-83.

Finer, Herman, *Mussolini's Italy.* New York: Holt, 1935.

Steiner, H. Arthur, *Government in Fascist Italy.* New York: McGraw-Hill, 1938. See also his "The Constitutional Position of the Partito Nazionale Fascista," *American Political Science Review,* 31:227-242 (1937).

For Fascist analyses, see:

Bortolotto, Guido, *Lo Stato e la dottrina corporativa.* Bologna: Zanichelli, 1930.

Bortolotto, Guido, *Faschismus und Nation.* Hamburg: Hanseatische Verlagsanstalt, 1932.

Bortolotto, Guido, *Massen und Führer in der fascistischen Lehre.* Hamburg, Hanseatische Verlagsanstalt, 1934.

Keim, Walter, *Die nationale Fascistische Partei.* Leipzig: Hans Buske, 1935.

Liuzzi, B., *Il Partito Nazionale Fascista nel Diritto.* Rome: Soc. edit. del foro ital., 1930.

Lo Verde, Giuseppe, *Die Lehre vom Staat im neuen Italien.* Berlin: Junker und Dünnhaupt, 1934.

Panunzio, Sergio, *Lo Stato fascista.* Bologna: Cappelli, 1924.

Panunzio, Sergio, *Il Sentimento dello stato.* Rome: Libr. del Littorio, 1929.

The National Socialist Party

See the following official or semi-official publications:

Huber, Ernst Rudolf, *Verfassung*. Hamburg: Hanseatische Verlags-anstalt, 1937.

Ipsen, H. P., "Vom Begriff der Partei," *Zeitschrift für die Ges. Staats-wissenschaft*, 100:309-336, 477-510 (1940).

Koellreutter, Otto, *Grundriss der Allgemeinen Staatslehre*. Tübingen: Mohr, 1933.

Lingg, Anton, *Die Verwaltung der Nationalsozialistischen Arbeiterparti*. Munich: Eher, 1940.

Neesse, Gottfried, *Partei und Staat*. Hamburg: Hanseatische Verlags-anstalt, 1936. See also *Die Nationalsozialistische Deutsche Arbeiter-partei—Versuch einer Rechtsdeutung*. Stuttgart: Kohlhammer, 1935.

Schmitt, Carl, *Staat, Bewegung, Volk*. Hamburg: Hanseatische Verlags-anstalt, 1933.

Valuable scientific analyses will be found in:

Abel, T., "Patterns of a Successful Political Movement," *American Sociological Review*, 2:347-352 (1937).

Boerner, A. B., "The Position of the N.S.D.A.P. in the German Constitutional Order," *Political Science Review*, 32:1059-1081 (1938).

Cantril, Hadley, *The Psychology of Social Movements*. New York: Wiley, 1941.

Gerth, Hans, "The Nazi Party: Its Leadership and Composition," *American Journal of Sociology*, 45:517-541 (1940).

Loewenstein, Karl, "Legislative Control of Political Extremism in European Democracies," *Columbia Law Review*, 38:591-622, 725-774 (1938). For Democratic counter-measures.

See also the special chapters dealing with the party in the general studies on National Socialism by Karl Loewenstein, F. M. Marx, James Pollock, Stephen Roberts, etc.

Chapter VI

THE CONTROL OF THE MASSES: INSTITUTIONAL FRAMEWORK

BASIC PRINCIPLES

The institutional framework of modern dictatorship has been extensively studied in numerous standard treatises. In addition to the works enumerated in the Bibliography for Chapter I, see the following:

Ashton, E. B., *The Fascist: His State and His Mind.* New York: Morrow, 1937.

Batsell, W. R., *Soviet Rule in Russia.* New York: Macmillan, 1929.

Brady, R. A., *The Spirit and Structure of German Fascism.* New York: Viking, 1937.

Duranty, Walter, *The Kremlin and the People.* New York: Reynal and Hitchcock, 1941.

Elwin, W., *Fascism at Work.* London: Hopkinson, 1924, with an introduction by Francesco Nitti.

Fraenkel, Ernst, *The Dual State; a Contribution to the Theory of Dictatorship.* New York: Oxford University Press, 1941.

Lichtenberger, H., *The Third Reich.* New York: Greystone, 1937.

Loewenstein, Karl, *Hitler's Germany.* Rev. ed. New York: Macmillan, 1940.

Munro, W. B., *The Governments of Europe.* 3rd ed. New York: Macmillan, 1938.

Neumann, Franz L., *Behemoth, the Structure and Practice of National Socialism.* New York: Oxford University Press, 1942.

Ogg, F. A., *European Governments and Politics*, 2nd ed. New York: Macmillan, 1939.

Roberts, St. H., *The House That Hitler Built.* New York: Harper, 1938.

Salvemini, Gaetano, *The Fascist Dictatorship in Italy.* New York: Holt, 1927.

Salvemini, Gaetano, *Under the Axe of Fascism.* New York: Viking, 1936.

Shotwell, James T. (ed.), *Governments of Continental Europe.* New York: Macmillan, 1940.

Spencer, H. R., *Government and Politics Abroad.* New York: Holt, 1936.

Webb, Sidney and Beatrice, *Soviet Communism: A New Civilization.* 2 vols. New York: Longmans, Green, 1935.

For official documents of dictatorial governments, the following English collections will be helpful:

Hill, N. J., and Stoke, H. W., *The Background of European Governments.* New ed. New York: Farrar and Rinehart, 1940.

Langsam, W. C., *Documents and Readings in the History of Europe Since 1918.* New York: Macmillan, 1939.

Pollock, J. K., and Heneman, J. H., *The Hitler Decrees.* 2nd ed. Ann Arbor: Wahr, 1934.

Rappard, W. E., and others, *Source Book on European Governments.* New York: Van Nostrand, 1937.

Centralization and Dictatorship

The specific German problem of federalism can be studied by following the extensive discussion during the Weimar Republic.

Consult the testimony of Otto Braun, the former Prussian Prime Minister ("the Red Czar" of Republican Prussia) in *Von Weimar zu Hitler* (2nd ed. New York: Europa Verlag, 1940).

For the National Socialist development, see:

Boerner, Alfred V., "Toward Reichsreform—the Reichsgaue," *American Political Science Review*, 33:853 ff. (1939).

Koellreutter, Otto, *Zur Entwicklung der deutschen Reichseinheit*. Jena: Frommansche Buchhandlung, 1935. A National Socialist interpretation.

Lepawsky, A., "Nazis Reform the Reich," *American Political Science Review*, 30:324-350 (1936).

Wells, R. H., "Liquidation of the German Länder," *ibid.*, 30:350-361 (1936).

On the "federal" structure of the Soviet Union, see:

Broda, R., "The Revival of Nationalities in the Soviet Union," *American Journal of Sociology*, 37:82-93 (1931).

Kohn, Hans, *Nationalism in the Soviet Union*. New York: Columbia University Press, 1933.

Stalin, Josef, *Marxism and the National and Colonial Question*. New York: International Publishers, 1936.

Institutional symbolism found its clearest expression in the British monarchy. See:

Keith, A. B., *The King and the Imperial Crown*. London: Longmans, 1936.

Martin, Kingsley, *The Magic of Monarchy*. New York: Knopf, 1937.

The upholding of constitutions worn thin and the creation of new ones may both serve the need for the crystallization of power; such a procedure is especially useful for fluctuating dictatorial governments. For a recent example, see the controversial discussion on the Soviet Constitution of 1936:

Brecht, A., "The New Russian Constitution," *Social Research*, 4:157-190 (1937).

Chamberlin, W. H., "Russia's Gold Brick Constitution," *American Mercury*, 42:181-186 (1937).

Coates, W. P. and Z. K., *From Tsardom to the Stalin Constitution*. London: Allen and Unwin, 1938.

Dean, Vera M., "The New Constitution of the U.S.S.R.," *Foreign Policy Reports*, XIII (April 15, 1937).

Pares, Sir Bernard, "Historical Commentary on the New Constitution of the U.S.S.R.," *International Conciliation,* No. 327 (1937).

Strong, A. L., *The New Soviet Constitution.* New York: Holt, 1937.

International Conciliation, No. 327 (February, 1937) and W. E. Rappard, *et al., Source Book on European Governments* (New York: Van Nostrand, 1937) contain an English translation of the full text.

On political representation, see:

Fairlie, John A., "The Nature of Political Representation," *American Political Science Review,* 34:236-248, 456-466 (1940).

Koellreutter, Otto, *Deutsches Verfassungsrecht.* 3rd ed. Berlin: Junker und Dünnhaupt, 1938.

Leibholz, G., *Das Wesen der Repräsentation.* Berlin: de Gruyter, 1929.

Mims, Edwin, *The Majority of the People.* New York: Modern Age Books, 1941.

Sait, E. M., *Political Institutions.* New York: Appleton-Century, 1938. Especially Chap. 20, pp. 467-499.

Triepel, Heinrich, *Hegemonie; ein Buch von Führenden Staaten.* Stuttgart: Kohlhammer, 1938.

Williamson, René de Visme, "The Fascist Concept of Representation," *Journal of Politics,* 3:29-41 (1941).

The significance of the "most democratic" electoral system, proportional representation, for the emergence of dictatorial rule has been emphasized in the following:

Hallett, G. H., and Hoag, C. G., *Proportional Representation—The Key to Democracy.* Washington: National Home Library, 1937. An opposite view.

Hermens, F. A., *Democracy or Anarchy? A Study of Proportional Representation.* Notre Dame: The Review of Politics, 1941.

Schauff, Johannes (ed.), *Neues Wahlrecht.* Berlin: Stilke, 1929.

On elections in dictatorship, see:

Salvemini, Gaetano, "Totalitarian Election in Italy Today," *Social Research,* 4:108-123 (1937).

Teper, L., "Elections in Soviet Russia," *American Political Science Review,* 26:926-931 (1932).

On plebiscites, see:

Koellreutter, Otto, *Deutsches Verfassungsrecht.* 3rd ed. Berlin: Junker und Dünnhaupt, 1938. The official Nazi view.

Wambaugh, Sara, *Plebiscites Since the World War.* Washington: Carnegie Endowment for International Peace, 1933.

Wambaugh, Sara, *The Saar Plebiscite.* Cambridge, Mass.: Harvard University Press, 1940.

Zurcher, A. J., "The Hitler Referenda," *American Political Science Review*, 29:91-99 (1935).

For a critical appraisal of the referendum in democratic government, see:
Friedrich, C. J., *Constitutional Government and Democracy*. Boston: Little, Brown, 1941. Pp. 536-563.
Laski, H. J., *Parliamentary Government in England*. New York: Harper, 1938. Pp. 105-107.
Schuman, F. L., *The Nazi Dictatorship*. New York: Knopf, 1936.

BUREAUCRACY

On historical background and contemporary problems, see:
Dorn, Walter L., "The Prussian Bureaucracy in the Eighteenth Century," *Political Science Quarterly*, 46:403-423 (1931), and 47:75-94 (1932).
Finer, Hermann, *The Theory and Practice of Modern Government*. New York: Dial Press, 1934. Part VI.
Friedrich, Carl J., *Constitutional Government and Democracy*. Boston: Little, Brown, 1941. Chap. 2, "The Core of Modern Government: Bureaucracy," pp. 36-58. The bibliography (pp. 599-601) refers to the valuable publications of Otto Hintze, Gustav Schmoller, Max and Alfred Weber, etc.
Friedrich, Carl J., and Cole, Taylor, *Responsible Bureaucracy*. Cambridge: Harvard University Press, 1932.
White, Leonard D., *Introduction to the Study of Public Administration*. Rev. ed. New York: Macmillan, 1939.

For bureaucracy and dictatorship, see the following:
Cole, Taylor, "Italy's Fascist Bureaucracy," *American Political Science Review*, 32:1157 ff. (1938).
Lasswell, Harold D., and Sereno, Renzo, "Governmental and Party Leaders in Fascist Italy," *American Political Science Review*, 31: 914 ff. (1937).
Lusignoli, A., "The Italian Civil Service," in L. D. White (ed.), *The Civil Service in the Modern State*. Chicago: University of Chicago Press, 1930.
Marx, F. M., "Germany's New Civil Service Act," *American Political Science Review*, 31:879 ff. (1937).
Marx, F. M., "Bureaucracy and Consultation," *Review of Politics*, 1:84-100 (1939).
Marx, F. M., "Bureaucracy and Dictatorship," *Review of Politics*, 3:100-117 (1941).

Pollock, J. K., and Boerner, A. V., *The German Civil Service Act.* Chicago: Civil Service Assembly of the United States, 1938.

Steiner, H. Arthur, *Government in Fascist Italy.* New York: McGraw-Hill, 1938.

Economics of the Garrison State

This is not the place even to outline the extraordinary changes that "economics" has undergone in recent decades. Undoubtedly, the concepts of "classical economy" and of "welfare economy" can no longer be simply taken for granted. However, the great influence of the writings of John Maynard Keynes should be mentioned.

The impact of war has unquestionably revolutionized economic thought in democracies as well as in dictatorships. Among the numerous studies on the economics of war, see:

Mendershausen, Horst, *The Economics of War.* New York: Prentice-Hall, 1940.

Pigou, A. C., *The Political Economy of War.* Rev. ed. New York: Macmillan, 1940.

Spiegel, Henry William, *The Economics of Total War.* New York: Appleton-Century, 1942.

For background studies, see:

Arnhold, Karl, *Der Betriebsführer und sein Betrieb.* Leipzig: Bibliographisches Institut. 1937. By the director of the influential *Dinta*, the German Institute for National Socialist Technical Work Training.

Burnham, James, *The Managerial Revolution.* New York: John Day, 1941.

Handman, Max, "War, Economic Motives, and Economic Symbols," *American Journal of Sociology*, 44:629-648 (1939).

Hansen, Alvin H., *Fiscal Policy and Business Cycles.* New York: Norton, 1941.

Hawtrey, R. G., *Economic Aspects of Sovereignty.* London: Longmans, 1930.

Heimann, Eduard, *Communism, Fascism or Democracy.* New York: Norton, 1932.

Higgins, Benjamin, "The Economic War Since 1918," in Willard Waller (ed.), *War in the 20th Century.* New York: Random House, 1940. Pp. 135-191.

Knight, Frank H., *The Ethics of Competition.* New York: Harper, 1935.

Lerner, Max, "Do Free Markets Make Free Men?" *Southern Review*, 3:625-639 (1938).

Marschak, J., "Peace Economics," *Social Research*, 7:280-298 (1940).

Meade, J. E., *The Economic Basis of a Durable Peace.* New York: Oxford University Press, 1940.

Staley, Eugene, *Raw Materials in Peace and War.* New York: Council on Foreign Relations, 1937.

On the "planned economy" of the U.S.S.R., see:

Dean, V. M., "Industry and Agriculture in the U.S.S.R.," *Foreign Policy Reports* (June 1, 1938), and "Labor and Management in the U.S.S.R.," *ibid.* (June 15, 1938).

Farbman, M., *Piatiletka: Russia's Five-Year Plan.* New York: New Republic, 1931.

Gordon, Manya, *Workers Before and After Lenin.* New York: Dutton, 1941.

Grinko, G. F., *Five-Year Plan of the Soviet Union.* New York: International Publishers, 1930.

Haensel, P. P., *The Economic Policy of Soviet Russia.* London: King, 1930.

Hirsch, Alcan, *Industrialized Russia.* New York: Reinhold, 1934. Preface by Maurice Hindus.

Hoover, Calvin B., *The Economic Life of Soviet Russia.* New York: Macmillan, 1931.

Johnson, Hewlett, *The Soviet Power.* New York: Modern Age Books, 1941. An appraisal by the Archbishop of Canterbury.

Maxwell, B. W., *The Soviet State.* Topeka, Kansas: Steves and Wayburn, 1934.

Stalin, Josef, *From the First to the Second Five-Year Plan.* New York: International Publishers, 1934.

State Planning Commission of the U.S.S.R., *The Second Five-Year Plan.* New York: International Publishers, 1937.

Yugov, A., *Russia's Economic Front for War and Peace.* New York: Harper, 1942.

On Italy's *stato corporativo,* see:

Field, G. L., *Syndical and Corporative Institutions of Italian Fascism.* New York: Columbia University Press, 1938.

Haider, Carmen, *Capital and Labor Under Fascism.* New York: Columbia University Press, 1930.

Palomba, G., "Le grandezze fonlamentali dell' economia corporativa," *Giornale degli Economisti.* 2 (N.S.):168-181 (1940).

Schmidt, C. T., *The Plough and the Sword.* New York: Columbia University Press, 1938.

Schmidt, C. T., *The Corporate State in Action.* New York: Oxford University Press, 1939.

Schneider, H. W., *The Fascist Government of Italy*. New York: Van Nostrand, 1936. Chap. 4.

Steiner, H. A., *Government in Fascist Italy*. New York: McGraw-Hill, 1938.

Welk, W. G., *Fascist Economic Policy*. Cambridge, Mass.: Harvard University Press, 1938.

On the German *Wehrwirtschaft*, see:

Balogh, T., "The National Economy of Germany," *Economic Journal*, 48:461-497 (1938).

Barth, Eberhart, *Wesen und Aufgaben der Organisation der gewerblichen Wirtschaft*. Hamburg: Hanseatische Verlags-Anstalt, 1939.

Brady, R. A., "Policies of National Manufacturing Spitzenverbände," *Political Science Quarterly*, 56:199-225, 379-391, 515-544 (1941).

Cole, Taylor, "The Evolution of the German Labor Front," *Political Science Quarterly*, 52:532 ff. (1937).

Crump, N., "The Economics of the Third Reich," *Journal of the Royal Statistical Society*, 102:167-212 (1939).

Frase, Robert, "A Study of Labor Market Control," in C. J. Friedrich, and E. S. Mason (eds.), *Public Policy*. Cambridge, Mass.: Harvard University Press, 1940.

Guillebaud, C. W., *The Social Policy of Nazi Germany*. New York: Macmillan, 1941.

Hamburger, L., *How Nazi Germany Has Mobilized and Controlled Labor*. Washington: Brookings, 1940.

Heneman, H. J., "German Social Honor Courts," *Michigan Law Review*, 37:725 ff. (1939).

Hitchcock, Dal, "The German Financial Revolution," *Harper's*, 182: 238-247 (1941).

Holt, J. B., *German Agricultural Policy, 1918-1934*. Chapel Hill: University of North Carolina Press, 1936.

Miller, Douglas, *You Can't Do Business with Hitler*. Boston: Little, Brown, 1941.

Palyi, Melchior, "Economic Foundations of the German Totalitarian State," *American Journal of Sociology*, 46:469-486 (1941).

Pelcovits, N. A., "The Social Honor Courts of Nazi Germany," *Political Science Quarterly*, 53:350 ff. (1938).

Poole, Kenyon, *Financial Policies in Germany, 1932-1939*. Cambridge, Mass.: Harvard University Press, 1939.

Possony, Stefan T., "National Socialistic Economics: The Contradictions of the 'New Order,'" *Journal of Politics*, 4:149-182 (1942).

Pratt, Fletcher, "German Planning for Total War," *Harper's*, 182:225-237 (1941).

Reimann, G., *The Vampire Economy*, New York: Vanguard, 1939.

Singer, H. W., "The German War Economy in the Light of German Economic Periodicals," *Economic Journal*, 50:534-546 (1940), 51:19-35, 193-215 (1941).

Spiegel, H. W., "Wehrwirtschaft: Economics of the Military State," *American Economic Review*, 30:713-723 (1940).

Stolper, Gustav, *German Economy, 1870-1940*. New York: Reynal and Hitchcock, 1940.

Sweezy, Maxine Y., *The Structure of Nazi Economy*. Cambridge, Mass.: Harvard University Press, 1941.

Tolischus, O. D., *They Wanted War*. New York: Reynal and Hitchcock, 1940.

Wunderlich, Frieda, "Germany's Defense Economy and the Decay of Capitalism," *Quarterly Journal of Economics*, 52:401-430 (1938).

DICTATORSHIP AND THE ARMED FORCES

On the relationship between military and civil authorities, see:

Herring, E. Pendleton, *Civil Military Relations*. Chicago: University of Chicago Press, 1940. Bibliographical notes on "Administrative Problems of Civilian Mobilization." See also his *Impact of War*. New York: Farrar and Rinehart, 1941.

Oncken, Herman, *Politik und Kriegsführung*. Munich: Max Hueber, 1928.

Rogers, Lindsay, "Civilian Control of Military Policy," *Foreign Affairs*, 18:280-291 (1940).

That armies are an integral part of the social institution and that changing military tactics have a most significant influence on the structure of social and political institutions has been proved by the writings of Hans Delbrück and Otto Hintze. For contemporary discussions, see:

Kähler, A., and Speier, H. (eds.), *War in Our Time*. New York: Norton, 1939.

Lasswell, Harold D., "The Garrison State," *American Journal of Sociology*, 46:455-468 (1941).

Lauterbach, Albert T., "Roots and Implications of the German Idea of Military Society," *Military Affairs*, 5:1-20 (1940).

Renn, Ludwig, *Warfare: The Relation of War to Society*. New York: Oxford University Press, 1939.

Speier, Hans, "The Effect of War on the Social Order," *Annals of the American Academy of Political and Social Science*, 218:87-96 (1941).

Waller, Willard (ed.), *War in the 20th Century*. New York: Dryden Press, 1940.

On total war, see:

Douhet, Giulio, *La guerre de l'air*. Paris: Les Ailes, 1936. Translation from the Italian.

Farago, Ladislas, and Gittler, L. F., *German Psychological Warfare*. New York: Committee for National Morale, 1941. Annotated bibliography and introductory article.

Farago, Ladislas, *The Axis Grand Strategy*. New York: Farrar and Rinehart, 1942.

Foertsch, H., *The Art of Modern Warfare*. New York: Veritas Press, 1940.

Forsthoff, Ernst, *Der totale Staat*. 2nd ed. Hamburg: Hanseatische Verlagsanstalt, 1934.

Jünger, Ernst, *Die totale Mobilmachung*. 2nd ed. Berlin: Junker und Dünnhaupt, 1934.

Ludendorff, Erich, *Der totale Krieg*. Munich: Ludendorff's Verlag, 1935. Translation: *The Nation at War*. London: Hutchinson, 1936.

Sigaud, Louis A., *Douhet and Aerial Warfare*. New York: Putnam, 1941.

Vagts, Alfred, *A History of Militarism*. New York: Norton, 1937. A fundamental study of the nature and history of militarism.

On the Red Army, see:

Kournakoff, Sergei N., *Russia's Fighting Forces*. New York: Duell, Sloan and Pearce, 1942.

Werner, Max, *The Military Strength of the Powers*. New York: Modern Age, 1939.

Wollenberg, Erich, *The Red Army*. London: Secker and Warburg, 1940.

X (Anonymous), "Russia and Germany, Political and Military Reflections," *Foreign Affairs*, 20:303-323 (1942).

Zacharoff, Lucien, *"We Made a Mistake"—Hitler*. New York: Appleton-Century, 1942.

On the complex relations between the Reichwehr and the Third Reich, consult:

Deuel, Wallace, *People Under Hitler*. New York: Harcourt, Brace, 1942.

Harsch, Joseph C., *Pattern of Conquest*. New York: Doubleday, Doran, 1941. Especially Chap. 5, pp. 138-169.

Rosinski, Herbert, *The German Army*. New York: Harcourt, Brace, 1940.

For the historical background, see:

Demeter, K., *Das Deutsche Offizierskorps*. Berlin: Hobbing, 1930.

Drucker, Peter, "What Became of the Prussian Army?" *Virginia Quarterly Review*, 17:28-42 (1941).

Endres, F. C., "Soziologische Struktur und dazugehörige Ideologie des Offizierskorps vor dem Weltkrieg," *Archiv für Sozialwiss.* Vol. LVIII (1927).

Kehr, E., "Zur Genesis des Preuss Reserveoffiziers," *Die Gesellschaft.* Berlin: Dietz, 1929.

Salomon, Albert, "The Spirit of the Soldier and Nazi Militarism," *Social Research*, 9:82-103 (1942).

Vagts, Alfred, "The German Army of the Second Reich as a Cultural Institution," in C. W. Ware (ed.), *The Cultural Approach to History*. New York: Columbia University Press, 1941.

On democratic militarism, see:

Beneš, Eduard, "Das demokratische Heer," *Gedanke und Tat*, 2:139-163 (Prague: Orbis Verlag, 1937).

McKinley, S. B., *Democracy and Military Power*. Rev. ed. New York: Vanguard, 1941.

Muret, Charlotte, and Rougemont, Denis de, "The Army of a Democracy," *Harper's*, 183:337-346 (1941).

Wavell, General Sir Archibald, *Generals and Generalship*. New York: Macmillan, 1941. The Lee-Knowles Lectures delivered at Trinity College, Cambridge.

DICTATORSHIP AND THE ESTABLISHED CHURCHES

For a historical treatment of the conflict between state and church in Italy, see:

Eckhardt, C. C., *The Papacy and World Affairs as Reflected in the Secularization of Politics*. Chicago: University of Chicago Press, 1937.

Halperin, S. W., *The Separation of Church and State in Italian Thought from Cavour to Mussolini*. Chicago: University of Chicago Press, 1937.

Halperin, S. W., *Italy and the Vatican at War*. Chicago: University of Chicago Press, 1939.

Hill, N. L., and Stoke, H. W., *The Background of European Governments*. 2nd ed. New York: Farrar and Rinehart, 1940. Pp. 526-529. For an abbreviated English text of the Lateran Accord.

Ridley, F. A., *The Papacy and Fascism*. London: Secker and Warburg, 1937.

Warren, Roland L., "Fascism and the Church," *American Sociological Review*, 6:45-51 (1941).

Williamson, Benedict, *The Treaty of the Lateran*. London: Burns, 1929.

For the U.S.S.R., see:

Gurian, Waldemar, *Bolshevism: Theory and Practice*. London: Sheed, 1933.

Hecker, J. F., *Religion Under the Soviets*. New York: Vanguard, 1927.

Johnson, The Very Reverend Hewlett, *The Soviet Power*. New York: Modern Age Books, 1941.

For Nazi Germany, consult:

Barth, Karl, *The Church and the Political Question of Our Day*. New York: Scribner, 1939.

Bergmann, Ernst, *Die Deutsche Nationalkirche*. Breslau: Hirt, 1933.

Bergmann, Ernst, *Die 25 Thesen der Deutsch Religion*. 3rd ed. Breslau: Hirt, 1934.

Faulhaber, Michael von, *Judaism, Christianity and Germany*. New York: Macmillan, 1934.

Gurian, Waldemar, *Hitler and the Christians*. London: Sheed, 1936.

Gurian, Waldemar, "Hitler's Undeclared War on the Catholic Church," *Foreign Affairs*, 16:260-271 (1938).

Hauer, Friedrich W., *Deutsche Gottschau*. 4th ed. Stuttgart: Gurbrod, 1936.

Kerrl, Hans, *Religion und Weltanschauung*. Berlin: Müller, 1937.

Mason, J. B., "Christianity Faces Caesarism," *Sewanee Review*, 47:461-472 (1939).

Micklem, N., *National Socialism and the Roman Catholic Church*. New York: Oxford University Press, 1939.

Niebuhr, Reinhold, *Christianity and Power Politics*. New York: Scribner, 1940.

Niemoeller, Martin, *God Is My Father*. New York: Philosophical Library, 1941. His last 28 sermons.

Pauck, W., "National Socialism and Christianity; Can They Be Reconciled?" *Journal of Religion*, 20:15-32 (1940).

Shuster, George N., *Like a Mighty Army—Hitler vs. Established Religion*. New York: Appleton-Century, 1935.

Spence, L., "Neo-pagan Movement in Germany," *Quarterly Review*, 275:66-80 (1940).

Tillich, Paul, "The Totalitarian State and the Claim of the Church," *Social Research*, 1:405-433, 1934.

Voegelin, Erich, *Die Politischen Religionen*. Stockholm: Bermann Fisher, 1939.

THE FAMILY UNDER TOTALITARIANISM

On Soviet Russia, see:

Fairchild, Mildred, "The Status of the Family in the Soviet Union Today," *American Sociological Review*, 2:619-629 (1937).

Grunfeld, Judith, "Women's Work in Russia's Planned Economy," *Social Research*, 9:22-45 (1942).

Halle, Fanina, *Women in Soviet Russia*. New York: Viking Press, 1933.

Halle, Fanina, *Women in the Soviet East*. New York: Dutton, 1938.

Kingsbury, Susan M., and Fairchild, Mildred, *Factory, Family and Women in the Soviet Union*. New York: Putnam, 1935.

For the background and recent development in Germany, consult:

Bäumer, Gertrud, *Die Frau im Deutschen Staat*. Berlin: Junker und Dünnhaupt, 1932.

Beyer, Hans, *Die Frau in der politischen Entscheidung*. Stuttgart: Enke, 1932.

Hankins, F. H., "German Policies for Increasing Births," *American Journal of Sociology*, 42:630-652 (1937).

Kirkpatrick, Clifford, "Recent Changes in the Status of Women and the Family in Germany," *American Sociological Review*, 2:650-658 (1937).

Kirkpatrick, Clifford, *Nazi Germany: Its Women and Family Life*. Indianapolis: Bobbs-Merrill, 1938.

Meusel, A., "National Socialism and the Family," *Sociological Review*, 28:166-186, 389-411 (1936).

Scholtz-Klink, Gertrud, *Verpflichtung und Aufgabe der Frau im Nationalsocialistischen Staat*. Berlin: Junker und Dünnhaupt, 1937.

See also the general studies on population trends and developments such as:

Glass, D. V., *Population Policies and Movements in Europe*. Oxford: Clarendon Press, 1940.

Thompson, Warren S., *Population Problems*. New York: McGraw-Hill, 1935.

Thompson, Warren S., *Danger Spots in World Population*. New York: Knopf, 1939.

EDUCATION IN UNIFORM

Italy

Ascoli, Max, "Education in Fascist Italy," in *Social Research*, 4:338-347 (1937).

Ascoli, Max, "The Fascisti's March on Scholarship," *American Scholar*, 7:50-59 (1938).

Gentile, G., *The Reform of Education*. New York: Harcourt, Brace, 1922. Translated by D. Bigongiari.

Hartmann, Hans, *Der Faschismus Dringt ins Volk. Eine Betrachtung über das Dopolavoro*. Berlin: Der Neue Geist Verlag, 1933.

Marraro, H. R., "New Education in Italy," *Current History*, 37:571-576, (1933).

Piccoli, D. S., *The Youth Movement in Italy.* New York: American-Italian Union, 1936.

Schneider, H. W., *Making Fascists.* Chicago: University of Chicago Press, 1929.

Soviet Russia

Harper, S. N., *Civic Training in Soviet Russia.* Chicago: University of Chicago Press, 1929.

Mehnert, Klaus, *Youth in Soviet Russia.* New York: Harcourt, Brace, 1933.

Nearing, S., *Education in Soviet Russia.* New York: International Publishers, 1926.

Pinkevich, A. P., *The New Education in the Soviet Republic.* New York: Day, 1929.

Rappard, W. E., *et al.*, *Source Book on European Governments.* New York: Van Nostrand, 1937. Part V, pp. 53-59. Gives the program of the Comsomols as adopted in 1936.

Watson, Goodwin, "Education in Soviet Russia," *Social Research,* 4: 360-370 (1937).

Woody, T., *New Minds: New Men?* New York: Macmillan, 1932.

National Socialist Germany
Among the National Socialist statements, see:

Bäumler, Alfred, *Politik und Erziehung, Reden und Aufsätze.* Berlin: Junker und Dünnhaupt, 1937.

Brennecke, Fritz (ed.), *The Nazi Primer. A Nazi Textbook for Primary Schools.* New York: Harper, 1938. Translation and preface by H. L. Childs.

Germany Speaks. London: Thornton Butterworth, 1938. Twenty-one essays by leading National Socialists, among them Bernhard Rust, Minister of Education.

Klagges, D., *Idee und System.* Leipzig: Armanen-Verlag, 1934.

Krieck, Ernst, *Nationalpolitische Erziehung.* 21st ed. Leipzig: Armanen-Verlag, 1938.

Schirach, Baldur von, *Revolution der Erziehung. Reden.* Munich: Eher, 1938.

For critical analysis, consult:

Hartshorne, E. Y., *The German Universities Under National Socialism.* Cambridge, Mass.: Harvard University Press, 1937.

Kandel, I. L., "The Making of Nazis," *Educational Yearbook of the International Institute of Teachers College,* New York: Columbia University Press, 1934. Pp. 413-552.

Kneller, George Frederick, *The Educational Philosophy of National Socialism*. New Haven: Yale University Press, 1941.

Lichtenberger, Henri, *The Third Reich*. New York: Greystone, 1937. On the "Spartan spirit" of National Socialist education.

Mann, Erika, *Education for Barbarians*. New York: Modern Age, 1938.

Mason, John Brown, "Nazi Concepts of History," *Review of Politics*, 2:180-196 (1940).

Waln, Nora, *Reaching for the Stars*. Boston: Little, Brown, 1939.

Wunderlich, Frieda, "Education in Nazi Germany," *Social Research*, 4:347-360 (1937).

For contrast, see:

Edwards, Newton (ed.), *Education in a Democracy*. Chicago: University of Chicago Press, 1942.

Kotschnig, Walter Maria, "Educating the Elite in Europe," *Journal of Educational Sociology*, 13:70-81 (1939).

Ulich, Robert, *Fundamentals of Democratic Education*. New York: American Book, 1940.

FEAR AS A POLITICAL WEAPON

On law and legal institutions in dictatorships, see:

Callcott, M. S., *Russian Justice*. New York: Macmillan, 1935.

Kirchheimer, Otto, "Criminal Law in National-Socialist Germany," *Studies in Philosophy and Social Science*, 8:444-463 (1940), and his "The Legal Order of National Socialism," *ibid.*, 9:456-475 (1941).

Laski, H. J., *Law and Justice in Soviet Russia*. London: Hogarth, 1935.

Loewenstein, Karl, "Law in the Third Reich," *Yale Law Journal*, 45:779 ff. (1936).

Loewenstein, Karl, "Dictatorship and the German Constitution, 1933-1937," *University of Chicago Law Review*, 4:537 ff. (1937).

Preuss, L., "Germanic Law Versus Roman Law in National Socialist Legal Theory," *Journal of Comparative Legislation and International Law*, 16:26 ff. (1934).

Steiner, H. A., "The Fascist Conception of Law," *Columbia Law Review*, 36:1267-1283 (1936).

The literature dealing with the "Political Trials" in the U.S.S.R. is numerous and inconclusive. See:

Davies, Joseph E., *Mission to Moscow*. New York: Simon and Schuster, 1941.

Koestler, Arthur, *Darkness at Noon*. New York: Macmillan, 1941. A significant analysis in novel form.

Mosely, P. E., "Recent Soviet Trials and Policies," *Yale Review*, 27:745-766 (1938).

The court proceedings of the Moscow trials, published by the People's Commissariat of Justice of the U.S.S.R., are available in English under the titles:

The Trotskyite-Zinovievite Terrorist Centre. (August, 1936.)
The Anti-Soviet Trotskyite Centre. (January, 1937.)

On the organized terror of modern dictatorship, see:

Balticus (pseud.), "The Two G's: Gestapo and GPU," *Foreign Affairs*, 17:489 ff. (1939).

Nenni, P., *Ten Years of Tyranny in Italy.* London: Allen and Unwin, 1932.

Roper, Edith, and Leiser, Clara, *Skeleton of Justice.* New York: Dutton, 1941.

Rowan, R. W., *Terror in Our Time.* New York: Longmans, Green, 1941.

Taylor, Edmond, *The Strategy of Terror.* Boston: Houghton Mifflin, 1940.

Tiltman, H. H., *The Terror in Europe.* New York: Stokes, 1932.

Among the numerous books of an autobiographical or semi-fictional nature, the following will be of some significance for a fuller evaluation:

Billinger, K., *Fatherland.* New York: Farrar and Rinehart, 1935.

Kent, Madeleine, *I Married a German.* New York: Harper, 1939.

Langhoff, Wolfgang, *Rubber Truncheon.* New York: Dutton, 1935. Translated from the German, *Die Moorsoldaten.*

Lips, Eva, *Savage Symphony.* New York: Random House, 1938.

Litten, Irmgard, *Beyond Tears.* New York: Alliance, 1940.

MacInnes, Helen, *Above Suspicion.* Boston: Little, Brown, 1941.

Nitti, F. F., *Escape.* New York: Putnam, 1930.

Rauschning, Anna, *No Retreat.* Indianapolis: Bobbs-Merrill, 1942.

Seger, Gerhart, *A Nation Terrorized.* Chicago: Reilly and Lee, 1935.

Valtin, Jan, *Out of the Night.* New York: Alliance, 1941.

Vance, Ethel, *Escape.* Boston: Little, Brown, 1939.

For the psychological make-up of the "dictatorial terrorists" consult:

Dollard, John, and others, *Frustration and Aggression.* New Haven: Yale University Press, 1941.

Fromm, Erich, *Escape from Freedom.* New York: Norton, 1941.

Chapter VII

THE CONTROL OF THE MASSES: PUBLIC OPINION AND PROPAGANDA

PROPAGANDA: SOME MISCONCEPTIONS

For a definition and general discussion of public opinion and propaganda, see:

Albig, William, *Public Opinion*. New York: McGraw-Hill, 1939.

Bernays, E., *Propaganda*, New York: Liveright, 1928.

Casey, Ralph D., "Propaganda and Public Opinion" in W. Waller (ed.), *War in the Modern World*. New York: Random House, 1940.

Childs, H. L. (ed.), "Pressure Groups and Propaganda," *Annals of the American Academy of Political and Social Sciences*, 179:1-239 (1935).

Childs, H. L., "By Public Opinion I Mean," *Public Opinion Quarterly*, 3:327-336 (1939).

Childs, H. L., *An Introduction to Public Opinion*. New York: John Wiley, 1940.

Doob, Leonard W., *Propaganda—Its Psychology and Technique*. New York: Holt, 1935.

Gallup, George, *Public Opinion in a Democracy*. Princeton: Princeton University Press, 1939.

Gallup, George, and Rae, S. F., *The Pulse of Democracy; the Public Opinion Poll and How It Works*. New York: Simon and Schuster, 1940.

Lasswell, H. D., Casey, Ralph D., and Smith, Bruce Lannes, *Propaganda and Promotional Activities, an Annotated Bibliography*. Minneapolis: University of Minnesota Press, 1935.

Miller, Clyde R., "Some Comments on Propaganda Analysis and the Science of Democracy," *Public Opinion Quarterly*, 5:657-665 (1941).

Odegard, Peter H., *The American Public Mind*. New York: Columbia University Press, 1930.

Palmer, Paul A., "The Concept of Public Opinion in Political Theory," *Essays in History and Political Theory in Honor of C. H. H. McIlwain*. Cambridge, Mass.: Harvard University Press, 1936. The evolution of the concept of public opinion.

Public Opinion Quarterly, Princeton University Press, 1937 ff. Contains an excellent discussion of pertinent problems and a running comment on the extensive literature in the field.

On World War I propaganda, see:

Bruntz, G. G., *Allied Propaganda and the Collapse of the German Empire in 1918*. Stanford: Stanford University Press, 1938.

Lasswell, H. D., *Propaganda Technique in the World War*. New York: Knopf, 1927. This is the standard work. See also his essay, "The Strategy of Revolutionary and War Propaganda" in Quincy Wright (ed.), *Public Opinion and World Politics*. Chicago: University of Chicago Press, 1933.

Mock, J. R., and Larson, Cedric, *Words That Won the War*. Princeton: Princeton University Press, 1939.

Paxson, F. L., *American Democracy and the World War*. Boston: Houghton Mifflin. Vol. I, 1936; Vol. II, 1939.

Peterson, H. C., *Propaganda for War: the Campaign Against American Neutrality, 1914-1917*. Norman: University of Oklahoma Press, 1939.

Riegel, O. W., *Mobilizing for Chaos*. New Haven: Yale University Press, 1934.

Thimme, H., *Weltkrieg ohne Waffen: die Propaganda der Westmächte gegen Deutschland*. Stuttgart: Cotta, 1932.

For interesting contributions by social psychologists on propaganda and public opinion see:

Allport, Floyd Henry, *Institutional Behavior*. Chapel Hill: University of North Carolina Press, 1933. Especially the chapter, "Psychology of Nationalism."

Bird, Charles, *Social Psychology*. New York: Appleton-Century, 1940. Chap. 9, "Propaganda"; Chap. 10, "The Behavior of Crowds"; Chap. 11, "Leadership."

Britt, Steuart H., *Social Psychology of Modern Life*. New York: Farrar and Rinehart, 1941. Especially Chapter 24, "Nationalism and War."

Brown, J. F., *Psychology and the Social Order*. New York: McGraw-Hill, 1936.

Cantril, Hadley, *The Invasion from Mars*. Princeton: Princeton University Press, 1940.

Cantril, Hadley, *The Psychology of Social Movements*. New York: Wiley, 1941.

Chakotin, Serge, *The Rape of the Masses*. New York: Alliance, 1940. This study by the well-known student of Pavlov represents an interesting attempt to apply the master's theory of conditioned reflexes in an analysis of totalitarian propaganda.

Freeman, Ellis, *Social Psychology*. New York: Holt, 1936.

Gundlach, Ralph H., "Emotional Stability and Political Opinions as

Related to Income and Age," *Journal of Social Psychology*, 10:577-590 (1939).

Gundlach, Ralph H., "The Psychology of Nationalism as a Major Factor for War," *Psychological Bulletin*, 37:590 ff. (1940), 37:613-620 (1940).

Klineberg, Otto, *Social Psychology*. New York: Holt, 1940.

La Piere, R. T., and Farnsworth, P. R., *Social Psychology*. New York: McGraw-Hill, 1936.

Sherif, Muzafer, *Psychology of Social Norms*. New York: Harper, 1936.

PROPAGANDA FOR WHOM?

On the spread and scope of modern propaganda, consult:

Atkins, H. G., *German Literature Through Nazi Eyes*. London: Methuen and Co., 1941.

Burke, K., "Rhetoric of Hitler's Battle," *Southern Review*, 5:1-21 (1939).

Childs, Harwood L., and Whitton, John B. (ed.), *Propaganda by Short Wave*. Princeton: Princeton University Press, 1942.

Desmond, R. W., *The Press and World Affairs*. New York: Appleton-Century, 1937.

Dovifat, E., *Rede und Redner; Ihr Wesen und ihre Politische Macht*. Leipzig: Bibliographisches Institut, 1937.

Friedrich, Carl J., "Press and Radio—The Control of Communications," in *Constitutional Government and Democracy*. Boston: Little, Brown, 1941. Pp. 475-505; bibliography, pp. 654-658.

Hettinger, H. S., "Radio: The Fifth Estate," *Annals of the American Academy of Political and Social Sciences*, 177:1-219 (1935). See especially the articles by Horst Dressler-Andress, "German Broadcasting," and Rose Ziglin, "Radio Broadcasting in the Soviet Union," *ibid.*, pp. 61-72.

Lazarsfeld, P. F., *Radio and the Printed Page: An Introduction to the Study of Radio and Its Role in the Communication of Ideas*. New York: Duell, Sloan and Pearce, 1940.

Lee, A. M., *The Daily Newspaper in America: The Evolution of a Social Instrument*. New York: Macmillan, 1937.

Lippmann, Walter, *Public Opinion*. New York: Macmillan, 1922.

Lippmann, Walter, *The Phantom Public*. New York: Harcourt, Brace, 1925.

Lueddecke, T., *Die Tageszeitung als Mittel der Staatsführung*. Hamburg: Hanseatische Verlags-Anstalt, 1933.

Odegard, Peter H., *The American Public Mind*. New York: Columbia University Press, 1930.

Rolo, Charles J., *Radio Goes to War, the "Fourth Front."* New York: Putnam, 1942.

Speier, Hans, "The Radio Communication of War News in Germany," *Social Research*, 8:399-418 (1941).

Speier, Hans, "Magic Geography," *Social Research*, 8:310-330 (1941). On the use of maps in propaganda.

On propaganda and education, see:

Doob, Leonard W., and Robinson, Edward S., "Psychology and Propaganda," *Annals of the American Academy of Political Science*, 179: 88-95 (1935).

Friedrich, Carl J., "Education and Propaganda," *Atlantic*, 159:693-701 (1937).

Lasswell, H. D., "The Study and Practice of Propaganda" in *Propaganda and Promotional Activities, an Annotated Bibliography*. Minneapolis: University of Minnesota Press, 1935. Pp. 3-27.

Lenin, V. I., *Agitation und Propaganda*. Vienna: Verlag für Literatur und Politik, 1929.

Lumley, Frederick E., *The Propaganda Menace*. New York: Appleton-Century, 1933.

Martin, Everett Dean, *The Meaning of a Liberal Education*. New York: Norton, 1926.

May, M. A., *Education in a World of Fear*. Cambridge, Mass.: Harvard University Press, 1941.

Odegard, Peter H., "Needed: New Symbols of Peace" in H. S. Quigley (ed.), *Peace or War?* Minneapolis: University of Minnesota Press, 1937.

On propaganda in dictatorship and democracy, see:

Childs, Harwood L. (ed.), *Propaganda and Dictatorship*. Princeton: Princeton University Press, 1936.

Lasswell, Harold D., *Democracy Through Public Opinion*. Menasha, Wisconsin: George Banta Publishing Co., 1941.

Marx, Fritz M., "Criticism in a One-Party State," *Public Opinion Quarterly*, 1:92-98 (1937).

Odegard, Peter H., "Propaganda and Dictatorship," in Guy Stanton Ford (ed.), *Dictatorship in the Modern World*. 2nd ed. Minneapolis: University of Minnesota Press, 1939.

See also the publications of the Institute of Propaganda Analysis. New York: 1939 ff.

Among the Third Reich's official and semi-official publications, in addition to Hitler's and Goebbels' writings, the following books should be mentioned:

Blau, A., *Propaganda als Waffe*. Berlin: Bernard and Graefe, 1937.

Hadamovsky, E., *Propaganda und nationale Macht*. Oldenburg: Stalling, 1933.

Six, F. A., *Die politische Propaganda der NSDAP im Kampf um die Macht*. Heidelberg: Winter, 1936.

TECHNIQUES OF TOTALITARIAN CONTROL

For the machinery of dictatorial propaganda, see:

Dreyer, E. A. *Deutsche Kultur im neuen Reich. Wesen, Aufgabe und Ziel der Reichskulturkammer*. Berlin: Schlieffen Verlag, 1934.

Kiefer, Alexander F., "Government Control of Publishing in Germany." *Political Science Quarterly*, 57:72-97 (1942).

Kris, Ernst, "German Propaganda Instructions of 1933," *Social Research*, 9:46-81 (1942). An analysis of important secret documents of the German Ministry of Propaganda. This study represents a sound discussion of the techniques and principles of National Socialist psychological warfare.

Larson, Cedric, "The German Press Chamber," *Public Opinion Quarterly*, 1:53-70 (1937).

Schrieber, Karl F., *Das Recht der Reichskulturkammer*. Berlin: Junker und Dünnhaupt, 1935.

Wilson, C. H., "Hitler, Goebbels and the Ministry of Propaganda," *Political Quarterly*, 10:83 ff. (1939).

For comparison, see:

Larson, Cedric, "The British Ministry of Information," *Public Opinion Quarterly*, 5:412-431 (1941).

Sharp, Walter R., "Methods of Opinion Control in Present-day Brazil," *Public Opinion Quarterly*, 5:3-16 (1941).

SYMBOLS AND MASS MANAGEMENT

Arnold, Thurman W., *The Symbols of Government*. New Haven: Yale University Press, 1935.

Brinton, Crane, "Revolutionary Symbolism in the Jacobin Clubs," *American Historical Review*, 32:737 ff. (1927).

Chakotin, Serge, *The Rape of the Masses*. New York: Alliance, 1940.

Corwin, E. S., "The Constitution as Instrument and Symbol," *American Political Science Review*, 30:1071 ff. (1936).

Ginsburg, J., "National Symbolism," in P. Kosok, *Modern Germany*. Chicago: University of Chicago Press, 1933. Chap. 17.

Lasswell, H. D., *World Politics and Personal Insecurity*. New York: McGraw-Hill, 1935.

Lerner, Max, "Constitution and Court as Symbols," *Yale Law Journal*, 46:1290 ff. (1937).

Loewenstein, Karl, "The Influence of Symbols and Politics," in R. V. Peel, and J. S. Roucek (eds.), *Introduction to Politics*. New York: Crowell, 1941. Pp. 62-83.

Marshall, James, *Swords and Symbols*. New York: Oxford University Press, 1939.

Merriam, C. E., *The Making of Citizens*. Chicago: University of Chicago Press, 1931.

Whitehead, A. N., *Symbolism, Its Meaning and Effect*. Cambridge, Mass.: Harvard University Press, 1938.

Chapter VIII

THE IMPACT OF PERMANENT WAR

Roots of Totalitarianism

For an authoritative exposition of National-Socialist and Fascist ideology, see:

Bäumler, Alfred, *Männerbund und Wissenschaft*. Berlin: Junker und Dünnhaupt, 1934.

Bäumler, Alfred, *Studien zur Deutschen Geistesgeschichte*. Berlin: Junker und Dünnhaupt, 1937.

Gentile, Giovanni, "The Philosophical Basis of Fascism," *Foreign Affairs*, 6:290-304 (1928).

Gini, Corrado, "The Scientific Basis of Fascism," *Political Science Quarterly*, 42:99-115 (1927).

Hitler, Adolf, *Mein Kampf*. New York: Reynal and Hitchcock, 1939.

Moeller van den Bruck, Arthur, *Das Dritte Reich*. Hamburg: Hanseatische Verlags-Anstalt, 1931. English translations: *The Third Reich* (London, Allen and Unwin, 1934), *Germany's Third Empire* (New York: Norton, 1941).

Mussolini, Benito, "The Political and Social Doctrine of Fascism," *Political Quarterly*, 4:341-356 (1933). Translation of an article in *Enciclopedia Italiana*, 14:847-851 (1932).

Rocco, Alfredo, "The Political Doctrine of Fascism," *International Conciliation*, No. 226. New York: Carnegie Endowment for International Peace, 1926.

Rosenberg, Alfred, *Wesen, Grundsätze und Ziele der National-Sozialistischen Deutschen Arbeiterpartei; Das Programm der Bewegung*. 19th ed. Munich: Eher, 1938.

Rosenberg, Alfred, *Der Mythus des 20. Jahrhunderts.* 153-156 ed. Munich: Hoheneichen Verlag, 1939.

Rosenberg, Alfred (ed.), *National Sozialistische Monate-Hefte.* (Monthly.)

Schmitt, Carl, *Der Begriff des Politischen.* Hamburg: Hanseatische Verlags-Anstalt, 1933.

Schmitt, Carl, *Volk, Staat und Bewegung.* Hamburg: Hanseatische Verlags-Anstalt, 1933.

Schmitt, Carl, "Totaler Feind, Totaler Krieg, Totaler Staat," *Völkerbund und Völkerrecht,* 4:139 ff. (1937).

Steding, Christoph, *Das Reich und die Krankheit der Europäischen Kultur.* Hamburg: Hanseatische Verlags-Anstalt, 1938.

For a critical analysis, consult:

Borgese, G. A., "The Intellectual Origins of Fascism," *Social Research.* 1:348 ff. (1934).

Borgese, G. A., *Goliath: The March of Fascism.* New York: Viking. 1938.

Butler, Rohan D'O., *The Roots of National Socialism.* New York: Dutton, 1942.

Coker, Francis, *Recent Political Thought.* New York: Appleton-Century, 1934. Pp. 460-496.

Coole, W. W., and Potter, M. F. (eds.), *Thus Speaks Germany.* New York: Harper, 1942.

Elliott, W. Y., *The Pragmatic Revolt in Politics.* New York: Macmillan, 1928.

Heller, Hermann, *Europa und der Faschismus.* Berlin: De Gruyter, 1929.

Kohn, Hans, *Force or Reason,* Cambridge: Harvard University Press, 1938.

Kohn, Hans, *Revolutions and Dictatorships.* Cambridge: Harvard University Press, 1939.

Kohn, Hans, "The Totalitarian Philosophy of War," *Proceedings of the American Philosophical Society,* 82:57-72 (1940).

Kolnai, Aurel, *The War Against the West.* New York: Viking, 1938.

Krebs, Gerhard, "Moeller van den Bruck: Inventor of the Third Reich," *American Political Science Review,* 35:1085-1105 (1941).

Leighton, J. A., *Social Philosophies in Conflict.* New York: Appleton-Century, 1937.

Mayer, Carl, "On the Intellectual Origin of National-Socialism." *Social Research,* 9:225-247 (1942).

McGovern, W. M., *From Luther to Hitler,* Boston: Houghton Mifflin, 1941.

Megaro, Gaudens, *Mussolini in the Making.* Boston: Houghton Mifflin, 1938.

Palmieri, Mario, *The Philosophy of Fascism.* New York: Fortuny's, 1936.

Rader, M., *No Compromise: The Conflict Between Two Worlds.* New York: Macmillan, 1939.

Rauschning, Hermann, *The Revolution of Nihilism.* New York: Alliance, 1939.

Stewart, W. K., "The Mentors of Mussolini," *American Political Science Review,* 22:843-869 (1928).

Vermeil, Edmond, *Doctrinaires de la revolution allemande,* Paris, 1938.

Viereck, Peter, *Metapolitics: From the Romantics to Hitler.* New York: Knopf, 1941.

Impact of War on State and Society

Extremely valuable material can be found in the monumental studies of the Carnegie Endowment for International Peace, *Economic and Social History of the World War* (New Haven: Yale University Press). Equally important for an analysis of the psychological moods and motivations of the war generations are the innumerable war novels. Unfortunately, these sources have hardly been tapped by students in the field. For preliminary investigations, see:

Cru, Jean Norton, *Témoins.* Paris: Les Etincelles, 1929.

Cysarz, Herbert, *Zur Geistesgeschichte des Weltkriegs. Die Dichterischen Wandlungen des Deutschen Kriegsbilds.* Halle: Max Niemeyer Verlag, 1931.

Grimrath, Hermann, *Der Weltkrieg im Französischen Roman.* Berlin: Junker und Dünnhaupt, 1935.

Pfeiler, William A., *War and the German Mind.* New York: Columbia University Press, 1941.

Schinz, Albert, *French Literature of the Great War.* New York: Appleton-Century, 1920.

Vic, Jean, *La Littérature de guerre.* 5 vols. Paris: Les Presses Françaises, 1923.

For a general evaluation of war and society, compare also the challenging interpretations:

Herring, E. Pendleton, *The Impact of War.* New York: Farrar and Rinehart, 1941.

Sorokin, P. A., *Social and Cultural Dynamics,* Vol. 3, *Fluctuation of Social Relationships, War, and Revolution.* New York: American Book, 1937.

Toynbee, Arnold J., *A Study of History.* New York: Oxford University Press, 1939.

Zink, Harold and Taylor Cole (eds.), *Government in Wartime Europe.* New York: Reynal and Hitchcock, 1941.

THE CONFLICT OF GENERATIONS IN GERMANY

The perennial problem of the age groups has become more articulate in modern times. It is by no mere accident that the 20th century started with Ellen Key's *Century of the Child* and with a promising youth movement in European countries. Some light has been thrown on this phenomenon in literature from Goethe's *Gespräche mit Eckermann* down to Phyllis Bentley's *Sleep in Peace* and Wassermann's *Kerkhoven's Dritte Existenz.* Some novels, such as Turgenev's *Fathers and Sons*, made this problem of generations the central theme.

Yet the scientific analysis of this important phenomenon has been considered only in borderline fields of the social sciences and almost exclusively in Germany and France. For art and literature, see:

Kummer, Friedrich, *Deutsche Literaturgeschichte des 19. Jahrhunderts. Dargestellt nach Generationen.* Dresden: Reissner, 1900.

Petersen, Julius, *Die literarischen Generationen.* Berlin: Junker und Dünnhaupt, 1930.

Pinder, Wilhelm, *Kunstgeschichte nach Generationen.* Leipzig: Pfeiffer, 1926.

Thibaudet, Albert, *Histoire de la littérature française.* Paris: Stock, 1936.

Compare also the earlier studies:

Dilthey, W., "Über des Studium der Geschichte der Wissenschaften vom Menschen," *Gesammelte Schriften.* Leipzig: Teubner, 1924. Bd.V, pp. 36-41.

Dromel, Justin, *La loi des révolutions, les générations, les nationalités, les dynasties, les religions.* Paris: Didier, 1862.

Lorenz, Ottokar, *Die Geschichtswissenschaft in Hauptrichtungen und Aufgaben Kritisch Erörtert.* Berlin: Hertz, 1886.

Lorenz, Ottokar, L. v. *Ranke, die Generationenlehre und der Geschichtsunterricht.* Berlin: Hertz, 1891.

For some first attempts at a systematic approach, see:

Behrendt, Richard, "Die öffentliche Meinung und das Generationsproblem," *Kölner Vierteljahrshefte für Soziologie,* 11:290-309 (1932).

Mannheim, Karl, "Das Problem der Generationen," *Kölner Vierteljahrshefte für Soziologie,* 7:157-187, 309-330 (1928).

Mentré, François, *Les générations sociales.* Paris: Editions Bossard, 1920.

Ortega y Gasset, José, *The Modern Theme.* New York: Norton, 1933.

Spranger, Eduard, *Psychologie des Jugendalters.* Leipzig: Quelle and Meyer, 1930.

Among the numerous demonstrations and "confessions" of the German youth, the following books may be mentioned:

Deubel, Werner, *Deutsche Kulturrevolution; Weltbild der Jugend.* Berlin: Verlag für Zeitkritik, 1931.

Dingräve, Leopold, *Wo steht die Junge Generation.* Jena: Diederichs, 1931.

Gründel, E. Günther. *Die Sendung der jungen Generation.* 3rd ed. Munich: C. H. Beck, 1933.

Hartmann, Hans, *Die junge Generation in Europa.* Berlin: Der Neue Geist Verlag, 1930.

Hotzel, Curt, *Deutscher Aufstand; die Revolution des Nachkriegs.* Stuttgart: Kohlhammer, 1934.

Matzke, Frank, *Jugend Bekennt: So sind Wir!* Leipzig: Reclam, 1930.

Moeller, van den Bruck, A., *Das Recht der jungen Völker.* Berlin: Der Nahe Osten, 1932. This collection of articles by the "Young Nationalist" contains the significant discussion of national Bolshevism with the Bolshevist Karl Radek.

For a critical analysis, consult:

Hartshorne, E. Y., *German Youth and the Nazi Dream of Victory.* New York: Farrar and Rinehart, 1941.

Linke, Lilo, *Restless Days; A German Girl's Autobiography.* New York: Knopf, 1935.

Neumann, Sigmund, "The Conflict of Generations in Contemporary Europe," *Vital Speeches,* 5:623-628 (1939).

WESTERN DEMOCRACIES AND THE REVOLUTION OF WAR

On Great Britain

While a comprehensive study of the effect of the war on British society is still lacking, much material can be found in numerous books on modern England, such as:

Brittain, Vera, *Testament of Youth.* New York: Macmillan, 1933.

Collier, John, and Lang, Jain, *Just the Other Day.* New York: Harper, 1932.

Graves, Robert, and Hooge, Alan, *The Long Weekend. A Social History of Great Britain, 1918-1939.* New York: Macmillan, 1941.

Hirst, F. W., *The Consequences of the War to Great Britain.* New Haven: Yale University Press, 1934.

Masterman, C. F. G., *England After the War.* New York: Harcourt, Brace, 1923.

Playne, Caroline E., *Britain Holds on, 1917-1918*. London: Allen and Unwin, 1933. Cf. also her other writings: *The Pre-war Mind in Britain* London: Allen and Unwin, 1928, *The Neuroses of the Nations* (New York: Boni, 1925): *Society at War, 1914-16* (London: Allen and Unwin, 1931).

Wingfield-Stratford, E. C., *The Harvest of Victory*. London: George Routledge, 1935.

The labor party immediately after the war appealed to the young war generation who, disappointed in the "old parties," joined this rising movement. See Wertheimer, Egon, *Portrait of the Labour Party*. New York: Putnam, 1929.

The difficulties and the only limited success of the two labor Cabinets and especially the crisis of 1931 led to a decline in prestige of the labor party among the younger generation. The impact of this crisis has unfortunately never been fully studied. British Fascism under the leadership of "young" Sir Oswald Mosley certainly gained its initial success partly as a result of its appeal as a "youth movement."

On the specific problems of the British ruling class after World War I, see:

Lord Halifax, "The Conflict of Youth," *Atlantic*, 163:737-743 (1940).

Hutton, Graham, "The Conflict Between the Generations in Britain," *Atlantic*, 161:190-196 (1938).

Laski, Harold J., *The Danger of Being a Gentleman*. New York: Viking, 1939.

Sheean, Vincent, "The Tory Leaders," *Harper's*, 1101:245-251 (1942).

Stolper, Gustav, "The Fable of Britain's Degeneracy," *Harper's*, 1099: 30-39 (1941).

On France

Aron, Robert, and Dandieu, A., *La révolution necessaire*. Paris: Grasset, 1933.

Benda, Julien, "Conflict of Generations in France," *Foreign Affairs*, 17:65-77 (1938).

Brogan, D. N., *France Under the Republic*. New York: Harper, 1940.

Daniel-Rops, Henry, *Notre inquiétude*. Paris: Perrin, 1926.

Daniel-Rops, Henry, *Le monde sans âme*. Paris: Plon, 1932.

Daniel-Rops, Henry, *Les années tournantes*. Paris: Editions de siècle, 1939.

Iswolsky, Helen, *Light Before Dusk: Recollections, 1923-1941*. New York: Longmans, Green, 1942. With a foreword by Jacques Maritain.

Luchaire, Jean, *Une génération realiste*. Paris: Valois, 1929. Especially two chapters: "Le retour des combattants" and "Le retour de vieux monde."

Pickles, D. M., "Intellectual Ferment in France," *Politica*, 2:56 ff. (London, 1936).

Schüler, Johann, *Strömungen in der französischen Jugend von heute*. Jena: Diss, 1935.

Chapter IX

DICTATORSHIP IN INTERNATIONAL POLITICS

BACKGROUND FOR TOTAL WAR

For an evaluation of dictatorship in foreign affairs, a general understanding of the Armistice period is necessary. To give here even a selection of the inexhaustible list of publications is impossible. Running bibliographies are easily accessible in the well-established guides of the pioneer institutions in the field. See the publications of:

The Royal Institute of International Affairs:

> *Survey of International Affairs* (Annual).
> *Documents on International Affairs* (Annual to 1937).
> *International Affairs* (Bi-monthly to 1938).
> *Bulletin of International News* (Fortnightly) and the excellent reports of special study groups.

The Council on Foreign Relations:

> *Foreign Affairs* (Quarterly).
> *Political Handbook of the World* (Annual) and numerous monographs of first rank.

Foreign Policy Association:

> *Foreign Policy Reports* (Fortnightly).
> *Foreign Policy Bulletin* (Weekly).

Carnegie Endowment for International Peace:

> *International Conciliation* (monthly).

For periodical articles, see the bibliographies in:

American Political Science Review (bi-monthly).

In re: Germany (monthly). New York: American Friends of German Freedom.

International Index to Periodicals.

Reader's Guide to Periodical Literature.

Valuable material has also been presented in the first descriptive attempts at a history of post-war Europe and in general treatises on international affairs, such as:

Benns, Frank L., *Europe Since 1914*. 5th ed. New York: Crofts, 1941.

Carr, E. H., *International Relations Since the Peace Treaties*. London: Macmillan, 1937.

Gathorne-Hardy, G. M., *A Short History of International Affairs, 1920-38*. New York: Oxford University Press, 1938.

King-Hall, Stephen, *Our Own Times, 1913-1934*. 2 vols. London: Nicholson and Watson, 1934-1935.

Langsam, Walter C., *The World Since 1914*. 4th ed. New York: Macmillan, 1940.

Lee, Dwight E., *Ten Years. The World on the Way to War, 1930-1940*. Boston: Houghton Mifflin, 1942.

Schmitt, Bernadotte E., *From Versailles to Munich, 1918-1938*. Chicago: University of Chicago Press, 1938.

Schuman, Frederick L., *International Politics*. 3rd ed. New York: McGraw-Hill, 1941.

Sharp, Walter R., and Grayson, Kirk, *Contemporary International Politics*. New York: Farrar and Rinehart, 1940.

Simonds, F. H., and Emeny, Brooks, *The Great Powers in World Politics*. 3rd ed. New York: American Book, 1939.

Steiner, H. Arthur, *Principles and Problems of International Relations*. New York: Harper, 1940.

Among thought-provoking analyses of the period the following books should be mentioned:

Armstrong, Hamilton Fish, *"We or They." Two Worlds in Conflict*. New York: Macmillan, 1936.

Armstrong, Hamilton Fish, *When There Is No Peace*. New York: Macmillan, 1939.

Armstrong, Hamilton Fish, *Chronology of Failure*. New York: Macmillan, 1940.

Baudin, Louis (ed.), *Free Trade and Peace*. New York: Columbia University Press, 1939. International Studies Conference, Bergen, 1939.

Birdsall, Paul, *Versailles Twenty Years After*. New York: Reynal and Hitchcock, 1941.

Carr, E. H., *The Twenty Years' Crisis, 1919-1939*. New York: Macmillan, 1940.

Chase, Stuart, *The Road We Are Traveling, 1914-1942*. New York: Twentieth Century Fund, 1942.

Dean, Vera Micheles, *Europe in Retreat*. Rev. ed. New York: Knopf, 1941.

Feis, Herbert, *The Changing Pattern of International Economic Affairs*. New York: Harper, 1940.

Fischer, Louis, *The Soviets in World Affairs.* 2 vols. New York: J. Cape, 1930.

Hanc, Josef, *Tornado Across Eastern Europe,* New York: Greystone, 1942.

International Studies Conference, *Peaceful Change.* Paris: International Institute of Intellectual Cooperation, 1938.

International Studies Conference, *Colonial Questions and Peace.* Paris: International Institute of Intellectual Cooperation, 1939.

Kranold, H., *International Distribution of Raw Materials.* New York: Harper, 1939.

Macartnay, C. A., *National States and National Minorities.* London: Oxford University Press, 1934.

Padelford, N. J., *International Law and Diplomacy in the Spanish Civil Strife.* New York: Macmillan, 1939.

Royal Institute of International Affairs, *Nationalism.* New York: Oxford University Press.

Royal Institute of International Affairs, *Southeastern Europe.* New York: Oxford University Press, 1939.

Schuman, Frederick L., *Europe on Eve.* New York: Knopf, 1939.

Schuman, Frederick L., *Night Over Europe.* New York: Knopf, 1941.

Schuman, Frederick L., *Design for Power.* New York: Knopf, 1942.

Seton-Watson, Robert W., *Britain and the Dictators.* Cambridge University Press, 1938.

Staley, Eugene, *Raw Materials in Peace and War.* New York: Council on Foreign Relations, 1937.

Staley, Eugene, *World Economy in Transition.* New York: Council on Foreign Relations, 1939.

Van Zeeland, Paul, "Report on International Economic Reconstruction," *International Conciliation,* No. 338 (March, 1938).

Wheeler-Bennett, John W., *The Forgotten Peace: Brest-Litovsk.* New York: Morrow, 1939.

Wolfers, Arnold, *Britain and France Between Two Wars.* New York: Harcourt, Brace, 1940.

Zimmern, Sir Alfred, *The League of Nations and the Rule of Law, 1918-1935.* London: Macmillan, 1936.

An indispensable source of day-to-day information will be found in the numerous man-on-the-spot studies and commentaries by outstanding correspondents and publicists, such as:

Chamberlin, W. H., *Russia's Iron Age.* Boston: Little, Brown, 1934.

Deuel, Wallace R., *People Under Hitler.* New York: Harcourt, Brace, 1942.

Duranty, Walter, *Duranty Reports Russia*. New York: Viking, 1934.

Duranty, Walter, *I Write as I Please*. New York: Simon and Schuster, 1935.

Duranty, Walter, *The Kremlin and the People*. New York: Reynal and Hitchcock, 1941.

Fischer, Louis, *Men and Politics*. New York: Duell, Sloan and Pearce, 1941.

Fischer, Louis, *Dawn of Victory*. New York: Duell, Sloan and Pearce, 1942.

Fodor, M. W., *South of Hitler*. Boston: Houghton Mifflin, 1939.

Fodor, M. W., *The Revolution Is On*. Boston: Houghton Mifflin, 1940.

Gedye, G. E. R., *Betrayal in Central Europe*. New York: Harper, 1939.

Gunther, John, *Inside Europe*. War ed. New York: Harper, 1940.

Harsch, I. C., *Pattern of Conquest*. New York: Doubleday, Doran, 1941.

Hindus, Maurice, *Humanity Uprooted*. New York: Cape and Smith, 1930.

Hindus, Maurice, *Hitler Cannot Conquer Russia*. New York: Doubleday, Doran, 1941.

Knickerbocker, H. R., *Is Tomorrow Hitler's?* New York: Reynal and Hitchcock, 1941.

Lengyel, Emil, *The Danube*. New York: Random House, 1939.

Lyons, Eugene, *Assignment in Utopia*. New York: Harcourt, Brace, 1938.

Matthews, H. L., *Two Wars and More to Come*. New York: Carrick, 1938.

Mowrer, Edgar A., *Germany Puts the Clock Back*. Rev. ed. New York: Morrow, 1939.

Murrow, Edward R., *This Is London*. New York: Simon and Schuster, 1941.

Sheean, Vincent, *Personal History*. New York: Doubleday, Doran, 1935.

Sheean, Vincent, *Not Peace But a Sword*. New York: Doubleday, Doran, 1939.

Shirer, William S., *Berlin Diary*. New York: Knopf, 1941.

Stowe, Leland, *No Other Road to Freedom*. New York: Knopf, 1941.

Strong, Anna Louise, *The Soviets Expected It*. New York: Dial, 1941.

Swing, R. G., *How War Came*. New York: Norton, 1939.

Tabouis, Geneviève, *They Called Me Cassandra*. New York: Scribner, 1942.

Thompson, Dorothy, *Let the Record Speak*. Boston: Houghton Mifflin, 1939.

Tolischus, Otto D., *They Wanted War*. New York: Reynal and Hitchcock, 1940.

Van Paassen, Pierre, *Days of Our Years*. Rev. ed. New York: Dial, 1940.
Van Paassen, Pierre, *The Time Is Now*. New York: Dial, 1941.
Voigt, F. A., *Unto Caesar*. New York: Putnam, 1938.
Werth, Alexander, *France in Ferment*. New York: Harper, 1935.
Werth, Alexander, *France and Munich*. New York: Harper, 1939.
Wolfe, H. C., *The German Octopus*. New York: Doubleday, Doran, 1938.
Wolfe, H. C., *Imperial Soviets*. New York: Doubleday, Doran, 1940.

Of equal importance are the reports of ambassadors and other active participants, such as:
Davies, Joseph Edward, *Mission to Moscow*. New York: Simon and Schuster, 1941.
del Vayo, J. Alvarez, *Freedom's Battle*. New York: Knopf, 1940.
Dodd, W. E., Jr., and Martha (eds.), *Ambassador Dodd's Diary, 1933-1938*. New York: Harcourt, Brace, 1941.
French Yellow Book, *Diplomatic Documents, 1938-1939*. New York: Reynal and Hitchcock, 1940.
Hambro, Carl J., *I Saw It Happen*. New York: Appleton-Century, 1940.
Harriman, F. J. (H.), *Mission to the North*. Philadelphia: Lippincott, 1941.
Henderson, Nevile, *The Failure of a Mission*. New York: Putnam, 1940.
Kleffens, E. N. van, *Juggernaut Over Holland*. New York: Columbia University Press, 1940.
Koht, Halvdan, *Norway, Neutral and Invaded*. New York: Macmillan, 1941.
Rauschning, Hermann, *The Revolution of Nihilism*. New York: Alliance, 1939.
Wilson, Hugh R., *Diplomat between Wars*. New York: Longmans, Green, 1941.

STRATEGIES OF CONQUEST

Psychological Warfare and National Morale
For a general bibliography see:
Child, J. L., "Morale: A Bibliographical Review," in *Psychological Bulletin*, 38:393-420 (1941).
Farago, Ladislas, *German Psychological Warfare: Survey and Bibliography*. New York: Committee for National Morale, 1941.
"National Morale," special issue of *The American Journal of Sociology*, 47:277-480 (1941).
Scherke, F. und Gräfin Vitztum, *Bibliographie der Geistigen Kriegsführung*. Berlin: 1938.

Among the numerous publications the following present a wealth of material:

Blau, A., *Geistige Kriegsführung*. Potsdam: Voggenreiter, 1938.

Childs, Harwood L., and Whitton, John B. (eds.), *Propaganda by Short Wave*. Princeton: Princeton University Press, 1942.

Farago, Ladislas, *The Axis Grand Strategy*. New York: Farrar and Rinehart, 1942.

Fernández, Artucio Hugo, *The Nazi Underground in South America*. New York: Farrar and Rinehart, 1942.

Jones, F. E., *The Attack from Within; the Modern Technique of Aggression*. London: Penguin Books, 1939.

Pinschovius, K., *Die seelische Widerstandskraft im modernen Krieg*. Oldenburg: Stalling, 1936.

Possony, "Defeatism," *Review of Politics*, 4:34-60 (1942).

Riess, Curt, *Total Espionage*. New York: Putnam, 1941.

Rowan, Richard W., *Terror in Our Time. The Secret Service of Surprise Attack*. New York: Longmans, Green, 1941.

Spivak, J. L., *Secret Armies; the New Technique of Nazi Warfare*. New York: Modern Age, 1939.

Taylor, Edmond, *The Strategy of Terror*. Boston: Houghton Mifflin, 1940.

For Geopolitics compare especially Karl Haushofer's numerous studies:

Dai Nihon. Betrachtungen über Gross-Japans Wehrkraft, Weltstellung und Zukunft. (Bln. E. S. Mittler und Sohn, 1913); (ed.), *Deutschlands Weg an der Zeitenwende* (Munich: Hugendubel, 1931); *Erdkunde, Geopolitik und Wehrwissenschaft* (Munich: Max Hueber, 1934); *Geopolitik der Pan-Ideen* (Berlin: Zentral Verlag, 1931); *Geopolitik des Pazitischen Ozeans* (3rd ed. Berlin: Vowinckel, 1938); *Grenzen in ihrer Geographischen und Politischen Bedeutung* (2nd ed. Berlin: Vowinckel, 1938); *Japan und die Japaner* (2nd ed. Leipzig: Teubner, 1933); *Der Nationalsozialistische Gedanke in der Welt*. (Munich: Callwey, 1933); *Wehr-Geopolitik. Geographische Grundlagen einer Wehrkunde* (Berlin: Junker und Dünnhaupt, 1932); *Weltmeere und Weltmächte* (Berlin: Zeitgeschichte Verlag, 1937); *Weltpolitik von Heute* (Berlin: Zeitgeschichte Verlag, 1937), and his *Zeitschrift für Geopolitik*.

See also:

Griswold, A. W., "Paving the Way for Hitler," *Atlantic*, 167:315-318 (1941).

Strausz-Hupe, R., "Geopolitics: Haushofer's Sinister Pseudo-Science Now Rules," *Fortune*, 24:110-112 (1941).

Strausz-Hupe, R., *Geopolitics: The Struggle for Space and Power.* New York: Putnam, 1942.

Weigert, H. W., "German Geopolitics. Workshop for Army Rule," *Harper's,* 1098:586-597 (1941).

On geography and international relations, see: N. J. Spykman, "Geography and Foreign Policy," *American Political Science Review,* 32:28-50, 213-236 (1938), and *America's Strategy in World Politics* (New York: Harcourt, Brace, 1942).

The Master Race
For an authoritative exposition of the National Socialist theory, see:

Darré, W., *Das Schwein als Kriterium fur Nordische Völker und Semiten.* Munich: Lehmann, 1933.

Darré, W., *Das Bauerntum als Lebensquell der Nordischen Rasse.* Munich: Lehmann, 1939.

Darré, W., *Neuadel aus Blut und Boden.* Munich: Lehmann, 1939.

Guenther, Hans F. K., *Rassenkunde des Deutschen Volkes.* Last edition. Munich: Lehmann, 1939.

Rosenberg, Alfred, *Der Mythus des 20th Jahrhunderts.* Munich: Hoheneichen Verlag, 1934.

The "official" 19th-century forerunners are:

Chamberlain, H. St., *Die Grundlagen des 19. Jahrhunderts.* Munich: Bruckmann, 1900.

Gobineau, Comte Arthur de, *Essai sur l'inégalité des races humaines.* Paris: Firmin-Didot, 1853.

For a critical evaluation, consult:

Barzun, Jacques, *Race. A Study in Modern Superstition.* New York: Harcourt, Brace, 1937.

Benedict, Ruth, *Race: Science and Politics.* New York: Modern Age, 1940.

Preuss, L., "Racial Theory and National Socialist Political Thought," *Southwestern Social Science Quarterly,* 2:1-16 (1934).

Radin, Paul, *The Racial Myth.* New York: Whittlesey House, 1934.

Snyder, Louis L., *Race; A History of Modern Ethnic Theories.* New York: Alliance, 1939.

Voegelin, Erich, "The Growth of the Race Idea," *Review of Politics,* 2:283-317 (July, 1940), and also his *Rasse und Staat.* Tübingen: Mohr, 1933.

For specific implications of the National Socialist race theory, see:

Janovsky, D. J., and Fagen, M. M., *International Aspects of German Racial Policies.* New York: Oxford University Press, 1937.

Riesman, David, "The Politics of Persecution," *Public Opinion Quarterly*, 6:41-56 (1942).

For the "New Order" in Europe, consult:

Ardenne, R., *German Exploitation of Belgium.* Washington: Brookings, 1942.

Borkenau, Franz, *The New German Empire.* New York: Viking, 1939.

Dean, Vera M., "Europe Under Nazi Rule," *Foreign Policy Reports*, 16:188 ff. (October 15, 1940).

Drucker, Peter F., "Germany's Plans for Europe," *Harper's*, 181:597-604 (1940).

Duff, Shiela Grant, *A German Protectorate: The Czechs Under Nazi Rule.* Toronto: Macmillan, 1942.

Einzig, Paul, *Hitler's "New Order" in Europe.* New York: Macmillan, 1941.

Evans, Jon, *The Nazi Order in Poland.* Toronto: Ryerson, 1941.

Hagen, Paul, *Will Germany Crack?* New York: Harper, 1942.

Harsch, Joseph C., *Pattern of Conquest.* New York: Doubleday, Doran, 1941.

Hediger, Ernest S., "Nazi Exploitation of Occupied Europe," *Foreign Policy Reports*, 18:66 ff. (June 1, 1942).

Hula, Erich, "Control of the Conquered," *Social Research*, 8:136-155 (1941).

Kernan, Thomas, *Paris on Berlin Time.* Philadelphia: Lippincott, 1941.

Lewis, Leona, *Nazi Europe and World Trade.* Washington: Brookings, 1941.

Lorwin, L. L., *Economic Consequences of the Second World War.* New York: Random House, 1941.

Moen, Lars, *Under the Iron Heel.* Philadelphia: Lippincott, 1941.

Palmer, Paul, *Denmark in Nazi Chains.* London: Drummond, 1942.

Porter, Roy P., *Uncensored France.* New York: Dial, 1942.

Reveilie, Thomas, *The Spoil of Europe.* New York: Norton, 1941.

Riess, Curt, *Underground Europe.* New York: Dial, 1942.

Royal Institute of International Affairs, *Europe Under Hitler: in Prospect and in Practice.* New York: Oxford University Press, 1941.

St. John, Robert, *From the Land of the Silent People.* New York: Doubleday, Doran, 1942. (Greece, Yugoslavia, Crete.)

Segal, Simon, *The New Order in Poland.* New York: Knopf, 1942.

World Economic Survey, *1939-1941.* Geneva and Princeton: League of Nations, 1941.

Worm-Müller, J. S., *Norway Revolts Against the Nazis*. London: Drummond, 1941.

For democracy in foreign affairs, see:

Barthélemy, J., *La conduite de la politique extérieure dans les democraties*. Paris: Publications de la Conciliation Internationale, 1930.

Friedrich, Carl J., *Foreign Policy in the Making*. New York: Norton, 1938.

Maddox, William P., *Foreign Relations in British Labour Politics*. Cambridge, Mass.: Harvard University Press, 1934.

Nicolson, Harold, *Curzon: The Last Phase*. Boston: Houghton Mifflin, 1934. Especially the final essay, "Some Remarks on the Practice of Diplomacy."

Nicolson, Harold, "British Public Opinion and Foreign Policy," *Public Opinion Quarterly*, 1:53-63 (1937).

Nicolson, Harold, *Diplomacy*. New York: Harcourt, Brace, 1939.

Poole, Dewitt C., *The Conduct of Foreign Relations Under Modern Democratic Conditions*. New Haven: Yale University Press, 1924.

Schuman, Frederick L., *War and Diplomacy in the French Republic*. New York: Whittlesey House, 1931.

Willert, Sir Arthur, *Aspects of British Foreign Policy*, New Haven: Yale University Press, 1928.

Young, George, *Diplomacy Old and New*. New York: Harcourt, Brace, 1921.

The Challenge to Democracy

The challenge to democracy has been taken up in the following books:

Barker, Ernst, *The Citizen's Choice*. Cambridge: Cambridge University Press, 1937.

Becker, Carl L., *Modern Democracy*. New Haven: Yale University Press, 1941.

Becker, Carl L., *New Liberties for Old*. New Haven: Yale University Press, 1941.

Chamberlin, W. H., *The World's Iron Age*. New York: Macmillan, 1941.

Cobban, Alfred, *The Crisis of Civilization*. London: Cape, 1941.

Curtis, Lionel, *Civitas Dei*. 3 vols. London: Macmillan, 1934-1937.

de Roussy de Sales, Raoul, *The Making of Tomorrow*. New York: Reynal and Hitchcock, 1942.

Earle, Edward M., *Against This Torrent*. Princeton: Princeton University Press, 1941.

Friedrich, Carl J., *The New Belief in the Common Man*. Boston: Little, Brown, 1942.

Hocking, William E., *The Lasting Elements of Individualism*. New Haven: Yale University Press, 1937.

International Conciliation, *Commission to Study the Organization of Peace, Preliminary Reports and Monographs*. New York: Carnegie Endowment for International Peace, 1941.

International Conciliation, *Commission to Study the Organization of Peace: Second Report—The Transitional Period*. New York: Carnegie Endowment for International Peace, 1942.

Kingsley, J. D., and Petegorsky, D. W., *Strategy for Democracy*. New York: Longmans, Green, 1942.

Kohn, Hans, *World Order in Historical Perspective*. Cambridge, Mass.: Harvard University Press, 1942.

Laski, Harold D., *The Strategy of Freedom*. New York: Harper, 1941.

Lerner, Max, *Ideas for the Ice-Age*. New York: Viking, 1942.

MacIver, Robert, *Leviathan and the People*. Baton Rouge: Louisiana State University Press, 1939.

Merriam, Charles E., *On the Agenda of Democracy*. Cambridge, Mass.: Harvard University Press, 1941.

Niebuhr, Reinhold, *The Nature and Destiny of Man*. New York: Scribner, 1941.

Niemeyer, Gerhart, *Law Without Force. The Function of Politics in International Law*. Princeton: Princeton University Press, 1941.

Perry, Ralph Barton, *Shall Not Perish from the Earth*. New York: Vanguard, 1940.

Sorokin, Pitirim, *The Crisis of Our Age*. New York: Dutton, 1941.

Stace, Walter T., *The Destiny of Western Man*. New York: Reynal and Hitchcock, 1942.

Stolper, Gustav, *This Age of Fable*. New York: Reynal and Hitchcock, 1942.

Streit, C. K., *Union Now*. New York: Harper, 1939.

Wallace, Henry A., *The Price of Free World Victory*. New York: Fischer, 1942.

SUPPLEMENTARY BIBLIOGRAPHY

The literature in the fields and subjects covered by the author has, of course, expanded considerably since this work was first published. This supplementary bibliography lays no claim to the comprehensiveness and erudition of the original one. However, it does represent an attempt to give the reader a survey of relevant works published after 1942. The publisher wishes to express his gratitude to Miss Sophia Sluzan for her invaluable help in the preparation of this bibliography.

Chapter I

MODERN DICTATORSHIP DEFINED

THE HISTORIC SETTING

General Works

Arendt, Hannah, *The Origins of Totalitarianism.* 2nd, enlarged ed. New York: Meridian Books, 1960.

Aron, Raymond, *L'Homme contre les tyrans.* New York: Editions de la Maison Française, 1944.

Barbu, Zevedei, *Democracy and Dictatorship.* New York: Grove Press, 1956.

Buchheim, Hans, *Totalitäre Herrschaft: Wesen und Merkmale.* Munich: Kösel Verlag, 1962.

Deutsch, Julius, *Wesen und Wandlungen der Diktaturen.* Munich: Humboldt Verlag, 1963.

Duverger, Maurice, *De la dictature.* Paris: Julliard, 1961.

Friedrich, Carl J. (ed.), *Totalitarianism.* Cambridge, Mass.: Harvard University Press, 1954.

Friedrich, Carl J., and Brzezinski, Zbigniew, *Totalitarian Dictatorship and Autocracy.* Rev. ed. Cambridge, Mass.: Harvard University Press, 1965.

Moore, Barrington, *Political Power and Social Theory.* Cambridge, Mass.: Harvard University Press, 1958.

Neumann, Franz L., *The Democratic and the Authoritarian State.* Glencoe: Free Press, 1957.

Nolte, Ernst, *Der Faschismus in seiner Epoche.* Munich: R. Piper Verlag, 1963.

Rauschning, Hermann, *Time of Delirium.* New York: Appleton-Century, 1946.

Talmon, Jacob L., *The Origins of Totalitarian Democracy*. New York: Frederick A. Praeger, 1960.
Talmon, Jacob L., *Political Messianism*. New York: Frederick A. Praeger, 1961.

Latin American Dictatorship

Alexander, Robert J., *Prophets of the Revolution*. New York: Macmillan, 1962. Profiles of Latin American leaders.
Johnson, John J., *Political Change in Latin America*. Stanford: Stanford University Press, 1958.
MacDonald, Austin F., *Latin American Politics and Government*. 2nd ed. New York: Thomas Y. Crowell, 1954.

The French Revolution

Gershoy, Leo, *The French Revolution and Napoleon*. New York: Appleton-Century-Crofts, 1964.
Geyl, Pieter, *Napoleon: For and Against*. New Haven: Yale University Press, 1963.
Thompson, James M., *Napoleon Bonaparte*. London and New York: Oxford University Press, 1952.

Studies on Revolution

Arendt, Hannah, *On Revolution*. New York: Viking Press, 1963.
Eckstein, Harry (ed.), *Internal War: Problems and Approaches*. New York: Free Press of Glencoe, 1964.

THE ORIGIN OF MODERN DICTATORSHIP

Soviet Russia

Abramovich, Raphael, *The Soviet Revolution, 1917–1939*. New York: International Universities Press, 1962.
Berdiaev, Nikolai A., *The Origins of Russian Communism*. 2nd ed. London: G. Bles, 1948.
Carr, Edward Hallett, *A History of Soviet Russia*. 7 vols. New York: Macmillan, 1951–64.
Schapiro, Leonard, *The Origin of Communist Autocracy*. Cambridge, Mass.: Harvard University Press, 1956.
Sukhanov, Nikolai N., *The Russian Revolution, 1917*. London and New York: Oxford University Press, 1955.
Wolfe, Bertram D., *Three Who Made A Revolution*. 4th rev. ed. New York: Dial Press, 1964.

Italy

Alatri, Paolo, *Le Origini del Fascismo*. Rome: Editori Riuniti, 1956.
Carocci, Giampieri, *Storia del Fascismo*. 3rd ed. Milan: Garzanti, 1963.
Chabod, Federico, *A History of Italian Fascism*. London: Weidenfeld and Nicolson, 1963.
Salomone, Arcangelo W., *Italian Democracy in the Making*. Philadelphia: University of Pennsylvania Press, 1945.
Salvatorelli, Luigi, and Mira, Giovanni, *Storia d'Italia nel Periodo Fascista*. Turin: Einaudi, 1962.
Tasca, A., *Nascita e Avvento del Fascismo*. Florence: La Nuova Italia, 1950. This work was published under a pseudonym (Rossi) in 1938. The preface is new.

National Socialist Germany

Bracher, Karl, *Die Auflösung der Weimarer Republik*. 3rd ed. Villinger: Ringverlag, 1960.
Bracher, Karl, Sauer, Wolfgang, and Schulz, Gerhard, *Die Nationalsozialistische Machtergreifung*. Cologne: Westdeutscher Verlag, 1960.
Brecht, Arnold, *Prelude to Silence: The End of the German Republic*. New York: Oxford University Press, 1944.
Clark, Robert, *The Fall of the Weimar Republic*. New York: Russell and Russell, 1964.
Eyck, Erich, *History of the Weimar Republic*. 2 vols. Cambridge, Mass.: Harvard University Press, 1962, 1963.
Holborn, Hajo, *A History of Modern Germany*. 2 vols. New York: Knopf, 1959, 1963.

Chapter II

THE LEADER

Definition by Contrast: Institutional Representation

General Works

Friedrich, Carl J., *Constitutional Government and Democracy*. Rev. ed. Boston: Ginn, 1950.
Graubard, Stephen R., and Holton, Gerald (eds.), *Excellence and Leadership in a Democracy*. New York: Columbia University Press, 1962.
Marvick, Dwaine (ed.), *Political Decision Makers: Recruitment and Performance*. Glencoe: Free Press, 1961.

Sereno, Renzo, *The Rulers*. New York: Frederick A. Praeger, 1962.

The British Prime Minister

Carter, Byrum E., *The Office of Prime Minister*. Princeton: Princeton University Press, 1956.

MacKintosh, John P., *The British Cabinet*. London: Stevens, 1962.

The United States President

Binkley, Wilfred E., *President and Congress*. 3rd rev. ed. New York: Vintage Books, 1963.

Hyman, Sidney (ed.), *The Office of the American President*. Philadelphia: American Academy of Political and Social Science, 1956.

Neustadt, Richard E., *Presidential Power*. New York: Wiley, 1960.

Rossiter, Clinton L., *The American Presidency*. Rev. ed. New York: Harcourt, Brace, 1960.

The President of the French Council

Earle, Edward M. (ed.), *Modern France: Problems of the Third and the Fourth Republics*. Princeton: Princeton University Press, 1951.

Thomson, David, *Democracy in France Since 1870*. 4th ed. London and New York: Oxford University Press, 1964.

Leadership in Wartime

Churchill, Winston S., *The Second World War*. 6 vols. Boston: Houghton Mifflin, 1948–53.

Ehrman, John, *Cabinet Government and War, 1890–1940*. Cambridge, England, and New York: Cambridge University Press, 1958.

Feis, Herbert, *Churchill, Roosevelt, Stalin*. Princeton: Princeton University Press, 1957.

DICTATORIAL LEADERSHIP

The Demagogue

Beaverbrook, William M. A., *The Decline and Fall of Lloyd George*. New York: Duell, Sloan, 1963.

Mussolini

Fermi, Laura, *Mussolini*. Chicago: University of Chicago Press, 1961.

Kirkpatrick, Ivone, *Mussolini: A Study in Power*. New York: Hawthorn Books, 1964.

Monelli, Paolo, *Mussolini, Piccole Borghese*. 4th ed. Milan: Garzanti, 1959.

Hitler

Bullock, Alan, *Hitler: A Study in Tyranny*. Rev. ed. New York: Harper, 1964.

Gisevius, Hans Bernd, *Adolf Hitler*. Munich: Rütten-Loening Verlag, 1963.

Heiden, Konrad, *Der Fuehrer: Hitler's Rise to Power*. Boston: Houghton Mifflin, 1944.

Stalin

Avtorkhanov, Abdurakhman, *Stalin and the Soviet Communist Party*. New York: Frederick A. Praeger, 1959.

Deutscher, Isaac, *Stalin: A Political Biography*. London and New York: Oxford University Press, 1949.

Fischer, Louis, *The Life and Death of Stalin*. New York. Harper, 1952.

The Marginal Men

Kinross, Patrick Balfour, *Atatürk*. New York: Morrow, 1965.

Papen, Franz von, *Memoirs*. London: André Deutsch, 1952.

Rhodes, Anthony, *D'Annunzio: The Poet as Superman*. New York: Obolensky, 1960.

Chapter III

THE POLITICAL LIEUTENANT

THE NUMBER TWO MEN, NATURE AND VARIANTS

Fest, Joachim C., *Das Gesicht des Dritten Reiches*. Munich: R. Piper Verlag, 1963.

Lochner, Louis P. (ed. and trans.), *The Goebbels Diaries*. Garden City: Doubleday, 1948.

THE COMPOSITE STRUCTURE OF THE ELITE

Armstrong, John A., *The Soviet Bureaucratic Elite: A Case Study of the Ukrainian Apparatus*. New York: Frederick A. Praeger, 1959.

Aron, Raymond, *The Opium of the Intellectuals*. Garden City: Doubleday, 1957.

Djilas, Milovan, *The New Class*. New York: Frederick A. Praeger, 1957.

Lasswell, Harold D., *The Comparative Study of Elites*. Stanford: Stanford University Press, 1962.

Lerner, Daniel, *The Nazi Elite*. Stanford: Stanford University Press, 1951.

Pipes, Richard (ed.), *The Russian Intelligentsia*. New York: Columbia University Press, 1961.

Schueller, George K., *The Politburo*. Stanford: Stanford University Press, 1951.

Scott, Derek J., *Russian Political Institutions*. 3rd rev. ed. New York: Frederick A. Praeger, 1965.

Waite, Robert G. L., *Vanguard of Nazism: The Free Corps Movement in Postwar Germany 1918–1923*. Cambridge, Mass.: Harvard University Press, 1952.

SUCCESSION IN LEADERSHIP IN A DICTATORSHIP

Pistrak, Lazar, *The Grand Tactician: Khrushchev's Rise to Power*. New York: Frederick A. Praeger, 1961.

Rush, Myron, *Political Succession in the U.S.S.R.* New York: Columbia University Press, 1965.

Rush, Myron, *The Rise of Khrushchev*. Washington: Public Affairs Press, 1958.

Chapter IV

THE AMORPHOUS MASSES EMERGE

General Works

Almond, Gabriel A., and Verba, Sidney, *The Civic Culture: Political Attitudes and Democracy in Five Nations*. Princeton: Princeton University Press, 1963.

Friedrich, Carl J., *The New Image of the Common Man*. Boston: Beacon Press, 1950.

Kornhauser, William, *The Politics of Mass Society*. Glencoe: Free Press, 1959.

Levy, Marion, *The Structure of Society*. Princeton: Princeton University Press, 1952.

Lipset, Seymour M., *Political Man*. Garden City: Doubleday, 1960.

Parsons, Talcott, *Essays in Sociological Theory*. Glencoe: Free Press, 1956.

Industrialization

Aron, Raymond, *Sociologie des sociétés industrielles*. Paris: Centre de Documentation Universitaire, 1959.

Dahrendorf, Ralf, *Class and Class Conflict in Industrial Society*. Stanford: Stanford University Press, 1959.

Gerschenkron, Alexander, *Bread and Democracy in Germany*. Berkeley: University of California Press, 1943.

Popitz, Heinrich, *Das Gesellschaftsbild des Arbeiters*. Tübingen: Mohr, 1957.

Smelser, Neil J. (ed.), *Readings on Economic Sociology*. Englewood Cliffs: Prentice-Hall, 1965.

Smelser, Neil J., *The Sociology of Economic Life*. Englewood Cliffs: Prentice-Hall, 1963.

Urbanization

Hatt, Paul K., and Reiss, Albert J., *Cities and Society*. Glencoe: Free Press, 1957.

Kornhauser, Arthur W., *et al.* (eds.), *Industrial Conflict*. New York: McGraw-Hill, 1954.

Chapter V

THE ONE-PARTY STATE

THE DEMOCRATIC PARTY SYSTEM

Alford, Robert R., *Party and Society: The Anglo-American Democracies*. Chicago: Rand McNally, 1963.

Bailey, Sydney D. (ed.), *Parties and the Party System in Great Britain*. New York: Frederick A. Praeger, 1953.

Binkley, Wilfred E., *American Political Parties*. New York: Knopf, 1962.

Campbell, Angus, *et al.*, *The Voter Decides*. Evanston: Row, Peterson, 1954.

Campbell, Peter, *French Electoral Systems and Elections 1789–1957*. New York: Frederick A. Praeger, 1958.

Duverger, Maurice, *The French Political System*. Chicago: University of Chicago Press, 1958.

Duverger, Maurice, *Political Parties; Their Organization and Activity in the Modern State*. New York: Wiley, 1961.

Ehrmann, Henry (ed.), *Interest Groups on Four Continents*. Pittsburgh: University of Pittsburgh Press, 1958.

Finer, Hermann, *Governments of Greater European Powers*. New York: Holt, 1956.

Holborn, Hajo, *The Political Collapse of Europe*. New York: Knopf, 1951.

La Palombara, Joseph, *Interest Groups in Italian Politics*. Princeton: Princeton University Press, 1964.

Lavau, Georges E., *Partis politiques et réalités sociales*. Paris: Colin, 1953.

Leiserson, Avery, *Parties and Politics*. New York: Knopf, 1958.

McKenzie, R. T., *British Political Parties*. Rev. ed. New York: Frederick A. Praeger, 1964.

Macridis, Roy C., and Ward, Robert E. (eds.), *Modern Political Systems*. Englewood Cliffs: Prentice-Hall, 1963.

Neumann, Sigmund (ed.), *Modern Political Parties*. Chicago: University of Chicago Press, 1956.

Rossiter, Clinton L., *Parties and Politics in America*. Ithaca: Cornell University Press, 1960.

Stewart, John D., *British Pressure Groups*. London and New York: Oxford University Press, 1958.

Williams, Philip M., *Politics in Post-War France*. London and New York: Longmans, Green, 1954.

CHARACTER OF THE TOTALITARIAN PARTY

The Soviet Party

Armstrong, John A., *The Politics of Totalitarianism*. New York: Random House, 1961.

Brzezinski, Zbigniew, *The Permanent Purge*. Cambridge, Mass.: Harvard University Press, 1963.

Fainsod, Merle, *How Russia Is Ruled*. Rev. ed. Cambridge, Mass.: Harvard University Press, 1963.

McCloskey, Herbert, and Turner, John E., *The Soviet Dictatorship*. New York: McGraw-Hill, 1960.

Reshetar, John S., *A Concise History of the Communist Party of the Soviet Union*. Rev. ed. New York: Frederick A. Praeger, 1965.

Schapiro, Leonard, *The Communist Party of the Soviet Union*. New York: Random House, 1960.

The Fascist Party

Germino, Dante L., *The Italian Fascist Party in Power*. Minneapolis: University of Minnesota Press, 1959.

Payne, S. G., *Falange: A History of Spanish Fascism*. Stanford: Stanford University Press, 1961.

The National Socialist Party

Heberle, Rudolf, *From Democracy to Nazism: A Regional Case Study on Political Parties in Germany*. Baton Rouge: Louisiana State University Press, 1945.

Matthias, Erich, and Morsey, Rudolf, *Das Ende der Parteien*. Düsseldorf: Droste Verlag, 1960.

Chapter VI

THE CONTROL OF THE MASSES: INSTITUTIONAL FRAMEWORK

BASIC PRINCIPLES

Bauer, Raymond A., Inkeles, Alex, and Kluckhohn, Clyde, *How the Soviet System Works.* Cambridge, Mass.: Harvard University Press, 1956.

Baumont, Maurice, Fried, John H. E., and Vermeil, Edmond (eds.), *The Third Reich.* New York: Frederick A. Praeger, 1955.

Brzezinski, Zbigniew, *Ideology and Power in Soviet Politics.* New York: Frederick A. Praeger, 1962.

Carson, George Barr, *Electoral Practices in the U.S.S.R.* New York: Frederick A. Praeger, 1955.

Hazard, John N., *The Soviet System of Government.* 3rd rev. ed. Chicago: University of Chicago Press, 1964.

Inkeles, Alex, and Bauer, Raymond A., *The Soviet Citizen.* Cambridge, Mass.: Harvard University Press, 1959.

Kulski, W. W., *The Soviet Regime.* Syracuse: Syracuse University Press, 1963.

Monnerot, Jules, *The Sociology and Psychology of Communism.* Boston: Beacon Press, 1960.

Moore, Barrington, *Soviet Politics—The Dilemma of Power.* Cambridge, Mass.: Harvard University Press, 1950.

Moore, Barrington, *Terror and Progress USSR: Some Sources of Change and Stability in the Soviet Dictatorship.* Cambridge, Mass.: Harvard University Press, 1954.

Neumann, Franz L., *Behemoth: The Structure and Practice of National Socialism, 1933–1944.* 2nd ed. New York: Octagon Books, 1964.

BUREAUCRACY

Armstrong, John A., *The Soviet Bureaucratic Elite: A Case Study of the Ukrainian Apparatus.* New York: Frederick A. Praeger, 1959.

Blau, Peter M., *The Dynamics of Bureaucracy.* Chicago: University of Chicago Press, 1961.

De Witt, Nicholas, *Soviet Professional Manpower: Its Education, Training and Supply.* Washington: National Science Foundation, 1955.

Granick, David, *The Red Executive.* Garden City: Doubleday, 1960.

Hyneman, Charles S., *Bureaucracy in a Democracy.* New York: Harper, 1950.

Merton, Robert K., *et al.* (eds.), *Reader in Bureaucracy.* Glencoe: Free Press, 1952.

Robson, William A. (ed.), *Civil Service in Great Britain and France.* London: Hogarth Press, 1956.

ECONOMICS

Dinerstein, Herbert, and Gouré, Leon, *Communism and the Russian Peasant.* Glencoe: Free Press, 1955.

Erlich, Alexander, *The Soviet Industrialization Debate, 1924–1928.* Cambridge, Mass.: Harvard University Press, 1960.

Hallgarten, George W., *Hitler, Reichswehr und Industrie.* Frankfurt, 1955.

Klein, Burton, *Germany's Economic Preparations for War.* Cambridge, Mass.: Harvard University Press, 1959.

Laird, Roy D. (ed.), *Soviet Agricultural and Peasant Affairs.* Lawrence: University of Kansas Press, 1963.

Schwartz, Harry, *Russia's Soviet Economy.* 2nd ed. New York: Prentice-Hall, 1954.

Schweitzer, Arthur, *Big Business in the Third Reich.* Bloomington: Indiana University Press, 1964.

Vucinich, Alexander, *Soviet Economic Institutions.* Stanford: Stanford University Press, 1952.

DICTATORSHIP AND THE ARMED FORCES

Brzezinski, Zbigniew (ed.), *Political Controls in the Soviet Army.* New York: Research Program on the U.S.S.R., 1954.

Craig, Gordon A., *The Politics of the Prussian Army, 1640–1945.* London and New York: Oxford University Press, 1955.

Erfurth, Waldemar, *Die Geschichte des Deutschen Generalstabes von 1918 bis 1945.* Göttingen, 1957.

Erickson, John, *The Soviet High Command.* New York: St Martin's Press, 1962.

Liddell Hart, B. H., *The Red Army.* New York: Harcourt, Brace, 1956.

Janowitz, Morris, *The Military in the Political Development of New Nations.* Chicago: University of Chicago Press, 1964.

Taylor, Telford, *Sword and Swastika: The Story of the Struggle Between the German Generals and Nazis in the Third Reich.* New York: Simon and Schuster, 1952.

Wheeler-Bennett, John W., *The Nemesis of Power: The German Army in Politics, 1918–1945.* 2nd ed. New York: St Martin's Press, 1964.

White, D. F., *The Growth of the Red Army.* Princeton: Princeton University Press, 1944.

DICTATORSHIP AND THE CHURCHES

Curtiss, John Shelton, *The Russian Church and the Soviet State*. Boston: Little Brown, 1953.

Ebenstein, William, *Church and State in Franco Spain*. Princeton: Center for International Studies, Princeton University, 1960.

Hochhuth, Rolf, *The Deputy*. New York: Grove Press, 1964.

Jannasch, W., *Deutsche Kirchendokumente: Die Haltung der Bekennenden Kirche im Dritten Reich*. Zurich, 1946.

Kolarz, Walter, *Religion in the Soviet Union*. New York: St Martin's Press, 1962.

Lewy, Guenter, *The Catholic Church and Nazi Germany*. New York: McGraw-Hill, 1964.

Niemöller, Wilhelm, *Hitler und die Evangelischen Kirchenführer*. Bielefeld: Bechauf, 1959.

Timasheff, Nicholas S., *Religion in Soviet Russia, 1917–1942*. New York: Sheed and Ward, 1942.

Webster, Richard A., *The Cross and the Fasces*. Stanford: Stanford University Press, 1960.

Zahn, Gordon C., *German Catholics and Hitler's War*. New York: Sheed and Ward, 1962.

DICTATORSHIP AND EDUCATION

Bereday, George Z. F., and Pennar, Jaan (eds.), *The Politics of Soviet Education*. New York: Frederick A. Praeger, 1960.

Fisher, Ralph T., *Patterns for Soviet Youth, A Study of the Congresses of the Komsomol, 1918–1954*. New York: Columbia University Press, 1959.

Kassof, Allen, *The Soviet Youth Program*. Cambridge, Mass.: Harvard University Press, 1965.

Klönne, Arno, *Hitlerjugend: Die Jugend und Ihre Organisation im Dritten Reich*. Hannover, 1962.

Laqueur, Walter Z., *Young Germany: A History of the German Youth Movement*. New York: Basic Books, 1962.

Samuel, Richard H., and Thomas, R. Henton, *Education and Society in Modern Germany*. London: Routledge and Kegan Paul, 1949.

FEAR AS A POLITICAL WEAPON

Delarue, Jacques, *The Gestapo*. New York: Morrow, 1964.

Leites, Nathan C., and Bernaut, Elsa, *Ritual of Liquidation*. Glencoe: Free Press, 1954.

Solzhenitsyn, Alexander, *One Day in the Life of Ivan Denisovich.* New York: Praeger, 1963.

Steinberg, I. N., *In the Workshop of the Revolution.* New York: Rinehart, 1953.

Tucker, Robert C., and Cohen, Stephen F. (eds.), *The Great Purge Trials.* New York: Grosset and Dunlap, 1965.

Weissberg, Alex, *Conspiracy of Silence.* London: Hamish Hamilton, 1952.

Wolin, Simon, and Slusser, Robert M. (eds.), *The Soviet Secret Police.* New York: Praeger, 1957.

Chapter VII

PUBLIC OPINION AND PROPAGANDA

Cantril, Hadley (ed.), *Public Opinion, 1935–1946.* Princeton: Princeton University Press, 1951.

Doob, Leonard W., *Public Opinion and Propaganda.* New York: Holt, 1948.

Friedrich, Carl J., *The New Image of the Common Man.* Boston: Beacon Press, 1950.

Hale, Oron J., *The Captive Press in the Third Reich.* Princeton: Princeton University Press, 1964.

Inkeles, Alex, *Public Opinion in Soviet Russia: A Study in Mass Persuasion.* 2nd ed. Cambridge, Mass.: Harvard University Press, 1958.

Key, Vladimer O., Jr., *Public Opinion and American Democracy.* New York: Knopf, 1961.

Kris, Ernst, *et al., German Radio Propaganda: Report on Home Broadcasts During the War.* Ithaca: Cornell University Press, 1944.

Milosz, Czeslaw, *The Captive Mind.* New York: Knopf, 1953.

Sington, Derrick, and Weidenfeld, Arthur, *The Goebbels Experiment: A Study of the Nazi Propaganda Machine.* New Haven: Yale University Press, 1943.

Chapter VIII

THE IMPACT OF PERMANENT WAR

Aron, Raymond, *The Century of Total War.* Garden City: Doubleday, 1954.

Black, Cyril E. (ed.), *The Transformation of Russian Society*. Cambridge, Mass.: Harvard University Press, 1960.

Klemperer, Klemens von, *Germany's New Conservatism*. Princeton: Princeton University Press, 1957.

Krieger, Leonard, *The German Idea of Freedom*. Boston: Beacon Press, 1957.

Meerloo, Joost A. M., *Total War and the Human Mind*. New York: International Universities Press, 1945.

Mises, Ludwig von, *Omnipotent Government*. New Haven: Yale University Press, 1944.

Mosse, George L., *The Crisis of German Ideology*. New York: Grosset and Dunlap, 1964.

Neurohr, Jean, *Der Mythos vom Dritten Reich*. Stuttgart: Cotta, 1957.

Stern, Fritz, *The Politics of Cultural Despair*. Garden City: Doubleday, 1965.

Chapter IX

DICTATORSHIP IN INTERNATIONAL POLITICS

Arendt, Hannah, *Eichmann in Jerusalem: A Report on the Banality of Evil*. New York: Viking, 1963.

Beloff, Max, *The Foreign Policy of Soviet Russia, 1929–1941*. 2 vols. London and New York: Oxford University Press, 1947, 1949.

Brook-Shepherd, Gordon, *The Anschluss*. Philadelphia: Lippincott, 1963.

Dallin, Alexander, *Soviet Conduct in World Affairs*. New York: Columbia University Press, 1960.

Deakin, Frederick, *The Brutal Friendship*. New York: Harper, 1963.

Eubank, Keith, *Munich*. Norman: University of Oklahoma Press, 1963.

Fischer, Louis, *The Soviets in World Affairs, 1917–1929*. 2 vols. Princeton: Princeton University Press, 1951.

Gibson, Hugh (ed.), *Ciano Diaries*. Garden City: Doubleday, 1946.

Kogon, Eugen, *The Theory and Practice of Hell*. New York: Berkeley Publishing Corporation, 1960.

Lemkin, Rafal, *Axis Rule in Occupied Europe*. Washington: Carnegie Endowment, 1944.

Mosely, Philip E. (ed.), *The Soviet Union, 1922–1962*. New York: Frederick A. Praeger, 1963.

Poliakov, Leon, and Wulf, Josef (eds.), *Das Dritte Reich und die Juden*. Berlin: Arani, 1955.

Reitlinger, Gerald, *The SS: Alibi of a Nation, 1922–1945*. New York: Viking, 1957.

Ritvo, Herbert (ed.), *The New Soviet Society*. New York: New Leader, 1962.

Toynbee, Arnold (ed.), *Hitler's Europe*. London and New York: Oxford University Press, 1954.

Walsh, Edmund, *Total Power*. Garden City: Doubleday, 1948.

INDEX

Action, a necessity in the New Order, 38-39, 228, 257
Acton, Lord, 42
Addison, on John Churchill, 52
Age composition, in British government, 252; in French politics, 252; of German economic leaders, 239; of Nazi party, 135-136, 243; of Reichstag, 238
Agricultural classes, 99-101
Agriculture, collectivization of, 159-161; legislation for, in Germany, 169-170
Air force, German, 180
All Quiet on the Western Front, 237
Ambiguity the essence of dictatorship, 258-259
Amman, Max, 81, 243
Andreyev, 79, 249
Anti-Bolshevists, Russian, 259
Anti-intellectualism in Nazi Germany, 197
Anti-party, 137
Anti-Semitism, 297-300
Anzilotti, 273
Appeasement, 138, 258-259
Armistice period, 6-9, 17-19, 22-26, 250-255, 258, 260, 261-281
Army as dictator's competitor, 94
    See also German army; Red army.
Asquith, 52
Astor, Lady, 160
Ataturk, Kemal, 60, 71-72
Austria, after the Armistice, 272-273; *Anschluss*, 278-279, 286, 287

Bagehot, 47, 231
Balance of power, 262
Balbo, 74, 76, 133
Baldwin, Stanley, 46-47, 251, 252, 253

Balkan Entente, 280
Balkanization of Europe, 7
Balkans, capture of, for German trade, 280-281
Bannasch, Monsignor, 184
Baptism of Fire, 221, 305
Barter trade, 173, 280
Bäumer, Gertrud, 191
Beard, Charles A., 51
Beck, Colonel, 175, 279
Begbie, Harold, 53
Beneš, 244, 271
Beria, 249
Berlin-Tokyo axis, 275
Bilateral treaties, 173, 280, 281-282
Birth rate, in dictatorships, 293; in Germany and Italy, 192; in Soviet Russia, 189
Bismarck, 22, 26, 143, 290
Black Shirts, 19, 132, 147
Blomberg, von, 243
Blum, Léon, 48, 89, 252
Bocchini, Arturo, 81
Bolshevism, fear of, 21, 282-283, 285; military character of, 132; split in theory and practice of, 157
    See also Communism; Soviet Russia.
"Bolshevist attempt" in Italy, 19-20
Bolshevist party, 123
Bolshevist Revolution, 9-14, 106, 222
Borgese, 28
"Boss rule," 80, 90-92
Bouhler, Philip, 79
Brauchitsch, von, 175, 176
Brave New World, 303
Bredow, General von, 174
Briand, 25, 251, 266, 274
Briand-Laval visit to Berlin (1931), 274
Britain and France Between Two Wars, 262